Understanding Third World Politics

Also by B. C. Smith

Regionalism in England
Field Administration: An Aspect of Decentralization
Advising Ministers
Administering Britain (with J. Stanyer)
Policy Making in British Government
Government Departments: An Organisational Perspective
(with D. C. Pitt)
The Computer Revolution in Public Administration
(edited with D. C. Pitt)
Decentralization: The Territorial Dimension of the State
Bureaucracy and Political Power
Progress in Development Administration (editor)
British Aid and International Trade (with O. Morrissey and
E. Horesh)

Understanding Third World Politics

Theories of Political Change and Development

B. C. Smith
Professor of Political Science
University of Dundee

First published 1996 by
MACMILLAN PRESS LTD
Houndmills, Basingstoke, Hampshire RG21 2XS
and London
Companies and representatives
throughout the world

ISBN 0–333–64404–2 hardcover
ISBN 0–333–64405–0 paperback

A catalogue record for this book is available from the British Library.

10 9 8 7 6 5 4 3 2 1
05 04 03 02 01 00 99 98 97 96

Copy-edited and typeset by Povey–Edmondson
Okehampton and Rochdale, England

Printed in Malaysia

To Jean, Rebecca and David

Contents

List of Tables and Figures

Tables

Figure

Preface

This book provides a critical introduction to the attempts of political scientists to understand the politics of less developed countries. While it provides a very wide range of empirical examples from many countries in several continents its central focus is on the issues and controversies that have dominated the social science of Third World politics since the 1950s and in particular on assessing the main theories that have been formulated that attempt to make systematic and rigourous sense of political development.

The book commences with discussions of two topics that are an essential preparation for what follows: the question of whether there is a 'Third World'; and the colonial backgrounds of most of today's less developed countries. To identify the types of society with which the book is concerned Chapter 1 deals with the concept of a 'third' world. It will soon become clear that different terminology is used to label the countries and the circumstances in which they find themselves – developing, underdeveloped, poor, less developed – as well as 'Third World'. These are not synonyms but denote interpretations of history. The significance of labels is that they define subjects for analysis. So Chapter 1 distinguishes the different meanings that have been attached to the term 'Third World', to explain why doubts have been expressed about the legitimacy of such a label. This also introduces us to the problems experienced by Third World countries and the major changes that have taken place in the period since the end of the Second World War.

An understanding of imperialism is necessary not only to know the nature of one of the most formative historical influences on today's Third World, but also to comprehend the debates within the social sciences about the legacy of that episode. Imperialism, a foundation of contemporary Third World status, has been defined in different ways: obtaining sovereignty; forceful annexation; a stage of capitalism; and colonialism. Imperialism is, however, mainly an economic concept, while colonialism is mainly social and political.

Not all Third World countries were colonies, but all have been affected by imperialism. The development of imperialism is briefly outlined, from pre-capitalist imperialism, through the transition from merchant capital to industrial capital, to the acquisition of colonies in the nineteenth century.

Chapter 2 draws a distinction between imperialism and colonialism, sets out the main elements of the economistic explanations of imperialism, particularly that of the nineteenth century, evaluates these and alternative explanations, and distinguishes between the different forms of European imperialism and their impact on indigenous society. It notes the variability of colonial intervention, the pragmatism contrasted with the assimilationism of colonial policy, and the variability of local conditions in terms of fertile land for cash cropping, the structure of communications, the presence of mineral wealth, climatic conditions, indigenous social structures, levels of urbanisation, and forms of political organisation. Consequently different forms of colonial presence were felt: plantations, mining enclaves, the encouragement of peasant cash cropping, European settlement, and combinations of these.

The second part of the book deals with the main theoretical perspectives on the overall quality of political change in the Third World, which try to understand the situation in which such societies find themselves in terms of 'modernisation, 'development', 'neo-colonialism' and 'dependency'. Chapter 3 locates the origins of modernisation theory in evolutionary social theory and its key concepts of continuity, progress, increased complexity and specialisation. It notes its appeal in the context of post-War optimism and US foreign policy. Five dimensions of modernisation theory are discussed: its neo-evolutionary perspective; the interrelationship between economic and social values which it embodies; the concept of differentiation derived from Durkheim and Parsons and entailing the specialisation of political roles; Weber's concepts of secularisation and rationality; and changes in cultural patterns, exemplified by Parsons' 'pattern variables' following the conceptualisation of modern and pre-modern social patterns produced by Tonnies in terms of *Gemeinschaft* (community) and *Gesselschaft* (association).

Criticisms of modernisation theory are then considered with particular reference to the concept of tradition, 'obstacles' to development, and rationality. Modernisation theory's perception of much of the conflict in developing societies in terms of tradition and modernity obscures more important conflicts. It is ideologically conservative and underestimates the influence of external forces. The static and uniform conception of tradition has also been criticised, as has the ethnocentricity of the unilinear view of modernisation. The problem with dichotomies in social analysis such as Parsons' 'pattern variables' is also discussed. Much modernisation theory can be reduced to tautologies. The psychology of modernisation theory is shown to be reductionist and to ignore ideological, economic, political and social structures.

Chapter 4 seeks to understand the main arguments of the functionalist perspective on comparative politics, especially the concepts of function and 'structural differentiation' when applied to political systems, the motivation behind this theoretical position, and the main criticisms that have been levelled against it. Functionalism requires social phenomena to be explained in terms of their 'functions' or what is needed to maintain the organism in a healthy state – here political development theory borrowed ideas from biology. The relationship between structure and function was seen as providing a theoretical framework that could cope with a bewildering variety of political systems. Functionalism became the political interpretation of modernisation theory because of the need to encompass traditional and modern political systems within a single framework of comparative inquiry.

The idea of neo-colonialism explored in Chapter 5 questions the significance of formal independence for post-colonial societies. A particular perception of the relationship between sovereign states and between political and economic freedom is conveyed by the term 'neo-colonialism'. It was assumed that constitutional independence would mean that indigenous governments, representing the interests of local people rather than alien groups, would have sovereign state power at their disposal. However, what the new rulers of many ex-colonies found was that the major proportion of the resources available to them were controlled from metropolitan centres that hitherto had ruled their countries directly. Within political science the *political* manifestations of this domination proved difficult to describe in concrete terms, except for those for whom politics was merely an epiphenomenon of the economic. The nature of the economic linkages could easily be described, but the domestic political effects were left to be inferred from them.

Chapter 5 examines the economic basis of neo-colonial politics in the failure on the part of colonialism to develop the economies of the colonised territories and the highly specialised state in which the colonial economy was left at independence, with one or two major commodities orientated towards export earnings and therefore foreign exchange. The theory is that the 'commanding heights' remained largely in the hands of foreign firms, and that adverse terms of trade forces dependence on loans from developed countries, investment by foreign firms and aid for capital which the foreign private sector will not provide. Theorists of neo-colonialism claim that continuing dependency on foreign capital caused a net *outflow* of capital from the developing to the metropolitan country. Chapter 5 also examines the controversy generated by Warren's claim that the term 'neo-colonialism' obscured the role played by the achievement of formal sovereignty and its consequences. Warren's optimism at the progressive, in Marxist terms, nature of Third World development did not go unchallenged.

Dependency theory, which had its roots in the crisis of US liberalism in the late 1960s and a major critique of modernisation theory, adds the idea of peripherality, or satellite status, to the concept of neo-colonialism. Chapter 6 shows how dependency theory originated in an analysis of Latin America where circumstances that might be expected under conditions of colonialism or only recently liberated ex-colonies were found in states that had been independent since the early or mid-nineteenth century. The main constituents of dependency theory are the idea of a hierarchy of states, the concept of 'underdevelopment', a view about the nature of capitalism, propositions concerning 'disarticulation', and the effect of economic dependency on the structure of political power.

The next part of the book moves on to specific institutional arrangements and the attempts by political scientists to produce valid theoretical statements about the most significant political institutions in Third World societies: the state, political parties, the bureaucracy and the military. Social science interest in the post-colonial state has in part been a reaction against the economic reductionism found in dependency theory and in part an extension of a resurgence of interest in the nature of the capitalist state within mainstream Marxist thought. In Chapter 7 a developmentalist view of the state, or political system, is contrasted with neo-Marxist theorising about the state in Third World societies.

Chapter 8 deals with theories explaining the importance of political parties in Third World politics. Ideological foundations in class, European political ideas, religion, ethnicity, and populism with its attendant factionalism and patronage politics are considered. The single-party system of government in the Third World has attracted much attention (and hostility). Explanations of this tendency are assessed. The conditions required for the survival of party systems, such as economic growth and social stratification, are considered. The survival of parties as institutions is also of concern as the movement for democracy gathers momentum in the Third World.

Bureaucracies are important political organisations in all political systems. Theories of the post-colonial-state have employed the concept of a bureaucratic oligarchy, clearly implying that government is in the hands of the paid officials of the state. Chapter 9 distinguishes between different concepts of bureaucracy and shows that all are contained in the analyses that have been carried out of the role of the bureaucracy in Third World societies and states. Chapter 9 discusses the bureaucratic features which have been taken to be signs of the emergence of a new kind of ruling class. Bureaucracy also implies a certain kind of rationality in the context of the official allocation of scarce resources. Thus Chapter 9 considers the theory of 'access'.

Chapter 10 examines military intervention and the coup d'état. Different types of military intervention in politics are distinguished and explanatory factors identified as accounting for the *coup* as the most extreme form of intervention are considered. The problems associated with statistical causal analysis as a means of explaining military intervention are outlined, since this has been a popular method of analysis in the past.

The final section of the book is about challenges to the status quo and therefore about the political instability which is so frequently found in Third World societies. First it deals in Chapter 11 with the demand for independence on the part of ethnic or national minorities: the phenomenon of *secession*. This is a very widespread feature of Third World politics. Three theories of separatism are examined: political integration, internal colonialism, and 'balance of advantage'. It is suggested that explanations of nationalism and secession need a class dimension because of the social stratification found within cultural minorities, the petty-bourgeois leadership of ethnic secessionist movements, and the significance for the outcome of nationalism of the reaction of the dominant class in the 'core' community to nationalist political mobilisation.

Chapter 12 poses the questions of why peasants and workers do not have more political power, given their numerical preponderance, and why peasant-based revolutions have occurred in some countries but not others with equally oppressed masses. Different forms of oppression are distinguished and key concepts are discussed: participation in 'normal' politics, 'rebellion' to redress wrongs, 'revolution' to change society, and the definition of 'peasantry'. Obstacles to political participation are explored and developments leading to changes in the political orientation of the peasantry, such as the declining political significance of the village, the spread of universal suffrage and its effects on patron–client relations, and improvements in education and literacy, are considered. Particular attention is paid to Moore's conclusions about the social structures and historical situations which produce or inhibit peasant revolutions.

The penultimate chapter addresses a theme that underlies most explorations of Third World societies and their politics, and which figures prominently in the discussions contained in earlier chapters – the preconditions for political stability. Political instability in the Third World seems indiscriminate and ubiquitous. Explanations of it have emphasised aspects of economic development such as levels of affluence, the rate of growth, and frustrated expectations. The theoretical or empirical weaknesses of these conclusions are identified, namely that correlation does not necessarily prove causality, that poor and underdeveloped countries can be stable especially if authoritarian, that political stability might *cause* affluence and economic growth, and that high rates of growth and stability have gone together in some countries. Problems with the concept of 'political stability' itself are addressed: its normative content, the question of whether the analysis is concerned with stable government whatever the type of regime or just stable *democratic* government, and the lack of a satisfactory operational definition of 'instability'.

I owe a debt of gratitude to a number of people for their support and inspiration at different stages in the making of this book. It was given its initial shape while teaching with Geof Wood and Edward Horesh at the University of Bath. Both taught me an immense amount about how to study political development, and I am pleased to acknowledge that here. At the University of Dundee I obtained valuable insights into theories of political change from Richard Dunphy. Susan Malloch and Anne Aitken never lost patience with my endless word-processing queries. The staff of Dundee University Library dealt efficiently with my many requests for inter-library loans. An earlier version of Chapter 9 appeared in *Politics, Administration and Change*, vol. 16, Jan–June 1991. Finally, I thank my wife Jean for her tolerance of my irritation when things went wrong, as they so often did. What I have done with the ideas of the theorists reviewed here remains my responsibility alone.

B. C. SMITH

Part I
Preliminaries

1
The Idea of a 'Third World'

1. Introduction

Since this chapter examines a controversy over the label 'Third World' it is appropriate to begin with a definition. In order to identify the subject-matter of this book, to convey the diversity of the social and economic conditions found within the Third World, and to provide an outline of the major changes taking place in Third World countries, an indication of the key characteristics of Third World status must be given. For the purpose of this survey the Third World will be defined as a group of countries which have colonial histories and which are in the process of developing economically and socially from a status characterised by low incomes, dependence on agriculture, weakness in trading relations, social deprivation for large segments of society, and restricted political and civil liberties. This definition acknowledges the process of change and therefore the probable diversity of countries within the group. The following examination of Third World status and trends will follow the components of the definition: the achievement of political independence; average income levels; industrialisation; integration into the world economy; social well-being; and human development (Thomas, 1994, p. 10). By this definition the Third World comprises approximately 100 states in Africa, Asia, the Middle East, Latin America and the Caribbean. Their combined population of some 4 billions accounts for 75 per cent of the world's total and their territories cover nearly 70 per cent of the world's land area (World Bank, 1993, pp. 238–9).

Political independence

Only a tiny minority of countries that would be regarded as part of the Third World by other criteria have not experienced colonialism at some stage in their recent histories. The picture of the Third World in this respect is becoming more complex with the dissolution

3

of the Soviet Union and the emergence of a number of independent states that were formerly part of it (Berger, 1994, p. 257). Most of these, such as Tajikistan and Uzbekistan, rank as lower-middle-income countries along with, for example, Senegal, Thailand and Peru. However, this is a less significant variation in Third World status than the length of time that countries have been independent from their colonisers, with most Latin American countries gaining political independence in the early nineteenth century and most African countries only after the Second World War.

There are still a few small territories that have yet to achieve independence from a European power (as distinct from territories within Third World states struggling to secede, such as Kashmir or East Timor): the French colonies of Guadeloupe, Martinique and French Guiana, for example.

Experience of imperial political control and economic penetration varied considerably, as did the routes to independence which were taken (roughly divided between constitutional negotiations and armed struggle). However, the legacy of imperialism and colonialism was everywhere profound, transforming political institutions and processes. New geo-political boundaries were drawn. Reactions against alien rule mobilised new political forces and alliances. Indigenous social structures were altered by European economic interventions and settlement. Valuable indigenous resources such as precious metals and labour were extracted by force.

Agricultural production was transformed by plantations and the control of smallholder production to produce cash crops demanded by European commerce. Colonial agriculture was incorporated into world trade. Food crops were transferred from one region of the world to another. Such agricultural changes had permanent ecological consequences. Handicraft production declined to be replaced by the cultivation and extraction of primary products for export rather than by an industrial manufacturing capacity. European investment in the economic infrastructure of colonies facilitated this trading regime and strengthened links with the imperial economy.

Average incomes

Most Third World countries are poor by international standards. The majority are found in the low-income or lower-middle-income categories used by the World Bank and defined in terms of gross national product (GNP) per capita. Though this indicator is by no means wholly satisfactory as a measure of economic well-being, examining changes in it enables some important variations and trends to be traced.

Differences in per capita incomes vary greatly between regions of the world and, as Table 1.1 shows, the regions of the Third World continue to lag behind the developed economies. The gap in real incomes between some Third World countries, such as those in East Asia and the industrialised countries, has narrowed considerably since 1945. But the gap between developed countries and other regions of the Third World has widened, so that many Third World countries have per capita real incomes that are well below that of the USA in the early nineteenth century (World Bank, 1991, p. 2). Equally disturbing is the fact that some 1115 million people in the Third World were living in poverty in 1985 and of these 630 million were extremely poor with an annual consumption level of less than $275.

In the last twenty-five to thirty years incomes in the Third World have in general been rising. Output per capita in low and middle income countries has grown on average by 2.5 per cent per annum since 1965. Income levels improved across East Asia and, more slowly and unevenly, in South Asia. East Asia's share of developing countries' real income increased from 22 per cent to 37 per cent. But

Table 1.1 *Historical trends in GDP per capita*

	1830	1913	1950	1973	1989	*Growth rate 1950–89*
Asia	375	510	487	1215	2812	3.6
Latin America		1092	1729	2969	3164	1.2
Sub-Saharan Africa			348	558	513	0.8
Developing economies		701	839	1599	2796	2.7
		(32)	(25)	(22)	(28)	
OECD members	935	2220	3298	7396	10 104	2.3

SOURCE: World Bank, 1991, p. 14.
NOTE: Benchmark values are 1980 international dollar estimates. Numbers in parentheses are regional GDP per capita as a percentage of GDP in the OECD economies.

in other regions of the Third World incomes have stagnated or fallen. The divergencies between regions mainly occurred in the 1970s, so that whereas by 1980 per capita GDP was growing at 6.7 per cent in East Asia and 3.2 per cent in South Asia, it was falling in Latin America and Sub-Saharan Africa. Per capita incomes in Sub-Saharan Africa have fallen in real terms since 1973. The region's per capita income was 11 per cent of the industrialised countries average in 1950; today it is 5 per cent. Such differences reflect variations between regions in levels of economic growth and investment which are themselves dependent on domestic economic policies and international economic forces (World Bank, 1990, pp. 7–15).

Industrialisation

Low per capita incomes are related to an economy's high level of dependence on agriculture. Incomes tend to rise as countries industrialise and the size of the manufacturing sector increases. Countries in the Third World tend to be more dependent on agriculture than on manufacturing sectors of industry. More of the labour force is employed in agriculture than in industry. In the period 1989–91 60.5 per cent of the labour force in developing countries was in agriculture compared with 14.4 per cent in industry and 25.1 per cent in services (see Table 1.2). In Africa and South Asia the number of people for whom agriculture is their main source of income actually increased in the 1980s by over 25 per cent in many countries (Thomas, 1994, p. 52).

Table 1.2   *Employment in developing countries, 1965–91*

	% of labour force in					
	Agriculture		*Industry*		*Services*	
	1965	*1989–91*	*1965*	*1989–91*	*1965*	*1989–91*
Least developed countries	83	72	6	8	11	20
Sub-Saharan Africa	79	67	8	9	13	24
All developing countries	72	61	11	14	17	25

SOURCE: UNDP, 1993, Table 17, p. 169.

The most notable exceptions to this general picture are the 'Asian Tigers' of Hong Kong, Taiwan, South Korea and Singapore – which at the end of the 1980s exported a greater value of manufactured goods than the rest of the Third World together – and other newly industrialising countries (NICs) in Asia and Latin America. Most of the world's manufacturing takes place in developed countries, though the Third World's share has grown since 1960. The proportion of GDP accounted for by the industrial sector of Third World economies increased from 27 per cent in 1965 to 34 per cent in 1988 and that of agriculture fell from 42 per cent to 31 per cent.

During the 1980s the fastest growth in manufacturing occurred in South-east Asia and the Middle East. Africa's record was generally poor and Latin America was held back by indebtedness which reduced investment in industrial development. There was negative growth in manufacturing production in Bolivia and Argentina, for example. It is significant for Third World development that its smallest share in world manufacturing is in machinery, the most valuable sector. Third World countries make their most significant contributions – about one-fifth – to three sectors: food, beverages and tobacco; textiles, clothing and footwear; and chemical, petroleum and related products. Much of this is accounted for by the movement of multinational corporations to areas of low labour costs.

Integration into the world economy

A Third World economy is typically characterised by a high level of dependence on the export of a very small number of commodities. Compared with the diversified exports of most developed countries, the value of Third World trade is still concentrated on a few primary commodities whose prices are liable to severe fluctuations (see Table 1.3). For example, during the 1980s the prices of many primary commodities fell to their lowest levels since 1945 (World Bank, 1990, p. 13). Africa has been particularly severely affected.

The Third World's export markets are predominantly in the developed economies – only a small proportion of trade is conducted between countries in the Third World and the majority of world trade takes place between developed countries. The problem for many Third World countries even today is that they are on the periphery of world trade.

Table 1.3   *Structure of Third World imports and exports (%), 1991*

	Exports (%)		Imports (%)	
	Primary commodities	*Manufactures*	*Primary commodities*	*Manufactures*
Sub-Saharan Africa	92	8	32	68
E. Asia	28	72	25	75
S. Asia	28	72	40	60
Middle East and N. Africa	90	10	27	73
Latin America and Caribbean	66	34	32	69

SOURCE: World Bank, 1993, Tables 15 and 16, pp. 267 and 269.

However, the trend has been towards a growth in the level of manufactured exports from the Third World. Between 1965 and 1988 these rose as a proportion of Third World exports from 16 to 64 per cent, mainly because of East Asian development. This is despite the fact that developing countries are confronted with considerable protectionism by Western industrialised countries. In the 1980s quotas and other measures are estimated to have cost the Third World in loss of export earnings almost as much as the value of official aid ($55 billions in 1980). Whereas most of the Third World experienced declining terms of trade as prices of primary commodities fell, the four East Asian NICs increased their share of total world trade and manufactured exports by over eight times between 1965 and 1989 (World Bank, 1991, pp. 105–6).

The full integration of the Third World in the global economy is still a long way off. Despite the fact that 75 per cent of the world's population live in developing countries, they produce less than 20 per cent of global output and account for only 17 per cent of world trade.

One way in which the Third World is integrated into the global economy, however, is through indebtedness. In the 1970s developing countries borrowed heavily to finance consumption, investment and oil imports. During the 1970s the volume of international bank lending increased by nearly 800 per cent to reach $800 billions. The scale of indebtedness reached crisis proportions in the early 1980s when a combination of high interest rates, adverse trade balances and the world recession caused severe debt servicing problems for many Third World countries. Interest payments grew by 40 per cent between 1980 and 1983 to $64 billions, a level equal to 3.2 per cent of GNP compared to less than 1 per cent at the end of the 1970s. Many developing countries had to negotiate a restructuring of their loans from commercial banks and foreign governments. By 1989 financial transfers to developing countries had become a net outflow of $30 billions compared with a net inflow of $36 billions in 1981. As a result, growth in GDP in the severely indebted countries of Africa, Latin America and the Middle East slowed down. The burden or severity of debt for a country is relative to its ability to earn foreign exchange from which to make repayments (see Table 1.4). So debt is a particular problem for Sub-Saharan Africa where it is equivalent to 329 per cent of the region's exports and 108 per cent of GNP. The problem of external debt in the Third World, amounting to over $1.3 trillion, remains a severe constraint on development (World Bank, 1991, pp. 23–4).

Table 1.4   *External debt ratios*

	Total external debt as % of Exports		GNP		Interest payments as % of exports	
	1980	*1991*	*1980*	*1991*	*1980*	*1991*
Sub-Saharan Africa	96.6	329.4	28.6	107.9	5.7	10.5
East Asia and Pacific	89.6	96.2	16.9	28.2	7.7	5.9
South Asia	160.4	287.1	17.0	35.6	5.1	11.5
Middle East and North Africa	114.4	185.8	31.0	58.8	7.3	8.4
Latin America and Caribbean	195.5	256.0	35.1	41.3	19.6	15.8

SOURCE: World Bank, 1993, Table 24, p. 285.

Social well-being

Social development has also been uneven across the Third World. Trends reflect overall economic performance. Progress was made between 1965 and 1985, with per capita consumption increasing by nearly 70 per cent in real terms, average life expectancy rising from 51 to 62 years, and primary school enrolment rates reaching 84 per cent. Progress in child mortality rates and primary school enrolments continued in the 1980s in most developing countries. In 1950 28 children in 100 died before their fifth birthday; this number had fallen to 10 by 1990. Smallpox has been eradicated, whereas it claimed more than 5 million lives annually in the Third World in the early 1950s (World Bank, 1993, p. 1).

Such averages conceal variations between countries, regions and, of course, social groups within countries. Sub-Saharan Africa, for example, a region with the highest infant mortality and lowest primary education enrolment, saw only a small improvement in infant mortality in the 1980s and a decline in the enrolment rate. Several Latin American countries, by contrast, saw infant mortality declining at a rate faster than that achieved in the 1960s and 1970s. Malnutrition is on the increase in Sub-Saharan Africa, while there is much greater variability in the countries of Latin America (World Bank, 1990, p. 45). In Pakistan it is estimated that 36 per cent of the population has no access to health care. Because of the economic recession of the early 1980s there have been substantial declines in real per capita spending on education and health in Sub-Saharan Africa and Latin America.

In East Asia the poor have access to primary education whereas in Sub-Saharan Africa few of the poor have even this level of schooling. Less progress in extending health care to the poor has been made in all regions of the Third World. Government spending on social services tends to be diverted away from those whose needs are greatest – the poor. Comparing social service indicators with the percentage of the non-poor in the population gives some idea of whether the poor are being reached. Table 1.5 shows the regional variations that are found and suggests that further coverage in health care and education will benefit the poor.

Many problems remain (see Table 1.6). Absolute mortality levels in developing countries are high, child mortality is ten times greater than in developed countries. Malnutrition is a major contributory factor. Maternal mortality ratios are thirty times higher. It is estimated that decades of improvement in mortality rates will be wiped out by the AIDS epidemic, predicted to cause 1.8 million deaths annually by the year 2000. Malaria is proving resistant to treatment and tobacco-related deaths are likely to double in the first

Table 1.5 *Social services and the poor, 1985*

	All developing countries	Sub-Saharan Africa	East Asia	South Asia	Europe, Middle East and North Africa	Latin America and the Caribbean
Non-poor in population (%)	67	53	79	49	75	81
Primary school net enrolment rate (%)	84	56	96	74	88	92
Children immunized (%)	58	47	73	43	63	65

SOURCE: World Bank, 1990, p. 43.

Table 1.6 *Social indicators*

	Life expectancy at birth (years), 1991	Adult illiteracy (%), 1990	Population per physician, 1990	Infant mortality,[a] 1991	Primary education enrolment (%) 1990	Maternal mortality,[b] 1988
Sub-Saharan Africa	51	50	23 540	104	46	686
East Asia and Pacific	68	24	6170	42	100	195
South Asia	59	54	2930	92	67	444
Middle East and North Africa	64	45	2240	60	85	151
Latin America and Caribbean	68	16	1180	44	88	162
High income economies	77	4	420	8	97	N/A

SOURCE: World Bank, 1993, Tables 1, 28, 29, and 32; pp. 239, 293, 295 and 301.
NOTES: (a) per 1000 live births
(b) per 100 000 live births

decade of the next century and grow to more than 12 million a year by 2025 (World Bank, 1993, pp. 1–3). To achieve significant improvements in health and education in the Third World requires higher levels of expenditure on the social sectors than have been achieved in the 1980s. It is difficult to see how these can be provided by governments that are under pressure to reduce public expenditure as part of economic restructuring.

Inequalities in social well-being, as indicated by health and education, are also found between urban and rural areas and between men and women. There is generally greater poverty in rural areas and more severe problems of malnutrition, lack of education, life expectancy and substandard housing. This applies to countries with high levels of urbanisation, such as those in Latin America. Table 1.7 compares the urban and rural incidence of infant mortality and access to safe water in selected countries and shows that higher levels of poverty in rural areas are accompanied by lower levels of social well-being.

Women in all regions of the Third World do worse than men in terms of health, nutrition and education. For example, in 1980 the literacy rate for women was only 61 per cent of that for men in Africa, 52 per cent in South Asia, 57 per cent in the Middle East, 82 per cent in South East Asia and 94 per cent in Latin America. Women can also be expected to work longer hours for lower wages than men. They face more cultural, legal, economic and social discrimination than men – even poor men (World Bank, 1990, p. 31).

Human development

One way of viewing human development is to measure it in terms of economic and social welfare. Rather than just taking per capita GNP as an indicator, human development can be measured by social as well as economic variables. The United Nations Development Programme (UNDP) does this in its Human Development Index (HDI), derived from scores given for life expectancy at birth, adult literacy levels, average years of schooling, and real GDP per capita (to indicate purchasing power). The two educational variables are combined but with different weightings, and growth in the human development value of increases in income

Table 1.7 *Rural and urban poverty in the 1980s*

	Rural population (% of total)	Rural poor (% of total)	Infant mortality (per 000 live births)		Access to safe water (% of population)	
			Rural	Urban	Rural	Urban
Sub-Saharan Africa						
Côte d'Ivoire	57	56	121	70	10	30
Ghana	65	80	87	67	39	93
Kenya	80	96	59	57	21	61
Asia						
India	77	79	105	57	50	76
Indonesia	76	91	74	57	36	43
Malaysia	62	80	:	:	76	96
Phillipines	60	67	55	42	54	49
Thailand	70	80	43	28	66	56
Latin America						
Guatemala	59	66	85	65	26	89
Mexico	31	37	79	29	51	79
Panama	50	59	28	22	63	100
Peru	44	52	101	54	17	73
Venezuela	15	20	:	:	80	80

SOURCE: World Bank, 1990, Table 2.2, p. 31

is assumed to fall after a certain level is reached. The three indicators are averaged to provide each country with a score from 0 to 1. Such analysis shows that countries with comparable levels of income can have very different levels of human development, and that relatively poor countries in purely economic terms can provide high levels of human development. China, for example, is a low income country but life expectancy is at the upper-middle-income country average. Table 1.8 compares regions of the world by their human development, weighted by population.

Table 1.8   *Human development by region, 1992*

Region	HDI
Latin America and Caribbean	0.000
Developing countries	0.468
Sub-Saharan Africa	0.263
South Asia	0.309
Arab States	0.515
East and South-East Asia	0.568
Latin America and Caribbean	0.728
Industrialised countries	0.919

SOURCE: UNDP, 1993, p. 15.

Again it is found that women's experience of human development is worse than men's. When a country's HDI is adjusted for gender disparity, every country's value declines. Rankings change too, showing that some countries do better than others. Costa Rica's ranking improves by two positions whereas South Korea's falls by three and Sri Lanka's by one. The most significant disparities for women lie in employment opportunities, earnings (also the main factors in industrialised countries), health care, nutrition and education. It has been estimated that in South and East Asia there are some 100 million women fewer than there would be were it not for maternal mortality rates, infanticide and the nutritional neglect of young girls (UNDP, 1993, p. 17).

Human development is often adversely affected by generalised inequality. In many countries the HDI falls considerably when adjustments are made to the income component of the index to

Table 1.9 *Government expenditure, 1991: selected countries and services (%)*

	Defence	Education	Health	Welfare[a]	Economic services
Low-income economies					
Sierra Leone	9.9	13.3	9.6	3.1	29.0
Bangladesh	10.1	11.2	4.8	8.0	34.4
Malawi	5.4	8.8	7.4	3.2	35.0
India	17.0	2.5	1.6	6.9	20.8
Kenya	10.0	19.9	5.4	3.9	20.7
Pakistan	27.9	1.6	1.0	3.4	11.6
Sri Lanka	9.4	8.3	4.8	18.4	24.6
Indonesia	8.2	9.1	2.4	1.8	27.1
Egypt	12.7	13.4	2.8	17.8	8.2
Lower-middle income					
Bolivia	13.1	18.7	3.3	18.8	16.9
Phillipines	10.9	16.1	4.2	3.7	24.7
Peru	16.4	21.1	5.6	0.5	N/A
Tunisia	5.6	17.5	6.3	18.3	24.4
Thailand	17.1	20.2	7.4	5.9	24.3
Upper middle income					
Botswana	13.3	20.5	5.1	16.2	16.8
Argentina	9.9	9.9	3.0	39.4	16.0
Mexico	2.4	13.9	1.9	13.0	13.4

SOURCE: World Bank, 1993, Table 11, pp. 258–9.
NOTE: [a] includes housing and social security.

Another threat to democracy in the Third World is posed by the rise of forms of religious fundamentalism which violate principles of toleration and equal rights. In India, for example, Hindu nationalism is believed by some experts to threaten the very survival of the political system as a pluralist democracy (Chiriyankandath, 1994, p. 32). To a considerable extent such movements reflect disillusionment with political and economic developments which leave large sections of the population marginalised both materially and politically as power is accumulated in the hands of new ruling classes. Religious fundamentalism provides an ideological focus which asserts the relevance of forms of traditionalism to the modern world.

2.   The concept of a 'Third' World

Gunnar Myrdal, winner of the Nobel Prize for economics in 1974, once said that in the relationship between rich and poor countries there has been diplomacy by language, meaning that in the developed, and to a lesser extent the underdeveloped, countries there has been a constant search for an acceptable label for this latter group. We sometimes refer to 'the South' rather than use 'developing countries'. Others prefer 'less developed countries' (LDCs), while still others prefer 'underdeveloped', a concept that has taken on a very specific meaning and which, as we shall see later, denotes a particular kind of interrelationship between countries and a particular process of change.

No one has come up with a label that claims universal acceptance. The search is fraught with difficulties, not least ideological ones. As Goulbourne points out, the terminology of comparative politics, particularly as far as the Third World is concerned, is largely expressive of attitudes rather than precise analytical concepts (Goulbourne, 1979, p. xii). Cannot all countries be described as 'developing' in some direction or another? If we reserve 'development' for movement in a particular direction, then it has to be made explicit what path should be regarded as development and what should not. 'Modernisation' similarly risks all the dangers of ethnocentric evolutionism, though as a conceptualisation of social and political change it has had an enormous impact on development studies and comparative politics. The influence of modernisation theory and its applications to political change will be examined in Chapters 3 and 4.

The concept of the 'South' reflects some of the frustrations felt when trying to differentiate between countries in terms of meaningful indicators that show why grouping countries is helpful to analysis. It is also possible to talk about rich and poor countries, but this draws a boundary between countries which many people interested in the Third World wish to treat as a single grouping. It is easy to understand the appeal of 'underdevelop' as a transitive verb in distinguishing those countries whose exploitation made possible the development of their exploiters. The idea that advanced societies secured their own advancement by underdeveloping poor countries is at the heart of dependency theory, which will be examined in Chapter 6.

Such difficulties form the substance of this chapter. The purpose of examining the concept of the 'Third World' is that one can gain a preliminary insight into some of the problems experienced by such countries by examining the validity of using a single category for such an amorphous group. Examining the concept of the Third World actually teaches us quite a lot about the history of developing countries, the alliances that have been formed among them, and the attempts that have been made to produce solidarity vis-à-vis the rest of the world.

3. Meanings and objectives

To be able to evaluate the different positions adopted by those who have entered into dispute about whether 'Third World' is a meaningful concept it is necessary to separate out the different perceptions that people have about the countries which they think deserving of the label.

Non-alignment

The original meaning of the term 'Third World' referred to a group of countries outside the great power blocs. There has been a lot of discussion as to who used the term first, but it is generally accepted that it was the French demographer and economic historian, Alfred Sauvy who coined the term in the early 1950s. However, there is also the view that it should have been translated as 'Third Force' because Sauvy seemed to have in mind the problem of power blocs during the Cold War, and of a Third Force distinct from the Western bloc and the Eastern bloc. 'Non-alignment' in the military and diplomatic spheres is one of the earliest qualities associated with Third World status (Wolf-Phillips, 1979 and 1987; Love, 1980).

Many Third World leaders, and notably Kwame Nkrumah, the first Prime Minister of Ghana, Nehru, the first Prime Minister of independent India, and Nasser, the first President of Egypt after the military *coup* of 1952, sought to convey their independence from the Great Powers, particularly at the height of the Cold War. The Third World was seen as a group of countries trying to demonstrate that they were neither pro-USA nor pro-USSR, but rather wanted to stand above the ideological conflicts threatening their very existence. This stance was most strikingly represented by the Bandung Conference, attended by the representatives of twenty-nine African and Asian countries in 1955.

Solidarity

'Third World' also conveys a common interest and solidarity among developing countries based on their primary producing economic status, their relative poverty, their dependence on agriculture and their distinctive forms of economic regime neither modelled on the Eastern bloc of planned economies nor the Western, free-market system. The Third World was seen to fall outside the first world of the advanced capitalist democracies and the second world of industrially advanced communist countries. As the British political scientist Samuel Finer pointed out (1970), the Third World was not just a residual category of states that were neither liberal-democratic nor communist-totalitarian. It was a significant grouping in that its members lay outside Europe, mainly south of the fortieth parallel, were mainly agrarian, were much poorer than northern states and had been subjected either to colonialism or 'deep diplomatic and economic penetration by the Western powers'(Finer, 1974, p. 98).

However, there was an important deviation from this perception of the world's economic divisions. China's Mao Tse-tung produced a very different categorisation in which the USA and the USSR constituted the first world, Japan, the European countries and Canada constituted the second world, while Africa, Latin America and most of Asia formed the third world. The claim being made here was that *both* the USA and the USSR were imperialistic, with their developed satellites as the second world and the primary producing former colonial possessions of the first and second worlds forming the third world. So the OPEC countries would, despite their wealth, fall into this third group (Muni, 1979; McCall, 1980, p. 539).

Mao was clearly influenced by current relationships between China and the USSR, worse at that time than between China and some capitalist states. From other socialist perspectives, developing countries have been seen as predominantly dependencies of the major capitalist powers. This led to the belief that one could only meaningfully talk about two worlds, not three, one capitalist, one socialist (Griffin and Gurley, 1985; Toye, 1987).

Anti-imperialism

Thirdly there has been the idea of an alliance against colonialism, neo-colonialism and racialism. So the Third World stood for solidarity against the continuing intervention and involvement of the powerful economies in the developing economies and polities of the world, in an attempt to strengthen economic sovereignty at a time when it was very obvious that political and economic autonomy did not necessarily go together, and that the achievement of constitutional independence did not guarantee freedom internally from external constraints. This idea will be taken up again when we come to look at the concept of 'neo-colonialism' and the way in which interpretations of political and economic development have been formulated in such terms. The idea of a Third World thus tries to capture a common experience of exploitation by richer and more powerful societies. All Third World countries have experienced such exploitation to some degree, and it was strongly felt by many Third World leaders that it was persisting even after independence.

Regionalism

Fourthly, Third Worldism has been associated with the idea of regional coherence through pan-nationalist movements. The Third World might not represent a grouping of countries all with identical interests, but within the Third World there could be groups of states that shared interests cutting across national boundaries – for example, the pan-Arab world or the pan-African world. Such concepts were important to political leaders in developing countries in the 1960s. Here was an attempt to prove that national boundaries were not going to be as important as they were in other parts of the world. National boundaries were seen as the creation of European colonialism, especially in Africa. Thus they were to some extent alien, reflecting a colonial past. Institutions were set up to reflect this internationalism and some still exist, though without the significance that they were originally intended to have.

A new international order

Since the early 1970s Third Worldism has reflected a campaign for a new international economic order under which developing countries would secure greater national control of their natural resources, and try to protect their economies by collectively agreeing to the prices of raw materials upon which so many of their economies were dependent. Third Worldism has been to some extent driven by a sense of grievance against the developed countries who appear to have rigged the rules of the international economy against LDCs (Rothstein, 1977, p. 51).

Third World countries also wanted to combine forces to gain greater access to markets in industrialised countries for their own manufactured goods by persuading the governments in those countries to lower the trade barriers that protected domestic industries from competition from Third World products. This call was taken up by the UN and the World Bank in 1992, both arguing for the liberalisation of global markets and a reduction in the level of protectionism in the OECD countries. The costs of protectionism in the rich countries of the world extend beyond blocking imports from the Third World to include negative capital transfers, higher real interest rates, unequal competition in international services and closed markets for technology. A more rapid transfer of technologies to give Third World countries access to the advanced technologies required by the industrialisation process, and which were proving so successful in some developing countries, also formed part of this aspect of Third Worldism.

All of these aspirations were echoed in the Brandt Report of 1980 but were rejected by the Western powers soon after. Other similar proposals have included a World Development Fund to which all countries would contribute on a sliding scale related to their national income; the development of the sea bed to provide new sources of food; and the international development of alternative energy sources. The objective has been to strengthen through collective action the position of individual Third World countries *vis-à-vis* their main trading partners and sources of foreign investment.

Through UNESCO Third World countries are also trying to act collectively to resist the pressures from the Westernised mass media, and the cultural, educational and scientific imperialism which introduces inappropriate technology and educational values into their societies.

Poverty

Finally there is the idea that Third World countries are poor. The fact that needs to be recognised is that although some of the countries that would conventionally be thought of as part of the Third World are relatively rich, particularly in the Middle East, nevertheless poverty continues to be a real and significant feature of Third World countries. Far from declining, this aspect of Third Worldism has increased since 1975. The World Bank's estimate is that over a billion people lived in poverty in 1985 compared with 770 million in 1975. This represents a third of the population of the developing world. Even if the policies for labour-intensive production and social service provision advocated by the Bank were adopted, poverty would fall only to 825 million by the year 2000, a forecast that is at least 100 million higher than the Bank's previous projection for the decline in absolute poverty, made in 1978.

Some progress was made in the reduction of Third World poverty in the 1960s and 1970s, but the 1980s were the 'lost decade' for the poor. Sustained economic growth in Asia, where most of the world's poor live, meant that living conditions improved. But in Latin America and Sub-Saharan Africa poverty has increased. Nearly half of the developing world's poor, some 520 million, live in South Asia, 280 million in East Asia and 180 million in Africa. Poverty is the condition of approximately half the population in South Asia and Sub-Saharan Africa (World Bank, 1990).

In symbiotic relationship with such poverty are low levels of productive capacity, low per capita incomes, low life expectancy. high infant mortality, illiteracy, the oppression of women, grossly unequal distributions of wealth, over-dependence on export earnings and foreign capital, and a small industrial sector. As a former President of the World Bank once put it:

> 800 million individuals trapped in absolute poverty, a condition of life so characterised by malnutrition, illiteracy, disease, squalid surroundings, high infant mortality, and low life expectancy as to be beneath any reasonable definition of human decency. (Quoted in Wolf-Phillips, 1979, p. 109)

Third Worldism is in part about reminding people that poverty is still a problem, and that in general there are widening gaps between the developed and developing countries. According to the UNDP the imbalance between the world's rich and poor is growing at an alarming rate. The wealthiest fifth of the world's population is now estimated to be 150 times better off than the poorest fifth, compared with a 30-fold difference in 1960 (UNDP, 1992). There are still enormous problems to be confronted arising from those disparities, including the 'silent genocide' of high infant mortality, poor nutrition and low standards of living.

4.   Changing worlds

The Third World has changed much since the earliest visions of solidarity and continues to do so. Consequently, a label that conveys a message of homogeneity of socio-economic conditions and political purpose is increasingly unacceptable to commentators from both North and South (Leftwich, 1983, pp. 163–4; Hume and Turner, 1990, pp. 7–8).

Cultural heterogeneity

The term 'Third World' has been considered by some as insulting to the diverse range of polities, cultures, histories and ideologies found within the Third World (Rothstein, 1977, p. 48; Naipaul, 1985). The conservative economist Peter Bauer adopts a similar view, though for different reasons. His purpose has been to contradict the view that responsibility for Third World poverty lies with the developed world, a view that Bauer finds patronising and condescending. Part of this condescension is to present the Third World as a 'uniform stagnant mass devoid of distinctive character'. The individuals and societies of the Third World are in this way denied identity, character, personality and responsibility. 'Time and again the guilt merchants envisage the Third World as an undifferentiated, passive entity, helplessly at the mercy of its environment and of the powerful West' (Bauer, 1981, pp. 83–4).

Disparities of wealth

Another reason why the label 'Third World' has become less acceptable as a way of thinking about poorer countries is that there are now great disparities of wealth within the Third World. Wide disparities are developing in per capita GNP, levels of food production, annual growth rates, levels of literacy and rates of industrialisation (Muni, 1979). Whatever measures one might feel are appropriate for deciding whether or not a country is progressing, the Third World is becoming increasingly differentiated. For example, in terms of growth and output the relative position of Africa worsened in the 1970s and 1980s. The East Asian economies, in contrast, have achieved impressive growth rates, and avoided the problems caused by debt and falling oil prices that have plagued Latin America and the OPEC countries by investment in manufactured exports and inward-directed strategies of industrialisation (Toye, 1987, p. 14).

Expert observers and international organisations such as the World Bank now distinguish between the rich poor countries, the middle poor and the poorest countries, even to the extent of referring to the last group as the Fourth World – the poorest of the poor or the least developed of the developing countries (Rothstein, 1977, pp. 53–4). World Bank statistics are presented in such divisions and other organisations such as the UN also differentiate in their policy-making (Hoogvelt, 1982, pp. 22–3). Some of the cut-off points between these categories are pretty arbitrary (Worsley, 1984, pp. 321–2) but nevertheless there are real differences when one compares Bangladesh with, say, Malaysia. Some aid donors, such as the British Government, distinguish between the poor and the poorest with the aim of directing their development assistance at the poorest countries, many of which are among the countries of the British Commonwealth, which fits nicely with its policy of directing its aid towards its ex-colonies.

Ideological differences

The three-fold classification implied by 'Third World' ignores ideological differences. Despite the current penchant for market economics rather than socialist planning, it is still possible to produce a four-fold classification if ideological as well as developmental criteria are applied. We could, after all, divide the developed and the less developed countries into capitalist and socialist (Worsley, 1980). Such a matrix is for some purposes more useful than the single category of 'Third World', though the categories produced are rather too crude for countries such as Tanzania and Zambia that would claim that they had produced their own original ideologies, or even India, which claims to operate a mixed economy along social democratic lines. The move away from centralised planning in Angola, Mozambique and even China also undermines the significance of this matrix. It has been argued that the 'globalisation' of market economics and pluralistic democracy, apparently heralded by the end of the Cold War, further challenges the validity of the concept of a Third World (Berger, 1994), although this ignores the uncomfortable fact that markets may dominate economies in societies in which tyrants dominate government.

Conflict within the Third World

The evidence of deep internal divisions within the Third World significantly reduces the credibility of the solidarity which the term was intended to convey by many Third World leaders forty years ago. That solidarity has been undermined by a number of developments. First, many organisations expressing regional common interests have been weak or have disappeared. Once independence was achieved national boundaries became as durable as any in Europe: governments in the Third World seem prepared to spill just as much blood to preserve the territorial integrity of their countries. So the pan-national movements and organisations have not received delegated sovereignty from the new national governments of the Third World.

Those organisations that have survived have been geared to the economic interests of particular regions, for example, the Central American Common Market, the Latin American Free Trade Association, and OPEC (which by the end of the 1970s was doing far more damage to the economies of the poor countries than the developed, especially when the world economic recession adversely affected the values of poor country exports). Regional groupings have not always wanted to share the benefits which they derive from the trading and other relationships which they have negotiated with industrialised countries (Rothstein, 1977, p. 49). The relationships have sometimes developed into international organisations with memberships cutting across the North–South divide, bringing together countries from the First and Third Worlds. An important recent example is APEC – Asia-Pacific Economic Co-operation – whose membership includes the USA, Japan, South Korea, Taiwan, Malaysia, Thailand, Singapore, China and Australia. (Mexico, Papua New Guinea and Chile were expected to join in 1994.) In 1993 the member-states of APEC accounted for more than half the world's economic output and two-fifths of its trade.

Secondly, solidarity has been undermined in Third World countries by domestic economic problems such as those reflected in demands for a new international economic order. Policy failures, mismanagement and debt have forced some Third World countries to become inward-looking, leading some to the conclusion that 'Third World solidarity has become a thing of the past' (Westlake, 1991, p. 16). Thirdly, the demise of communist regimes in eastern and central Europe and the former USSR has produced a degree of homogeneity between the First and Second Worlds, at least in terms of economic systems, which makes references to developing countries as a 'Third' group or force less and less meaningful.

But most significant of all with respect to internal divisions has been warfare. Even before the civil wars in (the former) Yugoslavia and the Confederation of Independent States we could only speak of the last forty years as 'the post-war period' by being excessively ethnocentric. Prior to the latest conflicts in Europe over 25 millions had died in warfare since the Second World War and that warfare had been almost exclusively located within the Third World. This is not to say that the First and Second Worlds – in Afghanistan, Vietnam, Central America and the Middle East – have not been significantly involved. But even leaving aside civil war, which can happen anywhere, warfare between states, and notably the Iran–Iraq conflict and the Gulf War, causing immense human suffering and economic loss, cannot be underestimated when considering Third World solidarity.

As some LDCs have welcomed or at least accepted the inevitability of foreign investment and the dependency that it brings, including subordination in the international division of labour, non-alignment is further undermined. So even by the end of the 1960s, Third World countries were by no means behaving in unity towards East–West relations. A stridently anti-communist group of Asian states emerged – Indonesia, Malaysia, Singapore, Thailand and the Philippines. This brought an end to the Third World as a coherent voting block in the UN, splitting it along ideological lines. Similarly in 1979 at the UN Conference on Trade and Development (UNCTAD V), the more industrialised of the Third World countries vetoed a code of conduct for multinational corporations (MNCs) that the less industrialised Third World states wanted to bring in, demonstrating their need to avoid antagonising MNCs on whose presence even the rich Third World countries so heavily depend for their development. Worsley has argued that the material, economic basis of non-alignment had become very weak by 1980, making it difficult for dependent economies to express political sovereignty and to form a solid bloc hostile to one or other of the major economic blocks in the developed world upon which they depend for foreign investment, technology, aid and technical assistance. Politically, the majority of Third World countries have been very 'aligned' for some time now (Worsley, 1984, p. 324).

Poverty within countries

Finally a serious objection to the concept of a Third World has been raised by people who find the association with poverty unacceptable. The concern is that if a group of countries is defined as poor it might obscure the fact that there are in such countries classes that enjoy immense wealth. To talk about poverty-ridden peoples in LDCs (Meier, 1976) might act as a form of mystification deflecting attention away from internal stratification: poor countries do not consist entirely of poor people – great internal disparities exist. The UNDP report on human development referred to earlier drew attention to the scale of the inequalities in some individual countries including the worst case, Brazil, where the income ratio of the top to the lowest fifth of the population was 26 to 1. There is no homogeneous 'hungry universe' that constitutes the Third World (Rodinson, 1977). The economic differentials between Third World countries has not eradicated poverty within the more successful ones. Inequalities persist and sometimes increase regardless of a country's overall economic performance (Toye, 1987, p. 16).

Third World conditions are even said to exist within some of the peripheral regions of First World countries and certainly within some of the new states of the former Soviet bloc. Many native Americans and Australian aborigines, for example, exist in conditions which correspond to those in which the rural and urban poor of many Third World countries live. The contrasts in living standards and political power between whites and blacks in South Africa, or European élites and indigenous people in Latin America, also call the term 'Third World' into question in so far as it implies geopolitical distinctiveness. At the same time élites in Third World societies often appear to have more in common with Western élites than with their own dispossessed masses (Berger, 1994, pp. 267–8).

Global stratification into rich, middle income and poor countries must not be allowed to conceal internal social stratification. This is not to say that the poverty that poor people in poor countries experience is solely to do with the domestic maldistribution of power; and it is not to say that it has nothing to do with dependence on the more powerful economies in the world. But it does alert us to the possibility that these two things are related – that dependency within the world economic system actually benefits some classes in the Third World. The term *comprador bourgeoisie* was coined to convey the idea of an alliance between an indigenous middle class and foreign investors, MNCs, bankers and military interests. There is thus a need to relate thinking about global stratification to how that division and the relationships between those global strata affect relations between internal social strata. To what extent would redistribution within a poor country be made easier if there was no dependence on more powerful trading partners and sources of foreign exchange?

There is thus a risk that the expression 'Third World' might obscure the heterogeneity of social classes, each with its own political objective. The concept of the Third World has consequently been denounced, notably by Regis Debray, as mystification designed to conceal dependency and exploitation, as well as a device allowing rulers of Third World countries to present a common interest between themselves and the masses to disguise their own alliance with metropolitan interests.

5. Conclusion: Third World values

Some think it is still important to keep the term 'Third World' in order to preserve and convey the values associated with it. It could be dangerous to stop talking about the Third World and so further fragment that group of countries – that their solidarity must be somehow preserved simply because as individual states they are bound to be weak in the relationships with the developed world. The 'Third World' is seen by one Indian scholar as 'a sound concept' and a 'flexible, resilient category'. Attempts to question its validity are mischievous and misleading. It implies neither inferior values nor some lower numerical order, but rather

> a set of specific characteristics that are unique in more than one way to the countries of Asia, Africa and Latin America. It represents the broadly similar, though not exactly identical, nature of these countries' experiences in the processes of development, processes that were arrested in the past, are discouraging and uncertain at present, and are likely to be unprecedented in the future. (Muni, 1979, p. 128)

Even if Third Worldism only means building regional alliances to present a united front economically, that in itself is important.

It has also been pointed out that to reject the concept because it treats the Third World as an undifferentiated mass ignores the psychological and political connotations of Third Worldism in favour of an interpretation that 'denotes an association of countries dedicated to the moral blackmail of a guilt-afflicted West' (Toye, 1987, p. 6). It continues to be the case that there is a group of countries which to varying degrees confront a common set of problems that are as significant today as they were when Robert Rothstein refused to abandon the concept of Third World in the mid-1970s: the dominance of subsistence production and self-employment in the absence of a significant modern industrial sector; low per capita incomes; low productivity; and over-dependence on export earnings and foreign capital flows (Rothstein, 1977, p. 50).

All of the problems which characterised the group of countries originally labelled the Third World by Western analysts, and which prompted solidaristic action by Third World leaders, are to be found today. Some of them are worsening. The poorest countries, with 75 per cent of the world's population, contain only 14 per cent of the world's industrial capacity (the 44 least-developed countries provide 0.21 per cent of it). Within this group of countries, 40 were poorer in 1989 than they were in 1980. The terms of trade for their primary products have declined. For example, rice, coffee, cocoa, sugar and cotton were on average 20 per cent cheaper in 1989 than in 1980. Debt remains the consequence: in 1989 Third World debt amounted to $1.3 trillion – 44 per cent of its GNP. The inability to raise capital for investment still creates dependence on loans and aid, and strengthens foreign intervention through the medium of multi-nationals. In the 1980s poor countries were as locked into a vicious circle of mounting debt, falling export values, pressure to export to earn foreign exchange with which to service debts, net out-flows of capital in interest and repayments, and dependence on foreign aid and loans, as they were in the decades immediately following political independence. The intensity of the accompanying social and ecological problems, such as illiteracy, malnutrition, disease and environmental degradation, equally suggests the need for a categorisation which reflects the obstacles to development confronting the world's poorest countries and which contrasts them with the world's richest. These characteristics are not found to the same degree in each developing country – Brazil ranks eleventh in the world industrially and fifty-nineth in terms of social development – but they are part of the common Third World experience.

Whether or not we accept the concept of a Third World, we are confronted with relative rather than absolute differences between the Third World and other, more developed, regions and countries. This is not to say that because some Third World countries are becoming richer they are therefore becoming more like the developed, industrialised West. Some of the richer countries of the Third World have vigorously rejected Westernisation in favour of their own cultural values, especially religious ones. It is rather the case that when we look at the politics of developing countries there are no absolute differences between their politics and those of the West or East, even in those two interconnected problems of establishing political authority and using public power to develop commerce, industry and trade which some observers see as the trademark of Third World status (Hawthorne, 1991). Many of the things that have been said about the role of the state in developing countries would equally apply in many developed countries (Leftwich, 1983, pp. 157–8).

The dependency which has featured in much of the discussion about the nature of the Third World has also been central to interpretations of the changes which are taking place there. In one sense the expression 'Third World' represents a challenge to 'development' as autonomous growth and progress. The controversies within the social sciences about development, underdevelopment and the consequences of contacts between rich and poor countries will form the substance of later chapters. Before taking up these issues, consideration must be given to the main type of encounter with advanced societies – imperialism – and the explanations that have been offered of it.

2

Theories of Imperialism and Colonialism

1. Introduction

An examination of the politics of underdevelopment must start with a consideration of imperialism and colonialism. The importance of imperialism in the histories of Third World countries cannot be exaggerated. So it is necessary to know what social scientists have said about it as a foundation upon which the present circumstances of underdevelopment rest.

The term 'imperialism' has been given many different meanings. Sometimes it is defined as sovereignty over what were formerly independent political entities. For some it has meant a relationship of dependency without necessarily involving the forceful annexation of territory which is then placed under alien rule. In classical Marxism, and especially for Hilferding, Bukharin and Lenin, imperialism referred to a stage of capitalism leading to political, economic and military rivalry and conflict between the advanced capitalist countries at the turn of the nineteenth century (Brewer, 1980, p. 80). In many formulations imperialism is equated with colonialism. Economic exploitation combines with political domination and the superimposing of European control over indigenous political authority (Cohen, B.J., 1973, ch. 1). It has been taken to mean the economic exploitation of weakness in another country, often associated more broadly with a policy that aims to reverse the power relations between two countries (Morgenthau, H.J., 1948, p. 42). After an exhaustive comparison of definitions of imperialism, Cohen concludes that there are three necessary elements for such a relationship between countries to be said to exist: inequality, domination, and a multiplicity of cause, not just economic. Imperialism 'simply refers to *any relationship of effective domination or control, political or economic, direct or indirect, of one nation over another'* (Cohen, B.J., 1973, p. 16, emphasis in original).

Imperialism should not, however, be equated with colonialism. Colonialism, meaning the annexation and direct government of one country by another, is a frequent but not universal adjunct of imperialism. The driving forces behind colonialism were additional to those motivating imperialism, and brought about the political domination of a territory by an alien power as an auxiliary activity to support economic control, not necessarily of the same territory. Imperialism is thus mainly an economic concept, whereas colonialism is a social and political concept. Colonialism was also sometimes regarded as a cost by imperial powers rather than a benefit, albeit a cost that in the context of international rivalry was unavoidable.

Not all Third World countries were colonies – the exceptions were Thailand, Ethiopia, Liberia, Iran and Afghanistan – but the vast majority were. More significantly, all Third World countries have as part of their histories some form of imperialism, if not direct colonial government of their territory. As Michael Barratt Brown pointed out, in addition to the 800 million people under colonial rule between the two World Wars (a third of the world's population), a further 500 million in China, 150 million in Central and South America, and 100 million in South-east Europe 'had very limited economic freedom of manoeuvre against the economic strength of the great industrial powers' (Barratt Brown 1963, p. 159). So imperialism does not necessarily mean taking political control of a country (Magdoff, 1972). As we shall see later, some analysts wish to talk about imperialism in the post-colonial era as a continuing phenomenon because they attach maximum emphasis to economic exploitation that does not necessarily involve political annexation.

China, for example, was never a colony but experienced imperialism through its economic relations with the Western powers. The establishment of 'treaty ports', around which industrialisation took place, was for the economic benefit of foreign investors rather than for domestic development. After the nationalist revolution in 1926 in China, British troops and warships were sent to protect the concessions made to foreign investors in those economic enclaves. In addition China lost parts of its own empire through invasion and annexation by other powers: Indo-China to the French, and Burma and Hong Kong to the British.

The first task in this chapter is to consider the major explanations of imperialism and colonialism. Particular attention will be paid to the political consequences for the dominated peoples. Criticisms of the dominant interpretations will also be considered. The defensive and critical literature on the subject of imperialism is vast. Even if attention is restricted to the 'new' imperialism of the late nineteenth century, with its associated colonialism and therefore direct political consequences for those colonised, there is far too large a body of literature to do justice to here. Only the most influential thinkers can be dealt with and even then the concentration will be on what they had to say about the effects of imperialism on colonised societies. This provides a more relevant foundation for subsequent discussion of theories of political change than would the long-standing debates about the causes of imperialism, its relationship to the development of mercantilism and capitalism, and its influence as a major cause of war between the European powers (Cohen, 1973, ch. 2; Kiernan, 1974, p. 24; Larrain, 1989, pp. 62–77).

Secondly, the different forms taken by colonial penetration and the forces shaping them will be identified. Finally, a brief look will be given at the debate within the social sciences on the relationship between imperialism and capitalism. The question is whether imperialism was a progressive force for colonies because it introduced capitalism, regarded as significant either because it is seen as a necessary stage of historical development, or because it is seen as an advanced and civilised way of organising an economy and society. This section acts as a prelude to later examination of the controversy over the significance of political independence to former colonies.

2. Explanations of imperialism

Pre-capitalist imperialism of the mercantilist period of European economic development, such as Spanish and Portuguese conquest in South America, involved the exaction of tribute and the control of trade routes to open up new markets. As capitalism developed, the nations of Western Europe engaged in territorial expansion and domination to acquire precious metals, luxury goods and slaves, and to interfere in local production so that exploitation could be intensified. From the mid-seventeenth to the late eighteenth centuries the object of imperialism was to secure the raw materials and food needed in the period of rapid growth in manufacturing which preceded the Industrial Revolution, and to provide markets for those manufactures.

During the nineteenth century the transition from an imperialism based on merchant capital to one based on industrial capital was completed. Warfare between competing European nations for the control of colonies was largely replaced by wars of conquest as new colonies were acquired. Between 1800 and 1878 the European nations extended their control from 35 per cent of the globe's land surface to 67 per cent. However, the rate of seizure between 1878 and 1914 was three times greater, represented most notably by the scramble for Africa and giving the imperial powers control over 85 per cent of the globe. This greater involvement in the world economy was primarily motivated by the transformation from competitive into monopoly capitalism (Cohen, B.J., 1973, pp. 23–31; Brewer, 1980, ch. 1; Magdoff, 1982).

The most systematic attempts to explain imperialism focused on the expansionism of Western European capitalist powers in the late nineteenth century, and were derived from a combination of largely but by no means entirely Marxist thinking. Marx himself wrote about imperialism, particularly in relation to India, in *Das Capital*. The English writer Hobson, not a Marxist but nevertheless radical, presented his ideas in *Imperialism, A Study*, published in 1902. This book had a great influence on Lenin, despite the fact that he regarded Hobson as a 'bourgeois social reformer' and 'social liberal'. Rosa Luxemburg analysed imperialism in her book *The Accumulation of Capital* (1913). Lenin's *Imperialism: the Highest Stage of Capitalism* was published in 1917. He was also influenced by the Austrian Marxist Rudolf Hilferding's *Finance Capital* published in Vienna in 1910; and by the leading Bolshevik Bukharin, whose *Imperialism and the World Economy* (written in 1915) was also based on Hilferding's work (Brewer, 1980, p. 79).

Karl Marx

These writers emphasised different aspects of the relationship between the development of capitalism and imperialism. Marx's own analysis of the capitalist mode of production saw capitalism as producing an international division of labour. Capitalism also gave rise to a world market for commodities produced by that division. The world was at the same time divided into nation-states whose ruling classes protected their own national interests. So there was an obvious contradiction, as capitalism developed, between the internationally unifying tendencies of these new economic forces and the competitive nature of nation-states. That contradiction was expressed in economic rivalries and imperial expansion in pre-capitalist societies. As capitalist enterprises in the advanced countries sought to expand their markets and maintain their levels of profit, they came into conflict with each other as they sought control of new outlets for investment, sources of raw materials and markets (Kemp, 1972, pp. 22–6). Marx placed great emphasis on the need for what were increasingly monopolistic enterprises to reduce the costs of raw materials such as the primary products that could be obtained from the tropical dependencies, and the need to export capital by building ports and railways in areas that had to be opened up to trade.

Marx examined the effects of colonisation on the colonised peoples in a fragmentary way, and was mainly concerned with Ireland and India. His treatment of the two was not always consistent (Leys, 1975, pp. 6–7). In Ireland, Marx believed colonialism had caused the expulsion of the peasantry through the establishment of capitalist agriculture and migration. Ireland's function was to supply raw materials, cheap labour, a market for manufactured goods and land for safe investment.

The effect on India of British industrial capitalism was a flooding of its markets with British textiles and the destruction of Indian handicraft textile production. State power was needed to make Asiatic society less resistant to penetration by trade. The destruction of the Indian village, in which land was held not privately but through membership of the community led to the *zamandari* system of large landed estates, and the *ryotwari* system of taxation which treated cultivators as individual proprietors or tenants.

The progressive features of imperialism in India included the creation of a labour force of dispossessed peasants, the accumulation of capital from trade and usury, industrial development supported by the building of railways, political unity supported by the electric telegraph, the seeds of self-determination supported by a

British-trained army, reconstruction supported by a free press, and the emergence of an educated middle class 'endowed with the requirements of government and imbued with European science' (Marx, 1969, p. 133). Imperialism was thus creating the conditions for industrial capitalism and a modern nation-state (Brewer, 1980, p. 58). It would produce the same consequences as it had for the colonisers – the development of society's productive forces, and misery and degradation for its workers.

In his later writings Marx emphasised the destructive aspects of imperialism: enforcing dependence on agriculture to supply the needs of the industrial world; draining capital from the colonies; and failing to complete the institution of private property (Carnoy, 1984, pp. 174–5). Earlier he had overestimated the strength of the forces making for change. Industry, transportation and communications were not having the impact he thought on caste and communalism, and were not to do so for many years, nor was agrarian capitalism providing the foundation for industrial capitalism (Kiernan, 1974, pp. 180–91).

Lenin

To some Marxists it seemed that national markets within the Western capitalist countries were unable to absorb the goods which capitalist enterprises were producing or the savings which needed to be invested. Markets had to be found elsewhere – hence the importance of colonies for trade and investment as well as for raw materials.

To many Marxists, and particularly Kautsky and Lenin, the First World War appeared to be a culmination of those tendencies that Marx had identified much earlier. Lenin was concerned to explain the international forces that brought about the First World War, and so systematised and popularised the Marxist theory of imperialism in his tract of 1916. He repeated what Marx had said about capitalism reaching a stage of surplus which could not be reinvested in the domestic European economies because local demand was insufficient to make that investment profitable. To create that market would have required the consumption power of the working classes to have been strengthened by increases in wages. But for employers and the owners of capital to do that would have reduced the level of surplus value created by labour and therefore the level of profits. So the European powers were forced to look elsewhere to increase the profitability of their investments. Exporting capital was for Lenin completely consistent with low costs of production, low wages and the use of cheap raw materials. The expansion of colonial conquests and annexations in the second half of the nineteenth century coincided with capitalism's transition from its competitive form, based on the export of goods, to its monopolistic form, based on the export of capital. 'The non-economic superstructure which grows up on the basis of finance capital, its politics and its ideology, stimulates the striving for colonial conquest' (Lenin, 1917, p. 84). He quoted Hilferding approvingly: 'Finance capital does not want liberty, it wants domination'.

Lenin was unable to deal with the political aspects of imperialism because his pamphlet was written for 'legal' publication in Russia and therefore had to pass the tsarist censorship. His non-economic references were mainly restricted to European conquests in Africa, Asia and the Americas. But he did risk noting that British and French imperialists saw the settlements for surplus population and the new markets provided by colonies as the means of avoiding civil war in Europe.

Lenin was also aware that finance capital could thrive without colonies. He thus raised another issue that was to become central to later debates about imperialism. There were other forms of dependency. Countries could be politically independent yet 'enmeshed in the net of financial and diplomatic dependence' (p. 85). Argentina was an example, so financially dependent on London as to be a British 'commercial colony', with firm bonds between British finance capital and the Argentine bourgeoisie, leading businessmen and politicians (p. 85). Yet another form of dependency was found between Britain and Portugal, a 'British protectorate' providing a market for goods and capital as well as safe harbours and other facilities.

During the period of capitalist imperialism the relations that have always existed between 'big and little states' became a 'general system' and part of the process of dividing the world: 'they became a link in the chain of operations of world finance capital' (p. 86). Other than this, Lenin did not give a detailed discussion of colonial areas. Like Bukharin, he took it for granted that imperialism would have a totally adverse effect on indigenous peoples (Kiernan, 1974, p. 46).

Rosa Luxemburg

Rosa Luxemburg also emphasised the importance of pre-capitalist societies as new markets which could be controlled rather than left open to intervention by other trading nations or left to be satisfied from within by domestic producers. But she also showed how imperialism had to destroy competition within pre-capitalist societies, by eradicating alternative sources of supply so that the market could be monopolised by the imperial power. That is what happened in India, where there had been a thriving local textile industry based on cottage-scale production. Britain needed a market for its own textiles, so imperialism required the systematic destruction of local manufacturing capacity. This was accomplished by a combination of discriminatory legislation, tariffs and sub-sidised competition.

For Rosa Luxemburg, colonialism represented capitalism's need to destroy what she called 'natural economy'. She was consequently more concerned than other Marxists with the effects of colonialism on the social, political and economic structures within the colonies themselves. In social organisations where 'natural economy' prevailed, such as simple peasant communities, there was no demand for foreign goods and no surplus production. In such economies the means of production and labour power were bound together by the rule of law and custom. 'A natural economy thus confronts the requirements of capitalism at every turn with rigid barriers' (Luxemburg, 1913, p. 369). Capitalism must therefore annihilate natural economy wherever it is encountered. In the non-European countries the methods used – coercion, taxation and commercial relations – were embodied in colonial policies. Capitalism was not content with the means of production that it could acquire through commodity exchange. Colonialism gave it access to the productive forces of 'vast tracts of the globe's surface'.

Any opposition mounted by the colonised peoples was met by further force: 'permanent occupation of the colonies by the military, native risings and punitive expeditions are the order of the day for any colonial regime' (p. 371). Luxemburg saw British policy in India and French policy in Algeria as the 'classic examples' of capitalism's capitalism's use of such methods. In India the British enforced the compulsory alienation of land for tax arrears, artificially created a landed aristocracy, and allowed the ancient irrigation system to decay in its efforts to disrupt the social organisation of the people. France, in its determination to universalise private property among the Arabs of Algeria and acquire land for French capitalists claimed uncultivated areas, established settlements for the colonisers, imposed oppressive taxation, and broke up joint family property, leading increasingly to 'reckless speculation in land, thriving usury and the economic ruin of the natives' (p. 384). Colonisation had also assisted European capitalism by the destruction of rural industries and small-scale commodity producers in North America and South Africa.

Hobson

Capitalism's need for new investment opportunities was a factor which Hobson had stressed earlier. Markets were too small to make further investment in productive capacity profitable within Europe. Hobson showed that contemporary imperialism acquired for Britain tropical and sub-tropical regions with which there was only an insignificant amount of trade. He also dismissed the prevalent belief among the proponents of imperialism that colonial expansion was necessary to accommodate a surplus of population. He saw the new wave of imperialism as being bad business for the nation but good business for certain classes and professions that benefited from the militarism involved. Arguing largely from the South African case, Hobson claimed that the greatest impulse for imperialism related to investment and what he called the 'cosmopolitanism' of capital (Hobson, 1902, p. 51). The period of 'energetic imperialism' was shown to coincide with a remarkable growth in the earnings from foreign investments.

However, Hobson's was not an entirely economistic interpretation of imperialism. He was well aware of ideological forces which provided the energy behind imperialism, which investors then manipulated and guided. Politicians, soldiers, philanthropists, traders and missionaries generated the patriotic forces and enthusiasm for imperialism, but the final determination of where that energy was directed lay with the power of finance controlling public opinion through an obedient press, educational system and church. Hobson's solution was radical reform at home which would increase levels of private and public consumption, expand home markets and remove the need for foreign ones. 'It is not industrial progress that demands the opening up of new markets and areas of investment, but mal-distribution of consuming power which prevents the absorption of commodities and capital within the country' (p. 85).

Hobson was also concerned to contest the statements by the protagonists of imperialism about the beneficial consequences of British rule in her dependent territories. Contemporary justifications for imperialism claimed that the subjects of the Empire enjoyed benefits which it was the duty of the British to bestow. Hobson dismissed this motive for imperialism as a mere dressing-up of the 'spirit of naked dominance', pointing out that the 'chivalrous spirit of Imperialism' never promoted any Western nation to 'assail a powerful State, however tyrannous, or to assist a weak state reputed to be poor' (p. 200). No power of self-government had been bestowed upon the vast majority of the population of the Empire. 'Political freedom, and civil freedom, so far as it rests upon the other, are simply non-existent for the overwhelming majority of British subjects' (p. 114). They enjoyed none of the important political rights of British citizens, received no training in the arts of free British institutions, and exercised no political privileges. The most important fact of Empire for Hobson was that

> we have taken upon ourselves in these little islands the responsibility of governing huge aggregations of lower races in all parts of the world by methods which are antithetical to the methods of government which we most value for ourselves. (p. 117)

He also challenged the view that imperialism was part of a necessary struggle for survival among the races so that only the most 'socially efficient' would flourish, exposing this way of thinking as no more than the ethical fallacy of assuming that the power to do something constitutes a right or even a duty to do it. Anticipating controversies that were to surface again in the sociology of development, Hobson warned that 'the notion that civilization is a single beaten track, upon which every nation must march, and that social efficiency, or extent of civilization, can be measured by the respective distances that the nations have gone, is a mischievous delusion' (p. 188).

In colonies the progress of local people was sacrificed to social order, both being subservient to the 'quick development' of profitable trade or 'the mere lust of territorial aggrandisement'. The missionaries used political intrigue and armed force in their competition for converts. The scientific knowledge possessed by the imperial powers was seldom used for 'light and leading' in relations with indigenous peoples. Slavery had given way to indentured and forced labour and other ways of compelling people to substitute wage labour for traditional life on the land, such as the confiscation of land and livestock, taxation, and the establishment of 'native locations', all designed to supply cheap labour for farms, mines and the military. In India, in which Hobson regarded the British presence as in many respects beneficial, a century of British rule had proved incapable of warding off starvation, had forcibly destroyed much Indian art and industry, and had subverted ancient village institutions.

Taken together these 'classical' explanations of imperialism saw the monopolistic aspect of capitalism in the second half of the nineteenth century as producing cartels and trusts needing protected markets in which to invest and having the power to control markets and the terms of trade between the European powers and their new dependencies. So part of the explanation of imperialism was in terms of 'push' factors. In addition there were the conditions in pre-capitalist societies which acted as a magnet pulling capital from the developed economies – cheap labour, cheap raw materials and agricultural commodities (tin, copper, zinc, cotton, rubber, coffee, tea, sisal, jute). The classical theorists of imperialism recognised to varying degrees the pernicious effects of colonialism on society, but their writings also indicate that some regarded the opening up of 'backward' countries as ultimately a progressive movement (Larrain, 1989, pp. 70–2).

Once these economic relationships were in place, a third set of factors came into play – the strategic or protective aspects of colonialism which applied to areas of no immediate economic benefit but which were important for protecting areas that were from rival colonial powers – areas such as Aden, protecting the approaches to India, were consequently of vital strategic significance. Colonies spawned other colonies, whose function was to support the imperial system (Sweezy, 1942). This was important for those who wanted to play down the economic impulse behind imperialism. Robinson and Gallagher (1961), for example, argued that the partition of Africa represented attempts to protect other acquisitions, such as Britain's need to guard its two routes to India. Such an explanation is partially accurate but it cannot be extended so as to exclude the significance of 'the great tidal force of capitalism' altogether (Kiernan, 1974, p. 76).

3.   Critiques of economism

The more economistic theories of imperialism have been criticised on a number of counts. Hobson's and Lenin's association of imperialism with war has been countered by the argument that war has other causes than competition between capitalist societies for colonies. The Austrian economist Joseph Schumpeter argued in *Imperialism and Social Classes* that war was an 'objectless disposition on the part of a state to unlimited forcible expansion'. Societies seek 'expansion for the sake of expanding, war for the sake of fighting, victory for the sake of winning, domination for the sake of ruling' (1951, pp. 5–6). Capitalism, according to Schumpeter, devotes its competitive energies to purely economic activities. It also provides the social context for opposition to war, arms expenditure, militarism and imperialism; and support for peace, international arbitration and disarmament. Although it may be true to say that imperialism cannot be blamed for war, Schumpeter's disassociation of war and capitalism is unconvincing.

Other historians of international relations and war deny that, with the possible exception of the Boer War, wars since 1870 have been waged for imperialistic motives. Imperialist rivalry was one of the causes of the First World War, but so were

> the interactions of the European alliance systems and nationalisms in a framework dominated by balance of power thinking, security apprehensions generated by militarism and armaments competition, and the conditions of international anarchy, that is, the absence of organisations adequate to ensure peaceful settlement of disputes. (Dougherty and Pfaltzgraff, 1981, p. 248)

The direction of trade and investment throws doubt on the importance of late nineteenth-century imperialism for European capitalist development. After 1870 most international investment flowed between European states or between Europe and North America or Australia. Imperial investment from Britain in the 1880s and 1890s, for example, took place mainly in Australia and Canada. Two-thirds of the great boom in British overseas investment between 1900 and 1913 went to the Americas: 'the new British colonial possessions in Asia and Africa, with the outstanding exception of South Africa, hardly received any capital for their development at all in this period, not 5 per cent of the total' (Barratt Brown, 1963, p. 94; Cohen, B. J., 1973, pp. 63–5). Between 1870 and 1914 the income from overseas investments received by Britain was greater than the capital exported, and most of what was sent overseas was in the form of loans to governments and public utilities and not transfers from banks or monopolistic companies to their subsidiaries (Barratt Brown, 1972, pp. 54–5). Before 1914 only 10 per cent of overseas investment from France went to its empire (Aron, 1968, p. 261). Few of the territories that were acquired in the wave of imperialism at the end of the nineteenth century were the best areas for capital investment.

Similarly, trade with colonial dependencies constituted a small proportion of European trade. The share of the colonies in markets for raw materials was less than some of the theorists of imperialism would lead us to believe (Cohen, B. J., 1973, pp. 60–2).

It is also significant that some non-imperialist countries experienced high levels of economic growth, international trade and foreign investment without imperialist acquisition. The Scandinavian countries are cases in points. Yet at the same time countries such as Italy and Portugal were imperialistic despite having relatively underdeveloped economies themselves and a scarcity of capital. Schumpeter saw the finance imperialism thesis as undermined by the fact that the United States, an increasingly powerful capitalist country in the second half of the nineteenth century, did not annex Canada or Mexico, both rich in resources but weak militarily (Schumpeter, 1951, p. 57). The USA was developing very powerful monopolistic forces within its own economy long before its relatively slight excursion into imperialism, notably in the Philippines. Other countries that developed in this way also showed no inclinations towards imperialism or colonialism (Emmanuel, 1972a).

Britain, a country of cartels and other forms of capitalist concentration, did. Monopoly capital and particularly finance capital was more a feature of German imperialism than of British or French.

The motivation behind the imperialistic adventures of the advanced and advancing industrialised economies of the West is varied and complex. Studies of specific imperialist annexations reveal combinations of many factors – diplomatic, strategic, geopolitical, cultural and racial, as well as economic. It is not possible to reduce all of these to economic pressures. Colonialism was often expensive, with only indirect benefits. The American political theorist Edward McNall Burns summarised the non-economic objectives of the new imperialism as follows:

> National pride played a part in it also; and so did the desire of zealous Christians to convert the heathen. Military and naval chieftains demanded bases, coaling stations, and new sources of able-bodied recruits. Politicians argued the need for territories where surplus inhabitants of the mother country could settle without being 'lost to the flag'. Few ever migrated, but the argument continued to be used that colonies were necessary to provide relief for population congestion in the developed nations. (McNall Burns, 1963, p. 505)

States were sometimes drawn into colonial expansionism as a result of conflict sparked off by the activities of traders, missionaries and explorers. When the stability of regions became threatened by internal conflicts among the indigenous communities and trade was thereby threatened, the European state was drawn in to restore order. It was sometimes a matter of trade following the flag, sometimes of the flag following trade. In West Africa, when indigenous leaders found themselves integrated and subordinated into an alien imperial system after believing that they had merely entered into trading arrangements with European companies, and expressed disquiet, alarm and outright hostility, they were quickly overcome by superior military technology, rapidly followed by an administrative apparatus.

The colonisation of parts of Africa is frequently represented as a competition between European nations from the late nineteenth century. This was not necessarily based on a sense of immediate economic advantage, but through fear that European competitors might pre-empt territory, forestalling subsequent opportunities for trade and the extraction of raw materials. The British and French in West Africa were caught up in this, wanting to stop each other gaining possessions as much as to occupy territory themselves. Hence the 'scramble for Africa' which could be explained partly in terms of trading routes, safe ports of call, and the protection of trading posts and strategically important areas, such as the Suez canal zone. A comparable competition can be seen earlier in the Indian sub-continent with the Portuguese in the sixteenth century, and later the French and British, entering into agreements with local power-holders over the establishment of ports, enclaves and control over the hinterland. These then provided bases for subsequent incursions into the interior. That process was particularly associated in West Africa with the slave trade, an important commodity in early imperialism.

Arghiri Emmanuel (1972b) added another factor to produce a more complete explanation of the 'costly and irrational' impulse to colonise in support of European economic expansion and exploitation. Emmanuel argued that the colonialists themselves, including not only the white settlers but also the colonial civil servants and employees of the trading companies, were an independent force behind colonialism. They promoted colonialism because they found their livelihood in it.

Motives and justifications for imperial control also included racial ideologies and cultural prejudices. There was the overriding stereotype of 'native' peoples as needing the guiding light of European civilisation, a view of tropical and sub-tropical societies that was used extensively to justify the annexation of vast territories and huge populations. Imperialism represented, in Thornton's words, 'an immense responsibility for human welfare and the opportunity for human betterment' (Thornton, 1959, p. 305). Some justifications of empire typically ignored its economic motivation in favour of a belief in 'a duty imposed by some Providence on Englishmen to use their power in the world as a power for good, without asking anyone else whether they wanted to have good done to them or not' (Kiernan, 1974, p. 70).

Imperialism for the imperialists meant bringing the benefits of their civilisation and technology, as well as of their liberty, justice, law and order to people whose societies were thought to lack these qualities. It was easy for the imperialists to convince themselves in their highly ethnocentric fashion that the so-called savage and primitive races were simply awaiting the benefits of Western civilisation, that indeed there was a high moral duty to carry those benefits into such backward areas. Gladstone, in a speech to the House of Commons in 1877, referred to 'the stupidity of those people who cannot perceive the wisdom of coming under our sceptre'. He had been asked why additions to the Empire so often involved so much bloodshed. The reply was that the ignorant would inevitably resist what they did not understand to be in their interest. Joseph Chamberlain described imperialism as 'knowledge in place of ignorance, civilisation in place of barbarism'. This is not the historian's interpretation of imperialism but the imperialists' attempts to justify the morally questionable if not indefensible.

The reality, according to Barratt Brown, was vastly different:

> Establish and maintain a native feudal aristocracy, hold back the emergence of a truly entrepreneurial class, divert the nationalist movement into safe channels, hold down the peasant in debilitating poverty – it is not too much to say that these have been the harsh realities, often openly pursued, behind the lofty phrases about the white man's burden and preparation for self-government. (1963, p. 181)

Two hundred years of British rule in India left over 80 per cent of the people illiterate, a record repeated throughout Asia and Africa. Seventy-five years of British rule in West Africa left one fever hospital for 30 million Nigerians, a ratio of doctors to inhabitants of 1:60 000, and only half the children of one province surviving beyond their fifth year.

It has also been argued that imperialism was sometimes engaged in for domestic political and ideological objectives, such as France's reaction to defeat in the Franco–Prussian war of 1870 and her need to reassert national glory and rebuild the army; or Germany's consolidation of the fatherland between the World Wars. Sometimes there was the motive of counter-expansionism against states that threatened to disturb the balance of power in Europe. Imperialism was thus as much a function of international politics in Europe as of national economic advantage. The argument that imperialism in the late nineteenth and early twentieth centuries was much more a political than an economic phenomenon has been forcefully put by B. J. Cohen. Colonies were attractive to the European powers in their struggle for international supremacy to secure their national security. As Germany, France and Italy threatened Britain's imperial interests in their attempts to gain prestige and diplomatic advantage, so Britain retaliated by further annexations to protect her existing possessions and sea routes. 'The contest for colonies became general' (Cohen, 1973, p. 79).

Technological developments in communications, transportation and weapons also affected Europe's relationships with the rest of the world. Progress in technology provided opportunities for acquisition of and control over other parts of the world. Technology made it possible to develop new trade routes and new routes into interiors (by, for example, the construction of railways) when hitherto European contact had been limited to coastal settlements. Advances in medicine enabled Europeans to survive inhospitable climates. Weaponry made possible the incorporation of communities with which the Europeans had formerly only traded into imperial systems of political control. However, the question of why the Europeans wanted to use their technological advantage in this way remains. Unless technological determinism – that once a more advanced society encounters a less advanced one it will inevitably be driven to enlarge the area of contact by the sheer force of its technological advantage – is accepted, the question of why technology should have been put to the use that it was needs an answer. The technological advantage argument is closely related to the self-justification which the Europeans themselves produced to defend what they were doing, the domination of one community by another.

4. Varieties of colonial intervention

The factors referred to so far produced a complex pattern of colonial intervention in the world's pre-industrial societies. In addition to the varying balance of economic, strategic and diplomatic interests, and cultural expansionism prompted by a confidence in the superiority of Western civilisation, there were highly variable local factors that conditioned the impact of European intervention. These included material conditions and the different political organisations encountered when the decision was taken to move from a purely commercial relationship with pre-industrial societies to their political incorporation into an imperial structure.

Nor did the European powers promote their cultures in the same way and to the same degree. It is possible to contrast the approaches of the British and French or Portuguese to their imperial possessions. Britain's approach to the dissemination of its culture was far more pragmatic than some of its continental neighbours, in that it sought to preserve indigenous cultures, values and social structures where it suited the colonial power politically to do so. It was possible for British imperialists to talk at one and the same time about the great benefits to their colonial dependencies of the liberties that followed the flag, while at the same time respecting and reinforcing caste and feudalism. Britain's need for political control and the maintenance of stability was consistent with the preservation of indigenous practices. In many parts of West Africa, for example, with the exception of inhuman punishments for criminal offences defined according to local customary law, existing customs and laws were left intact. It was far easier to keep a population quiescent when it was partly governed by its own institutions, laws and customs, although ultimately subject to the local representatives of the British Crown. A hierarchy of colonial officials extended from the Secretary of State for the Colonies at the apex down to district commissioners in charge of large populations and supervising the exercise of customary law by indigenous judges and lawmakers regarded as legitimate by the local population.

The French and Portuguese, by contrast, attempted assimilation. This meant that native peoples were to be turned into Europeans, particularly through Western education. This had significant implications for the development of areas in which local political élites identified closely with Europe and European culture. There was a much more vigorous policy, albeit in reality aimed at a select minority and with limited effect (Berman, 1984, p. 177), in French than in British territories of turning local people into local versions of the populations of the imperial power. The assumption was that local culture was an obstacle to the spread of European civilisation.

The availability of fertile land and the possibility of utilising it for peasant cash cropping or plantations for tea, coffee, sugar and cotton, were not constant factors. Sometimes the land could only be exploited for produce that was already indigenous to the area. The introduction of cash crops from abroad (such as rubber into Malaya from Brazil) was not always feasible. The availability of deep-water harbours which could be linked to the interior by railways and roads also affected the pattern of colonial intervention. The whole structure of communications and transportation was a highly variable factor. Initially rivers were the key to expansion, allowing penetration into the interior without any significant capital outlay. Traditional communication routes tended to determine the spatial pattern of colonial investment. The presence of minerals was another factor – copper in East Africa, gold and diamonds in Southern Africa, and tin in Bolivia, for example. Climatic conditions also differed, making East Africa far more conducive to European settlement than West Africa.

Another variable was the indigenous social structures of the colonised territories. Some local communities were extremely simple in their economic activities, being based on hunting and gathering. Some were nomadic pastoral communities, surviving on the basis of livestock which was grazed over regular transhumance routes. Other societies had complex agrarian systems with highly elaborate organisations for production, distribution and exchange. Levels of urbanisation varied considerably, too, with some societies based on towns that performed the roles of administrative and commercial centres. Some societies were highly feudalistic in terms of relations between landowners and their tenant cultivators, whereas elsewhere more egalitarian systems were found, with land held in common and individual plots cultivated by families without rights to alienate or accumulate. Concepts of rent and tenancy were absent from such cultures, as were the political relationships that accompany them.

Different forms of political organisation were encountered. There were centralised state structures immediately recognisable as such by Europeans: ancient kingdoms had clearly articulated forms of political authority and leadership, with state functionaries recruited according to explicit rules; traditional leaders were surrounded by civil and military officialdom; territorial divisions were created for purposes of administration, taxation, and the enforcement of laws. Such structures of government were highly suitable for the purposes of colonial administration, especially in the context of the pragmatic approach to managing dependent territories mentioned earlier. Indirect rule meant using the indigenous political structures for imperial objectives. There were obvious political advantages in using the legitimacy conferred upon traditional leaders who were at the same time loyal to, and dependent on, the colonial administration. The benefits of such indirectly acquired legitimacy were especially great under circumstances when this would otherwise have been extremely difficult, if not impossible, to achieve. Exploiting military and commercial superiority was thus made easier.

The colonial powers found it relatively easy to persuade indigenous rulers to accept this integration of their own traditional systems of decision-making and adjudication into the colonial state hierarchy. Claimants to the throne received the support of the colonial authorities in return for their loyalty and co-operation. Corrupt, incompetent or insubordinate rulers were easily deposed and there were always more co-operative princes, chiefs and emirs to replace them (Berman, 1984, p. 184). British officials became the real power behind the thrones of indigenous rulers, intervening according to the precise needs of the European presence. Such interventions had to be greater if there was a need to remove local people from their land through legislation and other instruments of colonial policy. Elsewhere there was simply a need to preserve conditions under which cash crops could be produced by peasant cultivators according to traditional methods of cultivation. Here indirect rule was a most appropriate form of colonial administration.

Indigenous political structures were not always so familiar and useful to colonial government. In the acephalous societies, without formal positions of permanent leadership, government was organised without separate institutions for making laws, adjudicating in disputes and performing other civil and military functions on behalf of the community. Far less familiar forms of authority were used to manage society's communal affairs, such as age groups, lineages, clans or elders. What was required was an interpretation of the wisdom of ancestors in order to solve disputes over land, family affairs or economic activities, make decisions concerning the welfare of the community, or deal with conflicts with neighbouring communities. In societies without obvious structures of chieftaincy or other political offices it was much more difficult to integrate indigenous political authority into an imperial system. Offices had to be artificially created for the purposes of colonial government, a source of great discontent and alienation in the communities affected, sometimes leading to political instability and problems of social order.

A consequence of such local economic, social and political variety, combined with the varying motivations of the imperialists, was that different forms of colonial intervention developed. In some areas plantations were set up in which industrialised forms of agricultural production were created, requiring large numbers of wage labourers and European managers. Elsewhere mining activities required the encouragement of the local population into the formation of an industrial labour force. In other areas imperialism required the encouragement of peasant cash cropping without changing the relations of production by the introduction of wage labour or new technology. Another variation on the colonial theme was European settlement on the best land available, leading to permanent commitments on the part of white minorities. It was common to find more than one form of colonial intervention in a single colony – as in Kenya and Tanganyika, where peasant production was combined with plantation and settler agriculture. Economically one form was usually dominant, as in the Gold Coast, where peasant commodity production dominated a colonial economy that included European-owned mining operations (Berman, 1984).

5. The introduction of capitalism

The variation in the forms taken by colonial penetration and imperialism and the different activities engaged in by the Europeans, combined with the different circumstances encountered by them, led to a debate among historians and social scientists about whether colonialism transformed pre-capitalist societies into capitalist societies through incorporation into a network of capitalist relations that extended from metropolitan centres as new territories were absorbed into empires; or whether capitalism simply traded upon pre-capitalist relations and modes of production that were part of traditional society, so that even though the firms extracting raw materials and agricultural produce from the colonies were capitalist, the actual processes of production remained largely unchanged. This controversy formed an important part of the debate about post-colonial 'dependency' and will be referred to again in that context in Chapter 6.

On the one hand, it was quite possible for cash crops and even raw materials to be produced for the imperialists by pre-capitalist methods. The earlier stages of imperialism did not find it necessary to affect the mode of production in the colonised society. Peasant production was in no way capitalist but could still produce the commodities that the West needed. Colonial interests were pursued through existing relations of production within peasant or tribal communities except in so far as mechanisms were introduced to increase the rate of exploitation of labour.

On the other hand, where there were mining enclaves, plantations and expatriate agricultural settlement the effect on the indigenous societies was most traumatic and was likely to transform peasant producers into wage labourers or capitalist farmers. European capital investment was relatively high in such areas, and some encouragement was given to the development of an industrial economy (Barratt Brown, 1963, p. 169). There was far less capital investment in areas without European settlement. Investment in primary production brought some changes to a colony through the creation of wage labour in ports and railways. In such cases capitalism can be said to have transformed indigenous social and economic systems. Sometimes the quest for raw materials led the Western powers to interfere in the relations of production and in market relationships, particularly changing the balance between food crops and cash crops to increase the production of the latter. Local political control was important in turning local producers away from subsistence agriculture towards exportable commodities for the European economies. Imperialism thus became associated with famine in some circumstances, as in parts of India.

So the extent to which imperialism actually affected or interfered with pre-capitalist modes of production varied a good deal. Probably nowhere were traditional pre-capitalist forms of production and the social relations accompanying them completely abolished, but nowhere were they left completely unchanged. Where a system of landlordism existed, for example, which the colonial authorities found convenient for the management of labour and other features of local society, the colonial authorities would at the same time tax the incomes of landlords who, as a consequence, were denied full access to the resources over which they had previously had command. Relationships with tenants and labourers was changed. This happened in India when the colonial authorities used the richer tenant classes for the management of society and the extraction of revenue (Kiernan, 1974, pp. 18–19).

Over a period of time changes in relations of production gradually took place under the influence of colonialism. This generated another controversy about the economic and political consequences of imperialism, and about whether colonialism encouraged or obstructed capitalist industrialisation (Sutcliffe, 1972). One interpretation is that imperialism did not provide a basis for industrialisation because wealth was remitted to metropolitan centres and natural resources were exploited using an artificially created and controlled proletariat. The terms of trade were adversely affected by dependence on a limited number of export crops and restricted markets. European investment in the infrastructure of railways, ports, roads, and the telegraph aimed solely to extract primary products for export (Barratt Brown, 1963, pp. 160–3).

Others, notably the Marxist economist Bill Warren, have argued that imperialism and colonialism did encourage the development of capitalism, acting as a 'powerful engine of progressive social change'. The significance of this controversy, which will be returned to when the concept of neo-colonialism is analysed in Chapter 5, for present purposes lies not so much in its implications for understanding the economic development of dependent societies as in its significance for understanding social development and therefore the emergence of political forces.

Colonialism changed colonial society in ways that eventually led to the emergence of new social groupings and political forces. The spread of urbanisation, the gradual opening up of the professions and the bureaucracy to local people, the development of an indigenous commercial middle class, and the acquisition of Western education by a privileged local élite, all provided a social basis for nationalist movements, demands for self-government, and the emergence of political parties and other organisations to represent the interests of sections of indigenous society (Barratt Brown, 1963, p. 180).

Colonialism also enabled imperialism to employ coercion to enforce the introduction of commodity production and wage labour. The colonial authorities exercised direct control over labour, deployed arbitrary political authority, adapted indigenous forms of social order such as caste, enforced laws restricting the free movement of workers including bonded labour, and interfered with the labour market to reduce its cost. Taxation, forced labour, the creation of official markets or trading centres, and compulsory crop production were widely used to ensure a supply of labour and export commodities: 'In sum, the recruitment of labour and the regulation of relations of production were increasingly assumed by colonial states, rather than being left to unpredictable "market" forces or the direct confrontation of labour and capital' (Berman, 1984, p. 170).

Taking the Indian sub-continent as an example, Wood itemises the extent of colonial state intervention designed to ensure the right conditions for the exploitation of labour in order to raise the level of the surplus value which it creates:

> tenancy legislation, revenue and rent fixing, head/poll taxes, monetizations of those obligations, registration of families, restrictions on their mobility, control of migrant workers and disposal of their incomes, expropriation of land to create homelands for expatriate settlement and plantations. (Wood, G. D., 1984b, p. 35)

Consequently political and economic relationships became fused, leaving 'little room for the legitimating support of bourgeois ideology'. This failure to convert labour into a commodity whose status is sustained by 'bourgeois freedoms' had profound effects on political development. The absence of laws and practices supporting the development of a labour force free to enter into wage contracts with employers removed an essential prerequisite of the liberal democratic state. Colonialism in its political and economic form was not consistent with the model of the bourgeois state. The role of the colonial state was inconsistent with the values and practices of liberalism. Colonialism could not provide an ideology to sustain liberal democracy. This may be colonialism's most important legacy for post-colonial societies.

Two further legacies of the colonial experience can be identified. From a comparative study of African colonies Berman concludes first that colonialism established the state as the source of economic development and therefore as the focus of a particular kind of political conflict. The process began when colonial administrators encouraged selective indigenous élites to participate in production and trade through institutions such as co-operatives which had been established by the colonial authorities. 'All of this meant that the administrators mediated access to many of the sources of accumulation and the state increasingly became the necessary focus of the emerging proto-capitalist class' (Berman, 1984, p. 186; see also Lonsdale, 1981, pp. 193–4). This trend was encouraged by post-war colonial development policies involving state-sponsored rural development programmes, commodity marketing boards, wage and labour laws, and public expenditure on the social and economic infrastructure. Consequently political power became much more than a matter of national sovereignty for the emerging nationalist élites.

Secondly, Berman notes that the colonial administrations fragmented African society through an informal policy of 'divide and rule'. This obstructed the development of alignments on a national scale by encouraging identification with ethnicity and locality. It was in the interest of colonial administration to prevent the development of class consciousness by any stratum of indigenous society. 'African political and social forces were fragmented, isolated and contained within the framework of local administrative units which . . . inhibited the coalescence of African opposition and resistance into a colony-wide challenge to the colonial order' (Berman, 1984, pp. 186–7). As we have seen, the administrative division of colonial society relied heavily on the co-option of traditional authority. In Africa, for example, chiefs were invested with more power than they traditionally enjoyed in return for their support and co-operation. Hoogvelt argues that this undermined their legitimacy in traditional society, leaving political space for new élites whose status rested on Western educational achievement. Thus a dual political structure was created of Westernised élites in the urban areas and traditional élites, supported by the administration through the reaffirmation of local law and custom, in the rural areas (Hoogvelt, 1978, p. 107).

The 'tribalism' thus encouraged persisted into the immediate post-independence period and became a major source of destabilising political conflict.

6. Conclusion

Colonialism has now all but disappeared: there are a few small pockets left in the world. National sovereignty is the rule. Latin

American independence had been achieved by the end of the nineteenth century, whereas in Africa and Asia colonialism came to an end largely as a result of the Second World War. Social scientists found themselves confronted by a growing number of newly independent states after that war and became interested in how these societies were going to progress and develop. This was of more than merely academic interest, it was important for the foreign policies of the great powers. They were interested in the way that modernising countries would change, whether they would achieve a stability that favoured Western interests and, if not, whether such regimes could be destabilised to produce a less hostile environment for Western economic, strategic and diplomatic aims.

Part II
Theories of Political Change

3
Modernisation and Political Change

1. Origins

Modernisation theory is a body of thought which attempts to incorporate a large number of societies, many of which were in the process of becoming new states, into a theory about change. It is a theory that must be located in a specific historical and global context. It had some of its roots in the optimism following the Second World War and the widespread belief that the countries achieving or approaching independence would not only be freed from exploitation by the First World but would also have benefited from contacts with the exploiter's technology, culture, liberal democracy and capitalism. The advanced countries were perceived as having poverty and inequality (especially in levels of education and welfare) under control. Democracy had triumphed over fascism in war and Marxism had been discredited by Stalinism. Social scientists in the West believed beneficial social engineering, based on a scientific understanding of the new states of the Third World, to be possible (Higgott, 1983).

Later this optimism changed to pessimism as, in the 1960s, political realities in the Third World became clearer and as social science adopted new paradigms. The second generation élites of the Third World were increasingly exposed as corrupt, and the state administrations and public sectors seemed incapable of stimulating development. Supposedly independent nation-states and sovereign governments were found to be constrained by external political and economic forces. The 'total pessimism that engulfed the later years of the first Development Decade' was accompanied by the influence on modernisation theory of economics, rational choice theory and the growth of a new political economy. The limitations of behavioural and liberal political theory were increasingly recognised (Higgott, 1983, p. 21).

The idea of modernisation was predominantly conceptualised by US social scientists, backed by generous government support. In the US modernisation theorists assisted foreign policy-makers concerned about the possibly destabilising effects of rapid economic change, and the consequences of any destabilisation for communist subversion and therefore the security of the USA in different parts of the world (Bernstein, 1971; Preston, 1982, pp. 72–9). Numerous cases of American developmentalist social theory being co-opted into foreign policy-making during the 1960s on such issues as the invasion of Cuba and the Vietnam war are cited by A. G. Frank to demonstrate the lack of 'role specificity' in the social science profession of an advanced industrial society (Frank, 1972c, pp. 330–2). The close relationship between government and academics in the generation and dissemination of ideas about Third World development is illustrated by the fact that Hoselitz's *Sociological Aspects of Economic Growth* was translated into twenty-five languages by the US Department of State and the essays published in Weiner's *Modernization: the Dynamics of Growth* were first prepared for *Voice of America* (Valenzuela and Valenzuela, 1978, p. 553). Changing perceptions of the Third World in the West on the part of both policy-makers and social scientists led the political science of development to reorientate itself in the second half of the 1960s towards the preconditions of political order, stability and the maintenance of regimes and élites, a change which will be described in Chapter 4.

2. Social evolution

Modernisation theory is concerned with the social transformations taking place in societies whose economies and social systems are changing rapidly. It has its roots in classical evolutionary explanations of social change. Western, and particularly US, social scientists interested in the problems of economic development, political stability and social and cultural change in the Third World societies emerging on to the world's stage as a consequence of independence from imperial control, inevitably turned to familiar approaches to social change. Ideas about modernisation were heavily dependent upon evolutionary theories (Tipps, 1973, pp. 200–1). Modernisation theory is thus a descendant of the idea that change is both quantitative and qualitative. It has its intellectual roots in the European evolutionists of the eighteenth and nineteenth centuries: the French philosophers and founders of modern sociology Auguste Comte and Emile Durkheim; the British philosopher Herbert Spencer; and of course Marx (Huntington, 1971, pp. 291–2; Bock, 1978; Varma, 1980, p. 34). All were in their different ways trying to explain the transformation from pre-industrial society into industrial society. Two elements in particular from that early theorising were carried over into debates about modernisation in the Third World. One is the belief that social change involves continuity and the other is the belief in progress (So, 1990, pp. 18–20).

The belief in continuity reflects the attempts of social theorists to emulate the natural sciences in the study of society, and to establish laws governing social change. This meant focusing attention on the causes of historical development and the possibility that changes in certain directions may be inevitable and predictable. A science of society should be capable of relating cause and effect in this way.

Continuity is not seen as neutral but as progressive. The early theorists of social evolution assumed that change implied advancement and improvement, a highly qualitative aspect of the transition from pre-industrial to industrial society. It was also common for such social theorists in the nineteenth century to think in terms of stages of development, and at the very least to distinguish between the traditional stage and the modern stage of social evolution. This is an idea that was incorporated into more recent thinking about the process of becoming a modern society (Hoogvelt, 1976, pp. 11–12; Bock, 1978).

Progressive continuity involves two sets of transformations: increased complexity, and greater specialisation in human organisation and activity in the social, economic and political spheres. Twentieth-century concepts of modernisation inherited all of these assumptions about continuity and progress. The conclusions about specialisation and complexity were particularly influential. Some theorists described these processes in terms of greater differentiation in society, a particularly important concept in modern versions of evolutionist thinking.

Modernisation theory, like other evolutionary explanations of society, has its own view of the end of the evolutionary process. Modernisation means advancement towards a condition corresponding to the industrial capitalist societies of the West. A society that is becoming modern is one that acquires characteristics common to more developed societies, achieving things that modern societies have in common. This belief is made most explicit by Eisenstadt:

> Historically, modernization is the process of change towards those types of social, economic and political systems that have developed in western Europe and North America from the seventeenth century to the nineteenth and have then spread to other European countries and in the nineteenth and twentieth centuries to the South American, Asian, and African continents. (Eisenstadt, 1966, p. 1)

Traditional societies will gradually eliminate their economic, political and particularly cultural institutions and values, replacing them with modern ones.

Such ideas were the concern of policy-makers as well as academics, because it was believed that official interventions could speed up the process of modernisation. This belief affected the financial and technical assistance given by the richer to the poorer countries. Education in particular was seen as a way of developing human resources to serve the needs of modern industrial production by providing the skills and knowledge required for technological progress. Special training programmes were launched on the premise that the required psychological motivation could be encouraged to overcome barriers to modernisation, what some social psychologists referred to as the 'need for achievement', a characteristic of modern man and needing to be imbued in traditional people (see below, pp. 75–9). As they became more modern, traditional people would acquire this 'need' but it could be encouraged by training, education and example. The mass media were consequently regarded as vitally important for the dissemination of modern values. So it became particularly important for some policy-makers that people in the rural areas of backward societies should have access to radio, newspapers and literacy programmes.

The attributes needed for modernisation were seen as interrelated. Economic and social values were linked through such individual values as the work ethic, needed to support the kind of activities upon which modern industrial society depended but not found in traditional society. Modernisation theory thus relied heavily on Max Weber's view of religious beliefs as sustaining certain kinds of economic relationships. Modernisation theorists, while not necessarily wanting to disseminate Protestantism, nevertheless accepted that normative values were extremely significant as a foundation for launching new kinds of economic initiatives.

The special social and cultural characteristics associated with being modern can be grouped under three headings. First there is the idea of an increasing level of social differentiation. Secondly, modernisation meant the diffusion of secular or rational norms within a culture. This requires changes in cultural patterns, presented as two contrasting models, the traditional and the modern. The path of progress between them is divided into stages. Thirdly, modernisation involved the transformation of the individual personality.

3. Differentiation

Social differentiation was an idea developed most fully by the French philosopher and sociologist Emile Durkheim, who applied the idea of the division of labour to society generally. As societies grow and become more complex, the level of specialisation increases and specialised roles become more interdependent. Social activities become divided among a multiplicity of institutions. As population size and density increase, urbanisation spreads and communications improve, this division of labour is extended.

This process can be seen in the transformation of subsistence agriculture. As production is organised on a larger scale, as consumption is no longer on the basis of subsistence but comes to depend on exchange, as distribution has to be organised, and as the processes of production become more complex, so more specialised roles are required to perform far more functions than were earlier performed by the subsistence farmer.

Durkheim described the process of becoming modern as the development of 'organic solidarity'. The growing division of labour means a transformation in the nature of social solidarity. Mechanical solidarity signifies a society in which the individual personality is absorbed into a collective personality. 'Individuality is something which a society possesses'. In contrast, the organic solidarity brought about by the division of labour presumes differences between individuals, each having a special sphere of action or personality:

> It is necessary, then, that the collective conscience leaves open a part of the individual conscience in order that special functions may be established there, functions which it cannot regulate. The more this region is extended, the stronger is the cohesion which results from this solidarity. In effect, on the one hand, each one depends as much more strictly on society as labour is more divided; and, on the other, the activity of each is as much more personal as it is specialised.

Occupations and professions give greater scope for the free play of initiative. Society becomes more capable of 'collective movement' as each of its elements gains greater freedom. The solidarity due to the division of labour is organic because 'the unity of the organism is as great as the individuation of the parts is more marked' (Durkheim, 1965, p. 213).

Differentiation thus refers to an increasing level of institutional specialisation and greater heterogeneity within society. For example, in traditional society the family as one structure performs a number of roles – reproductive, economic, educational – whereas in modern society there are specialised institutions for economy, education, and socialisation, developed outside the family. The family's role becomes more specific and restricted while new institutions are elaborated to perform these and additional roles that modern society demands. Specialisation of political roles was seen by the neo-evolutionists as part of becoming a modern polity. The main exponent of this process of differentiation was the US sociologist Talcot Parsons, the leading figure in the functionalist school of sociology, dominant in the US from the 1940s to the 1960s.

The historian S. N. Eisenstadt noted how structural differentiation affected stratification. The process of modernisation fragments social status, so that different people hold positions of high status in different social spheres. It is not just that roles become more specialised. Leaders in different institutional spheres – bureaucrats, entrepreneurs, the military leaders, intellectuals, political élites – do not form definite strata or classes, whereas the tendency is 'in many premodern societies for most property, power and status relations either to coalesce or to be segregated in a rather rigid hierarchical order' (Eisenstadt, 1966, p. 8).

4. Secularisation

Secularisation is a process by which societies become more rationalised; it occurs when people perceive that the circumstances around them are changeable by human intervention. If religious belief, such as fatalism, prevents society from seeing the environment in that way, then religion may become an obstacle to modernisation. A rational or secular basis of social values does not accept as unalterable or sacred the facts of life. Secularisation means enabling people to differentiate between the sacred and the profane, the religious world and the world of material objects. It does not interpret everything in terms of a set of beliefs about what is sacred and what is handed down from time immemorial. Those beliefs may remain but people begin to separate them from secular concerns, the latter then being exposed to rational scrutiny.

The precursor of this aspect of modernisation theory was the German sociologist Max Weber, whose theory of social action distinguished between actions determined by reason and actions determined by habit or emotion. Rationalisation for Weber meant subjecting a growing number of areas of life to calculation that enable predetermined ends to be achieved efficiently. For Weber capitalism represented the model of such calculation in the economy and was almost synonymous with the idea of rational economic thought producing the most efficient distribution of a society's material resources. What distinguished modern capitalism from earlier forms of economic enterprise and exploitation was that it had been

strongly influenced by the development of technical possibilities. Its rationality is today essentially dependent on the calculability of the most important technical factors. But this means fundamentally that it is dependent on the peculiarities of modern science, especially the natural sciences based on mathematics and exact and rational experiment. (Weber, 1965, p. 1527)

Bureaucracy was Weber's model of rational government. In the domain of the state, bureaucracy epitomised the idea of linking means to ends, and of defining an objective and calculating what needed to be done to achieve it. Bureaucracy, based on rules, expertise, plans and calculations, was the ideal form of authority for the rationalisation of politics. Rational-legal authority combines the idea of means being related to ends with the idea that rules, offices and public action would no longer reflect heredity, tradition, custom or charisma. Rules reflect an understanding of cause and effect in the political sphere. Rather than respect rules simply because they are endorsed by custom, religion or traditional values, rules are respected because they are instrumental. Moreover, capitalism has need of rational structures of law and administration, of

a calculable legal system and of administration in terms of formal rules. Without it adventurous and speculative trading capitalism and all sorts of politically determined capitalisms are possible, but no rational enterprise under individual initiative, with fixed capital and certainty of calculations. Such a legal system and such administration have been available for economic activity in a comparative state of legal and formalistic perfection only in the Occident. (Weber, 1965, p. 1257)

Greater rationality is supported by the growth of scientific and technological knowledge. M. J. Levy wrote that society was 'more or less modernized to the extent that its members use inanimate sources of power and/or use tools to multiply the effects of their efforts' (Levy, 1966, p. 11). Black associated modernisation with the adaptation of institutions to 'the rapidly growing functions that reflect the unprecedented increase in man's knowledge, permitting control over his environment' (Black, 1966, p. 7). Rustow saw modernisation as resulting from man's 'rapidly widening control over nature' (1967, p. 3). Moore equated modernisation with 'the process of rationalisation of social behaviour and social organisation', defining rationalisation as the 'normative expectation that objective information and rational calculus of procedures will be applied in pursuit or achievement of any utilitarian goal', an example being the use of sophisticated technology in industry (Moore, W. L., 1977, pp. 34–5).

Modernisation theorists do not assume that rational behaviour is universal, especially in the economic realm (Valenzuela and Valenzuela, 1978, p. 539). Individuals in developing countries are believed to 'behave in ways that are "irrational" or "non-rational" as judged on economic grounds' (Moore, 1964, p. 292; Huntington, 1971, p. 287).

Modernisation theory requires us to have some sort of perception of non-modern or traditional society. It also requires us to think about the way in which traditional social structures and values somehow hinder or present obstacles to modernisation (Higgott, 1978, p. 31). The values and institutions of traditional society are seen as causing underdevelopment and blocking modernisation. Development policies have been designed to overcome 'obstacles' to modernisation which take the form of traditional values. For example, traditional societies are sometimes said to have failed to understand the problem of over-population and therefore fail to adopt appropriate methods of birth control. Or they fail to see the dangers of over-urbanisation, leading to the appalling squalor of Third World slums and shanty towns. These failures of perception are associated with what is seen as a lack of rationality in the sense of being able to relate means to ends and so produce policies, strategies and interventions that will deal with problems. So part of the idea of a society becoming modern is of a society which not only develops the administrative capability to embark upon policies but also develops the very way of thinking that permits phenomena to be confronted, a mode of thought which accepts that things can be changed by human agency, by setting goals and working out the means of achieving them.

5. Cultural modernisation

Secularisation and rationalisation require changes in cultural patterns. These changes were categorised by Parsons as 'pattern variables', variable patterns of related values with which people make judgements about other members of their society or the way people orientate themselves within social relationships. He argued that social change was essentially a matter of how we perceive people with whom we come into contact, whether in the family, wider social organisations, territorial communities, or occupations.

From community to society

Parsons followed the conceptualisation of modern and pre-modern social patterns produced by the German sociologist Tonnies, who distinguished between two historically fundamental forms of social organisation. *Gemeinschaft* is usually translated as 'community' and *Gesselschaft* as 'society' or 'association'. According to Tonnies, communities are groups in which relationships between members are derived from strong codes and conventions based on emotion, sentiment and belief in a pre-ordained order. There is a common understanding of where each member stands in relation to others handed down from generation to generation, and enunciated from time to time by members of the community whose authority is recognised as falling within that sphere. In contrast, a society characterised by the relationships of association is one in which people stand in impersonal, contractual and calculative relations with each other. They come together not because they are bound by an interpretation of their society which links everyone in an established order defining a kinship or lineage group, but for purely instrumental reasons, offering each other reciprocal benefits to achieve something that cannot be achieved by people acting in isolation. People are not associated with because they are recognised as a member of a particular exclusive community, but because co-operation will enable a common goal to be achieved.

The modern industrial organisation represents the archetypal form of association, in which people are recruited into abstractly defined roles and integrated in a social structure to achieve some independently defined objective. For Tonnies, *Gemeinschaft* was represented by 'all intimate, private and exclusive living together' – the family, marriage, religious communities, communities of language, folkways, mores and beliefs, and by certain sorts of property (Tonnies claimed 'there exists a community of ownership in fields, forest and pasture'). In contrast *Gesellschaft* stood for public life, political institutions, the realm of business, travel or sciences, and commercial companies:

human *Gesellschaft* is conceived as mere co-existence of people independent of each other. . . . Accordingly, *Gemeinschaft* should be understood as a living organism, *Gesellschaft* as a mechanical aggregate and artifact. (Tonnies, 1965, pp. 191–2).

Pattern variables

The pattern variables described by Parsons tried to break these concepts down into further discrete sets of factors (Parsons, 1951). Traditional society is defined as characterised by *particularism*, whereas modern society is characterised by *universalism*. A particularistic judgement of or response to a fellow member of society applies special values because of a unique relationship between the people involved. Members of a kinship group or family will judge each other according to criteria applicable to that group relationship alone. When one only has values that can be utilised in the context of unique social relations a society is at the traditional end of the continuum. When judgements can be made on universal criteria, regardless of other dimensions of social relationships, society is at the modern end. When there are standards which can be applied to any individual regardless of their position in society, universalism is said to exist. Criteria of performance that are defined independently of the status of those being evaluated constitute a pure form of universalism.

Parsons then contrasts *ascribed status* with *achieved status*. The former implies the existence of inherent qualities associated with the specific individuals concerned. For example, in a society which respects the wisdom of its older members, as soon as one becomes an elder that wisdom is assumed to exist by definition. It is not appropriate to apply independent tests of competence. Achieved status depends upon a capacity to satisfy independent and abstract criteria that are defined independently of the other qualities of the individual concerned. When status is inherent in the person, society is traditional. Where status is acquired by the achievement of abstract qualities defined in terms of objective criteria, such as educational qualifications, society is modern. Ascriptive political office would be represented by an inherited position, whereas achievement would be exemplified by a bureaucrat recruited on the basis of acquired characteristics defined as necessary for particular tasks to be performed.

A third pair of cultural patterns contrasts *affectivity* with *neutrality*. 'Affectivity' refers to emotional attachments between people. Neutral attachments are based on instrumentality and objectives external to personal relationships.

Finally *diffuseness* is contrasted with *specificity*. Diffuse relations refer to the complex web of interconnections that link people together involving many roles and aspects of their lives. Here judgements can only be made about a total person: different roles cannot be separated for purposes of evaluation and the definition of social relationships. When society is formed on the basis of specificity, it is possible to distinguish the different roles performed by individuals and to be concerned with just one of them – as employer or employee, landlord or tenant, for example. Individuals in modern societies are seen as involved in a multiplicity of single-stranded relationships. Specificity signifies the separateness of social relations and their relative independence from each other, whereas diffuse relations combine all aspects of the individual's role in society and it is not possible to exclude consideration of some of these different aspects when individuals interrelate – relationships are multi-stranded; no individual can abstract one of those relationships and give it an independent existence.

Such variables enable us to see how far a society has changed along different dimensions. Each set of pattern variables represents an analytical model to which no reality corresponds exactly.

From tradition to modernity

Building upon these theoretical foundations, post-war modernisation theorists emphasised features of the process by which it was thought the undeveloped societies of the world would become modern. First, they contrasted the characteristics of an ideal type which was designated 'modern' with one that was designated 'traditional'. Development was then viewed as the transformation of the former into the latter (Nash, 1963). Development is seen as evolutionary, implying the bridging of a gap formed by observable differences between rich and poor countries 'by means of an imitative process, in which the less developed countries gradually assumed the qualities of the industrial nation' (Blomstrom and

Hettne, 1984, p. 20). Parsons' pattern variables were utilised for the purpose of comparison, notably by the US economist Hoselitz (1964).

An elaborate scheme of sociological concepts was produced by M.J. Levy in *The Structure of Society* (1952) which sets out the structures of relationships that are required in industrial society, arguing that the patterns dominant there inevitably spill over into other areas of life, especially the political system, where values must be compatible with those of the economy. The sociologist Neil Smelser emphasised the importance of structural differentiation in the social changes accompanying economic development. Differentiation, or the 'evolution from a multifunctional role structure to several more specialised structures' (1963, p. 34), occurs with the transition from domestic to factory production, the replacement of family and church by the school in the education function, and the substitution of the complex political party structure for tribal factions. Structural differentiation in the system of social stratification increases as ascription declines and individual mobility through occupational hierarchies increases. Integrating mechanisms are increasingly required to co-ordinate the growing social heterogeneity.

Theodorson also argued that 'an increase in universalism, achievement, suppression of immediate emotional release (affective-neutrality), and specificity all accompany industrialisation in the long run' (1953, p. 81). The adjustment of man to machines and the effect that this adjustment has on family life lead to an individual's relationships becoming

less diffuse, because he has less time to know them thoroughly. They are less particularistic because there are fewer groups in which he and his neighbours are integrated. Because he is dealing with relatively unfamiliar people on a specific-universalistic basis his relations with them will be less emotionally involved. (p. 82)

Machines also demand selection by achievement, not ascription. Ability is a specific demand, so diffuse standards become irrelevant. It becomes increasingly difficult to combine particularism and achievement. 'Achievement-universalism will be fostered not only by the demand for efficient labour for the expensive machines, but also by the demands imposed on the factory unit by competition, (p. 82).

The demands of the machine and the organisational hierarchy in which it is located lead to new relationships with authority:

> Before the introduction of the machine the relation of the individual member of the working group to those who possessed authority was diffuse. In the factory situation the relation of the individual towards his superiors becomes very specific. The superiors are only interested in those aspects of the individual which are relevant to the efficient use of the machines. (p. 83)

Similarly, relations with fellow workers become specific in place of the diffuseness characteristic of relations when people know others as total individuals. The more the economic system becomes separated from other systems in society, the less relevant are diffuse and particularistic considerations. If old cultural elements are preserved in the face of demands by the factory system, there will be strains such as less productivity and delays in the achievement of economic goals. The modern market also requires specific orientations towards others. Nor can political authorities any longer deal with citizens on the basis of diffuse standards.

Stages of modernisation

The evolutionary approach to modernisation required the identification of stages along the path from tradition to modernity. Parsons divided social evolution into the primitive, advanced primitive, intermediate and modern stages (Parsons, 1960 and 1966). The American economist W. W. Rostow, in his books on *The Process of Economic Growth* (1952) and *The Stages of Economic Growth* (1960) identified five stages of economic development:

- traditional society with a mainly agricultural economy and using more or less unchanging production methods;
- transitional society, when the possibility of economic progress is recognised, usually as a result of some external influence and spreading within either the established élite or some disadvantaged group keen to take the initiative for both economic and political reasons;
- the 'take off' stage when, because of rises in the rate of investment, changes in production techniques, increases in per

capita output, and political, social and institutional change supporting innovation, economic growth becomes more or less automatic;

- the 'drive to maturity' when modern technology is spread throughout the economy, approximately 10–20 per cent of national income is invested, output exceeds population increase, and society trades off old values against new according to the demands of efficient production; and
- the age of high mass consumption when, because of rises in real incomes and changes in the structure of the labour force, production shifts towards consumer durables and services, and resources can be allocated to social welfare and security.

Among the preconditions for 'take off' Rostow identifies two which connect his work with the sociological analysis of modernising culture – achieved status and rationality (Rostow, 1960, p. 19).

6. The modernisation of personality

A psychological view of modernisation emphasises the importance of the individual's personality traits. Psychologists such as Everett Hagen, Alex Inkeles and David McClelland contributed to the theory of modernisation with ideas about the nature of a modern personality and the 'need for achievement' as a necessary condition of economic progress.

McClelland was influenced by Weber's description of the 'spirit' of capitalism, concluding that the Calvinistic doctrine of predestination forced people to strive for perfection and to rationalise every aspect of their lives – that they had a strong need for achievement. If there was such an association between a need for achievement (n Achievement or n Ach) and the economic development recorded in the early stages of capitalism, it could be expected to be found elsewhere:

a high average level of n Achievement should be equally associated with economic development in ancient Greece, in modern Japan, or in a preliterate tribe being studied by anthropologists in the South Pacific. (McClelland, 1963, p. 76)

Among those credited with having achieved economic development because of their high level of *n* Achievement were the Russians and Chinese under communism.

It is a curious paradox that the Communists have managed to produce rapid economic growth in a country like Russia not, as they believe, because of socialism, but because of their fanatical belief in its superiority. That is, here, as elsewhere, a conviction in one's superiority has spread the *n* Ach virus, which is more directly responsible for accelerating the rate of economic growth than the socialist type of economic organisation. (McClelland, 1966, p. 38)

A need for achievement is a characteristic of a modernising individual regardless of culture or ideology. The need is for the satisfaction of a sense of personal accomplishment. This is what motivates modern man. Economic growth has in part to be explained by rising levels of the need for achievement. This need produces the entrepreneurial spirit. McClelland hypothesised that 'a society with a generally high level of *n* Achievement will produce more energetic entrepreneurs who, in turn, produce more rapid economic development' (1961, p. 205). He wanted to prove that psychological forces ultimately determined the rate of economic and social development, and that man was not a creature of the natural or social environment. Following Schumpeter's emphasis on the activities of entrepreneurs in creating Western industrialisation, McClelland argued that the business entrepreneur was the link that explained how 'a particular type of human motive in a population leads to a complex social phenomenon like economic growth' (1963, p. 82).

However, McClelland's researches also suggested to him that '*n* Ach' is by no means all there is to modernisation: 'it does not automatically lead one into socially useful activities or projects'. Research in India led McClelland to conclude that 'conscience' is another 'input' into modernisation. People with high levels of *n* Ach wanted to do things not just for themselves but for the common good. He found this theme of concern for the common good in the textbooks used by children in countries that had experienced rapid development, in contrast to references to tradition and habit in the books used in slowly developing countries.

It was almost as if some countries realized that in order to get people thinking about modernisation, they had to replace their normal traditionalism with a concern for the welfare of others who might even be strangers to them. Furthermore, it is probably in this way that one may most easily explain the correlations that have been found between investments in health and education and subsequent rates of economic growth. . . . In short, the impulse to modernisation in ideal psychological terms seems to consist in part of a personal virtue – *n* Ach – and in part of a social virtue – interest in the welfare of the generalised other fellow. (McClelland, 1966, p. 36)

Hagen similarly dichotomised the creative personality of modern society with its high needs for achievement, autonomy, order and understanding of natural and social systems, and the uncreative personality of traditional society which tolerates hierarchical, authoritarian and inherited status structures (Hagen, 1962 and 1963). Daniel Lerner identified what he believed to be a 'psychic gap' between traditional man's rejection of innovation and Western man's purposive rationality and 'mobile personality'. The 'mobile' person can identify with changes in his environment. He can 'enlarge his identity' through empathy:

high empathic capacity is the predominant personal style only in modern society, which is distinctly industrial, urban, literate and *participant*. Traditional society is non-participant – it deploys people by kinship into communities isolated from each other and from a centre. . . . Whereas the isolated communities of traditional society functioned well on the basis of a highly constrictive personality, the interdependent sectors of modern society require widespread participation. This in turn requires an expansive and adaptive self-system, ready to incorporate new roles and to identify personal values with public issues. (Lerner, 1958, pp. 50–1)

For Lerner, psychic mobility is largely the result of physical mobility, urbanisation, exposure to the mass media, and the spread of literacy.

Inkeles and Smith contrasted modern man's (*sic*) readiness to adopt innovations, belief in his own ability to effect change, independence from traditional influences and informed participation in affairs, with traditional man's passivity, lack of efficacy, fear of innovation, isolation, dependence on traditional authority, narrow preoccupations, limited ambitions and undervaluing of education. They claimed not only that modern attitudes and values change behaviour, but also that such behaviour was necessary for rapid economic growth and effective government (Inkeles and Smith, 1974).

These propositions quite clearly combine the descriptive with the prescriptive: that as people become more modern they will acquire this need for achievement; but that things need to be done to make it easier for such a need to be satisfied. Development assistance, for example, should in part nurture entrepreneurialism through special training programmes for selected élites in the Third World. For example, McClelland's plan for accelerating economic growth in underdeveloped countries involved

> mobilising more effectively the high *n* Achievement resources of a developed country to select and work directly with the scarcer high *n* Achievement resources of underdeveloped countries particularly in small and medium-sized businesses located in provincial areas. (1961, p. 437)

More young men (*sic*) should be given an 'entrepreneurial drive'. General acceptance of an achievement-orientated ideology should be fostered by the agencies responsible for speeding up economic development:

> this ideology should be diffused not only in business and governmental circles, but throughout the nation, and in ways that will influence the thinking of all parents as they bring up their children.

The legal and social rights of women should also be promoted: 'if the sons are to have *n* Achievement, the mothers must first be reached'. Governments in underdeveloped countries should adopt rigid achievement-orientated standards of performance so that people are judged by these and not by their family or political connections, or by their skill at rationalising poor performance in population control and the provision of capital or skilled manpower. The professionalisation of management should be encouraged to develop more competent business leadership.

The idea of cultivating a need for achievement has been influential, and indeed still is, in some approaches to development assistance. Much current development theorising, such as in the World Bank, is currently taking an entrepreneurial stance, seeing the private entrepreneur as the key to faster growth. Developing countries are seen as having gone too far in the direction of state planning. They need, it is argued, to leave decisions about economic allocations to private producers and sovereign consumers interacting according to the laws of supply and demand. Assumptions about what makes for successful development still rest heavily on ideas about the individual motivations of people in pursuit of their own individual interests.

7. Criticisms of modernisation theory

Modernisation theory has been subjected to extensive critical scrutiny from which it has emerged distinctly the worse for wear. The most telling criticisms are summarised below, grouped together by reference to the concepts which pose the most serious problems for anyone wishing to advance their understanding of change in the Third World.

The concept of tradition

The concept of 'tradition' as deployed by modernisation theorists poses numerous problems. First, there is the emphasis on obstacles to development and the way modernisation theory draws upon earlier evolutionary modes of thinking in order to characterise as 'traditional' anything in developing societies which appears to be such an obstacle. The people who applied such theories in the field, by devising public policies which they believed the governments of developing countries would do well to implement, often adopted a critical stance towards tradition, seeing it as impeding progress. They decried parochial and primordial values. The key question is of course: whose progress? This tended not to be asked by the modernisation theorists. Consequently, practitioners came away from the field, after visits as consultants or official aid donors, frustrated that local people could not see that the introduction of, for example, some new technology would really make a difference to agricultural productivity or health. Resistance to such progress was seen in terms of the burden of tradition and an inability to break with outmoded ways of perceiving the world.

However, the local people directly affected may have been making very rational calculations about the economic and political risks that are inevitably associated with disturbances to the status quo. The tendency of modernisation theory was to encourage the view that such reactions were a refusal to be dragged into the modern world, when what is happening is not due to a lack of rationality but to a different system of incentives operating under conditions that include poverty and dependency, and affecting all classes of society. For example, the interests of dominant socio-economic groups have often been best served by continuing dependency on the West rather than by self-sustaining autonomous development (Valenzuela and Valenzuela, 1978, pp. 545–51).

Modernisation theory's perception of much of the conflict in developing countries in terms of a clash between tradition and modernity. It fails to see that the secular and the rational may benefit some groups in society much more than others. A family planning programme may be readily taken up by wealthy families if they do not need children to assist in the cultivation of their land. It might not be accepted so readily by a poor family that cannot hire labour and whose existence as an economic unit depends upon its children; or by people who know that when they get old there will be no welfare state, or community care.

The resurgence of religion, especially as a foundation for political mobilisation, in parts of the Third World indicates that modernisation does not necessarily bring about secularisation, though the appeal of religious movements such as the Iranian Shi'ites is not unrelated to secular concerns such as growing social inequality, political repression, corruption, foreign exploitation and cultural division (Banuazizi, 1987). In this context, modernisation theory appears elitist and in contrast to the experience of the masses. Modernisation theory depicts religion as a less real, evolved and rational alternative to politics, doomed to secularisation, when in the otherwise contrasting cultures of Latin America, the Middle East, Central and Southern Africa, and South-east Asia, religion remains a source of popular mobilisation, alternative notions of legitimacy, resistance and even insurrection. It has come to fill an ideological vacuum. It can be revolutionary or reactionary (or evolve from one to the other). Where religion is identified with the state it tends to be a conservative force (as in Saudi Arabia) but where it is distanced from politics it tends to be anti-establishment, as in Central and South America (Kamrava, 1993, pp. 148–9).

Liberation theology in Latin America has challenged the authority patterns of the Catholic Church as well as political regimes in its clerical populism, its ideology of democratisation and equality, its stimulation of collective organisation and its recognition of the poor as a valid source of religious values and action. Its fusion of religion, social analysis (drawing inspiration from Marxism) and political activism has implications for the secular presuppositions of modernisation theory, in that religious values are not secondary to social and political reform. Religion is not merely being used as a convenient instrument of political mobilisation and solidarity. It represents a new spirituality as well as a new awareness of class, conflict, exploitation – the spirituality of the exploited poor (Levine, 1986 and 1988).

Secularisation of the state by technocratic élites in some Middle Eastern countries has magnified the ideological significance of Islam, especially for the poor and other excluded classes. As well as spiritual guidance it has provided a political framework and an alternative to the materialism and immorality associated with modernisation and secularism (Kedourie, 1992; Omid, 1992).

Ethnic conflict is similarly seen by modernisation theory as a by-product of tradition. Modernisation theorists could see that colonialism often meant grouping societies together in an arbitrary way. But ethnic conflict after independence tended to be seen as a conflict between the primordial values of tribe and race and the modern values of nationalism, when people think of themselves as individual members of a nation-state rather than as members of some sub-national collectivity such as a linguistic group. Again, there may be very 'modern' reasons, such as economic exploitation or political discrimination, for conflict between groups identified by reference to 'traditional' attributes and perceptions.

Modernisation theory can also be charged with ideological conservatism in the way it blames backwardness on the traditions of a people rather than on internal conflicts or external interventions, such as imperialism, and in the way it implicitly rules out the need for revolutionary change in the process of change. 'Evolution' may appear a strange concept to employ in descriptions of histories that in both the developed and underdeveloped worlds have been so significantly affected by revolutions and wars. Modernisation theory is striking for what it leaves out in its attempt to produce an explanation of change, notably class conflict, colonialism and revolution (Rhodes, 1968).

The influence of external forces is the most noticeable omission from the modernisation perspective. At the very most, external influences are perceived as limited to the diffusion of Western cultural attributes to non-Western societies. The colonial episode is notably problematic and can only be integrated into the 'traditional/modern' dichotomy with great difficulty, either as a hybrid or as a 'transitional' stage of evolution. Tipps is particularly critical of the way modernisation theorists underestimate or ignore external influences on social change in favour of indigenous structure and culture (Tipps, 1973, p. 212).

The static and uniform conception of tradition has also been criticised, notably by J. R. Gusfield, who warns that it is 'fallacious to assume that a traditional society has always existed in its present form'. Traditional cultures and social structures not only consist of diverse norms and values, they also contain 'moral bases for materialistic motivations and for disciplined and rational pursuit of wealth'. Nor are old traditions necessarily displaced by new norms and social structures – they can and do exist side by side. Elements of both as defined by modernisation theory may be fused, may co-exist or may be mutually reinforcing (Whitaker, 1967). New products, modes of decision-making and religions do not necessarily displace older practices and beliefs. Modern developments depend for their acceptance, rejection or modification on specific traditions. This is overlooked if 'traditional' society is abstracted from its specific cultural and historical setting.

The problem with modernisation theory's conception of 'tradition' is that it is a residual concept, defined by reference to the logical opposites of 'modern': 'The modern ideal is set forth, and then everything which is not modern is labelled traditional' (Huntington, 1971, p. 294; see also Valenzuela and Valenzuela, 1978, p. 538). Characteristics attributed to societies considered modern are used to measure a society's progress (for example, see

Black, 1966, pp. 68–75 and Almond, 1960, p. 64). 'Tradition' is not defined by reference to observed facts and knowledge of societies prior to their contact with the West. If the dichotomy does not reflect reality, all societies must be 'transitional' and modernisation theory loses all value as an aid to understanding historical change (Huntington, 1971, pp. 295–7). Modernisation theory obscures the variability found both within and between traditional societies (Tipps, 1973, pp. 212–13). Modernity is also an ambiguous concept as there are many routes to be taken and many models to be followed (Gusfield, 1967).

Unilinearity

This brings us to the idea of a unilinear path to modernity, and the presupposition that developing countries were destined to become like those in the West. The German economist Andre Gunder Frank produced one of the most penetrating critiques of the faulty historical assumptions of modernisation theory in denying under-developed countries their own histories, in ignoring the connections between these histories and the histories of developed countries, in overlooking the fact that penetration by foreign influences had not produced development or led to 'take off', and in misrepresenting the histories of today's developed countries as not having been dependent on the exploitation of today's underdeveloped societies (Frank, 1972c). Western imperialism had been part of the process of 'modernisation' for developing countries in a way that distinguished their path to modernity very clearly from that of contemporary modern societies.

Modernisation theory may thus be criticised for its ethnocen-tricity, judging progress by reference to Western, and largely Anglo–American, values and institutions. It is difficult to avoid the conclusion that the modernisation theorists' perspective on change was determined as much by ideological leanings as by rigourous scientific investigation (Tipps, 1973, p. 207; see also Bendix, 1967; Nisbet, 1969). Tipps argues that modernisation theory was heavily marked by 'widespread complacency towards American society, and the expansion of American political, military and economic interests throughout the world', and so constituted a form of cultural imperialism (1973, pp. 208–10).

The teleological quality of unilinear models of change is rejected by Kothari. There can be no pre-ordained path to development for all societies. Cultures and traditions vary too much from one society to another, and the process of modernisation varies from one time period to another (Kothari, 1968, p. 279).

Tipps points out that developing societies do not need to replicate the technological developments of the West. They exist, and are ready for adoption (1973, p. 215).

Rostow's stages of growth illustrate the difficulties involved in dividing evolution into stages. Kuznets has shown how blurred and therefore analytically weak the lines are between the stages, especially the crucial ones of 'take-off' and 'drive to maturity', and how the idea of a recurring take-off stage is not supported by the economic histories of many countries (Kuznets, 1973).

Dichotomous models

Modernisation theory provided ideal types or models of traditional and modern society to show along which dimensions they could be said to differ. But these tell very little about the dynamics of transition from one cultural state to another (Larrain, 1989, pp. 87–91).

For example, in terms of Parsons' pattern variables, developed countries can be shown to be particularistic in the behaviour of their social classes and private interests. Developed countries are also highly ascriptive, especially at the higher levels of business management and among the poor. Recruitment may be achievement-based, but reward is often based on age and family obligations (for example, in Japan). Roles are frequently 'diffuse' rather than functionally specific within such power structures as the military–industrial complex of the US (Frank, 1972c).

Conversely, underdeveloped countries frequently demonstrate universalism in their educational systems and mass media, in labour unions and in liberation movements. The economic and political leadership thrown up by military *coups* and emerging bourgeoisies throughout the Third World cannot be described as normatively ascriptive (Frank, 1972c, p. 334).

Role assignment by achievement is also widely found among the poorer classes of poor societies. In the distribution of rewards achievement accounts for more than ascription in underdeveloped countries. Roles may be found to be functionally diffuse in underdeveloped countries, especially among the poorest and richest strata, though the middle-class military officers, police officers, bureaucrats, junior executives and administrators are functionally specific in their roles. In Frank's view, however, these people 'serve specific functions of making the whole exploitative system function in the diffuse but particular interests of those who have achieved control' (1972c, p. 335). In Latin America, for example, it is the middle class that supports military dictatorship and grows rich at the expense of the poor. Neither 'tradition' nor 'modernity' can be seen as packages of attributes. Modernisation may be selective, with rapid social change in one area obstructing change in others, rather than tradition being the obstacle to development. Hence the eventual realisation among political scientists of the modernisation persuasion that modernisation and political stability do not always go together: modernisation in one sphere does not necessarily produce compatible ('eurhythmic') change in another (Tipps, 1973, p. 215).

Once it is recognised that traditional values and practices may persist in otherwise modern societies, doubt is thrown on the idea that tradition impedes change. Furthermore, if the destruction of tradition proves not to be necessary for 'modernisation', except in purely tautological terms, then traditional societies must be seen as being able to develop in directions other than towards 'modernity' (Tipps, 1973, p. 214).

Thus the characteristics attributed by modernisation theory to developed and underdeveloped countries 'present a distorted and inadequate conception of social reality'. The important determinants of development *and* underdevelopment lie elsewhere than in ideal-typical models of tradition and modernity. In addition to questioning the empirical validity of the pattern variable approach, Frank also argues that it is theoretically inadequate not to differentiate between the importance of the roles to be affected by modernisation and not to recognise that the determinants of underdevelopment extend beyond the family, tribe, community or even a whole poor country taken in isolation. Frank's understanding of underdevelopment, to be examined further in Chapter 6, led him to question the 'social whole' whose role patterns are to be changed by modernisation (Frank, 1972, p. 321).

Tautologies

Tipps also argues that modernisation theory is over-ambitious in its attempt to incorporate all social change since the seventeenth century. Consequently the key concepts are too vague and open-ended, often reducing theoretical propositions to 'meaningless tautologies' (Tipps, 1973, p. 218; see also Varma, 1980, p. 49). Modernisation theory proceeds by way of assumptions about change based on the prior definition of concepts. Concepts take the place of facts (Tipps, 1973, p. 222).

The psychology of modernisation

This dimension of modernisation theory suffers from reductionism. It derives the attributes of social processes from statements about individuals. Explanations of social behaviour are reduced to psychological statements. The individual constitutes the only social reality.

Social structures and processes cannot be reduced to individual attributes such as self-accomplishment, self-development, or achievement because these things cannot have meanings outside specific social and cultural settings. Ideas about individuals' needs for achievement cannot be abstracted and universalised (Portes, 1976; Larrain, 1989, pp. 98–100). To do so simply proves to be highly ethnocentric, amounting to the selection of certain approved attributes of our own society and the claim that they will develop in all people regardless of their cultural, social and economic contexts. The idea of there being a 'modern' personality also overlooks the effect on economic development of factors such as imperialism which often stifled indigenous entrepreneurial spirit, the absence of which cannot be ascribed to tradition (Rhodes, 1968).

A. G. Frank ridicules the psychology of McClelland, Hagen and others and their view that society can be changed by having its individuals taught to 'get a hold on themselves and raise their need for achievement', by not letting themselves be beaten down, and by interpreting China's economic development exclusively in terms of n Achievement, ignoring Marxism, economic, political and social structures, and revolution. For Frank, modernisation theory rests on the same 'twin gods' that sustain the USA generally: Santa Claus and Sigmund Freud:

How are the people in the underdeveloped countries to achieve economic development? By waiting for Christmas and then accepting the gift of diffusion from Santa Claus in the North. What gift does Santa Claus bear for the peoples of the underdeveloped countries? The latest message of Sigmund Freud. . . . Can it be any wonder that the people of the real underdeveloped world must, and will, look beyond what some others dream possible to find a theory of economic development and cultural change which is empirically congruent with, theoretically adequate for, and politically acceptable to their reality, needs and desires? (Frank, 1972, p. 396).

8. Conclusion

What has been referred to as modernisation theory was built up by the contributions of many scholars from a wide range of disciplines. Only the major lines of thought have been identified here. Undoubtedly, too, many refinements and nuances have been omitted. Justice has not been done to the impressive array of methodologies which modernisation theorists utilised. Nor has it been possible in this brief survey to capture the interaction between scholars of the modernisation persuasion as they responded to each others' refinement and modification of key ideas.

The most durable aspect of modernisation theory is its interdisciplinarity. This is its major bequest to the study of social change. Economic and political changes are related in various ways to fundamental changes in social values and social structures. Secularisation also has important political consequences both for the role of the individual in the political system and for recruitment into political office. The emergence of rational-legal authority has profound implications for the nature of the state, not least in the opportunity which it opens up for bureaucratisation. Clusters of pattern variables provide models of social organisation in which the political significance of universalism, achieved status, neutrality and specificity is plain. Of particular importance to the study of political development, as will be seen in the next chapter, is the effect of structural differentiation on the specialisation of political roles in transitional societies.

4

Development and Structural Differentiation

1. Introduction

The application of modernisation theory to politics has sometimes been labelled 'functionalism'. This refers to a theory which takes its inspiration from a particular approach to social anthropology. It had a major impact on the comparative study of politics when it appeared that the existing tools of political analysis were inappropriate for the task of including within a comparative analytical framework the new states appearing in the international political arena after the Second World War. Functionalism was seen as the way forward by a particularly influential group of political scientists in the 1950s and 1960s.

The key figures in the movement, which centred on the Committee on Comparative Politics of the US Social Science Research Council, were Gabriel Almond, Lucian Pye, Dankwart Rustow, Myron Weiner, James Coleman, Joseph LaPalombara and Ralph Braibanti, who between them edited and contributed to volumes of essays on political development, including the key text *The Politics of the Developing Areas* containing the group's theoretical position and five area studies. (For the story of the rise and fall of the movement see Riggs, 1981; Higgott, 1983; Smith, T., 1985, pp. 533–4; and Randall and Theobald, 1985.) The Committee sponsored research projects, workshops, conferences and publications. It provided a rewarding context for hundreds of scholars to exchange information and ideas about concepts and methods. It has even been suggested that a new scientific community was thus established (Ricci, 1977). It was a strongly anti-Marxist community that denied 'the legitimacy of the critical perspective on the study of politics and societies one finds in Marx'. A major impulse behind the study of development was the Cold War, and research funding came from agencies unlikely to support theoretical approaches threatening to major US interest groups (Pratt, 1973, pp. 98–101).

2. The organic metaphor

The very term 'function' suggests among other things an analogy between a society and a biological organism. In biology 'function' refers to the contribution which different parts of an organism make to its maintenance. The function of a leaf on a plant is the production of food by photosynthesis, for example. This biological analogy is useful to remember in order to get a grip on the presuppositions that were articulated about politics and government by this school of thought.

Emile Durkheim was the main precursor of this way of thinking about society. He was the first social theorist to assert the importance of determining any correspondence between social phenomena and 'the general needs of the social organism' in his *Rules of Sociological Method* published in 1895. Other major influences were the anthropologists Malinowski and Radcliffe-Brown, the sociologists Talcot Parsons and Robert Merton, and the political scientists David Easton and Herbert Hyman (Almond, 1965, p. 184; Varma, 1980, p. 58; Almond, 1987, pp. 437–44).

Functionalism requires social phenomena to be explained in terms of their functions. In this way it is possible to understand things that otherwise appear to make no sense. For example, the native Hopi people of North America had as part of their culture a rain dance. This manifestly did not produce rain. What it did was to perform the social function of strengthening social solidarity, reinforcing people's faith in the community and helping the society to cope with drought. Functionalism is thus a way of explaining phenomena that are inexplicable in literal terms. Durkheim himself wrote about religion and its importance in the reaffirmation of core values and the maintenance of social cohesion. The function of religion was not to assert the existence of a deity but rather to achieve a social objective. For Almond organisations such as political parties or administrative agencies had little meaning until it was known what purposes they serve for the functioning of the organism as a whole (Almond, 1965, p. 184).

Socially functional prerequisites

If one is talking about an organism, the next step is to ask what needs must be satisfied to maintain an organism in a healthy state. Similarly in sociological functionalism the question was whether there are any needs which all societies must satisfy. Are there general functional prerequisites in society? Parsons argued that there were. The first was *adaptation*, so that a social system can survive in its environment. The second was *goal attainment* – the need to be organised so as to achieve collective objectives such as waging war. Thirdly, there was the function of *integration* or maintaining social support for the system. Fourthly, Parsons identified the function of *pattern maintenance*, or the need for stability and continuity. However different societies might be in other respects, they all have to develop ways of performing these essential functions if they are to survive. Social structures have to exist in order to perform functions. The task of the social scientist is to identify and classify the structures that are developed in different societies for this purpose.

Adaptation was thought to be particularly important. If that could be achieved, then societies could change in response to changes in the environment. This modifies the idea of maintaining stability and continuity. In the natural world biological organisms can adapt to a changing environment, albeit over very long periods of time. They can cope with change and survive. Societies, it was argued, have to do the same. Almond translated the system-maintenance and adaptation functions into the recruitment and socialisation of incumbents into various political roles (diplomats, military officers, tax officials and so on). He interpreted goal attainment as dependent on the political systems conversion functions:

> In every political system there is a set of political structures which initiates or processes inputs, and converts them into outputs. The demands entering the political system are articulated, aggregated, or combined; converted into policies, rules, regulations; applied, enforced, adjudicated. (Almond, 1965, p. 194).

Political development theory borrowed two other key ideas from biology: *interdependence* and *equilibrium*. Interdependence means that when one component of an organism changes, the organism as a whole is affected. Almond gives the example of the emergence of mass political parties, or the mass media which 'changes the performance of all the other structures of the political system, and affects the general capabilities of the system in its domestic and foreign environments' (Almond, 1965, p. 185). If the change is dysfunctional to the system 'the dysfunctional component is disciplined by regulatory mechanisms, and the equilibrium of the system is re-established' (p. 185). Social systems tend towards equilibrium. Institutions preserve their character or change slowly. The concept of system implies 'the interdependent interaction of structures performing functions in such a way as to maintain the social system in equilibrium' (pp. 185–6).

Structure and function

Social structures are sets of roles performed by individual members of the set. Roles are distinguished from persons. When roles are performed in a particular set, they constitute a social structure. Individuals thus make up numerous different structures. A member of the role set of the family contributes to that structure as well as to the other structures to which he or she contributes roles – at work, in religious ceremonies, in the interpretation and enforcement of law and custom, in community associations, in political organisations, and so on. In pre-modern societies, age may determine which set an individual contributes to. Age grades then become an important structure for the performance of social functions.

The relationship between structure and function gave rise to the label 'structural functionalism' because the theory addressed the key question of how functions are performed for the social organism. (For a history of functionalism, and its relationship to structural functionalism, see Moore, W. E., 1979). For a while this was an extremely influential theory that, ironically, was all but abandoned by sociologists outside the USA when it was taken up by US political scientists in their efforts to devise a means of comparing all known political systems. Political functionalism also proceeded despite damaging criticisms of systems approaches to politics, notably by Gouldner (see, for example, Almond, 1965, pp. 186–7). Political science's need was for a theoretical framework that could cope with a bewildering variety of exotic political systems that could not be accommodated within existing modes of comparison (Eulau,

1963; Holt and Turner, 1972; O'Brien, D. C., 1972; Varma, 1980, p. 58). As Gabriel Almond put it 'Comparative politics of the 1950s and 1960s was a massive, enthusiastic, primarily American effort to encompass this novel and heterogeneous reality' (Almond, 1987, p. 456). A youthful social science had not had much time to produce theories of political organisation and change that could embrace such a varied set of political systems.

Structural functionalism seemed to provide such a comparative framework of analysis, especially since the Hopi Indian phenomenon appeared to be very prevalent in the political sphere. Very unfamiliar things seemed to be going on, yet familiar functions seemed to be performed. In non-Western societies unfamiliar structures were performing functions that seemed to be needed in all political systems. New concepts were needed to understand such phenomena. The concepts of contemporary political science were not, it was decided, equipped for the task. Western political science up to this point had been based on the comparison of institutions and, even more restrictedly, institutions found in the developed, industrialised societies and their processes of democratisation.

Once again biology provided the required insight:

> The problem of developing categories to compare the conversion processes of different kinds of political systems is not unlike the problem of comparative anatomy and physiology. Surely the anatomical structure of a unicellular organism differs radically from that of a vertebrate, but something like the functions which in the vertebrate are performed by a specialised nervous system, a gastro-intestinal tract, are performed in the amoeba by intermittent adaptations of its single cell (Almond, 1965, p. 195).

By analogy, complex political systems have specialised structures for performing distinctive tasks to enable political inputs to be converted into outputs, whereas simple ones do not.

3.   The analytical framework

Functionalism became the political interpretation of modernisation theory because it was necessary to find a way of addressing societies that were rapidly achieving the status of nation-states with apparently modern political institutions such as legislatures, parties, constitutions, and executives grafted on to structures that were totally unfamiliar to most Western observers other than anthropologists. As Almond and Powell put it: 'If political science is to be effective in dealing with political phenomena in all kinds of societies, regardless of culture, degree of modernization, and size, we need a more comprehensive framework of analysis' (1966, p. 16).

It was known that those unfamiliar structures were performing key political functions. The functionalists therefore abandoned comparative methods based on structures in favour of one based on functions. If structures were persisted with, the cultural context of contemporary political institutions in new states would not be comprehensible; the analytical tools would be totally inappropriate. The search for constitutions, parties, pressure groups, legislatures and bureaucracies would be fruitless in societies whose government did not depend on such structures.

Borrowing from earlier varieties of social anthropology, functionalism claimed that all societies have to perform certain political functions and that the analysis of politics should not be constrained by the concepts and language of Western political structures. A set of functions has to be performed in all societies no matter how complex or simple, industrialised or agrarian. The task is to establish what these are and then seek out the structures that perform them in different societies. Comparative politics could no longer prejudge the question of structures. If communities are found to enforce their rules not by courts, police forces, prisons and the other institutions of the state but by contests between the injured parties, tempered by public opinion within lineages, as in the Nuer of the southern Sudan, it should not be assumed that such societies are disorganised, chaotic or without the means of governing themselves. They might be societies without Governments but they were not societies without government or regular ways of performing necessary political functions. Structures existed to perform those functions. Familiar legislative structures might not exist to make legally binding rules, but other social structures would exist to perform this function of articulating rules, perhaps by age-groups. Lucy Mair, in her book *Primitive Government*, describes how the Kikuyu of East Africa and the Dinka of the Sudan traditionally gave the task of making rules to an age group. Rule enforcement also existed, but not through police forces and courts of law.

Boundaries

Another major contrast drawn by the functionalists between developed and developing societies was in the existence of boundaries between social, political and economic systems. In traditional societies these often appeared to be lacking, whereas in a modern society, according to the functionalists, it was possible to separate structures that were primarily economic from those that were primarily social or political. For example, in pre-industrial society social and economic roles were inextricably entwined in the family, a productive as well as a reproductive unit. Social, economic and political decisions could be bound up with initiation rituals, wedding ceremonies, the movement of pastoral nomads, religious observance, and the conduct of family affairs. In a modern society groups would be found articulating different political demands. In traditional societies with powerful chiefs and monarchs, such as the Kabaka of Buganda in East Africa, there was no articulation of society's demands and needs except through leadership, whose role it was to interpret the needs of different groups in society.

Traditional political systems

Social anthropologists divided pre-industrial political systems into two broad patterns. First there were the so-called 'acephalous' societies, without formal and stable positions of political leadership. The settlement of disputes between individuals, families or clans, the application of custom and convention to conflicts within and between societies, and the performance of rituals and ceremonies that were deemed necessary for the survival and prosperity of the community, were responsibilities that individuals, age groups or descent groups exercised according to immemorial custom (Mair, 1962; Cohen and Middleton, 1967). Executive leadership and hierarchical structures of authority were lacking. Societies without states, political leadership and the other institutions of government familiar to Western social science could not be incorporated into existing methods of comparative analysis and were thus particularly significant in the formulation of an alternative that concentrated on the things which they did have in common with other societies with different political structures. Such societies were clearly 'governed' but in ways that needed to be systematically compared and contrasted with the political processes of complex, industrialised and modernised societies.

The other category consisted of the pre-industrial states, sometimes with apparently feudalistic features. Here government centred upon a hereditary leader surrounded by a court and officialdom made up of judges, military commanders and tax collectors. Officials had specialised tasks to perform. The level of specialisation was greater than in the acephalous societies and the structures were more familiar to Western observers: they could be identified as comparable to those found at stages within their own political histories.

The significance of such societies for political science was that despite the absence of familiar social structures, especially in the stateless or acephalous societies, these communities were orderly, governed and stable, with legitimate forms of authority: government existed without the state. Consequently the functionalists needed both a theory of the political system – a more appropriate label than 'state', given the existence of stateless societies – and a theory of change or development. Like the modernisation theorists, they wanted to incorporate into their thinking the idea of progressive change. Societies were seen as not merely moving from one condition to another but from being traditional to being developed, implying improvement and progress in the way that societies are governed.

4. The political system

The functionalist theory of the political system rests on five key concepts: politics; system; structure; culture; and function.

Politics

By 'political' the functionalists refer to social relationships involving the legitimate monopoly of physical coercion, following the Weberian definition of the state, but with modifications drawn from the more recent work of M. J. Levy, Lasswell, Kaplan and Easton (Almond and Coleman, 1960, pp. 5–7; Almond, 1965, pp. 191–2). Political activities, whether inputs or outputs, demands or policies, are directed at control of or influence over the use of coercive power (Almond, 1965, p. 193). Whatever the values prompting demands for action by the authorities, and whatever the nature of the action called for, ultimately these relate to the coercive power of the political system.

System

The concept of system conveys the interrelationships between the parts of a polity so that when there is change in one part of the system other parts will be affected. The use of the sociological concept of role leads to the proposition that there are boundaries between the different systems making up a total society. In particular there is, asserts Almond, 'a boundary between the polity and the economy' (Almond, 1965, p. 188). The most worrying and controversial aspect of the 'boundary' issue – its seemingly artificial separation of the political from other spheres of life – is best illustrated by the version provided by Almond and Powell's comparative politics text, which adopted a developmental approach:

> a political system is made up of the interacting roles of nationals, subjects, voters, as the case may be, with legislators, bureaucrats and judges. The same individuals who perform roles in the political system perform roles in other social systems such as the economy, the religious community, the family and the voluntary associations. As individuals expose themselves to political communication, form interest groups, vote, or pay taxes, they shift from non-political to political roles. One might say that on election day as citizens leave their farms, plants and offices to go to the polling places, they are crossing the boundary from the economy to the polity. (1966, p. 18; see also Almond, 1965, pp. 187–8)

The political system is made up of particular roles involving the monopoly of physical force and the establishment and maintenance of a process by which inputs are converted into outputs. The political process generates both demands for policies and a number of supports for governmental outputs. Those demands and supports on the input side are converted into outputs through political processes. All societies have ways of converting inputs into outputs – they constitute its political system. In all societies there are interactions which produce political outputs by means of the employment or threat of employment of legitimate physical compulsion.

This is how societies could bring about change. The political system is a legitimate set of interrelated structures for maintaining order and responding to the changing pressures of the environment. Those structures will in part be regulative and coercive, concerned with the suppression of dissent. They will also be distributive, shifting resources between sectors of society. Extractive structures would draw resources from society through such means as taxation.

Structure

The idea of structures as sets of interrelated roles that make up the political process enables the functionalists to identify how functions could be performed without preconceived ideas associating particular functions with corresponding structures. So a legislature, for example, is a set of interrelated roles performing the function of making the rules by which outputs will be effected.

Culture

Functionalists developed the idea of culture and brought into the framework of political analysis the idea that all societies contain discernible attitudes and dispositions towards politics. Parson's pattern variables are utilised in political development theory, sometimes to dichotomise traditional and modern systems of politics, as in F. W. Riggs' (1957) models of Agraria and Industria, and sometimes to demonstrate a 'dualism' of political structure found in all societies, as in Almond's distinction between primary and secondary structures in societies where primitive or pre-modern political structures persist in modern political systems:

> This dualism of political structure is not only characteristic of modern Western political systems but of non-Western and primitive ones: i.e. there are both primary and secondary structures in primitive and traditional political systems and the secondary structures have modern (specific, universalistic, and achievement) features. (Almond, 1960, p. 23)

What differentiates a Western from a traditional society is the greater differentiation and significance of secondary structures and relationships in the former. Primary structures in modern societies tend to be modernised by the secondary ones. Almond also uses pattern variables to distinguish between the 'style' of interest articulation:

> the more latent, diffuse, particularistic, and affective the pattern of interest articulation, the more difficult it is to aggregate interests and translate them into public policy . . . the more manifest, specific, general and instrumental the style of interest articulation, the easier it is to maintain the boundary between the polity and society, and the better the circulation of needs, claims and demands from the society in aggregable form into the political system. (p. 36)

A society in crisis is often a society in which the dominant political culture is being undermined by competing sets of beliefs. It can no longer sustain the level of support needed by the political system for it to survive. The political culture thus consists of values about how politics should actually be conducted, and how the processes of government should be carried on. The legitimacy adhering to the structures and processes of government is expressed through a society's political culture. The obligations that are the consequence of that legitimacy relate to the rules of the political system.

In any given society there may well be different political cultures that give rise to conflict. One of the problems of becoming modern was seen in cultural terms as a problem of persuading people to accept the boundaries of the nation-state as legitimate when those boundaries had their origins in alien rule. The processes of government might also lack legitimacy if they were based on unacceptable forms of authority again derived from an alien source. Adaptation to forms of democracy inherited from outside may be difficult. This is frequently referred to as the problem of political integration, a major source of political instability in Third World societies. The 'problem' of political integration will be returned to in Chapter 11, when different explanations for nationalism and secession are considered.

Political functions

Finally there is the concept of function, central to the needs of the comparative analyst as perceived by the developmentalists. The universal attributes of political systems cannot be conceptualised in terms of structures because of the infinite variability of them. It can only be done in terms of functions. The functionalists claimed that every society, however organised politically, and whatever the political structures through which it conducts its processes of government, will perform eight political functions.

First there is *interest articulation*, or the ways in which demands are formulated and brought into the political arena so that the conversion process can transform demands into outputs. What for the West might be the most typical structure performing that function (pressure groups and similar forms of association) will not necessarily be found in pre-industrial societies. For example, in Sub-Saharan Africa, the interests to be articulated are those of stratification and differentiation by sex, race, age, wealth, occupation, class, lineage or locality. In societies where the lineage is the basic socio-economic unit, economic and religious interests are combined in the interests of the lineage as a corporate group. In more highly stratified societies the interests of craft groups have to be articulated, though not through guild organisations or structures, but rather through occupational classes 'in which members of a particular occupation constitute a class differentiated from other occupational classes in a highly stratified system of prestige ranking' (Coleman, 1960b, pp. 323–4). The effect of modernisation has

> altered the traditional modes of interest expression as a result of the erosion of traditional authority and lineage bonds and the progressive decline in traditional crafts. It has also given birth to specific interests requiring new modes of expression consonant with a secular authority structure and appropriate to a modern territorial society. (pp. 324–5)

The transitional nature of African society is reflected in the fact that 'the articulation of functionally specific interests is, with few exceptions, transcended by and considered to be the function of one's race, tribe, religion, or other group whose survival or primacy has first priority' – Asian traders' organisations, or trade unions in which occupation and tribe coincide, for example (p. 326).

Secondly, demands and expressions of political interest have to be combined. This is the function of *interest aggregation*. Coalitions have to be formed that are powerful enough to overcome other combinations of interests. In an absolute monarchy or an African chiefdom interests of different sections of the community would be 'aggregated' by rulers enjoying the right to interpret the wishes of their people. In a modern society the classic structure for interest aggregation was, for the functionalists, the political party.

Thirdly, the function of *rule making* has to be performed in all societies by some type of political structure. Political systems have to make authoritative and legitimate rules that can be supported by legitimate sanctions. Modern societies will have developed specialised structures – known as legislatures – for this. In traditional societies such structures will be absent but the function will be performed somewhere in the political system.

Fourthly, rules once made have to be enforced and applied. The modern structure for the function of *rule application* is bureaucracy. Conflicts arising from the application of rules to specific cases and circumstances require structures for adjudication. *Rule adjudication* was therefore identified as a universal political function. In modern societies the judiciary would be the specialised structure performing this function.

All political systems equally require means for the communication of demands and rules between the authorities and the people. In modern society the mass media constitute the social structures responsible for the function of *political communication*. In traditional society structures would reflect the technology available as well as the type of social organisation that had developed.

Societies then have to transmit their dominant political values from generation to generation. The functionalists believed not unreasonably that all societies have ways of conveying to the younger generation what they ought to believe about political obligation, authority and the rightful exercise of power. How the function of *political socialisation* is performed varies considerably from one society to another. The relative prevalence of the family, educational institutions, or other associations will differ from society to society.

Finally, individuals have to be recruited into roles and offices. Processes of political succession have to be devised – election, inheritance, merit, physical might, and other principles by which people are recruited into political roles and perhaps permanent offices. The function of *political recruitment* requires some kind of routinisation in both traditional and modern societies. The roles that perform the universal functions regardless of structure have to be filled by acceptable methods. These clearly change over time.

5. Political change

The functionalists were trying to do more than just provide a new language for identifying the universal features of political systems. They were trying to provide a framework for understanding change. In practice the functionalists were more concerned with the characteristics of societies in some process of transition, rather than with the elaboration of models for 'simple' or 'primitive' societies. Their major areas of interest were the new nation-states emerging on the international scene into which virtually all traditional societies had been more or less fully incorporated, usually through the operation of colonialism. The great effort that was put into comparative politics was designed to explain the effects of the interactions between the traditional structures and cultures of communities incorporated into these new states that had been produced by colonialism, and nationalistic reactions to it.

The most important change for the political functionalists was the association of increasingly specialised structures with single functions in modern societies. Political change is seen as the movement away from traditional politics towards the modern political system. Change takes place in both structure and culture.

Structural specialisation

Structures, it was argued, become more specialised and differentiated as societies become more modern. This is an application of those parts of modernisation theory that postulate the growing differentiation, specialisation and complexity found within modernising societies. As societies become more modern, their political functions come to be performed by specialised structures. Whereas in a traditional, absolute, monarchical polity there would be found, bound up in a single structure – that of the royal court – a multiplicity of functions such as rule making and rule adjudication, in a modern society with its pluralist democracy there would be found specialised structures performing single functions. Traditional social structures were described as typically 'multifunctional'. As societies develop, structures become less multifunctional.

Secularisation

When dealing with change in political cultures, the functionalists applied the idea of secularisation from modernisation theory. Secularisation is as important to political development theory as it was to modernisation theory's interpretation of social change generally (Coleman, 1960a, p. 537). Secularisation in political life was associated with rationality. Almond and Powell illustrate the point by comparing a political leader in a modern democracy with one in a traditional African political system:

> A modern democratic political leader when running for office, for instance, will gather substantial amounts of information about the constituency which he hopes will elect him and the issues of public policy with which that constituency may be concerned. He has to make estimates of the distribution and intensity of demands of one kind or another; he needs to use creative imagination in order to identify a possible combination of demands which may lead to his receiving a majority of the votes in his constituency. A village chief in a tribal society operates largely with a given set of goals and a given set of means of attaining those goals which have grown up and been hallowed by custom. (1966, ch. 2)

The process of secularisation in South-east Asia, for example, is revealed in the way the scope for religious influence on social and political life has been reduced by Western influences. However, the domination of secular attitudes is by no means complete:

> secular education, the weakening of family ties, the change from village to city life, have all contributed to a decline in the formal position of religion in the lives of Southeast Asians. On the other hand, religion still remains one of the principal bases for social identification, playing an important part in defining the communal groups in most of the countries. The nationalist

movement in Indonesia and Burma first took the form of religious activities. All the countries of the region, except the Catholic Philippines, have had political parties based on religion. (Pye, 1960, p. 104)

The rationalisation of government was seen as a distinguishing mark of modernity. As societies develop they acquire systems of government that are problem-orientated and designed to perceive, analyse and meet the needs of society as articulated through political demands. In addition, members of a modern society would experience cultural change in the direction of individuality. In terms of modernisation theory's pattern variables, people would begin to think of themselves and others in terms of universalism rather than specificity. The assertion of the individual's value in universalistic terms would in turn support political equality and mass participation on an individual basis. Individuals would not see political roles as being ascribed by tradition and custom to predetermined groups. Political power could be enjoyed by all on an equal basis.

Integration

In functionalist development theory political change affects both structure and culture. A combination of changes in these two spheres produces integration into the modern nation-state. A developed political system, it is assumed, would resemble the modern nation-state. The secularisation of government would be directed in part towards nation-building. This process of development involves the political system in overcoming sub-national loyalties such as tribe or religion, seen as parochial and pre-modern. It involves creating a consensus to support the new order, and mobilising the community to regard the nation-state, not some primordial grouping, as the legitimate political unit. Communities would be mobilised to articulate demands and supports; communications between leaders and led would be improved. This is all part of not just becoming modern but of producing an integrated society, a major achievement of a developed political system. Rustow and Ward, for example, defined a modern polity as having differentiated and functionally specific government organisations, rational and secular decision-making procedures, a widespread sense of identity with the nation-state, political roles allocated by achievement rather than ascription, and a secular and impersonal system of law (Rustow and Ward, 1964, pp. 6–7).

Capability

A further aspect of change in developing societies emphasised by functionalists is the 'capabilities' of political systems to formulate policies, enforce decisions throughout the territory, and develop a problem-solving capacity, especially through bureaucracy, so that public policies can be executed effectively and efficiently. Almond classified capabilities into five groups: extractive, regulative, distributive, symbolic and responsive (Almond, 1965, pp. 198–201), having earlier defined political change in terms of the acquisition by a political system of some new capability and its associated changes in political culture and structure (Almond, 1963). A modern political system would, unlike traditional polities, be able to use such concepts as effectiveness and efficiency. Such a capability was seen as dependent on the system's resources in terms of powers to regulate, powers to extract and powers to distribute. The more modern the political system, the more able it would be to build up its resources and in turn that would be dependent on the existence of differentiated and specialised political structures (see, for example, Pye, 1965).

There is, then, a kind of progressive circularity in functionalist thinking. The more specialised structures become, the greater the capacity of government, and the more modern the political system. The more modern the political system, the more specialised its political structures. There is a developmental syndrome which the idea of capabilities completes, taking us back to the importance of differentiation. A central case in point is the bureaucracy. Only with a highly efficient bureaucracy, based on the principle of merit recruitment and organised rationally as a specialised institution, can a political system develop its full capabilities to provide itself with resources and powers.

6. Assessment and critique

Functionalism has had many detractors. Yet much of what is expressed has become almost commonplace and integrated into our ways of thinking and communicating about politics. So it is common, for example, to find the concept of interest articulation widely used, rather than just references to pressure groups, acknowledging implicitly that different societies perform this function through different structures. Its enormous appeal is quite understandable. It made a great impact on political studies. Although it attracted much criticism, particularly in its developmental aspects because it is not entirely developmental, but a way of organising information about political phenomena, it has become an integral part of political science. It is also questionable whether students of comparative politics have developed superior theories. It has been argued that structural functionalism was rejected because it failed an unfairly severe test, that of providing comparative politics with a scientific unity and an all-encompassing theory of politics (Lane, 1994).

Secondly, functionalism drew attention to the importance of seeing societies as consisting of interdependent parts so that one could adopt a dynamic rather than static approach to the analysis of systems of government. The study of politics had to a very large extent adopted a rather insular, normative and legalistic format which functionalism completely changed, even though one of the major criticisms of functionalism was that it built boundaries around different systems to an artificial degree. But at least it acknowledged the possibility of boundaries becoming weakened and of the interpenetration of economy and polity. And in terms of the political, it showed how the parts of a system are interdependent.

Political development theory inspired the production of a large number of monographs – over 200 by 1975 – yet many would share Eckstein's assessment that the result of all this effort was 'mostly muddle' (Eckstein, 1982, p. 451). However, the many criticisms to which functionalism has been subjected have themselves formed an important part of the process of acquiring a clearer understanding of political change in the Third World. A debt is owed to functionalists for stimulating so much debate about political change and for forcing critical assessment of their ideas.

The problem of integration

Functionalism exaggerated harmony and integration in modern society. It tended not to accommodate the idea of conflicting interests and the differential power of groups in conflict with others.

The idea that different parts of the political system are supportive of everything else, producing a functional unity, seems a distorted way of describing any society. The functionalists directed their attention mainly towards the factors in society which maintain consensus and stability. This is understandable, given the areas of natural science which they and their social anthropological precursors chose as analogous to social science. Functionalists emphasise the importance for society of finding ways to socialise new generations into current values and they look for the contribution which political functions make to the maintenance of social equilibrium. Their central focus is on what holds societies together, what structures and values are functional to its survival.

Functionalism's systemic theorising sees society in organic terms, with specialised and interdependent parts functioning to satisfy the requirements of the whole for survival. The tendencies in society that are central to the analysis are those that lead to stability and inertia through mechanisms of adjustment and social control. The structures of the political system are presented in a neutral light as a mere arena for the resolution of conflict that is impartial as regards the contestants.

The conception of society as a functional unity seems to be an unjustifiable way of interpreting modern societies, and a mystification of social reality. However, we should remember that one of the sociological forefathers of functionalism, Robert Merton, explored the 'dysfunctions' that threaten social cohesion. This reminds us that what is functional for one group in society may be dysfunctional for another, perhaps to the extent of undermining the vitality of the whole. Functionalists tended to focus on mutually supporting parts of a political system and its survival through adaptation, but there are some important exceptions to this.

Functionalism can be criticised for being more concerned with the integration of interests into a single normative pattern than with instability and conflict as sources of social change. Conflicts over the allocation of scarce resources are seen as resolved within a framework of common values. Functionalism can be faulted for not being capable of explaining the very changes that were its *raison d'être* because it concentrates on the prerequisites of the maintenance of the status quo. The tendency to regard everything that exists, including the characteristics of the political system, as functional and therefore desirable becomes normatively supportive of the perpetuation of existing social arrangements. Social inequality and stratification, for example, are functional because society has motivated people to seek higher rewards and induced people to perform the duties attached to their station in life. Functionalism begins to look like an arbitrary selection of values in so far as it fails to show how choices can be made between the values which, though functional to an existing system, would be dysfunctional to an alternative one.

The concept of 'system', stressing the interdependence and integration found in biological organisms, when applied to human societies obliges us to view them as organisms in which the parts are subordinate to the whole. Utility is thus found in all patterns of behaviour. Conflict becomes regarded as pathological or abnormal. 'If shared values define the system, it is difficult to treat major conflict and deviance in the area of values as part of the system. And if one assumes stability of values, major structural change in the system is excluded by definition' (Cancian, quoted in Pratt, 1973, p. 99). Such a view of society will be favoured by some 'parts' (or interests) but will work to the disadvantage of others. Political realities present a challenge to the functionalist paradigm. One practical consequence of developmentalism was that the human dimension of development, and particularly the costs and benefits of different developmental strategies to different social groups, were totally neglected (Pratt, 1973, p. 89).

Change and causality

In biology the analysis of function is related to the analysis of causality. In sociology and political science the move from description to causality was never really achieved. So the claim of functionalism to be a *theory* has been seriously questioned. It has been acknowledged as an elaborate description and classification, able to describe the social practice which we find strange and difficult to comprehend. But as explanation of causality function-alism suffers from the fact that it is tautological – no explanation can be disproved because things are defined in relation to themselves. A practice is said to persist because it contributes to the maintenance of society. Its persistence is taken to prove that the society is motivated to maintain itself. If the practice ceases, this has to be taken as indicative that it was no longer 'functional' to

society's maintenance. Statements about the causes and consequences of social and political practices are merely true by
definition, not proved by explanation (Dowse, 1966).

So originally developmentalists offered no theory of change.
Huntington points out that *The Politics of the Developing Areas*, for
example, does not deal with development. It, and similarly inspired
works, employs concepts to compare systems presumed to be at
different stages of development. But there is no explanation of a
dynamic process. Later work, such as that by Almond and Powell
(1966) and Pye (1966) identified the key changes that occur as a
society becomes more developed politically, associating political
development with social modernisation: greater political equality,
governmental capacity and institutional differentiation (Pye, 1966,
pp. 31–48); subsystem autonomy, cultural secularisation and
structural differentiation (Almond and Powell, 1966); rationalisation, national integration, democratisation and mobilisation
(Huntington, 1965, pp. 387–8). Even then, however, 'the stress
was on the elaboration of models of different types of political
system, not different types of change from one system to another'
(Huntington, 1971, p. 307).

The problem was that political development was taken as given.
Meanings had then to be attached to the concept. Hence the
proliferation of definitions and 'conceptual entropy'. No account is
given of the forces that must, for the developmentalist's approach to
work, be driving societies along the development path (Eckstein,
1982, p. 466).

This problem with development theory was closely related to the
emphasis placed on system maintenance and the capacity of societies
to achieve equilibrium in the patterns of social interaction. Change
therefore appears unnatural. Forces placing the system under stress
have to be compensated for by other forces restoring stability. Such
a conceptual framework is of little use in analysing development
from one state to another (Huntington, 1971, p. 308).

When the shortcomings of political development theory in solving
the problem of explaining political change were eventually acknowledged, theorists abandoned the attempt to predict the direction of
change, concentrating instead on relationships between specific
variables indicative of development identified by different theorists
as particularly significant. For example, Huntington focused on the
causes of political stability in any society, however 'developed',

claiming the key variables to be levels of political participation and political institutionalisation (Huntington, 1965 and 1968). Other theorists of change also focussed on the destabilising effects of developments within the political system, but the important point is, as Huntington points out, that they were not dependent on definitions of 'modernisation', 'tradition' or 'development'. The central question became: what type of change in one component of a political system (culture, structures, groups, leadership, policies and so on) can be related to change or its absence in other components? (1971, p. 316).

Functionalism does not provide explanations of causes of change so much as definitions of key concepts: political function, structure, system and culture. The difficulty which some of the contributors to *The Politics of the Developing Areas* had in fitting the categories and concepts to 'traditional' society in the regions that they analysed from a functionalist perspective supports the critical opinion that political development theory was only able to describe the current situation, not explain how it had come about. When, for example, Myron Weiner had to say something about interest aggregation in South Asia he could only refer to the 'aggregative character' of modern organisations such as Congress in India: 'Before independence, interests were aggregated on two levels: by the colonial British government and by the nationalist movements' (Weiner, 1960, p. 218). Coleman observes that in Sub-Saharan Africa the 'principal aggregators' were chiefs, colonial governments and political parties (1960b, p. 327). Pye (1960) similarly describes rule adjudication by reference to the impact of Western legal systems, and rule application in terms of the characteristics of transitional society and the impact of colonialism. Political communication in the Near East is described in terms of the mass media, though reference is made to 'the largely autonomous systems of face-to-face communication in the villages and among the tribes' (Rustow, 1960, p. 442).

It is rare for this group of functionalists to explain processes of change in terms of structural differentiation and specialisation other than in the abstract. One critic of these area studies believes they 'speak more for the ingenuities of the authors than for the articulateness of the framework', since the concepts and models do not generate hypotheses that can be tested scientifically (Varma, 1980, p. 63).

Biological analogies

The analogy with biological organisms is insufficiently close to provide valid explanations of social and political phenomena. It is very difficult to talk about the normal or pathological functioning of society in the way that we can about organisms, without making massive value judgements. Societies can change their structures; organisms do not. It is not possible to examine the numerous instances of the same social function as it is with biological organisms. The analogy thus leads social explanation up a cul-de-sac. It does not provide the opportunity for theoretical explanation that the assumed parallel between natural and social science appears to offer.

Teleology

Many of the propositions of functionalism are not amenable to empirical assessment. Ultimately a functionalist perspective requires the reification of society. Whole societies are seen as having needs and goals which they satisfy or achieve through functional structures. But only individuals have wills, power and purposes: societies cannot be endowed with the characteristics of the members who make them up. Functionalism is teleological in explaining causes by their effects. Functions which meet the needs of a system for stability and continuity imply that societies have goals, needs and purposes; they cannot be empirically assessed as antecedent causes. Furthermore, defining 'development' in terms of direction rather than content means that anything that happens in developing countries must be seen as part of the process of development. The concept loses its utility as it loses precision and specific content: 'Political development thus loses its analytical content and acquires simply a geographical one' (Huntington, 1965, p. 390; see also Huntington, 1971, p. 303).

Conservatism

A conservative bias in functionalism has been identified and criticised (Abrahamson, 1978). Some functionalists, such as Merton, have argued that functionalism is radical. Institutions and practices are given no inherent value, only their consequences matter; they are only preserved until they cease to be of utility to society. That allows for as much change as a society feels it needs to achieve its goals. However, the main thrust of functionalism is towards a conservation of what is already in place. The tenor of much functionalist enquiry encourages a search for the benefits of surviving institutions. New generations have to be socialised into the existing mores of society. Functionally-orientated social scientists approach structures expecting them to have positive, functional consequences, and so contribute to the persistence of a society. There is no other way of thinking about functionalism as a method other than one that guides enquiry towards explanations of how societies maintain themselves and survive under their present arrangements. Institutions are assumed to contribute to the health of the whole social fabric. Approaching institutions by seeing them as supportive of society implies some normative consensus which is then endorsed by the investigator, who credits those institutions with positive values by deeming them to be functional.

From a non-consensus viewpoint, which finds it hard to think of political systems as consisting of mutually supporting elements, functionalism appears to adopt a very conservative stance, orientated towards preserving the status quo and leading to suspicion of and hostility to change. If it is assumed that society is a functionally integrated organic entity, a bias is introduced against disturbance to the system. That mode of analysis is hostile to criticism of what is happening in a particular society and to proposals for change that will disturb a set of structures that are functional to the continuing existence of that society.

This objection to functionalism had already been made before it had its major impact on political studies. For example, the anthropologist Malinowski was criticised for serving the interests of European colonialism by his bias towards preserving pre-industrial, simple societies rather than 'modernising' them (including, of course, the achievement of political autonomy). The conservative bias of functionalism became increasingly visible as the focus of attention moved towards explanations of crisis, instability and disorder. Crisis is seen to be a problem for élites. So a crisis is what the current élite deems to be so. Authoritarianism is then seen as a legitimate way for élites to manage crisis. Order is made the highest political good. Opponents of regimes are described as 'system wreckers': 'the interest in order of those at the top is given logical precedence over the interest in social justice of those below'

(Sandbrook, 1976, pp. 180–1). Supposedly value-free, scientific models of political development end up leaving an ideological message.

Definitions

The definitions of functionalism have also been found to be flawed. 'System' is defined in terms of what a system does. So a political system which does not perform the functions which such systems are defined as performing ceases by definition to be a political system. Again, the explanatory power is reduced to a tautology. Any statement about the political system is either true by definition because that particular system is doing what all political systems do, or is not about political systems at all. The same is true of 'structure': when structures are perceived and qualified by their salient functions – when the question is not what a structure *is* but what it is *for* – it is not possible to distinguish between structure and function and thus provide accurate descriptions of the former (Sartori, 1970, p. 1047).

The term 'function' is equally problematic. The word is used in different ways without the differences being fully acknowledged. 'Function' can mean maintaining something: for example, the function of the political system is to integrate society and allow it to adapt. Function can also mean merely a task, such as when the 'function' of a political organisation is to articulate an interest. The functionalist literature tends to switch from the more mundane meaning to the almost mathematical meaning of function as the result or consequence of some other factor in the social equation.

Other definitions of key concepts vary too much in their use to be of analytical value. The definition of 'political system' in terms of the legitimate use of physical coercion excludes some of the very societies – the stateless ones – for which the whole conceptual apparatus was designed. It also fails to distinguish between 'politics' and 'government'. The concept of boundary is also used ambiguously and without definitions of the non-political systems beyond the boundaries of the political system (Finer, 1970).

Ethnocentricity

Functionalist approaches to political development also appear ethnocentric, though purporting to be scientific, in that it is quite clear that a developed political system looks very much like Anglo–American pluralist democracy. This emerges very clearly in LaPalombara's search for a definition in modern terms:

> one could certainly use the Anglo-American political system as a working example of the kind of arrangement of institutions and behaviours that is desired and then proceed to raise and answer the questions concerning the conditions under which political development might or might not move in the desired direction. (1963, p. 37)

If the development of a political system is towards differentiated and specialised structures, each performing their own individual function, the end-state appears to be the system of government in the country producing the major exponents of the theory (Holt and Turner, 1966, pp. 13–16; Galtung, 1971). When a society becomes modern, pressure groups articulate and parties aggregate interests; legislatures make rules; judiciaries adjudicate; bureaucracies implement; the mass media communicate; a plurality of institutions socialise. The end-state is very familiar to a particular ideological and constitutional position.

There is nothing wrong *per se* in wishing to advocate the desirability of the separation of powers, to which Almond's 'output' functions clearly correspond. The distinction drawn by the functionalists between the 'input' side of the political equation, conceptualised in terms of socialisation, recruitment, interest articulation and aggregation, and communication; and the output functions of rule making, application and adjudication, is important (Varma, 1980, p. 65). It asserts the relationship between the mechanisms for public participation and those for liberal government. The input functions imply mass participation on the basis of political equality in a modern society. However, such advocacy is a far cry from a supposed science of political change.

It is one thing to say that, in Indonesia, poorly organised trade unions and business associations 'are not the important interest articulating structures', but that interests are articulated through status and kinship groups, lineages and anomic phenomena (Almond, 1960, p. 13). It is another thing altogether to say that it is to be underdeveloped not to have functions performed to the same specialised degrees by structures familiar in Western cultures. Indonesia is categorised as less developed because interest articulation is not through differentiated and specialised structures such as pressure groups, trade unions and business associations. This is either a tautology because 'underdeveloped' has been defined in terms of non-pluralist political features or it simply says that Indonesia is different.

The concept of 'boundary' produces a similar problem. If political systems could not be clearly differentiated from the economic and the social as, say, in China or the Soviet Union, it was heavily value-laden to say that they were, as a consequence, less developed than a society where it is assumed that state and economy operate in their own self-contained spheres. It may or may not be justifiable to prefer such separation, or *laissez faire*, but it is not a developmental stance to say that a more modern society creates clear boundaries between polity and economy. That begins to look like a subterfuge for saying that societies where there is heavy state involvement in the economy are backward. This leaves aside the problem of assuming capitalist societies themselves demarcate between politics and economics. In all societies people move from one system to the other by virtue of the different roles which they perform. The boundaries are blurred, even if we wish to distinguish between societies where polity and economy are closely integrated because of public ownership, state planning, or collectivisation, and societies where that is less so. Almond wanted to argue that it was regressive scientifically not to insist on an analytical boundary being drawn between the processes of politics and those of social integration and adaptation, or between the political system on the one hand and churches, economies, schools, kinship, lineages and age sets on the other (Almond, 1966, p. 5). Nevertheless, a political system defined in part by reference to boundaries either leaves non-boundary systems non-political systems or makes statements about political systems true by definition and untestable empirically (Holt and Turner, 1966, pp. 17–19).

The definition of a developed political system proves to be flawed on other counts. As we saw in our review of modernisation theory, elements of traditionalism are found in all political systems. Particularistic principles and ascribed status are important in many developed societies. The fact that elements of modernity and tradition may be found co-existing within the same system suggests that simple dichotomous models are being postulated with specific cases being placed in one or the other, with the rest in an increasingly large transitional class. That kind of typology can lead to mistaken assumptions about the nature of traditional society – that, for example, it was static prior to European contact and colonisation; that traditional societies were socially and politically homogeneous; that traditional social structures are replaced by, after some conflict with, modern structures and values.

Unilinear development

Finally there are unilinear assumptions within this mode of analysis – the idea that societies can be placed upon a continuum between traditional and modern, along which all societies progress or have progressed during their histories. The major fallacy here was the proposition that the new states appearing on the international scene as a result of political independence, particularly after the Second World War (the phase of liberation from colonialism with which this school of thought was most concerned), were replicating the European experience from the sixteenth to the nineteenth century. New states are supposed to be progressing along the path trodden earlier by the modern states of the world. (Huntington, 1971, p. 292)

This approach ignores a very fundamental difference: that the history of the advanced societies does not include colonisation by more powerful countries. This makes it impossible to think of a unilinear developmental process. The new states of the world were structured by the old in a way which does not apply to the histories of countries whose own development was made possible by their exploitation of pre-industrial and pre-capitalist societies (Pratt, 1973, p. 95). The West's development was built, some would say, on the active *underdevelopment* of weaker societies and economies (see Chapter 6 below).

Ignoring the significance of such historical factors was compounded by a lack of consideration of continuing relationships with the powerful economies of the West. Developmentalists were concerned with internal factors, 'ignoring the more important continuities that persist in the social and economic structure of new nations' and that call the significance of their political independence into question, especially economic and military aid programmes, interventions by international financial organisations such as the World Bank, and investments by multinational corporations (Pratt, 1973, pp. 88–92).

In 1987 Almond attempted to rebut the charge that development-alism was ethnocentric and its theory of change unilinear, arguing that developmentalist comparative politics always recognised that new states might develop authoritarian rather than democratic, pluralist tendencies. He also claimed that the school never neglected international influences on domestic politics. However, it is noticeable that he restricts his refutation of the unilinearity charge to an awareness of authoritarianism, citing approvingly Coleman's view that modernisation 'is an open ended process consisting of trends towards increasing structural differentiation leading to increased governmental capacity and trends towards equality in the legal, participatory and distributive senses' (Almond, 1987, p. 449).

Almond does not attempt to answer the criticism that developmentalists ignored the implications of colonialism and continuing economic dependency for the current autonomy of Third World countries. His lively critique of dependency theory does not dispel doubts that developmentalist political science could provide a framework for understanding the unique relationships between rich and poor countries, or if it did it was only after the impact of dependency theory had been felt. He reminds us that in 1970 he himself argued explicitly 'against the simple diffusionist notion of unilinearity in the early 1960s' (Almond, 1987, p. 449). However, the interaction of economics and politics which Almond insists was always a feature of comparative studies of political development, such as the political consequences of industrialisation or the distributional effects of economic growth, does not encompass the factors which critics regarded as significant and distinctive of Third World status (Almond, 1987).

7.   Changes of emphasis

As O'Brien (1972) and Higgott (1983) have shown, the pessimism about Third World politics that set in after what was perceived to be the failures of the UN's first 'Development Decade', together with US preoccupations with problems of political order at home and abroad, led to subtle changes of emphasis in political development theory. Of particular significance here was US support for authoritarianism when directed towards the containment of revolutionary forces. It is possible to discern three such changes.

First, the possibility of regression as well as progression was recognised. For example, Almond and Powell (1966, ch. 12) warn against drawing any inference from developmental concepts such as 'structural differentiation' and 'cultural secularisation' that trends in such directions are inevitable. Huntington similarly warned that development theory's commitment to progress excluded the possibility that political systems might 'decay' (Huntington, 1965, pp. 392–3).

The second significant reorientation of political developmentalism was towards an emphasis on political stability and social order (O'Brien, D. C. 1972). The literature became increasingly concerned with factors associated with the maintenance of regimes and élites, with social and political order and with the restrictions on the capability of systems of government to produce decisions, policies and interventions that can be enforced successfully. In his 1965 survey of the diverse definitions of political development, Lucian Pye notes that 'development' for some meant the political prerequisites of economic growth; for others a capacity to maintain certain kinds of public order and to mobilise resources; and for yet others 'political stability based on a capacity for purposeful and orderly change' even to the extent of seeing democracy as a political liability to economic and social development (Pye, 1965). This change of emphasis in the political development literature from the preconditions for democracy of the late 1950s and early 1960s to problems of political order and stability in the late 1960s and 1970s (Huntington, 1987) was particularly damaging for some of the evolutionary assumptions of functionalist political science.

The third area of emphasis is that of political integration, which frequently appears as another way of analysing political stability and social order. Political development theory has recognised the problem of producing a political consensus in the face of cultural diversity. New states experience many obstacles to the creation of a sufficiently widespread sense of loyalty and obligation to the nation and its government. In addition to the problem of state-building, or providing governmental capacity, there is the problem of nation-building, or creating loyalty and commitment (Almond and Powell, 1966, ch. 2; Wriggins, 1966). Myron Weiner identified five different uses of the term 'integration' in the political science literature. First there is the process of creating a sense of territorial nationality in place of subordinate parochial loyalties to culturally and socially discrete sub-groups.

Second, 'integration' is a way of conceptualising the problem already referred to of establishing central government authority over subordinate political units. Territorial integration 'refers to the objective control which central authority has over the entire territory under its claimed jurisdiction' (Weiner, 1965, p. 53). The third use of the terms refers to a 'gap' between the aspirations and values of élites and masses which can lead to conflict, coercion and even civil war. The concept of integration is thus one way of approaching the phenomenon of political instability. Weiner himself admitted that 'there are clearly situations when it is hard to see how anything short of an authoritarian government could maintain an integrated state' (Weiner, 1966, p. 209). Similarly, integration as the establishment of a value consensus again places emphasis on the problem of maintaining social order and producing widespread unanimity on the means and ends of politics.

Finally, there is 'integrative behaviour', or the extent to which people can organise themselves for some collective purpose. Weiner saw all these meanings as united by a common concern: 'to define what it is *which holds a society and a political system together . . . at a level commensurate with what their political leadership needs to carry out their goals*' (1965, p. 54, emphasis in original). Analysis of the politics of developing societies in terms of 'integration' is thus a way of conceptualising the general orientation of development theory in the 1960s towards explanations of crisis, instability and the 'innumerable ways in which societies and political systems can fall apart' (Weiner, 1965, p. 64).

8. Conclusion

Some of the criticisms of political development theory *as theory* have been very dismissive indeed. Holt and Turner, for example, find no theoretical value in the work of the school at all: the available data on politics in developing countries was not used rigourously or precisely; key concepts were used in different ways by different scholars; others were defined too loosely to be of scientific value; the publications produced by members of the school did not advance the development of theory at all (Holt and Turner, 1975). Rather than producing new scientific explanations of political change, political development theory was sociological orthodoxy based on the American liberal tradition (Ricci, 1977, p. 31). David Apter refers to the 'rush to functionalism' as not amounting to much: 'considering how much time, money and effort went into the enterprise and in so many places, the results have been by and large disappointing, almost as disappointing as development itself' (1980, p. 264). Huntington pointed to the 'gap' between theory and reality shown by the development of authoritarianism, instability, ethnic conflict, and institutional decay instead of democratisation, order, nation-building and institutional rationalisation and differentiation (Huntington, 1965, pp. 391–2).

The attempt to establish a rigourous mode of analysis centred on the concept of political development was eventually abandoned. The pressures were too many for it to bear. Dependency theory, derived substantially from a critique of modernisation and development theorising, gained in popularity. Definitions of 'development' proliferated, reflecting a fragmentation of interests into specialised studies of institutions, areas and processes. Disillusionment with 'development' in many parts of the Third World made earlier theorising appear 'naïvely optimistic'. Even Almond had to admit that 'as the new and developing nations encountered difficulties and turned largely to authoritarian and military regimes, the optimism and hopefulness faded, and interest, productivity and creativity abated' (Almond, 1987, p. 444). US scholars turned their attention to domestic problems (a kind of 'neo-isolationism' set in, according to Riggs). Concern about 'limits to growth', the environment, hunger and disease came to outweigh interest in political institutions and behaviour. In the USA the flow of financial support for research on political development dried up (Huntington, 1965 and 1971; Riggs, 1981). We must, therefore, consider alternative ways of conceptualising Third World political change.

5
Neo-Colonialism and Sovereignty

1. Constitutional independence

The two decades following the Second World War saw the final and most dramatic wave of independence sweep across the European empires in Asia, the Middle East and Africa, either as a result of more or less peaceful negotiations between the leaders of the nationalist movements and the European powers, or as the outcome of wars of liberation. What Michael Barratt Brown called 'one of the great transformations in modern history' occurred when all but a few million of the 780 million people living in the colonial possessions of the imperial powers 'freed themselves from subject status' (Barratt Brown, 1963, pp. 189–90).

Politically it was assumed that indigenous governments, representing the interests of local people rather than alien groups, would have sovereign state power at their disposal. Their relationships with the governments of other sovereign states would be those of independent nation-states entering into treaties and agreements within the framework of international law. Economically it was assumed that following independence the process of 'diffusion' would continue, as capital, technology and expertise spread. Foreign aid and investment would increase the productive capacity of the less developed economy (Rosen and Jones, 1979; Mack and Leaver, 1979).

2. Neo-colonial relations

A different perception of the relationship between sovereign states is conveyed by the term 'neo-colonialism', originally coined by mainly Third World leaders who found that the achievement of constitu-

120

tional independence and sovereignty did not give total freedom to the governments of the newly formed nation-states. Political autonomy was found to be something of a facade behind which lurked the continuing presence of powerful Western financial and economic interests. The end of colonial government was seen by leaders such as Kwame Nkrumah, the first Prime Minister of Ghana and author of a book entitled *Neo-colonialism: the Last Stage of Imperialism*, as not ending economic colonialism (Nkrumah, 1965).

The core of the neo-colonialist argument is that a distinction between political and economic freedom misses the point that there can be no real political independence while economic dependency remains. Economic colonialism has serious political consequences. So political autonomy had not really been achieved with the formal and constitutional ending of colonial government. Supposedly independent societies and their sovereign governments were found to be lacking in control of their economies. 'Independence for these former colonies has meant trading the direct political control of colonialism for the indirect economic, political and cultural controls of neo-colonialism' (Berman, 1974, p. 4). The expression 'neo-colonialism' tries to encapsulate the idea that economic power and the political power that flows from it still reside elsewhere, even when 'independence' has been achieved. O'Connor (1970), for example, defined neo-colonialism as 'the survival of the colonial system in spite of formal recognition of political independence in emerging countries' which had become the victims of an indirect and subtle form of domination by political, economic, social, military and technical forces' (O'Connor, 1970, p. 117). But those subtle and indirect forms of domination had as their root cause the economies bequeathed by the colonial powers at the time of constitutional independence.

The new rulers of the former colonies found that the major proportion of the resources available to them were controlled from metropolitan centres that hitherto had ruled their countries directly. Independence appeared largely symbolic. For Nkrumah,

> the essence of neo-colonialism is that the state which is subject to it is, in theory, independent and has all the outward trappings of international sovereignty. In reality its economic system *and thus its political policy* is directed from outside. (Nkrumah, 1965, p. ix, emphasis added)

According to Julius Nyerere, the first President of Tanzania, his country achieved 'political independence only' in 1961. It attained neither economic power nor economic independence.

> We gained the political power to decide what to do; we lacked the economic and administrative power which would have given us freedom in those decisions. . . . A nation's real freedom depends on its capacity to do things, not on the legal rights conferred by its internationally recognised sovereignty. (Nyerere, 1973, p. 263)

3.   The economic basis of neo-colonial politics

In dependency theory, as will be shown later, there is the view that imperialism created economies that had been and still are positively and actively *underdeveloped* by dominant economies. Neo-colonialism as an interpretation of post-colonial history did not express itself in those terms. It did, however, recognise a failure on the part of colonialism to develop the economies of the colonised territories beyond the small but important sectors needed by the European economies and for which colonial exploitation was carried on. If, for example, European commercial interests were to acquire groundnuts, cocoa, palm oil and other agricultural commodities, then production was encouraged regardless of the consequences for other products such as food. Goods for export were needed by the colonialists, not goods for consumption. The phenomenon continues today as countries such as Ethiopia, Kenya, Zimbabwe and Colombia supply the West with fresh flowers, the most polluting form of agricultural produce, instead of their own populations with food. In 1992 Zimbabwe had to borrow $70 millions to import maize while exporting 6 million kilos of flowers. This is one of the latest methods by which foreign firms repatriate profits.

At independence colonial economies were left in a highly specialised condition, with one or two major commodities orientated towards export earnings and therefore foreign exchange (Harrison, 1979, ch. 18). Further development of the economy required foreign exchange which had to be acquired from the export of a very limited range of primary products. In the case of Ghana, for example, 61 per cent of its total export earnings came from one commodity, cocoa, as late as 1970. In Zambia in the same year 97 per cent of export earnings came from copper. Furthermore these were commodities for which world prices fluctuated alarmingly. This feature of neo-colonialism continued throughout the 1980s as the world market prices of the primary products on which the economies of so many Third World societies are dependent for their foreign exchange earnings have declined. Even the oil-producing countries have been disproportionately affected by fluctuations in oil prices.

Neo-colonialism operated according to a number of distinct processes: through the terms of trade; the need for aid; the repatriation of profits; and technological dependency.

The terms of trade

The neo-colonial economy is one in which the terms of trade operate to its disadvantage. This leads to foreign exchange crises as the purchasing power of the neo-colonial economy declines (Berman, 1974, p. 6). The economy thus becomes dependent on loans from developed countries and investment by foreign firms. A growing proportion of the neo-colonial economy's wealth is withdrawn from the country in the form of profits or interests on loans. This leads to increasing demands on foreign exchange to service foreign creditors rather than finance imports of industrial equipment or consumer goods. Consequently a neo-colonial society could find that it owed its total anticipated export earnings to repay foreign debts. For example, in 1965 India's foreign debt amounted to the equivalent of its total anticipated export earnings. Today governments in Sub-Saharan Africa spend 20 per cent of their public expenditure servicing debts amounting to $150 billion, 2 per cent more than on health and education. In 1970 Uganda serviced its debt with 3 per cent of its export earnings. By 1989 it had to use 45 per cent.

The problem for the neo-colonial economy is not just that it is dependent on a small number of export items to a much greater degree than rich economies. It is also that it is dependent on primary products – minerals, fuels and crops – to a much greater extent that rich economies. This combination of circumstances means that Third World countries suffer from the greater price fluctuations found with primary products than with manufactured goods. The net effect over time of such fluctuations is a 'decay' in the value of primary products compared with a general increase in the value of manufactured goods. Consequently market prices favour the advanced industrial economies and disadvantage the less developed primary exporters. For Nkrumah the terms of trade were one of the mechanisms of neo-colonialism:

> On the economic front, a strong factor favouring Western monopolies and acting against the developing world is international capital's control of the world market, as well as of the prices of commodities bought and sold there. From 1951–61, without taking oil into consideration, the general level of prices for primary products fell by 33.1 per cent, while prices of manufactured goods rose 3.5 per cent (within which machinery and equipment prices rose 31.3 per cent). In that same decade this caused a loss to the Asian, African and Latin American countries, using 1951 prices as a basis, of some $41 400 million. In the same period, while the volume of exports from those countries rose, their earnings in foreign exchange from such exports decreased. (1965, p. 241)

There is a structural problem with world markets: 'Billions of dollars are implicitly taken from the poor and given to the rich through the impersonal mechanisms of freely negotiated international trade pricing' (Rosen and Jones, 1979, pp. 249–50). During the 1980s Africa's exports rose by 25 per cent in volume but declined in value by 30 per cent due to low commodity prices.

If foreign exchange crises are met by loans from a multilateral agency such as the IMF or the World Bank, conditions are likely to be attached, such as a requirement to cut public expenditure programmes, particularly food subsidies and social services. This can lead to political unrest, as in Morocco, the Sudan and Tanzania in the 1980s.

The declining value of Third World exports is now to be exacerbated by biotechnology. Research is under way to replace the basic commodities produced in developing countries, such as coffee, tobacco, sugar, cocoa, pyrethrum and palm oil, with genetically engineered substitutes and synthetics based on crops grown in the North, such as frost-tolerant coffee. Already corn syrup is replacing sugar. It is predicted that the consequences of genetic engineering include significant losses of foreign exchange earnings in low-income countries, greater exploitation of workers, and the devastation of single-commodity economies (de Selincourt, 1993).

Aid

For development in which private capital will not invest, the neo-colonial economy requires foreign aid. This may be forthcoming, but it is also used as a lever to determine domestic government policy. Nkrumah illustrated the range of conditions that could be attached to aid:

> the conclusion of commerce and navigation treaties; agreements for economic co-operation; the right to meddle in internal finances, including currency and foreign exchange, to lower trade barriers in favour of the donor country's goods and capital; to protect the interests of private investments; determination of how the funds are to be used; forcing the recipient to set up counterpart funds; to supply raw materials to the donor; and use of such funds – a majority of it in fact – to buy goods from the donor nation. The conditions apply to industry, commerce, agriculture, shipping and insurance, apart from others which are political and military. (1965, p. 243)

Donors can withdraw vital aid if the neo-colonial governments fail to adopt policies favouring the interests of the donor government or firms based in the donor economy. In this way it secures strategic and diplomatic advantages, as in 1983 when the US Congress made economic assistance to developing countries conditional upon support for US foreign policy. Economic interests which the donor represents secure a profitable policy environment, as in 1966 when the USA threatened to withdraw food aid from India if the government did not allow Standard Oil to sell fertiliser at its own price. Multilateral agencies such as the World Bank enforce ideological objectives in return for development assistance, as in 1973 when the Bank made it a condition of its aid that the formation of socialist villages in Tanzania should be slowed down. Other conditions on which aid is given include the purchase of arms and the award of contracts to firms in the donor country.

Aid affects the power structure of neo-colonial society (Mack and Leaver, 1979). It increases the power of those in command of the state apparatus relative to any opposition and the power of the bureaucracy is enhanced by aid, this being the channel through which aid flows. Also, technical assistance programmes to national defence and police forces strengthen these sections of the political élite: much of the aid from developed countries is in the form of military assistance which has affected the distribution of political power in neo-colonial society. Food aid distorts the neo-colonial economy by enabling recipient governments to avoid land reforms and changes in methods of agricultural production which would reduce external dependency and the power of the landed classes. Radical critics of aid have been joined by conservatives such as Lord Bauer, claiming that aid empowers the state at the expense of free markets and increases the power of ruling groups at the expense of the people generally (Bauer, 1971). Aid has also biased development towards urban rather than rural society (Lipton, 1977).

Repatriated profits

Theorists of neo-colonialism also claim that continuing dependency on foreign capital causes a net *outflow* of capital from the developing countries to metropolitan centres. Repatriated profits, royalties, services, interest payments and debt repayments actually outweigh investment in the Third World. In Sub-Saharan Africa between 1960 and 1967 private investment amounted to $2.249 billion, but repatriated profits amounted to $3.6 billion (Berman, 1974, p. 5). In its *Human Development Report 1992* the UN showed that since 1985 the net transfer from developing to developed countries exceeded $250 billion. This would not be so damaging if such costly investment increased GNP by an amount greater than the net outflow. But foreign capital (investment and aid) substitutes for, rather than supplements, domestic savings. Domestic investors put their money into low risk, high profit multinationals rather than weak indigenous enterprises. Hence the modern and dynamic sector of the neo-colonial economy comes increasingly under the control of multinational corporations. The backward sectors are left to local capital (Roxborough, 1979, p. 59). So if profits *are* reinvested locally this increases the share of domestic industry controlled by foreign capital. Foreign investment is said to 'decapitalise' the host economy through a net outflow of capital, with more being extracted in excess profits than being invested locally (Rosen and Jones, 1979).

In the neo-colonial economy, the profits which foreign investors and multinationals earn are used only in small part to finance new enterprises, and these add to the sector owned or controlled by foreign interests at independence. What is most significant in this expansion of expatriate economic activity is that investment tends predominantly to be in equipment, tools, plant and personnel imported from the 'metropolitan' country. The expansion thus contributes to the expansion of the metropolitan market rather than the industrial development of the neo-colonial society.

Wages may also be 'repatriated', so reducing the value of foreign enterprise to the neo-colonial economy which tends to employ a small percentage of the labour force at low wages. A small proportion of the revenues accruing to foreign firms are returned to the domestic economy through wages. For example, in the 1950s in the Middle East less than 5 per cent of oil revenues were paid in wages to 0.34 per cent of the population employed in the oil industry. The wages paid to expatriate workers are of course 'repatriated'. Local wage-earners receive too little to save and their consumption expenditure may be concentrated in company housing and stores, stocked from overseas. Wages therefore do not form a basis for indigenous investment or markets to encourage local production. Such trends contributed to the anxieties of political leaders in the new states of the 1960s.

Technological dependency

Even if the Third World economy tries to substitute public ownership and investment for foreign control, it still has to obtain technology from abroad. In the early years of independence this tended to be capital intensive and labour-saving. But as this is the only way for a developing country to compete on the world market the high cost of such technology has to be met, despite the fact that it displaces an already over-abundant supply of labour. Furthermore, a monopolistic control over advanced technology gives the multinationals additional leverage through the supply of industrial processes, machinery, patents, blueprints and spares. So technological dependency benefits external interests in various ways. When, in the late 1960s, Tanzania called in an international firm of consultants to advise on a fertiliser manufacturing project, the consultants rejected the use of local deposits of potash and opted for the supply of raw materials and plant from abroad. These oil-based raw materials increased in price fourfold soon after completion of the project in 1973, resulting in a supply of fertiliser too expensive for the average peasant producer and a serious drain on the country's scarce foreign reserves.

4.   The political analysis of neo-colonialism

The *political* manifestations of foreign economic involvement proved difficult to describe in concrete terms, except for those for whom politics was merely an epiphenomenon of the economic. One reason for this was that much contemporary political science accepted the constitutional formalities as accurate representations of reality. Another was that the economy was seen as a completely separate sphere or system of action. In 1973 Henry Bretton, writing mainly about Africa but in terms that had wider applicability, complained that 'The degree of economic power at the disposal of the decolonising state *vis-à-vis* the nominally independent one is not considered. The political influence that flows from that power is not even remotely acknowledged' (Bretton, 1973, p. 22). Liberal political science, represented most potently by the functionalists, acknowledged that the formation of new states had been profoundly influenced by the existence of old ones, but did not allow that conclusion to lead to 'the logical question of how precisely an old state might influence the formation of a new one' (p. 24).

Even if this is thought too harsh a judgement, it will nevertheless probably be accepted that political science had largely concerned itself with institution-building during the decolonisation process and the 'preparations' for independence in those colonies where the relationships between nationalists and the imperial powers could be described as such, involving more or less peaceful diplomacy and negotiation rather than wars of liberation. Thereafter politics was seen as the concern of an internally and externally sovereign state. Conflicts with other sovereign states, including the former colonial powers, were interpreted as matters of international law and diplomacy and left to the specialists in those fields. The political aspects of international economic relations were overlooked.

Yet even the political scientists and political economists who recognised the continuing economic dependency of post-colonial states rarely demonstrated how the mechanisms of the internal political consequences operated. The nature of the economic linkages could easily be described and disputed over, but the domestic political effects were left to be inferred from them. Bretton himself stated without further elaboration that 'The preponderance of one or two commodities among the exports of 19 African states . . . tells part of the story of African independence'. The uneven distribution of primary resources among new states was said to have a greater effect on governmental orientations than internal interests. The power of foreign interests could even be measured by 'the ratio of export–import trade to overall GDP of the host country' (p. 205). Mining concerns were said to constitute 'rival governments' (pp. 25–6). General policy constraints on post-colonial governments were noted, such as limitations on monetary policy by the high propensity to import (Hymer, 1982). Bretton concluded that 'The international power and influence flow is indeed so massive, concerning as it does the major share of the national resources available to the new rulers, that in many instances it is not possible to determine where national prerogatives end and foreign ones begin' (Bretton, 1973, p. 22). Integration into colonial economic blocks further strengthened external influences on the room to manoeuvre of domestic governments and indeed domestic economic interests. Economic infiltration took place via investment, loans, development assistance, technical assistance and military aid.

It was, however, possible to identify neo-colonialists as an organised interest, an interest having political significance internally but mainly externally orientated economically and carrying more political weight than economically marginal local groups. Foreign corporations, banks and trading houses could be described as 'positioned at the control points of the power and influence flow', resisting and countering nationalistic economic pressures. Within the context of an undeveloped economy the commanding heights were largely in the hands of foreign firms. In the immediate post-independence years indigenous, small-scale capital entrepreneurs had nothing like the same influence as the multinationals. Companies such as Unilever, the Firestone Corporation or United Fruit dominated the economies of the new states.

Organisations representing external interests were able successfully to contain the range of policy and ideological choices open to governments within limits acceptable to themselves (Berman, 1974,

p. 7). Multinationals can inhibit development planning by limiting the government's tax-raising capacity through transfer pricing and the movement of production from one country to another (Hymer, 1982; Sutcliffe, 1972, p. 188). Foreign owners and managers of foreign capital received special advantages. In francophone Africa, for example, *'la presence francaise'* meant the complete penetration of public life by such interests and their pressure groups. In Kenya, European organisations representing the agriculture-based industries exerted great influence on policy-making because of dependence for competitiveness on European involvement. In the 1960s the foreign owners of the greater part of non-agricultural capital were also represented locally by 'a substantial bureaucracy employed by the branches of foreign firms . . . mainly themselves foreigners', although increasingly including Kenyan Africans. As this ownership spread, so the political power of foreign capital increased (though in the interest of nationalist economic ideology and rhetoric it had to be ritually humiliated: Leys, 1975, p. 174).

In Senegal and the Ivory Coast the influence of French interests on government boards, chambers of commerce and informal meetings of businessmen exceeded the power of parliaments, cabinets and political parties (Bretton, 1973, pp. 204–8). After independence in the Ivory Coast French private interests were dominant in the commodities which formed the basis of the economy (coffee, cocoa and cotton). Manufacturing and processing were mainly in foreign hands, and governments had to obtain the approval of big foreign firms with the equipment, trade outlets, capital, and skills for groundnut-shelling, cotton-ginning and cocoa-cleaning before formulating any policies towards indigenous producers.

Nkrumah understood well the 'rights' and privileges that could be demanded by foreign interests as a result of their economic power: land concessions, prospecting rights, exemptions from customs duties and taxes, and privileges in the cultural sphere: 'that Western information services be exclusive; and that those from socialist countries be excluded'. So, for example, agreements for economic co-operation offered by the USA often included the demand that the US Information Agency ('a top intelligence arm of the US imperialists') be granted preferential rights to disseminate information (Nkrumah, 1965, pp. 246–50). Cultural neo-colonialism also rested on the dependence of newly independent states on Western ideas and methods in education, administration and the professions (Berman, 1974, pp. 7–8). The top executives of the subsidiaries of multinationals, the largest corporations in the country of operations, are influential in the social and cultural life of the host country as well as in its politics. Governments dependent on the information coming from such sources are unable to work out their own solutions to the problems, such as poverty, which are of no particular interest to foreigners (Baran, 1957, p. 194; Hymer, 1982).

The anti-colonialists of the post-independence era found neo-colonialism to be operating in diverse ways other than legitimate pressure group activity. Nkrumah described how neo-colonialists 'slip past our guard' through military bases, advisers, media propaganda, evangelism and CIA subversion. Military dependence on the former colonial powers for arms, training, advisers and basic military doctrine has been seen as one of the most visible aspects of neo-colonialism. The success or failure of a *coup d'état* was often dependent on the level of external encouragement. In Africa the 'metropolitan centres, especially France, have assumed the role of arbiters of the survival of particular regimes' (Berman, 1974, pp. 6–7). France's neo-colonial role has continued into the 1990s in Rwanda, Zaire, Gabon and Togo.

Other important political features of neo-colonialism are the common interests of local élites and external organisations, whether they be foreign governments, multinational corporations or international agencies. Baran described merchants 'expanding and thriving within the orbit of foreign capital', forming a '*comparador* element' of the native bourgeoisie which, together with 'native industrial monopolists', act as 'stalwart defenders of the established order'. Large landowners not only benefit from foreign capital but find outlets for their produce, employment opportunities for members of their families, and rising land values in the neo-imperial connection (Baran, 1957, pp. 194–5).

The multinationals have an effect on the class structure and power distribution in less developed countries by creating dependent classes of local merchants, financiers and privileged sections of the labour force – 'satellite classes whose interests are tied to the *dependencia* syndrome' (Rosen and Jones, 1979, p. 254). Under neo-colonialism the imperial power is represented by 'collaborative classes within post-colonial society, some more dependent on foreign interests than others'. Petras draws the following distinctions:

Large-scale industrialists involved in production for the local market and with a powerful presence in the state are more likely to be *associate power-sharers* with imperial interests. Import–exporters tied to foreign markets, shipping and credits are likely to be *dependent power-sharers*. Joint ventures, in which industrialists produce for foreign markets, drawing on foreign technology, capital and management, and with little direct representation in the state, are likely to be *subordinate* collaborators. (Petras, 1981, p. 18)

Indigenous élites, the most important being the bureaucracy and indigenous management cadres employed by foreign companies, develop an interest in maintaining economic arrangements in which foreigners hold a major stake. The close contacts between members of the national politico-administrative élite and external organisations 'makes the distinction between domestic and international affairs meaningless' (Berman, 1974, p. 9).

The foreigners are usually the dominant partners because of their superior resources, information and negotiating skills compared with national governments. With the possible exception of the military, governments, labour organisations and most non-business institutions and associations are 'far behind' multinationals in terms of financial, technological and administrative strength (Hymer, 1982). While foreign interests are thus included in the policy process, indigenous interests not represented by the élite are excluded. Institutions for representation and participation (parties, local governments, trade unions, youth organisations) have been left powerless relative to the bureaucracy. In the case of African states: 'the centre is thus itself an enclave, oriented towards and responsive to external interests, and largely impenetrable at the policy-making level to the population of its own periphery' (Berman, 1974, p. 11).

5. The Warren controversy

The view that formal political independence had not substantially modified the relations of domination and exploitation between the capitalist imperialist powers and the new states of the Third World received a major challenge in the early 1970s by the British Marxist Bill Warren (1973 and 1980). He questioned whether the evidence corroborated 'the neo-colonial thesis that political independence has meant only marginal changes in the economic ties between ex-colonies and their former masters' (Warren, 1980, p. 171). Although not denying that imperialism persisted 'as a system of inequality, domination and exploitation' (1973, p. 4) Warren challenged the conclusion that independence had not improved the prospects for economic development, and especially industrialisation, in the periphery. The term 'neo-colonialism' obscured the role played by the achievement of formal sovereignty and its consequences. His conclusions about the significance of formal constitutional independence for colonial societies and economies are particularly relevant to the central tenet of neo-colonialist explanations – that independence was largely a formality and dwarfed in importance by continuing foreign economic domination.

The Warren critique

In Warren's view, the post-war achievement of independence, together with other socio-political and economic trends, created the conditions for significant industrialisation. These trends included international rivalries and competition; the willingness and ability of foreign firms to invest in the Third World; the adoption by some developed countries of more liberal trading policies; and collaboration between imperialist and Third World governments to suppress anti-capitalist movements.

Warren argues that since independence, rates of growth and structural economic change, including industrialisation, have been significant. In the period studied by Warren, annual growth rates in Third World manufacturing industry were on average higher in the Third World than in the First. Manufacturing grew by about 7 per cent per annum between 1960 and 1968, compared with 6 per cent in advanced capitalist economies. Between 1971 and 1976 the rate of average annual increase was more that twice that for developed capitalist countries. This represented a momentum since 1945 sustained for a longer period than any previously recorded (1980, pp. 241–3). Foreign capital had been attracted by low costs into textile manufacturing, automobile assembly, shipbuilding and chemicals. By 1970 the export of manufactured goods accounted for 25 per cent of the value of Third World exports. Foreign investment had actually been beneficial to local economies (1980, p. 176).

Warren specifically addressed the contention that neo-colonialism is derived from balance of payments problems and the extraction of surplus capital. He showed that during the later 1960s the balance of payments of the LDCs improved on the whole, in part due to a growth in the volume of exports. In the 1960s and 1970s exports rose more rapidly than imports. He argued that a 'drain' of capital might well be a price worth paying for the creation of productive facilities, especially when it creates or encourages indigenous investment rather than suffocating it. Furthermore, some balance of payments difficulties had been caused by policy errors rather than the conditions ascribed to neo-colonialism (1980, pp. 177–8; see also Parfitt and Riley, 1989).

The import of technology had also constituted a net gain to developing countries. Its assimilation via the industrialisation process contributed to the development of indigenous technical capacity. Capabilities for assimilating technology were improving rapidly year by year and were more important than monopolistic foreign control for technological transfer and progress (Warren, 1973, pp. 30–1). The importation of technology had led to 'amazing achievements' and the abandonment of Western technology would be disastrous. Warren cites the case of DDT in Sri Lanka, where a ban on its use contributed to a rapid rise in malaria, previously almost eliminated in the country (1980, p. 180).

A number of dependent economies had also produced impressive growth in per capita incomes. The post-war record of the Third World compares favourably with its pre-war performance and with relevant periods of growth (for example, in the eighteenth and nineteenth centuries) in the developed market economies (1980, pp. 191–9). This is not so say that there have not been the inevitable inequalities associated with fast growth which had sometimes been politically destabilising. However, the rapid economic progress since 1945 had not *generally* been associated with worsening aggregate inequality. Experience has been mixed. The record also shows improvements in welfare between 1963 and 1972 according to indicators for nutrition, health, housing and education (1980, pp. 200–35).

Political independence, far from being a sham, was a significant change in the internal politics of former colonies because it provided a focus for the domestic state management of economic processes. The newly independent state became the focal point of economic development. Formal independence gave Third World states 'institutional control' over their domestic economies. The power to establish central banks and para-statals, enforce export and import currency controls, and implement taxation and public spending 'stem directly from independence' and effect far more than industrialisation, especially the reinforcement of capitalist social relations of production, commodity production in agriculture, and economic restructuring 'along lines more suitable to a successful indigenous capitalism' (1973, p. 13). The state exercised powers to direct investment and channel external capital whether from aid, multinationals or foreign countries and controlled the development of capitalist relations and modes of production. This led to it becoming a significant actor in the national political system and not totally subject to external political forces.

Domestic state management of the economy had significantly increased revenues from resource-based industries such as oil, expanded training for indigenous personnel, increased the demand for local inputs, and spread local shareholding and investment in manufacturing enterprises: 'all have been strengthened and their advance accelerated by deliberate policy' (1980, pp. 172–4).

New states had successfully negotiated with foreign investors over profit levels, wages, rents, pricing policies, volumes of output, transportation needs, sources of supply, taxes on multinationals, export policies and other interventions in the domestic economy. Third World states had shown themselves capable of taking controlling action against foreign firms located in their territories, such as nationalisation, the acquisition of majority shareholdings, joint ventures and service contracts. In some countries (for example, Ghana and Nigeria) specified areas of the economy have been reserved for local enterprises. Alliances with foreign capital have established conditions for indigenous capital accumulation. Indigenous capital, far from being swamped by foreign capital, has been able to form important alliances and create opportunities for profitable enterprise with foreign capital. The bargaining power of newly independent countries was further increased by collective organisations such as OPEC and the Andean Pact.

Governments in LDCs have learned to exploit conflict within the First and Second worlds. Independence broke the monopoly of colonialist powers, creating conditions in which Third World countries could utilise rivalries between the imperialist powers, foreign firms and the power blocs of East and West.

Independence also encouraged the development of social movements which gave added momentum to economic development. New ruling groups, often petty bourgeois in nature, could mobilise. The absence of a fully-formed national bourgeoisie has been compensated for by a state apparatus which has assumed the role of a bourgeois ruling class. So Third World societies had acquired their own indigenous ruling class, not in the form of a private property-owning bourgeoisie but in the form of a public property-directing state apparatus, particularly the bureaucracy. Conditions will increasingly exist for the formation of a national bourgeoisie and therefore the forms of control, management and politics that such a class requires. Independence also stimulated popular, diffuse, indigenous pressures for higher living standards, a major internal influence sustaining industrialisation policies. Economic nationalism, whether under left-wing, liberal or even extreme right-wing regimes, assisted underdeveloped capitalist countries to become more advanced (Warren, 1973, p. 11). The state has become a focal point of political pressure of an urban petty bourgeoisie demanding higher standards of living and consumption, all of which encourages manufacturing and industrialisation.

Warren recognised that for poor countries there are many problems that are part of the imperialist legacy, such as stagnation in agricultural production, excessive urbanisation, unemployment and even 'premature socialism' before capitalist development had been completed. But the relationship between new states and their former colonial powers is basically non-antagonistic and represented for Warren no more than the normal rivalries between competing national capitalist economies. There had not only been considerable progress in Third World industrialisation and economic development, it has been *independent* development. The expansion of manufacturing had been based on the home market. The industrial sector had become increasingly diversified; direct foreign investment had been less significant than the pessimists had claimed; local subsidiaries and branches of multinationals were largely funded from local sources and re-invested earnings:

the idea of 'neo-colonialism' – that the formal political independence of almost all the former colonies has not significantly modified the previous domination and exploitation of the great majority of humanity in Asia, Africa, and Latin America by the advanced capitalist world – is highly misleading and affords an assessment of post-war world capitalism that omits most new developments. (1980, pp. 184–5)

What the concept of 'neo-colonialism' had achieved, in Warren's view, was to indicate that newly-independent governments could not *immediately* exert their bargaining power, because of skills shortages and delays in establishing effective state institutions and representation on international bodies. It had also provided ideological support for, and international acceptance of, 'Third World bourgeois nationalism' – 'a fundamental ideological condition for the creation of modern nation-states out of states previously characterised by feudal particularism, religious and communal division, and all varieties of patriarchal backwardness' (1980, p. 185; see also Twitchett, 1965, p. 319).

Other assessments of imperialism have confirmed the significance of the ending of formal colonialism. Cohen argues that independence removed the direct power of the colonists, who were forced to rely on 'more subtle and indirect means of compulsion or persuasion in order to achieve the same ends' (Cohen, B. J., 1973, p. 221). Changes in the composition of government élites meant that their regimes do not remain *comprador* for very long. Independence provided opportunities for the national bourgeoisie, liberal reformers, democratic socialists, communists or military populists to alter relationships with rich countries. Independent governments could enter into alliances and trade agreements that were not open to them before, strengthening their bargaining positions in international economic relations, notably through UNCTAD and regional organisations such as OPEC.

Responses to Warren

Warren's optimism at the progressive, in Marxist terms, nature of Third World development did not go unchallenged. The reply of Warren's critics to his claim that there had been a rapid expansion of manufactured exports was that in the late 1970s 81 per cent of

Third World exports were still in the form of raw materials, foodstuffs and fuels, whereas 82 per cent of the imports into Third World countries from developed countries were manufactured goods, indicating that Third World economies still exhibited the neo-colonial distortion (Petras, 1981, pp. 118–24). In all regions of the developing world, with the exception of the oil-rich Middle East, the trade gap was increasing. Growing foreign reserves merely indicated increasing foreign debt or an incapacity to absorb capital. Debt problems resulting from declining prices of export commodities had led to austerity programmes, credit freezes, devaluations, bankruptcies, reduced living standards and political repression. The burden of debt had reached crisis proportions, and it was precisely the most industrially advanced regions of the Third World that were having the greatest difficulty in repaying loans.

Warren was also accused of exaggerating the benefits of foreign investment. Emmmanuel argued that foreign capital continued to displace profitable growth industries in developing countries because of its own monopolistic and dynamic superiority. The loss to the Third World economies resulting from the raw materials acquired by foreign investors was several times greater than the short-term gains provided by foreign investment in them. Emmanuel supported Warren in his view of capital as neutral as regards its source, the use to which it is put being more significant. But he claimed that the net inflow was derisory compared with what was needed:

> The mere arrival of foreign capital in a country does not 'block' anything. It enslaves or develops the country just as much as any other capital, neither more nor less. Consequently, if it should happen that capital from New York were to flow into Calcutta as it flows into San Francisco, we should have no reason to suppose that Calcutta would not one day be, for better or worse, the equal of San Francisco. Unfortunately – and this is where Bill Warren's mistake begins – (a) capital has never flowed into Calcutta; (b) under present conditions it seems improbable, if not impossible, that it will flow into Calcutta in the future; indeed (c) Calcutta is not underdeveloped because it has been invaded by foreign capital but, on the contrary, because it has been starved of this capital. (Emmanuel, 1974, p. 75; 1976, pp. 762–3)

Other critics, nqtably McMichael (1974), accused Warren of exaggerating the significance of popular pressures released by independence and of omitting any analysis of the social forces exerting pressures on government or the linkages between ruling groups and external interests: 'Capital is mobilized, bargaining takes place, pressures are exerted, nationalization (of sorts) takes place by something described as the "underdeveloped countries"' (p. 93).

The range of experiences of different class-based regimes was not assessed by Warren. Independence has not itself achieved development – it has only made possible the release of forces which in some countries have produced industrial advance. Some of the Third World countries that have made the greatest advances in Warren's terms have been least independent from foreign controls (Brazil, Indonesia and Zaire, for example), and have experienced extreme repression rather than popular pressures as the conditions under which such advances have occurred.

Warren was thought to have paid insufficient attention to the 'intensive political and economic integration of the international capitalist economy' during the period studied. He failed to distinguish the period of popular mobilisation, leading to national independence, from the post-independent *demobilisation* of such forces to enable dependent industrialisation to take place in countries such as India, Algeria, Indonesia, Nigeria and Kenya. Non-popular, pro-imperialist regimes, often resting on alliances between the military and propertied classes, have been the prerequisite of industrial growth. (McMichael *et al.*, 1974, p. 94)

The countries with the highest rates of industrialisation not only have the highest concentrations of foreign capital, they also have the highest rates of exploitation of labour, and the lowest rates of working-class mobilisation. They are in effect police states.

Warren also assumed rather than proved that multinationals and foreign capital brought benefits, and that Third World governments acquired leverage or national control over their operations. Sutcliffe had shown that while there had been rapid industrial growth in some LDCs in the early 1960s, this had not been matched by growth in employment or change in the type of goods available. Industries used foreign capital and techniques to produce the goods that used to be imported, reinforcing the pattern of income distribution and therefore the social structure (Sutcliffe, 1972, pp. 185–6).

Other criticisms were that Warren ignored 'internal colonialism' between regions of Third World countries, equated development with industrialisation, and exaggerated growth rates by the misuse of statistics. If economic growth rates are calculated per capita rather than nationally, they 'dwindle into insignificance' and do not compare favourably with advanced capitalist countries because capital-intensive industrialisation has not absorbed the labour available: 'More and more the developing countries show a structural distortion, providing highly rewarding employment for a small minority, and a very large amount of barely productive poverty-line employment, or no employment, for the masses' (Hoogvelt, 1978, p. 81).

It has also been shown that an increasing share of manufacturing in total production merely reflects declining production in the agriculture sector. Averaging the export record of the Third World concealed the fact that over half of it was accounted for by five countries. Any averaging of the developing countries conceals wide variations, including countries with very large populations and very poor records of industrial performance which are disguised by the impressive performance of some very small countries.

As far as the politics of neo-colonialism are concerned, the main issue dividing Warren from his critics is the consequences of capitalist industrialisation and growth for different classes within Third World societies. Warren's critics were anxious to establish that development usually meant the political repression and economic exploitation of workers and peasants. As we have seen, Warren did not deny this – as a Marxist he was hardly likely to. His conviction, however, was that growth and development were based on increasingly autonomous, nationalistic, political leadership and that this produced conditions for the development of capitalism *significantly* different from those preceding formal independence. Capitalist forces might have been exploitative (must have been, in fact) but at least they were national. Leys found supporting evidence in Kenya, where a class of agrarian capitalists is able to use its strong representation in the state apparatus to increase the rate of indigenous capital accumulation through policies on trade licensing, monopolies, state finance capital, private credit and state capitalist enterprise (Leys, 1978).

It is this point that raised the most serious objections from Warren's critics, rather than the quality of the regimes that served those interests best. Warren's argument was that national classes and their political representatives acted autonomously towards subordinate classes and foreign interests. The importance of Warren's conclusion about national independence and the power of the new national bourgeoisies for Marxists was that it identified the fundamental division as between classes, not nations (Brewer, 1980, pp. 293–4). His critics maintained that these classes and their regimes continued to be the instruments of foreign capital, and that as a consequence the economic record was not as good as Warren made it out to be, let alone the political and social record for those whom capitalism exploits.

6. Conclusion

Much of the literature on neo-colonialism was concerned with the real, rather than symbolic, significance of independence from a colonial power. Those who wrote about neo-colonialism separated the post-independence phase from the pre-independence. They were not particularly concerned with placing continuing economic relationships between poor and rich countries into a broad theoretical framework which produced an interpretation of the continuity between imperialism and independence. There had, however, been in existence a body of ideas that was trying to do precisely that. The idea of neo-colonialism was incorporated into a theory about an international system of economic subordination that had a very strong impact on countries long after their independence. This is generally referred to as dependency theory. It is a far more elaborate and sophisticated approach to development, or rather the lack of it, than the idea of neo-colonialism and the partial nature of political independence, and is the subject of the next chapter.

6

Dependency, Peripherality and Development

1. Introduction

Dependency theory had its roots in the crisis of US liberalism in the late 1960s (particularly associated with the war in Vietnam), the failure of many Third World societies to move in prescribed directions, and doubts about the credibility of social science's claims to be neutral and value-free (Higgott, 1983, p. 9). Other influences included the Cuban revolution, de-Stalinisation and Maoism (Leys, 1977, p. 98). It was in part a critical response to modernisation theory's assumption that 'backwardness' was the result of the isolation of LDCs from the rest of the world, rather than their exploitation by more advanced countries under various forms of imperialism (Phillips, 1977, pp. 7–8). The major contributors to what Foster-Carter (1976) has called a new paradigm in the study of development were Latin American Marxist economists such as Dos Santos, Cardoso, Sunkel and Faletto, non-Marxist Latin American economists such as Furtado and Prebisch, and North American neo-Marxists such as Bodenheimer, Petras, Magdoff and A. G. Frank (Ray, 1973, p. 6; O'Brien, 1975, p. 11; Higgott, 1978, p. 32).

2. Origins of dependency theory

Dependency theory adds the idea of peripherality or satellite status to the concept of neo-colonialism. This was achieved in two phases. The first was concerned with dependency as a function of primary

142

production, a very similar concern to that of theorists who saw a form of colonialism continuing after independence, with poor countries depending on a small number of primary products for their export earnings. The second phase developed the idea of 'peripherality'.

Export dependency

The first phase of dependency theory originated from the analysis of Latin America. It is thus not entirely straightforward to apply the theory to other parts of the Third World. There is something particularly significant in the fact that it was Latin American experience that originally prompted this particular perception of the poor country's problems. This is that the societies of Latin America had long ago achieved independence but nevertheless displayed problems of poverty in large sections of the population, regional inequalities alongside social inequalities, and sectoral divisions in the economy that were very similar to countries that were still colonies or had only recently achieved independence. Circumstances that might be expected under conditions of colonialism or in only recently liberated ex-colonies – especially economic exploitation and social inequality – were found in states that had been independent since the early or mid-nineteenth century. This observation led to the elaboration of the concept of 'dependency' by a mixed group of structuralist and neo-Marxist social scientists (O'Brien, P. J., 1975; Bernstein, 1979).

Dependency theory began as a critique of international trade theory and an explanation of why import substitution was needed. It then explained the failure of this strategy by reference to the structures introduced by industrialisation (Leys, 1977, p. 97; O'Brien, P. J., 1975, p. 7; Philip, 1990, p. 486). The general thesis of the first phase of dependency theory was that until about 1929 and the onset of the Great Depression, countries in Latin America had been trying to survive economically on the basis of exporting primary commodities. The Depression revealed the fragility of that strategy by removing the demand for many such exports. The effect of the Depression was consequently very severe. Political leaders and experts in Latin America reacted by arguing that these weaknesses meant that they were not equal but dependent partners in their relations with the richer countries with which they traded. Consequently fluctuations in the pattern of international demand for commodities produced dramatic social and regional dislocation from time to time. Past strategies had consisted of turning from one primary commodity (say sugar in the case of Brazil) to another (for example, coffee) when the market for the first product collapsed.

Continuing dependency and dislocation could be avoided, it was argued, by a strategy of import substitution. The manufacture of formerly imported goods would reduce dependency on the highly volatile markets for primary products. When the Economic Commission for Latin America (ECLA) was set up in 1948 such ideas were dominant among the technocrats influential in that organisation. ECLA was a major force behind the strategy of industrialisation, to be instituted where possible behind protective barriers, and if necessary with a high degree of state intervention and planning (Hirschman, 1961, pp. 12–20; Hoogvelt, 1982, pp. 167–8). The state would ensure that capital would be directed towards manufacturing industry (Dos Santos, 1973).

This strategy had political dimensions, in addition to reducing dependence on foreign trade and creating a locally controlled economy. It was intended that greater economic sovereignty would follow. Secondly, (and here there are echoes of modernisation theory) it was predicted that industrialisation would weaken traditional society. Manufacturing activities need different pattern variables from traditional societies. In Latin America this would mean that the status and power of the traditional landed oligarchy would be undermined. If this almost feudalistic stratum could be weakened, the way to greater democracy would be paved. Thirdly, industrialisation would start to make a real impact on the extreme inequalities found in Latin American societies. It would also contribute to the integration of the rural masses into the main activities of society. New occupational opportunities would be created. The problem of landlessness would be overcome by economic development in sectors other than agriculture. The rural masses, formerly isolated on plantations and *haciendas*, would become closely incorporated into society through new economic opportunities and improved standards of living. This would then contribute to the reinforcement of political stability. While the rural masses were marginalised by semi-feudal forces dominating the rural areas, political stability was always threatened.

Integration would produce not only stability, but greater democracy. The state would gain legitimacy by its association with the industrialisation process and by contributing to social and political equality as well as economic efficiency. National sentiment would be strengthened, especially for rural people hitherto allied economically and politically with rural oligarchies rather than the state. The consciousness of rural people focused on local landed and religious élites rather than the nation-state. Thus a secular goal for the import-substitution strategy was political integration into a liberal democratic society (Dos Santos, 1973).

Import dependency

Phase two of dependency theory was prompted by the apparent failure of this import-substitution strategy to solve the problem of dependency or to produce the intended political outcomes. By the end of the 1960s a very different state of affairs had developed. A new international division of labour had emerged, with the rich countries (usually referred to as 'metropolitan') exporting capital goods, and underdeveloped countries producing consumer goods with foreign capital. Import substitution had increased dependency, now upon foreign capital goods – machine tools, plant and technology. Automobiles were the classic example of this new kind of dependency. Goods for mass consumption were not being produced. Nor were goods that could have used indigenous technology and capital in significant quantities. Import substitution had created a manufacturing sector dependent upon foreign economic interests (Johnson, 1972).

The economic consequences of the strategy included an accelerated volume of imports in order to shift the composition of production towards capital goods, exacerbating problems of indebtedness, trade imbalance and inflation, and reinforcing the power of metropolitan capital. Monopolistic control over advanced industrial technology gave multinationals leverage in supplying the machinery and processes required.

Income distributions were found to have become more, not less, unequal. This inequality had developed a new dimension, that between the rural and urban areas. People displaced from the land were not being absorbed into new industrial activities and thereby integrated into the social fabric, largely because the new industries were capital rather than labour intensive. New forms of marginalisation were created in the slum populations gathered on the fringes of the major urban and industrial centres. Instead of integration into a modern economy, disparities in social and spatial terms and new forms of marginalisation were brought into being as a growing proportion of the population found themselves without jobs, education, political influence, security or proper shelter. Such people were politically highly volatile and therefore not committed to political stability. Their exclusion from politics did not engender consensus towards the state.

The state, it was argued, had become subservient to the multinational companies that controlled the industrialisation process. Greater sovereignty had not been achieved. Rather than liberal democracy and pluralism developing, politics became more authoritarian and repressive as governments tried to cope with the social strains brought about by the industrialising process. Managing the industrial labour-force as well as the marginalised masses seemed to require military dictatorship rather than pluralist democracy.

3. The elements of dependency theory

The dependency theorising of the late 1960s and 1970s attempted to explain the failure of industrialisation and import-substitution strategies. The perception of what was happening was summed up by Cardoso (1972) as 'dependent development', a somewhat controversial label, since the main thrust of dependency theory was to argue that no development had occurred: poor countries had been underdeveloped, not developed. A. G. Frank, one of the leading theorists of this phase, elaborated on the idea of one country 'underdeveloping' another. A new term was added to the lexicon of development studies: underdevelopment as a transitive verb. Poor countries had not just been left in an undeveloped state by the imperial powers, they were still being underdeveloped by metropolitan centres that deserved to be regarded as imperialist.

There are five main strands in dependency theory: the idea of a hierarchy of states; the concept of 'underdevelopment'; a view about the nature of capitalism; propositions concerning 'disarticulation'; and the effect of economic dependency on the structure of political power.

Hierarchy

Frank's studies of Brazil and Chile produced a 'centre–periphery' model to describe the impact of foreign investment in dependent societies. Others have preferred to talk about 'metropolitan-satellite' relations, referring to the great world centres of capital and the economies that are dependent upon them. A hierarchy of centres and peripheries is said to connect all levels of exploitation between one country and another and within the countries of the periphery. There is a steady extraction of surplus through the different levels in the hierarchy: from peasant to landlord; from landlord to local merchant; merchant to subsidiary of a multinational; subsidiary to headquarters of the MNC; headquarters to the major financial institutions of the West:

> it is this exploitative relation which in chain-like fashion extends the capitalist link between the capitalist world and national metropolises to the regional centres (part of whose surplus they appropriate), and from these to local centres, and so on to large landowners or merchants who expropriate surplus from small peasants or tenants, and sometimes even from these latter to landless labourers exploited by them. (Frank, 1969a, p. 7)

Mining, commercial, agricultural and even military centres within the peripheral satellites constitute 'micrometropolises' in relation to their hinterlands of small towns, mines and *latifundia*, which themselves relate in the same way to isolated workers. Similar relations of exploitation link industrial firms to the suppliers of components; large merchants and financiers to small traders and moneylenders; and city merchants and landowners to small rural producers and consumers (Frank, 1969a, pp. 16–17).

The idea of there being a hierarchy of states also implies a hierarchy of power relationships within poor countries. National capitals exploit the provinces and provincial metropolises are centres for the exploitation of the underdeveloped communities surrounding them (Frank, 1966, p. 19).

Underdevelopment

'Underdevelopment' refers to a continuing relationship of exploitation, where at any one level in the chain the full economic surplus is not available for re-investment at that level. It is removed, ultimately accumulating in the metropolitan centres (Dos Santos, 1970). Chile, for example, had at all stages of its history of contact with developed countries experienced expropriation of a significant part of the economic surplus produced within the country. The appropriation of surplus by foreigners worked through ownership (for example, of mines) or a monopolistic buying power over products and their sale elsewhere. Some dependency theorists explained capital flows from periphery to centre in terms of a process of unequal exchange rather than deterioration in the terms of trade between rich and poor countries. Lower wages in peripheral economies enable surplus to be siphoned off to the centre (Emmanuel, 1972a; Amin, 1976; Wallerstein, 1980). Foreigners owned or controlled facilities associated with the export of surplus-generating goods (storage, transport and insurance) (Frank, 1969a, pp. 7 and 18). At every stage in the chain, whether it be at the point of production, local exchange, taxation or trade, there is a removal of part of the economic surplus to a higher level: 'the metropolis expropriates economic surplus from its satellites and appropriates it for its own economic development. The satellite remains underdeveloped for lack of access to their own surplus' (Frank, 1969a, p. 33). Far from experiencing development as a result of ties with metropolitan centres (which is what modernisation theory tells us occurs), such ties hold the peripheral economy and society back.

Frank was particularly critical of the idea that there was a clear demarcation between backward and modern societies and that the histories of the backward societies would move from stage to stage along a path leading to modernity. He argued the reverse: that the condition of backwardness arises from the subordination of poor countries to the development of today's rich countries. The explanation of that backwardness could not be in terms of an earlier stage on the path. The circumstances under which advanced countries progressed cannot be repeated: 'The now developed countries were never *under*developed, though they may have been *un*developed' (Frank, 1966, p. 18). Dependency is a continuing relationship; not confined to an imperialist past but continuing in the neo-imperialist present. Formal political control is not necessary for a relationship of dependency and exploitation to be maintained through structures of foreign capital intervention.

A satellite within this hierarchical structure will only experience development when its ties to the metropolis are weak: 'no country which has been firmly tied to the metropolis as a satellite through incorporation into the world capitalist system has achieved the rank of an economically developed country' (Frank, 1969a, p. 11).

In Latin America the periods of autonomous industrialisation have occurred historically during periods when trade and investment ties with Europe were loosened by European wars and economic recessions. The Depression of the 1930s and the war and reconstruction period of the 1940s gave Latin America opportunities for nationalistic programmes of industrialisation and the expropriation of foreign capital (as in the case of the oil industry in Mexico). Public and private *domestic* capital was invested in the production of capital goods. The same applies, according to Frank, to relatively isolated regions within peripheral societies: the less integrated into the world mercantilist and then capitalist systems, the greater the growth of manufacturing and exports. The incorporation of a satellite into the metropolitan-led hierarchy chokes off development, making it more difficult for industrialisation and sustained development to take place.

What industrialisation has taken place has not produced national or independent development, with an accumulation of çapital under national control, self-sustaining economic growth, increased employment and growing levels of income, consumption and welfare (Bernstein, 1982). Rather, it has been accompanied by increased foreign control. The peripheral economy is made up of firms and sectors which are not highly integrated among themselves, but which are strongly integrated into networks centring on the developed capitalist world. Consequently sectors and regions producing exports important to the development of metropolitan capital experience growth which is followed by rapid decline as soon as metropolitan demand falls. So the least developed and most 'feudal-seeming' regions today are those which had the closest ties to the metropolis in the past. These are the regions that were once the great exporters of primary produce for the world's metropolises, such as the sugar-exporting regions of the West Indies and north-eastern Brazil, the ex-mining regions of Brazil, Peru and Bolivia, and the silver-producing regions of Mexico (Frank, 1969b).

The development of capitalism

Frank's interpretation of the significance of capitalism to under-development addressed the question of what happens to relations of production in an economy that is being underdeveloped. The answer to this question has implications for an understanding of politics and the nature of government in such societies.

Frank believed that there was a 'myth' that feudalism charac-terised parts of the economies of Latin America. His interpretation was that once an unbroken chain is created between rich and poor countries, a complete and total capitalist system is brought into existence. So the societies that become integrated into such hierarchies of core–periphery relations in the international econom-ic sphere are not backward in the sense of having pre-capitalist relations of production. Rather they become part of the capitalist system, and in the case of Latin America had been so since the sixteenth century, when the mercantilist economies of Spain and Portugal had implanted the seeds of capitalism. Peripheral societies may be subordinate in their relations with richer countries, but nevertheless they are part of an extended system of capitalist relations.

It was thus a myth to claim that the problems of peripheral countries could be attributed to the retention of pre-capitalist economic and political relationship in a 'dual' society of progressive and traditional economies, namely feudal forms of political authority and economic structure (Frank, 1969b, ch. 1). The so-called feudalistic institutions were as much the product of capitalist development as the more obviously modernised capitalist sectors. Whether the metropolis was controlled by mercantilist, industrial or finance capital, 'in the peripheries . . . the essential nature of the metropolis–satellite relations remains commercial, however "feudal" or personal seeming these relations may appear' (Frank, 1966, p. 18–20).

Thus Frank interpreted capitalism in terms of trade and exchange. Incorporating a society into a network of world trade was sufficient for it to be designated capitalist. Chile and other Latin American countries have been plagued by an 'open, dependent, capitalist export economy' since the sixteenth century (Frank, 1969a, p. 5). This of course has implications for the analysis of the political situations in such countries. The political relationships that we associate with capitalism – namely liberal democracy based on the institutions of private property, freedom of contract, and political rights – should have accompanied the incorporation of those societies into a capitalist world system.

Disarticulation

The fourth strand in dependency theory argues that the peripheral economy is 'disarticulated' by incorporation into such a system. This concept attempts to distinguish between forms of international dependency. One developed capitalist economy may be dependent upon another such economy. Therefore it may be thought that dependency is not peculiar to poor countries and weak economies. The UK economy is dependent on the US economy in terms of foreign investment, foreign ownership of economic resources and the interventions of US-based multinationals. Increasingly there is a similar dependency on Japan. Dependency theorists, however, argued that there is an important difference between that kind of dependency and the dependency experienced in the Third World (Amin, 1982).

When there are two developed economies with a degree of interpenetration of capital between them, the advanced nation remains an independent centre of capital accumulation (Roxborough, 1979, p. 64). This has consequences for the structure of political forces in that society. When, however, a peripheral society experiences dependency, a distinctive form of capitalism is produced. The poor society's economy is conditioned by the expansion of the stronger economy in ways which are quite different from the relationships between two developed economies. The conditioning or 'disarticulation' of the poor economy discourages internal growth by transferring the benefits of growth abroad (Frank, 1972a, p. 23).

Unlike in the first phase of dependency theory, dependency is here being characterised not so much as peripheral economies producing primary goods – wheat, cocoa, rice, coffee, cotton, jute (a number of developed economies such as Canada and Australia are still dependent on such commodities) – but rather as being on the periphery, which means that most trade is with the core economies of the world system. Developed economies carry out most of their exchanges amongst themselves.

Politically this has an effect on the class structure. It produces a dominant class of merchants not engaged in production, which is primarily in the hands of foreign enterprises who benefit from the transfer of commodities and profits from the Third World. The emergence of an industrial bourgeoisie is blocked. So the emergence of the political institutions upon which a domestic bourgeoisie thrives, the institutions of the liberal democratic state, are blocked too. The nature of dependency has a profound impact on the development of the state and political forces with it. The idea of disarticulation suggests that the capitalist state in its democratic form requires a certain kind of ruling class, one whose interests will be protected by such a state. If it does not have such a unified ruling class because of external dependency, the political consequences will be some kind of authoritarian regime.

Changes in class structure reflect changes in centre–periphery relations. For example, the two world wars and the Depression of the 1930s created economic and political conditions making industrialisation possible and therefore 'the emergence of stronger national bourgeoisies, industrial proletariats . . . and of their associated nationalistic and populist ideologies and policies' (Frank, 1972a, pp. 39–40).

Disarticulation thus means more than the presence of foreign capital, true of many advanced economies. It means that the capital-owning classes of the peripheral society are fragmented, particularly into those who are allied to indigenous capital and those who are allied to foreign interests, preventing the emergence of a national bourgeoisie. That the internal bourgeoisie is unable to complete the internal development of capitalist relations of production produces a very different kind of dependency from that which exists when advanced economies are dependent on one another.

The whole class structure of peripheral society is determined by the position of that society in the international division of labour – whether the country has been predominantly an agricultural export economy with a rural-based oligarchy, an enclave economy based on the extraction of natural resources, or an import-substitution economy with an industrial and financial bourgeoisie. None of these ruling classes have a vested interest in the reproduction of a working class through better health, housing and education, because there is a surplus of labour in excess of industry's needs created by a combination of stagnating agriculture, population growth and capital intensive industrialisation (Hein and Stenzel, 1979).

The structure of political power

The ruling classes of the Third World (merchants, landowners, financiers, industrial capitalists and state bureaucrats) are seen by dependency theorists as junior partners within the structure of international capital:

> once a country or a people is converted into the satellite of an external capitalist metropolis, the exploitative metropolis–satellite structure quickly comes to organize and dominate the domestic economic, political and social life of that people. (Frank, 1969a, p. 10)

The development of a national bourgeoisie is blocked. Instead, a bourgeoisie dependent on the imperialist metropolis and closely allied to its interests is created. These 'clientele classes' have a vested interest in the existing international system and perform domestic political and economic functions on behalf of foreign interests. They enjoy a privileged, dominant and 'hegemonic' position within society 'based largely on economic, political or military support from abroad' (Bodenheimer, 1971, p. 163). The policies of governments reflect the vested interests of the ruling class in the continuation of dependency:

> This colonial and class structure establishes very well-defined class interests for the dominant sector of the bourgeoisie. Using government cabinets and other instruments of the state, the bourgeoisie produces a *policy of underdevelopment* in the economic and political life of the 'nation' and the people of Latin America. (Frank, 1972b, p. 13)

Cardoso provided evidence of how dependency conditions or constrains the choice of development policies of countries located at the periphery when he analysed the overthrow of Brazil's populist regime by a military *coup* in 1964 and its consequences. Groups 'expressing the interests and modes of organisation of international capitalism' gained disproportionate influence over policy-makers. An ideological as well as economic affinity between the holders of economic power and the 'antipopulist' sectors of the military and technocracy enabled the latter to gain in influence not only in modernising the administration, but also in the repressive functions of the state. Other sections of the ruling class – including agrarian, merchant and some industrial interests, the traditional bureaucratic component of the middle class, and career politicians – declined in power, while organised sections of the working class were successfully marginalised.

Changes in the relative power position of different élites and classes were expressed through the accumulation process, requiring that 'the instruments of pressure and defense available to the popular classes be dismantled' so that wage levels could be kept low. This included unions and political organisations through which wage-earners had defended their interests during the populist period. In allowing the military to repress the working class, parts of the bourgeoisie lost control of the political process, especially the party system, elections, press freedom, and liberal education (Cardoso, 1973, pp. 146–59).

Cardoso identified different 'patterns of dependence' as account-ing for shifts in the relative power of different classes at this period of Brazil's history. The underlying factor was a movement away from an international division of labour in which some countries only exported raw materials and imported manufactured goods, to one in which manufacturing was increasingly shifted by interna-tional corporations from the 'hegemonic countries' to countries that had achieved a measure of industrialisation. Moving beyond import substitution in an attempt to reduce dependency meant moving away from a stage of development that in Cardoso's view was 'significantly controlled by the local bourgeoisie' (1973, p. 157). The role of international monopolies became comprehensive, including the remaining areas of primary exports, the private manufacturing sector and even public enterprises such as the state oil monopoly PETROBRAS. The political consequence of this economic realign-ment was an autocratic, developmentalist, military-bureaucratic regime.

4. Criticisms

Dependency theory, especially its second phase, has been subject to many criticisms. Exhaustive coverage of them is beyond the scope of this chapter (for a review see Larrain, 1989, pp. 188–93). The most damaging have specified the economistic nature of the argument; the 'myth' of feudalism; the tendency to underestimate Third World development; the level of generality at which the theory is pitched; the concept of 'hierarchy' in international economic relations; and the theory's policy implications. These will be discussed separately, though there are obviously interlinkages between them.

Economism

The main problem for students of Third World politics is that dependency theory does not make a systematic attempt to demonstrate the political consequences of dependency. It was predominantly an explanation of economic relations, leaving political relationships to be derived from them. It has a distinct tendency to see the state as epiphenomenal – that there is nothing to be explained in terms of the state, social classes and movements, politics and ideology other than as derivatives of the economy and without an independent role of their own. The state is merely a consequence of relationships and power structures that lie elsewhere, namely in the economy (Leys, 1977, p. 95; Goulbourne, 1979, pp. 11–17; Hoogvelt, 1982, p. 169).

This weakness is reflected in the over-generalised treatment of social classes. The absence of a sound analysis of the class content of the metropolitan-satellite 'chain' means that the qualities of the different social relations within it are left unspecified. As Luton put it: 'The relationship of the ruling class of the United States to that of Brazil is . . . of a different order than the relationship of a Brazilian peasant to his landless brother-in-law' (Luton, 1976, p. 577). The analysis of class in dependency theory is insufficiently dynamic. Dependency theorists did not examine changes in class relationships within the periphery which could influence relationships with external interests. Petras claims that 'shifts in peripheral economic activity and relations with the metropolis are in many cases products of rising new class forces taking power', as when metropolitan interests were 'displaced' from the agro-mineral sector by national social forces such as peasant and industrial labour movements or the petty bourgeoisie (Petras, 1975, p. 305). However, this line of criticism may understate the importance of the transition from dependence on primary products to dependence on multinational corporate investment.

Dependency theory's revolutionary and socialist solution to the problem of dependence does not carry conviction in the absence of a structural analysis that demonstrates there are classes or movements on which a revolution could be based. There is very little analysis of oppression, exploitation or class-based organisations. The failure to explain underdevelopment by reference to the interplay of political, social and economic forces exposes dependency theory to the charge that it is a-historical (Leys, 1977, pp. 98–9).

Roxborough sees the weakness of the class analysis springing from a conflation of spatial entities and social classes. Relations between classes, such as landlords and peasants, are presented as comparable to relations between geographical tiers in the metropolitan-satellite hierarchy. Relations of exploitation among classes are identified with transfers of value between spatial regions. The implication is that an exploiting class at one stage in the centre–periphery hierarchy is exploited by the class at the next higher stage. Such an assumption provides no basis for an analysis of the political behaviour of different socio-economic groups (Roxborough, 1976, pp. 121–6). Brewer also attacks the equation of a geographical hierarchy with a hierarchy of exploitation as superficial when 'the real relation of exploitation is a direct wage relations between the workers and the corporation as a unit of capital' (Brewer, 1980, p. 173).

Dependency theory leaves much work still to be done on the problem of societies that are supposedly capitalist finding it so difficult to sustain the institutions and forms of state that we associate with the development of capitalism. However, the concept of 'disarticulation' takes us a bit further than saying that if the propertied classes do not like what is happening under parliamentary government they do not hesitate to support military intervention; or that there is a contradiction between the material inequalities of capitalism and the political equality of democracy. That contradiction is an inadequate explanation in many Third World countries where there is no fully-developed working class.

The myth of feudalism

There was by no means total agreement with Frank's analysis of capitalism in terms of relations of exchange. It is more widely thought that capitalism exists more in terms of the relations of production – private property, free wage labour, and freedom of contract (Laclau, 1971; Barratt Brown, 1974; Taylor, 1979). These features were absent in many of the societies on the periphery. It was possible for the goods that were traded and exchanged to be produced under pre-capitalist relations of production. Social relations of production underpinning structures of political authority need not necessarily be capitalist at all for a rich country to be interested in what is produced. Just because the commodities emerging from a Latin American *hacienda* find their way into other parts of the international economy does not mean that they were produced through capitalist relations of production. Such relations may be highly feudalistic, involving peasant production on tenancies closely controlled by landlords – a control that extends far beyond what is bought by the payment of a wage. Imperialism often sustained the production of goods through feudalistic tenancies, bonded labour, controls over the movement of the population, and other non-capitalist controls exercised at the point of production. The penetration of foreign capital should not be confused with the installation of capitalist relations of production or indeed the political forms of the capitalist state (Brewer, 1980, pp. 160–72).

In addition to having a disarticulated economy and a fragmented bourgeoisie, many Third World societies had the remnants of pre-capitalist political authority, particularly in the rural areas. Landed oligarchies dominated the local peasantries in ways that are inconsistent with capitalist forms of political authority. Political equality and the political freedoms that are the necessary corollary of economic freedom are incompatible with the power of such landed oligarchies. Feudalism was not the 'myth' that some assumed it to be and the remnants of feudalism were among those factors that made it difficult for democratic government to survive.

Underestimating development

A further line of criticism concerns the process of 'underdeveloping' another country. This may underestimate the rate of development that has actually taken place in Third World societies. As we saw in the previous chapter, Warren was concerned to rehabilitate the orthodox Marxist position that imperialism had been the 'pioneer' of capitalism, performing a progressive role in bringing about the stage of capitalism which all societies have to move through on their way to socialism. Others have made similar criticisms of dependency theory, pointing out that in most Third World countries development has occurred because of, not despite, capitalism. Nove, for example, reminds us that in Zambia, Saudi Arabia and Sri Lanka it is the capitalist sectors that have developed, when foreign investment has been used to produce for world capitalist markets. What has held back development is lack of know-how, enterprise and capital and pre-capitalist social and political traditions (Nove, 1974). Relations between centre and periphery are non zero-sum games, so 'economic relations with the metropolitan centre may act as an enormously powerful engine of growth in the periphery' (Cohen, B. J., 1973, p. 217). Foreign capital, even with a net outflow, can add to the total of domestic capital by the multiplier effect of investment-generated local payments such as wages, taxes and purchases of local supplies (Ray, 1973, pp. 13–18). Developing countries can also reduce their dependency by using bargaining strength derived from the developed economies' dependence on them (Philip, 1990, p. 497).

The newly industrialised countries (NICs) have been interpreted by some as undermining dependency theory. These countries have been transformed into industrial manufacturers and exporters with high growth rates. Singapore's average annual growth rate in GNP per capita throughout the 1970s was 7.4 per cent, higher than many southern European countries such as Greece and Yugoslavia and with a higher GNP per capita in 1980 than either of them. South Korea similarly had a growth rate in GNP per capita of 6.9 per cent on average throughout the 1970s and 1980s. How does dependency theory explain this, when it seems to deny the possibility of both development and an autonomous political role for a national bourgeoisie dominating the state?

The NICs show how significant the state can be in autonomous, national economic development and how significant the national bourgeoisie can be in using that state apparatus in order to promote high rates of growth along capitalist lines. The NICs have been classified among the most *dirigiste* regimes, with state intervention at all levels in support of private capital. They are among the most planned and, some would say, corporatist economies. In supporting private capital the state has interfered with the free operation of market forces by the suppression of organised labour, the lowering of wages, and the weakening of political opposition to government policies. The economy has been opened to foreign investment. Public sector employment has been used as a political resource and patronage deployed to reward supporters and punish opponents. Protected enclaves have been provided, such as free-trade zones for high growth activities in which enterprises qualify for tax relief and enjoy a docile labour force, and where import tariffs and export licences are easily available. All this has been provided on behalf of what appears to be a dominant property-owning class. There is not much sign of the disarticulation to which the dependency theorists attached so much importance.

So the NICs require us to think again about the dependency framework. Their recent histories strongly suggest that not everything is determined by the international division of labour, and that political leaders can exploit, within limits, commercial links (to diversify trade), domestic assets (or even liabilities, such as debt), and a range of external sources of aid and loans (Seers, 1981).

Attempts to test dependency theory empirically, with particular reference to the economic consequences of dependency, have sometimes failed to show that dependency produces adverse economic effects, though they have only occasionally shown an opposite relationship. Analysis of cross-sectional aggregate socio-economic and political variables for twenty Latin American states in the 1960s found the greater the dependency, the higher the level of political participation, the better the government's democratic performance and the less military intervention is likely, though the greater the level of civil strife. These would not be the expectations aroused by dependency theory.

An analysis of data on thirty tropical African countries in the middle and late 1960s found measures of dependency unrelated to economic performance variables. In the mid-1960s African countries with high ratios of exports and imports to GNP and high levels of foreign capital had the best economic records. However, when this research made a distinction between 'market dependency' (a generalised feature of the international capitalist system) and 'economic power dependency' (meaning an economy is conditioned by the decisions of individuals, firms and agencies in metropolitan centres), it found the former to be positively related and the latter negatively related to economic performance (McGowan, 1976; McGowan and Smith, 1978, pp. 192–221).

Another study of Africa in the 1960s found that dependence and inequality were related (in line with hypotheses derived from dependency theory) but that dependency did not necessarily mean poor economic performance. However, it was admitted that the second finding may have resulted from the methodological inadequacy of the empirical test rather than from defects in the theory (Vengroff, 1977). The difficulty with this type of test lies in the operationalisation of concepts. The serious limitations of aggregate data techniques are shown by some of the indicators used to measure aspects of a 'dependent' economy and society – the level of unionisation and voting turnout as measures of class structure, for example (Kaufman *et al.*, 1974). (This is a problem that will be encountered again in Chapter 10, when studies of military intervention are examined.) Measuring degrees of dependence by means of quantifiable variables also fails to capture the essence of dependency – the class conflicts arising out of relations between dominant and dependent economies (Larrain, 1989, pp. 178–80).

Levels of generality

Dependency theory operates at too high a level of generality and conceptual imprecision for it to be refutable at the macro-level or applicable at the micro-level (Leys, 1977, p. 96; Higgott, 1983). Frank's over-generalisation about dependency has been criticised for obscuring much variability in dependency relations (Hopkins, 1975, p. 16). There are specific circumstances and particular historical processes that are the consequence of the impact of capitalism on peripheral countries; dependency theory tends to underestimate the importance of these: 'the empirical meaning of "underdevelopment" has to be pretty slight if it must embrace India and Brazil as well as Haiti and Tanzania' (Leys, 1977, p. 95). It is too static and unhistorical to explain the distinctive elements of economic and political development in backward countries, and the mechanisms of social reproduction, modes of social transformation, and modes of politics. Operating at such a high level of generality makes it difficult to focus on the specifics of a particular country at a particular moment in history and how important they have been to development prospects (Philip, 1990, p. 490). The size of a developing country's population, its ethnic or linguistic composition, its degree of self-sufficiency in natural resources (particularly energy), its physical location in relation to countries better endowed in terms of population, technology or military threats – such factors make a great deal of difference to the prospects for development, but tend to be overlooked by dependency theory. They cannot be described merely as features of world capitalism or the chain or hierarchy of metropolitan–periphery relationships. As factors affecting the room for manoeuvre which governments have, they would not disappear if the international capitalist system did not exist – so any explanation which overlooks such details must be deficient (Seers, 1981).

Nor are the actual mechanisms of dependency spelt out in detail. Dependency theorists tend to 'lose the parts in the totality'. Everything is seen as connected to everything else, but how and why often remains obscure. The failure to provide a clear analysis of the use made of the surplus that is transferred from satellite to metropolis means that it is impossible to explain why underdevelopment rather than development (predicted by classical Marxism) should result from the exploitation of an area's economic resources (Brewer, 1980, pp. 174–6). Past politics and policy instruments in particular receive only cursory treatment (O'Brien, P. J., 1975, p. 23). The function of the state in Third World societies cannot be reduced to external, international economic influences. Legacies of authoritarian government, ideologies of corporatism and populist nationalism, patterns of patron–client relations, the aggregation of local interests, the internal evolution of social and political forces – all produce variable styles of state action that are not wholly externally induced (Smith, T., 1979; Long, 1977, p. 91). Hence the importance of considering the evidence supporting different theories of the Third World state (as we shall later).

Hierarchy

Dependency theory has been criticised for restricting the idea of a hierarchy of national economies to relations between those that are developed and those that are underdeveloped. Dependency theory stands accused of painting too strong a contrast between development and underdevelopment. Dependency is a continuous rather than a discrete variable (McGowan and Smith, 1978, pp. 189–90).

There are two major strands to this line of criticism. In the first place, a certain degree of dominance and a great deal of influence characterise relations between advanced countries. The critics of dependency theory have denied that there are qualitative as well as quantitative differences between rich and poor countries which make their dependency distinctive in international terms. Dominance, dependence, influence and the interpenetration and internationalisation of capital apply just as much at the core or centre of the world capitalist system as at the periphery (Lall, 1975; Kay, 1975, p. 104; Bernstein, 1979). Brewer refers to 'interdependence' and 'dominance' because 'dependence' implies that some countries are economically independent, which is not true (1980, p. 178).

Dependency theory's argument is that in the core economies cultural, legal and political institutions are the product of indigenous development in the way that they are not in peripheral and particularly ex-colonial societies. Here institutions have developed from those originally imposed from outside; the class structure of dependent societies is also more a reflection of external economic interests than of the distribution of material resources and interests within the country (Larrain, 1989, p. 180). What is significant in Third World dependency is the representation in some general sense of external foreign interests rather than a class structure – and political configurations representing it – which are purely contained within the borders of that country. There is greater symmetry in the relations between rich countries and more chance of a reversal of roles. For example, it is possible that the UK could again become a richer country than the USA, whereas under the present world system there is no chance of Brazil (let alone Bangladesh or Tanzania) becoming richer than the USA. The interrelationships between the core economies of the world system are mutually beneficial rather than exploitative, whereas the relations between rich and poor countries work predominantly to the advantage of the rich.

But does this provide a firm analytic base for distinguishing dependent from non-dependent countries? Are the factors cited by dependency theory specific to rich–poor country relations? There seem to be hierarchies of developed countries. The USA among Western developed economies is at the apex of a hierarchy. There is mutual benefit between advanced economies only in the sense that the dominant classes benefit and not in the sense of some holistic notion of social benefit. This does not seem to differ from class relations in poor countries, where the rich benefit from mutual interests with the rich in rich countries. As to the 'alien' institutions, alien is a value-laden term. Many LDCs, particularly those that have experienced great economic success in terms of growth rates of output, productivity and GNP, could well benefit from an injection of external values if they included respect for civil rights, the rule of law and democracy. So perhaps all societies are in the pyramid of social, political and economic dominance with the apex occupied by the most powerful capitalist country and the bottom by the poorest countries. It is difficult to find some special horizontal dividing line which separates dependent from independent economies and societies. This debate has yet to be resolved.

The other strand of this particular line of criticism tackles the claim that dependent economies are deeply penetrated by foreign capital, with foreign capital-intensive technology; that they specialise in the export of primary commodities; that their élites have consumption patterns which distinguish them markedly from the mass of society; and that they have growing inequalities of income, with increased marginalisation of the urban poor in the sense of a declining rate of access to basic necessities and a decent standard of living – food, clothing, shelter and health.

It can be shown, however, that some economies that would always be classified as advanced also exhibit some of these characteristics. Dependency theory does not satisfactorily explain which the important ones are. If we find some of the factors to be part of the economic and social scene within rich countries, how do we decide which criteria indicate that a country is being under-developed by its dependence on a richer country? Canada and Belgium are more dependent on foreign investment than India or Pakistan. Other advanced countries such as Denmark depend heavily on foreigners for their industrial technology. There are growing inequalities of income in the UK. Conversely, some of the poorest countries of the Third World, such as Nepal, Chad, Burundi and Afghanistan are also some of the least dependent countries. The causal relationship between economic dependency and economic development is by no means clear (Mack and Leaver, 1979). If features associated with underdevelopment can be found in societies that would never be classified as such, they may be important measures of economic status, but they are not in themselves enough to allow a fundamental division between countries to be made or even states to be arranged in a hierarchy (Lall, 1975; O'Brien, P.J., 1975). The importance of such factors will depend on the specific context in which they occur.

Policies to counter dependency

Finally, there are the policy implications of dependency theory. (For a summary of the economic policies of different dependency theorists see Godfrey, 1980.) The original motivation behind it was highly relevant to public policy choices. It looked at economies it believed to be too orientated towards the export of primary commodities and recommended import substitution to overcome foreign exchange crises and provide a basis for independent development. Subsequently the policy implications of dependency theory became vague as far as responses to multinationals, technical transfer, unemployment, income distribution, and the marginalisation of the poor are concerned (O'Brien, P.J., 1975, pp. 24–5). All possible solutions to a Third World country's problems – import substitution, industrialisation, international aid, government planning – always turned out to be part of the problem (Leys, 1977, p. 97).

Some dependency theorists are reformist, others are revolutionary, and some are populist. Others were technocratic, especially in the early phase of dependency theory (O'Brien, P.J., 1975, p. 24). There is no distinctive ideology and therefore there are no policy prescriptions that can be derived from the theory.

One noticeably absent policy prescription is for the condition of non-dependency. Leys shows how important it is to specify what 'development' would involve when it has been asserted that LDCs cannot follow the same path as the countries that underdeveloped them (Leys, 1977, p. 94). The implication of dependency theory is that development can only be achieved outside the capitalist world market. However, dependency is not restricted to capitalism, but has been found in association with non-capitalist and pre-capitalist stages of economic development. Ray cites the case of Cuba, which left the capitalist work market to become part of the communist trading bloc. Consequently Cuba abandoned rapid industrialisation in favour of specialising in the export of sugar, leaving its economy structurally dependent. The economic reality of comparative advantage applied equally to both capitalist and communist trade blocs (Ray, 1973, pp. 14–16). Now that there is no longer a communist trading bloc this alternative is not on offer.

5. Conclusion

The critique of dependency theory can be summarised as a doubt that dependence can be causally related to underdevelopment. Dependence is either so general that it fails to have any explanatory value in the context of poor societies, or it arbitrarily selects certain features of international capitalism to produce a definition of dependence. Those features similarly do not allow the important distinctions between rich and poor, developed and underdeveloped, independent and dependent to be made in the way that dependency theory wants to.

Nevertheless, dependency theory served an important function in the analysis of development, especially in Latin America (Larrain, 1989, pp. 193–200). Its emphasis on the weak and relatively dependent position of the less advanced economies of the world was timely and a necessary corrective of much development theorising at the time, especially ideas about unilinear economic development and 'dual economies' (Luton, 1976). It called attention to the ideological implications of pluralistic and structural-functional development theorising, challenging the conventional wisdom that economic development in Latin America is inevitably consistent with American interests (Ray, 1973, p. 6). Its 'militant critique' of a highly ideological developmentalism that ignored social classes and treated the state as an instrument of popular will or the public interest showed that underdevelopment was not a 'primal' or 'original' condition. Dependency theory 'stimulated the empirical study of institutional and structural mechanisms of underdevelopment' such as multinationals, fiscal policies, capital expenditures and aid programmes (Leys, 1977, p. 93). It showed that capital does not necessarily break down non-capitalist modes of production, but can bolster 'archaic political and economic forms' through alliances with pre-capitalist social forces (Kay, 1975, p. 104).

Third World trends in the 1970s underlined the importance of understanding the limitations imposed by the international context, while at the same time revealing some of the gross oversimplifications that formed part of development theory's conclusions. The two concerns at the core of dependency theory – the limits on capitalist development at the periphery and the relative importance of external and internal variables in determining those limits – are of lasting significance. The core propositions of dependency theory are now part of the conventional wisdom (Philip, 1990, p. 491). Despite its weaknesses, dependency theory created a major opportunity for the effects of integration in an international system to be analysed, including those NICs such as South Korea which might be thought to undermine the dependency thesis (Bienefeld, 1980, pp. 5–10; Godfrey, 1980, pp. 1–4).

The excursions into different ways of explaining development that have been the subject of the last four chapters provide a foundation for the next stage of the operation being undertaken here, which is to consider the political entity known as the state in developing societies. References have frequently been made in the earlier discussion to the form of the state and the configuration of political interests sometimes articulated by the state and sometimes suppressed by it. As Goulbourne put it, the 'organic link' between the Third World and the international economy has implications for politics and the state, one of the most important of which is that all classes recognise the state as the point where class contradictions must be resolved 'since capital has always used the state in these societies as a leeway into production' (1979, p. 27).

The study of political change cannot work without some idea of the nature of the state. This is as central to this branch of political studies as to any other. So the way in which students of politics in the Third World have defined the state, perceived its roles and identified important structural characteristics will be dealt with next. The liberal democratic model will be examined first, to see its association with a particular approach to development and modernisation, before moving on to some important and influential Marxist interpretations of the state and the way in which some contemporary Marxists have drawn upon certain parts of classical

Marxism in order to obtain a grasp on what has happened in developing countries, particularly in the immediate post-independence period. The concept of the authoritarian state as a means of understanding Third World politics will also be examined.

Part III
Institutions

7

The State and Authoritarianism

1. Introduction

We have spent the time so far in looking at different attempts to explain the nature of Third World politics in terms of encounters with richer countries, whether through imperialism, dependency or the modernising influences that underdeveloped economies are supposed to experience as a result of their colonial interlude.

We now turn to the nature of the state in the Third World and what different social scientists have had to say about the form of the state in developing societies, focusing in particular on those societies that have a colonial history. This emphasis is partly explained by the fact that there are very few Third World countries that have not had such an experience, and partly by the importance which social scientists of very different ideological points of departure have attached to colonialism as a formative influence on the contemporary politics of developing countries. First we review some major interpretations of the state. This will be followed by an examination of how these have been developed in the context of post-colonialism.

It was a theory about the post-colonial state that in recent years has had the greatest impact on the study of the politics of developing countries. Particular attention will be paid to that set of ideas. Interest in the state and its class base was in part a reaction against the economic reductionism found in dependency theory, implying that the dominant class in a peripheral society could only play a *comprador* role. Theorising about the post-colonial state was further encouraged by a resurgence of interest in the nature of the capitalist state within mainstream Marxist thought as exemplified by debates in the 1970s between Miliband, Poulantzas, Anderson, Therborn,

171

Habermas, O'Connor and others. In the context of Third World studies the debate focused on the scope for indigenous classes to control the state (even if the dominant class was a bureaucratic bourgeoisie) under circumstances which varied according to the level of foreign capital penetration, the resources available for exploitation, the presence of settler capital, the level of colonial impact and the availability of indigenous capital (Higgott, 1983, pp. 65–70).

2. The state as pluralist political system

Political developmentalists preferred the language of the political system to that of the state, encouraging us to think of the institutions and processes at the centre of government in politically neutral terms. We are presented with an image of what other political theorists refer to as the state, which is central to a pluralistic interpretation of politics. Following the ideas of the German sociologist Max Weber, many schools of social science, including the functionalist, have seen the state or the political system as a set of social relationships for converting, through the use of legitimate physical compulsion, demands and supports into outputs – decisions, statutes, laws, regulations, investments and so on (Almond, 1960 and 1965, p. 193; Almond and Powell, 1966, ch. 2). The 'authoritative structures of government' (Pye, 1965, pp. 7–8) are a neutral set of arrangements consisting of political institutions and recognised procedures for interpreting political demands, resolving political conflicts and converting them into outputs that satisfy those demands.

The state is perceived as an arena in which conflicting interests compete for scarce resources. It is a means of managing competition, so that the state is recognised as a legitimate way to settle such disputes. The pluralist view of the political system sees its governmental functions as neutral in relation to the interests of different groups in society. It may be likened to an umpire, administering impartially the rules of the game without bias in favour of any particular player. The pluralist view of the state sees modern society as divided into competing elements which nevertheless find a kind of equilibrium. None is persistently more dominant than any other. None gets its way to the exclusion of others to a disproportionate extent. In this respect pluralists are building upon traditional ideas of liberal democracy and the role of the state, though rather than focus on the individual as the unit of analysis they are focusing on groups. They see society as consisting not of atomised individuals – the egotistical, rational person seeking his or her own interests in a society which the state has a duty to preserve – but of groups and associations. Only by co-operating with similarly placed and like-minded people can individual interests be protected. Complex modern societies produce such associations for the articulation of political interests.

Pluralism is a key attribute of modern society for functionalists (Coleman, 1960a, p. 535). Pluralists believe there will be an equilibrium in terms of the power of different groups partly because of cross-cutting loyalties. No group will have an interest in pushing its demands excessively to the exclusion of other groups in society because individuals are members of a multiplicity of groups and associations. As producers our demands for higher incomes for wages will not be pushed to an excessive degree because we are also consumers who have to pay the price of those increased costs of production. Attachments and loyalties cut across other groups as well. There is not only a balance of competing forces, but there is also multiple membership of different and sometimes overlapping groups. This serves to reduce the extremism of the demands of interest groups.

In the context of poor and developing societies the pluralist view of the state assumes that as pre-capitalist social structures and economic arrangements are replaced by capitalism and industriali-sation, so the authoritarian political institutions associated with the pre-capitalist era, especially feudalism, will also be swept aside. They will be replaced by the institutions of the liberal democratic state, perhaps in the form of a parliamentary democracy in which interests are protected by freely-formed associations, freely-competing electoral alliances, and freely-articulated ideas about public policy, preserved and protected by civil and political rights such as freedom of speech and association, universal suffrage and freedom of the press (Carnoy, 1984).

Such an approach to the state is also likely to see a sharp distinction between society and polity. It does not reveal how much state intervention there will be. Those on the extreme right of the liberal democratic spectrum of ideas will reduce the role of the state to the minimum, whereas those at the social democratic end will allow a considerable role for the state. But the extent of intervention will be an outcome of the interaction between competing groups. It will be the result of the success that some groups have in protecting their interests via publicly funded state interventions as opposed to the success that other groups have in protecting their interests by maintaining levels of state activity, public expenditure and taxation at a minimum, thereby maximising the level of private incomes. But even though there might be considerable state intervention, even including elements of public ownership, polity and economy are seen as separate and independent spheres of social action.

Another feature of the pluralist state is to play down the significance of class divisions in society. Liberal democratic and pluralist assumptions about society are that it may be disaggregated along occupational, gender, ethnic, or religious lines, but not into classes. Class may be used as a summation of some of those other more significant factors indicating occupation, income and lifestyle. But class is not seen as an identity around which people form alliances in order to compete for scarce resources politically. If a concentration of power is found, as in some undeveloped political systems, it is assigned to particular groups or élites, such as the executive and bureaucracy in a 'tutelary democracy', the military in a 'modernising oligarchy', or a dynasty in a 'traditional oligarchy' (Almond, 1960). But a notion of class that involves mutual antagonism and irreconcilable economic and political interests is rejected. So there is no sense in the pluralist model of the state of diametrically opposed interests, one gaining only if another suffers.

This view of the state, though not particularly well-articulated, was adopted by some of the imperial powers in their attempts – often hesitant, partial and delayed – to prepare colonies for independence. These were the assumptions of the constitution-builders when independence seemed inevitable and even desirable. They were also the assumptions of many within colonial society who collaborated with the processes of constitutional design. The leaders of some nationalist movements had similar views about the nature of the state. Many had, after all, been educated in the prisons and universities of the British Empire. Where they departed from it was less in the direction of Marxism than in the direction of some indigenous modification such as African socialism or the traditions of Indian village communities. Nationalist leaders such as Nyerere and Gandhi hearkened back to what they regarded and interpreted as a golden era preceding European intervention, and though not being so romantic as to think that the clock could be turned back, nevertheless advocating that there were values which had been lost and which could be retrieved to the advantage of a society that would henceforth be developing according to its own prescription.

3. A Marxist view of the post-colonial state

The pluralist view of the state has been systematically attacked, and some would say demolished, by an interpretation of the state which has its origins in the political economy of Marx. Many social scientists who have studied Third World politics have been influenced by Marxism, seeing society in terms of material interests that are often irreconcilable. They view society in terms of exploitation rather than accommodation between competing interests. The state is seen as an instrument of class domination.

If we turn to Marxism for a view of the state, we find not one but four or five (Jessop, 1977; Ziemann and Lanzendorfer, 1977). There is the idea of the state as a kind of parasite, particularly through a privileged, bureaucratic caste. The state extracts resources from society not for purposes of social reproduction, but to sustain an élite. There is the idea of the state as epiphenomenon, when economic and property relations are given such a determining significance that other institutions – political, legal, cultural and ideological – are merely a reflection of them and entirely explained by their dependence on prevailing economic relations. There is the idea of the state as an instrument of class domination, an executive committee for managing the affairs of the whole bourgeoisie. This comes close to being a view of the state as a neutral instrument which can be controlled equally effectively by any class which achieves a position of economic dominance. The state is not pluralistic in the sense of being a neutral arbiter, but is a set of institutions existing independently of social forces and which at different stages in history will be controlled in the interest of a dominant economic class, whether it be the landed aristocracy in a feudal economy or the industrial bourgeoisie of early capitalism.

Then there is the notion of the state as a factor of cohesion, where the state is involved in regulating struggles between antagonistic classes and using both repression and concession to moderate and manage those conflicts while sustaining the economic and political dominance of the most powerful economic class and preserving the social relationships which a capitalist economy requires.

That is very close to yet another view of the state found in Marxism – and here we come to one that has had the greatest impact on development studies – which is the Bonapartist. The idea of the state being a factor of cohesion, managing and manipulating class struggles without fundamentally damaging the economic system that preserves the dominance of a particular economic class, is close to the idea of the state as something that can stand aloof from the immediate interests of even the dominant economic class in society for a longer-term aim – that of moderating class conflict and preserving the social and economic system. This formulation is derived from Marx's analysis of French history between 1848 and 1852 when the nephew of Napoleon Bonaparte staged a *coup d'état* and overthrew republican parliamentary government. Marx's interpretation of that episode was that different factions of the bourgeoisie were in conflict with each other to such an extent that they were, particularly in the context of republicanism and political liberty, making it possible for the working class to win power through parliamentary institutions. The *coup d'état* was to save capitalism from itself – from its own destructive factionalism and from the contradiction between a capitalist economic system and a democratic polity. Capitalism was founded on the exploitation of man by man, whereas the democratic polity was founded on the principle of political equality, implying that the majority rule. In early capitalist society the majority would want to redistribute wealth in their own favour, inevitably harming the interests of capital.

Bonapartism, following Marx's *The Eighteenth Brumaire of Louis Bonaparte*, is a model of the state not simply as the product of a dominant class and an instrument to be wielded by whichever socio-economic group is dominant. It is not simply an executive committee of the bourgeoisie (although in the *Communist Manifesto* Marx does refer to the *whole* bourgeoisie, thus not excluding the possibility that the state preserves the long-term interests of that 'whole bourgeoisie' against its own internal factionalism such as that between industrial and finance capital). The state is, rather, almost autonomous and able to free itself to a degree from civil society, not to manage it neutrally in the interests of all sections, but in the long-term interests of a bourgeois class against the irreconcilable interests of other classes.

This interpretation seemed to some social scientists examining the post-colonial state to be enormously perceptive and resonant. Post-colonial society equally appeared to have a number of competing bourgeois factions whose conflicts needed to be managed in the long-term interest of capitalist growth and the social institutions upon which such development depended, in particular private property and the right to accumulation. A paper published by the Pakistani sociologist Hamza Alavi in 1972 applied this model of the state to a particular episode in the history of Pakistan which contained its first excursion into military government (see also Alavi, 1990). It seemed to Alavi that Pakistan had experienced a form of Bonapartism which, though very different in its social origins from the Bonapartism of mid-nineteenth century France, nevertheless had some parallels in terms of class structure and political conflict.

Although Alavi's paper was about Pakistan, it provided inspiration for a number of social scientists in their attempt to analyse other societies, sometimes pointing to the limitations of the model, sometimes enabling modifications to be made to the theory of the post-colonial state. The Bonapartist thesis held out the possibility of analysis in which the state was not simply reducible in its performance and structures to the interests of a single, dominant class.

Alavi examined a particular set of historical circumstances, paying especial attention to the period between independence in 1947 and the first *coup* in 1958, a period of tumultuous politics and instability threatening to the interests of a middle class emerging mainly in West Pakistan. The *coup* brought Ayub Khan to power, and throughout the 1960s his government set about vigorously to transform his own status from that of an Army General and Chief Martial Law Administrator into that of a civilian President. He tried to legitimise his own power in civilian terms through a structure of 'Basic Democracies', or local governments that constituted an electoral college for the presidency.

Alavi could see that there was more to this process than one man's desire to become the legitimate leader of Pakistan. He could see that Ayub Khan had been supported by an alliance between the bureaucracy and the military. Alavi wanted to understand the relationships between those parts of the state apparatus and the prevailing propertied classes in Pakistan. He conducted an analysis of what appeared to him to be a military-bureaucratic oligarchy by reference to class interests, rather than in the terms that prevailed in other parts of the social sciences where the military and bureaucracy were seen as modernising élites and where it was not found surprising or even disturbing that they enjoyed the most power. They represented the skills and values that developing countries required if they were to move down the path to modernity. Some of the functionalists had written about the modernising role of this part of the state apparatus. F. W. Riggs, a leading US political scientist, had also pointed to the colonial inheritance of a powerful bureaucracy, more powerful than other political institutions bequeathed at independence (Riggs, 1963). There are parallels between functionalism and Marxism in some of their references to the power of the bureaucracy after independence and to the colonial legacy (see Chapter 9). For both schools of thought colonialism meant the overdevelopment of the bureaucracy relative to other political institutions.

The main elements of Alavi's post-colonial state thesis are: relative autonomy; the overdeveloped state and its bureaucratic apparatus; and the high level of involvement of the state in the economy.

Relative autonomy

Relative autonomy refers to the controversy within Marxism about whether the state can free itself from class conflict in order to manage and control it. It is a difficult concept to use without ambiguity (Moore, M., 1980; Wood, G. D., 1980). Alavi argued that the state in Pakistan in the 1950s was not merely a set of institutions controlled by a dominant class. Its autonomy was not complete because it was not totally neutral or independent of all class forces. The state was neither autonomous in the pluralist sense, nor was it the prisoner of a single, dominant class. To support the idea of the state as relatively autonomous there has to be an accompanying analysis of class. The specific circumstances of the propertied classes in Pakistan meant that three could be identified: a national bourgeoisie whose interests centred on the ownership and control of industrial capital; an indigenous landed class dominant in the agricultural sector and consisting of a relatively small number of wealthy and powerful rural families owning large tracts of cultivatable land; and a 'metropolitan bourgeoisie'. Whereas the significance of a national bourgeoisie can be readily appreciated because they are actively present in the economy and polity, the metropolitan bourgeoisie is much less visible or tangible. The interests of these three propertied classes were found to be competing, but not contradictory. This is why instead of a more orthodox Marxist analysis which would interpret the state as directed by a single class, Alavi chose a formulation which reflected the more complex pattern of propertied classes found in Pakistan at that time. This involved in particular a significant presence of external capital whose base was outside Pakistan in one of the great metropolitan centres of the world economy.

These classes were in conflict, competing with each other for the resources which were under the control of the state. The landed aristocracy was important because the society had not been completely transformed under colonialism into a capitalist society. It was in transition, with surviving feudalistic relations in the rural areas reflected in the relationships between landlords and tenants. Agriculture was based on a mode of production which was far from capitalistic and which retained many elements of a pre-capitalist society and economy, particularly in the control of rural tenants and labour. By the end of the 1960s there were still large estates in which landlords could control the persons as well as the labour of their tenants and workers in ways not conceivable under market relationships between employer and employee, landlord and tenant. The landed classes were keen to retain their control over the agricultural sector, not because they wanted to transfer their surplus into industrial investment or even into a more capitalistic way of farming – rather they wanted to retain their pre-capitalist, feudalistic privileges and powers over the local population. They were less interested in the loss of status and control that would be brought about by a transformation of the forces of production in agriculture. The political consequences of that in the rural areas were very risky: modernisation would undermine traditional relationships between landowners and their dependents.

The interests of this class were not identical to those of the other two propertied classes. There was tension between the landed class and a bourgeoisie that wanted industrialisation to achieve higher levels of productivity and more surplus for indigenous investment, low wages supported by cheap food for the cities, and cheap raw materials for industrial processing. The metropolitan bourgeoisie was interested in investments that would not be of equal benefit to the national bourgeoisie. US aid was found to have forced policies on the government of Pakistan which were to the detriment of domestic interests but in favour of US investors. Corruption was another method by which the metropolitan bourgeoisie promoted its interests. It was in competition for control over different levels of the economy, the kinds of investment to be included in development plans, and the partnerships between indigenous and foreign capital that would be authorised by the state. At times the state seemed to act on behalf of international capital, representing it locally. Sometimes it would defend the interest of indigenous interests against foreign capital by setting up protectionist tariffs against the importing of finished manufactured goods. Though the national bourgeoisie was in a subordinate, client status to the metropolitan bourgeoisie, its collaboration did not imply an identity of interest – hence the need for the state to play a mediatory role.

The state essentially performed a function of mediation between conflicting propertied classes. Their interests were not contradictory, since they all had in common one essential value, the preservation of private property in the social relations of production. But they had clearly competing interests. The preconditions for the expansion of the national bourgeoisie required its dominance over agriculture to maintain in its own favour the terms of trade between agricultural and industrial goods. The exploitation of East Pakistan, later to become Bangladesh, was a key part of this competition.

It seemed to Alavi that a particular kind of state was most appropriate for this mediating role, one that could free itself to a degree from the direct control of a faction of the bourgeoisie. Such a state needed what he called a 'bureaucratic-military oligarchy'. It was no accident that this kind of regime emerged in Pakistan. It was historically appropriate (though morally objectionable). Such a regime would be sufficiently removed from the immediate interests of any one of those three classes to be able to exercise independent power and manage conflict, provided it did not challenge their common interest in private ownership of the means of production. So whereas the national bourgeoisie in a developed, capitalist society, or the metropolitan bourgeoisie in a colony, could establish their dominance, this was not possible in post-colonial conditions where 'none of the three propertied classes exclusively dominates the state apparatus or subordinates the other two. This specific historical situation confers on the bureaucratic-military oligarchy in a post-colonial society a *relatively autonomous* role' (Alavi, 1972).

The overdeveloped bureaucracy

What is specifically post-colonial about this situation, which might be expected in any society in the early stages of industrialisation with a predominantly agricultural economy and a high dependency on foreign capital? This is where the second element in the model comes in, the idea of an overdeveloped, bureaucratic state apparatus. Colonialism had produced a distorted state structure. Certain institutions which had been particularly significant for colonial government and which had a relatively long history, had been highly developed – namely the bureaucracy, the military and the police. A central feature of colonial government was a heavy reliance on these institutions. Colonialism required a state structure which would enable control to be exercised over all indigenous classes. This state apparatus had to be bureaucratic. The bureaucratic-military nature of the colonial state represented the 'institutionalised practices' of an overdeveloped state. 'It might be said that the "superstructure" in the colony is therefore "overdeveloped" in relation to the "structure" in the colony' (Alavi, 1972).

Depending on which region of the empire one examines it is possible to see different levels of indigenous recruitment into those institutions. In India indigenous people had been recruited into the bureaucracy, military and police for many years before independence. The first Indian District Collector was appointed well before the end of the nineteenth century. In other colonies there was much less recruitment of indigenous personnel before independence, because there were too few nationals with the requisite training. But in all cases these institutions had developed to a greater degree than the institutions of political democracy. A universal feature of colonial government was that it developed bureaucracies while neglecting legislatures, parties, local councils and other bodies able to maintain control and accountability.

The Indian subcontinent had probably had the longest history of democratic development of any part of the empire, but even here the bureaucracy appeared to Alavi to be overdeveloped. How much more this would be the case in countries where there had been virtually no experience of parliamentary and representative government before independence. In territories where nothing had been done to prepare them for democratic self-government, the distortion was even greater. In the Belgian Congo, for example, far from having established political institutions that could operate in the absence of an imperial state, the departing colonialists sabotaged as far as they could the apparatus bequeathed to the new government. Experience of parliamentary government prior to independence varied enormously. Even where it was considerable, the bureaucracy still emerged with prestige, power and status, monopolising the knowledge and expertise required for running a government and developing a society. Government was the main source of employment for professional people and the highly educated. Government absorbed the supply of technical expertise. For example, long practice in the mobilisation and organisation of people for political ends through the Congress movement in India still did not produce a capacity to control a highly developed administrative system in the years immediately following independence.

The bureaucratic-military oligarchy, with its distinctive set of practices, codes, rules and standards, almost totally unaccountable to outsiders under the imperial state, was recruited from the wealthier sections of society. In Pakistan there was an imbalance in recruitment between the East and West, with much of the recruitment into bureaucracy and military coming from the West. The underrepresentation of people from the East was a factor in the subsequent break-up of the country. The oligarchy was not classless: it had its social attachments. But it could mediate between classes more easily than legislative assemblies in which the representatives of warring factions sit. Legislative assemblies are also likely, under universal suffrage, to contain representatives of propertyless classes. They constitute a threat to those who are economically privileged. A state is thus required that can mediate between the propertied classes and subjugate other classes in the interest of the existing distribution of wealth.

State intervention

The third element of the explanation is the disproportionate involvement of the state in managing the economy. Where the private sector is small, where the market as a basis for the arrangement of production and distribution is weak, and where the economic activity of the state is significant, the state becomes the major employer. It also plays a prominent role in managing the flow of international finance from aid, loans and foreign investment. The state becomes the source of capital and it controls the use of that capital. An extensive state apparatus supports an emerging capitalist system. Public sector management; state marketing and rationing of scarce foreign exchange and consumer goods; state ownership; the provision of an infrastructure of communications, energy supply and transportation; the creation of a legal structure for commercial transactions; maintaining political stability to create confidence among investors – all are the responsibility of the state.

This model had a great impact in the 1970s on the political sociology and political economy of development. Attempts were made to apply the mode of analysis elsewhere in the Third World. In particular, scholars specialising in East African politics wanted to see if the post-colonial state under the particular conditions pertaining there fitted the Alavi description. Two political scientists in particular took Alavi's thesis and applied it to East Africa: Colin Leys in Kenya and John Saul in Tanzania.

4. Applications

If we examine how others have used the model in other contexts, we can appreciate its limitations as well as its strengths. More importantly, it provides a way of understanding the different circumstances that are found in other parts of the Third World. Alavi was concerned with a particular country at a particular period in its history. Testing whether the theory works in other countries will reveal factors that will not fit. The reason why the attempt to theorise about Pakistan in this particular way had so much appeal is that it seemed to offer a far more convincing approach to Third World states than the prevailing ones. Those who tried to apply the model elsewhere may have found it did not fit in all respects, but they certainly thought that it was more useful than earlier descriptions of politics in post-colonial societies, especially the pluralistic assumptions of functionalism.

Class development in Tanzania

The first attempt to apply Alavi's analysis was made in the study of Tanzanian post-independence politics (Saul, 1974). The particular experience of this part of East Africa, especially in its colonial history, was very different from the experience of the Indian sub-continent. Tanzania had been a German colony until the First World War but the German influence had been slight, restricted to some coastal plantations growing sisal. There was little trade with the interior. The European presence had little impact on the way the indigenous people produced agricultural and other goods. After the first World War, Tanganyika became a Protectorate of the UK under the dispensation of the League of Nations. That particular status restricted under international law the rights of the protector. So the British presence in Tanganyika was also limited, though the development of some cash crops, particularly tea and coffee, was encouraged. The first and clearest contrast with the Indian sub-continent was that imperialism and foreign capital were far less intrusive in Tanganyika.

The internal social structure of Tanganyika was consequently very different at the time of independence in 1961. The ethnic composition of the society was relatively untouched by European intervention: it consisted of a large number of small ethnic groups with no pattern of inter-ethnic dominance. One group in the region of Mt. Kilimanjaro, the Chagga, had benefited from the introduction of cash crops. A class of relatively rich peasant cultivators developed, but not a class of large landowners receiving part of their wealth in rents. Some of the richer peasant producers became petty-capitalist, investing in other activities such as local trade, but the extent to which this constituted any kind of new socio-economic class was very limited.

The relations of production within the different societies that made up Tanzania were communal, based on settlements consisting of kin-groups, and lacking landlords or employers of landless labour. The relationships between producers were those of kinship and ethnicity. Population density was relatively low and land was readily available. Some societies, notably the Masai, were pasturalist. By the time of independence a class structure, brought about by the combination of indigenous economy and foreign intervention, hardly existed. Rural people produced goods on the basis of small-scale communities with land held in common and land could not be alienated and accumulated: rights to occupancy and cultivation alone attached to individuals and families. There was a relatively small basis for a landed oligarchy or an industrial or commercial middle class, the last being mainly Asian in origin. An embryonic working class was also beginning to emerge at the time of independence, based on textiles, motor transport and tobacco processing.

The most powerful African class in the process of formation was what some analysts referred to as a petty-bourgeoisie of teachers, civil servants, prosperous traders, and farmers. The East African colonial state had subordinated pre-capitalist, though non-feudal, social formations to the needs of colonial capitalism, rather than the 'native social classes' referred to by Alavi. This pre-capitalist agriculture had moved towards commercialisation without 'quasi-feudal stopovers' and the indigenous bourgeoisie was confined to mainly Asian traders (Shivji, 1973 and 1975; Saul, 1974).

Society further differed from India in that there had not been in this part of East Africa extensive exposure to Western culture and education. There were, for example, throughout Africa few African graduates or professionals. By the early 1960s all that had happened in terms of Westernisation was some incorporation of educated Africans into the lower levels of the public service and related professions such as teaching.

Thus class conditions in Tanzania differed considerably from those described by Alavi in Pakistan. It is correspondingly more difficult to think of the state as having to mediate between well-articulated class interests, including those owning capital and those with only their own labour, as well as divisions within the capital-owning classes, including capital located outside the country. The metropolitan bourgeoisie, most notably represented by multinational corporations, was much more powerful than indigenous classes. The post-colonial East African state had nevertheless not become international capital's 'executive committee'. It retained a measure of autonomy because of its role in the production process and strategic position within the economy. The growing level of state intervention in the economy, with the state as the country's major employer and the main vehicle for social mobility for those able to obtain educational qualifications (Kasfir, 1983), again appeared to parallel the Pakistan situation. The state was a means to economic power, rather than an instrument of an already dominant economic class. Saul found Debray's conclusion concerning the Latin American petty-bourgeoisie applicable to the East African case:

> it does not possess an infrastructure of economic power before it wins political power. Hence it transforms the state not only into an instrument of political domination, but also into a source of economic power. The state, culmination of social relations of exploitation in capitalist Europe, becomes in a certain sense the instrument of their installation in these countries. (Debray, 1967, p. 35 quoted in Saul, 1974, p. 354)

The overdeveloped Tanzanian state

There was another way in which the form of the Tanzanian state appeared to be comparable to that in post-colonial Pakistan. That was in respect of the overdeveloped nature of the state in relation to civil society, particularly in its bureaucratic manifestations. Colonialism had left a relatively highly developed bureaucracy, although one that had not been extensively penetrated by Africans. Furthermore it represented the power of the colonial state over all the elements of civil society rather than any internal, domestic interests. The colonial state had developed even fewer institutions for negotiating with indigenous interests than in India. It was paternalistic rather than mediatory. The state apparatus, particularly in its bureaucratic form, was more overdeveloped in relation to civil society and the private sector, where capitalism either in agriculture or industry had hardly begun to emerge – with the exception of the one group that as a result of cash-cropping was beginning to emerge as a richer stratum of rural society. However, Africans were only recruited into positions of influence in meaningful numbers on the eve of independence, when it was essential to replace expatriate officialdom with local people. The overdeveloped state seemed to fit the Alavi model.

The case of Kenya, in particular, seemed not to support the observation that the post-colonial state was overdeveloped. It sustains a more orthodox position: that the state cannot be anything other than a reflection of a dominant class interest. Leys asked why, particularly in East African circumstances where there were no strong indigenous classes to be subdued, an overdeveloped state should be needed. The colonial state at the time of independence in East Africa did not appear to be particularly strong in terms of civil and military personnel or percentage of national income taken by government revenues and expenditure, let alone overdeveloped: 'the states of the ex-colonies actually tend to be small, relative to both population and the size of the economy, compared with the states of the advanced capitalist countries' (Leys, 1976, p. 42; see also Ziemann and Lanzendorfer, 1977; Crow, 1990, pp. 211–12). The post-colonial state was, according to Leys, also typically less involved in the ownership of productive forces or interventions in social life than in most advanced capitalist societies.

Leys felt that the distinction between the relations of state to society and of the bureaucracy to other state institutions must be sharpened if a case like Kenya is to be properly understood. Overdevelopment, if it could be said to exist at all, was a temporary feature of the immediate post-independence period, quickly giving way to control by a dominant class. In Kenya the dominant class was the metropolitan bourgeoisie. This was the interest that the post-colonial state articulated. The state in such a peripheral economy supported metropolitan capital against its main rival, a newly emerging property-owning middle class. The struggle did not have to be mediated – it had been won by metropolitan capital. The state performed municipal functions on its behalf. Domination of the mass of the population by foreign capital required the existence of domestic class interests, in this case the petty bourgeoisie, allied to foreign capital and 'which uphold their joint interests in economic policy and enforce their dominance politically' (Leys, 1975, p. 271). State power was not relatively autonomous, but rather was 'asserted' by the 'currently dominant combination of classes' in the form of policies to protect the petty bourgeoisie and subdue the unions and by means of clientelism, ideological domination and official repression. 'The "middle class" whose interests the Kenyan government wished to defend . . . was largely a foreign one. Its real economic and political power lay abroad' (Leys, 1975, p. 208).

The distinction drawn here between the metropolitan bourgeoisie and its national auxiliary corresponds to that between a ruling class and a governing class applied to Tanzania by Michaela von Freyhold (1976). For her, the ruling class was the metropolitan bourgeoisie and, in the absence of a strong indigenous bourgeoisie or a landed class, the governing class consisted of state personnel and politicians who had inherited their offices from their colonial masters.

Levels of state development

Other writers have stressed the temporary nature of the over-developed state. Classes and institutions have developed to capture the state and bring the bureaucracy under control. In India, for example, as society has become more complex and the private sector has grown stronger and more diversified, so the political institutions representing classes in society and the bureaucracy has taken on a more subservient role. G. D. Wood, for example, argues that in the case of India a significant bourgeoisie has emerged which, despite the presence of foreign capital, has captured control of the state. When, as in India, independence meant the continuation and strengthening of formal democratic institutions, allowing the articulation of interests within civil society and particularly those of the national bourgeoisie, the bureaucracy loses its dominance:

> Control over the post-colonial state does not lie autonomously in the hands of its apparatus – e.g. the bureaucracy, military and police. The administration is obliged to declare an instrumental role for itself and to relinquish control over policy. . . . The post-colonial society may inherit an 'overdeveloped apparatus of state', but not for long. (Wood, G. D., 1977, p. 309)

Kasfir makes a similar case for post-colonial Africa (1983, p. 8). However, class formation may take time, and African experience confirms that in the interim the state can independently act in a mediatory role and affect the process of class formation by the success or failure of its policies (for example, in protecting local firms from foreign competition).

Warren's evidence is also relevant to the debate. It will be recalled that he claimed that economic growth benefited indigenous classes and that capitalism and the state had developed in a far more orthodox manner than either dependency theorists or post-colonial state theorists would have us believe.

Bureaucracy in Mali

Claude Meillasoux developed a parallel piece of analysis to Alavi's in a study of Mali in which he also drew attention to the concentration of power in the state bureaucracy. He emphasised the legacy of colonial bureaucracy and its continuing political power. The bureaucracy was also central to the career opportunities of the small middle class in Mali and was the focus of political competition. In the absence of other fully developed institutions, political pressure and lobbying was directed towards the bureaucracy, which became the arena in which political conflict was fought out. Meillasoux's analysis differs from Alavi's in that the class analysis is Weberian. The internal characteristics of the bureaucracy account for their political power – their expertise, prestige and social status, another legacy of the colonial era when administrators were regarded with great deference, partly because of their power, partly because they were recognised as being the powers behind the thrones of traditional leaders, and partly because of genuine respect for people who were believed to be bringing progress to the country. In Mali the bureaucracy was overlaid on a feudal class structure that had been largely unaffected by colonialism. In the rural areas traditional patterns of political authority remained intact: a landed aristocracy controlled the countryside. Mali thus had a strange configuration of forces consisting of a powerful Westernised bureaucracy and a feudalistic class of landowners, in conflict with each other as they sought economic advantage from state policies. Class relations had been less affected by colonialism than in Tanzania and as such contrasted even more strongly with Pakistan as interpreted by Alavi.

The kind of analysis discussed above connects with some of the factors identified by dependency theorists as being central to the nature of the state in the Third World. In particular the role of the bourgeoisie and its level of development are central to both lines of enquiry. Peripherality is seen to retard the development of a bourgeoisie. Foreign capital is part of the class structure of the peripheral state. It does more than compete with the national bourgeoisie, however. It affects the rate and direction of its development. Indigenous classes do not develop autonomously: they are distorted by the presence of foreign capital, which is not merely another class in competition with indigenous classes but actually affects the formation and coherence of indigenous classes. In so far as it prevents indigenous classes from developing their own control over capital, it strengthens the mediatory role of the state free from class control.

The literature on the post-colonial state provides a useful framework for analysis and comparison. It could not be argued that Alavi's model of the post-colonial, relatively autonomous and bureaucratically oligarchic state can be applied everywhere: the range of historical conditions in the Third World is too great for that.

5. The bureaucratic-authoritarian state

An alternative attempt to theorise about the Third World state is based on Latin American experience and especially the work of the Argentinian political scientist Guillermo O'Donnell, who developed a 'bureaucratic-authoritarian' (BA) model of politics. The problem that motivated this approach was the presence and persistence of military regimes and other evidence suggestive of state over-development in countries that are quite economically advanced and that have been independent for over 150 years (Ziemann and Lanzendorfer, 1977, p. 145). Experience in Latin America again runs counter to a certain genre of development theorising which predicted that as countries develop economically, politics becomes more pluralistic and the state becomes more democratic. Latin America during the twentieth century should not have become more authoritarian politically. It is useful to compare the bureaucratic-authoritarian model with Alavi's post-colonial state model, because of the argument against Alavi that as societies develop economically and socially his model become less viable. Latin America seems to present evidence of bureaucratic-authoritarianism accompanying and even growing as societies become more economically advanced.

The line of explanation is different from Alavi's. It examines dependent societies where the process of modernisation has not led to the gradual enrichment of mass politics but to the collapse of political systems in which the working classes and lower-middle classes were important participants in, and beneficiaries of, the dominant coalitions. Populist politics, notably in Argentina under Peron, produce movements that seek mass support to maintain an élite rather than promote an ideological position. It is a form of politics in which the masses can engage and acquire influence and benefits. The important question is why populism so often degenerates into repressive authoritarianism, often of a military character, and the regressive redistribution of wealth in favour of the economically privileged. More advanced levels of industrialisation, growing GNP per capita and other aspects of economic development are linked to a reversal from democratic competitive politics and an increase in inequality.

Political constellations

O'Donnell (1979) compared Brazil, Argentina, Chile, Uruguay and Mexico, identifying an underlying common historical sequence starting with oligarchical political systems in which power, both economic and political, is held by a small number of families. This is then followed by a phase of populist politics eventually degenerating into bureaucratic-authoritarianism. Three factors in 'constellation' are said to account for the stage reached by any particular country: regime, coalition, and policies. By *regime* is meant the existence of civil rights, freedoms, electoral competition, and organised interests – compared with repression, intimidation, gerrymandering, ballot-rigging and the other practices which undermine and destroy the democratic process. *Coalition* refers to the class and sectoral composition of the dominant political group. *Policies* refers to the distribution of resources among different classes and sectors of the economy. Each constellation is seen as the result of relationships between three key aspects of socio-economic modernisation: levels of industrialisation; levels of political activism among the lower classes (or what is rather confusingly called the 'popular sector'); and the growth of technocratic occupations in both the public and private sectors. Constellations of regime, coalition and policies reflect constellations of levels of industrialisation, activism and technocracy.

Bureaucratic-authoritarianism is characterised by a *regime* in which electoral competition is eliminated and other forms of political participation are closely controlled by the authorities; a *coalition* of high level military and civil technocrats working with representatives of foreign capital; and a *policy* of promoting advanced industrialisation.

Industrialisation

This particular kind of political system is interpreted as a reaction to problems associated with a particular phase of import-substitution policy. This phase is brought to an end by the lack of a domestic market to support further industrial expansion. It is a phase marked by the high cost of imported intermediate goods and capital equipment that cannot be produced locally. This cost is quickly reflected in balance of payments deficits, foreign debt and inflation. There is a pressing need to overcome this problem by the development of a manufacturing sector geared to intermediate and capital goods rather than consumer goods. The policies aimed at that objective seek to acquire technology, managerial expertise and capital largely from the multinational sector, to deal with economic crisis, and to create long-term stability. This is the industrialisation part of the constellation associated with bureaucratic-authoritarianism.

Political activism

The political activism factor refers to the political opposition to such policies from lower-income groups adversely affected by shortages of consumer goods, the effect of inflation on wage levels, and unemployment arising from a switch to more capital-intensive production. Protests, strikes and crisis within the system of democratic politics have to be managed and controlled.

Technocratic development

The spread of technology produces higher levels of social differentiation associated with modernisation (echoes of earlier modernisation theory). The particular development identified here as more significant than others is the greatly increased role of technocrats in society. Technocrats do not have a great deal of time for democracy. Participation, consensus-building, negotiation and compromise all run counter to the values of the technocrat. Democracy is seen as an obstacle to economic growth. The bureaucracy and the military are identified in Latin America as being the main repositories of such technocracy on the state side, forming a natural coalition with the technocrats leading the private sector. Managers and engineers, rather than shareholders, are the dominant influences in industry. A new professionalism within the military supports technocratic views of the economy and society generally. Problems are seen as needing solutions that can only be provided by those with the training and qualifications. This is a very distinctive perception of the nature of social problems and is found in varying degrees in all societies. The technocrats form a natural '*coup* coalition' to establish an alliance between the military, the civil bureaucracy and the technocrats in the private sector. Democracy gives way to the power of those with knowledge. This line of analysis touches upon other interpretations of military intervention in Third World politics. A coalition between civil and military officials seems natural, not just because they have the same paymaster but also because they espouse the same technocratic approaches to politics.

According to this perspective, the origins of bureaucratic-authoritarianism lie in the need for governments to satisfy the demands of national entrepreneurs and the indigenous middle class, while at the same time enacting policies in support of foreign capital. Different countries have had different degrees of success in handling this contradiction. Brazil was better than Argentina at integrating the national bourgeoisie after establishing political and economic stability to ensure large injections of foreign capital. The case of Chile shows that the pre-*coup* crisis and post-*coup* repression in the 1970s were so extreme that there was great difficulty in attracting foreign investment.

6. Applications

The relevance of this theoretical scheme to other regions of the Third World is not immediately obvious. It seems productive in the Latin American context, but may have limited use beyond this. 'Bureaucratic-authoritarianism' is a fair description of Latin America's militarised regimes, provided that the differences in the regimes and their economic policies are also recognised. As an analytical model it declined in significance in the 1980s as civilian politics was restored, competitive party systems were established and economic liberalism enforced (Cammack *et al.*, 1993, p. 79). Collier (1979) identifies key problems that need to be resolved if the concept and origins of 'constellations' are to prove explanatory frameworks in any setting, Latin America included.

First, the highly variable quality of the separate factors into which 'bureaucratic-authoritarianism' and other forms of state can be disaggregated – regime, coalition and policy – needs to be recognised. For example, there are numerous indicators of 'regime' and different ways in which a regime can be characterised. These include the form of electoral competition, the role of political parties and trade unions, and the extent and level of official repression. Populism as a contrasting political system to, and a cause of change towards, authoritarianism is also highly variable. Further conceptual refinement is needed in each factor of a 'constellation' in order to appreciate the degree and nature of differences between bureaucratic-authoritarianism and other types of state.

Secondly, there are grounds for doubting that bureaucratic-authoritarianism is exclusively associated with later phases of industrial modernisation in Latin America. There must be similar grounds for raising this question in relation to other regimes, where it seems equally likely that the phenomenon has appeared at different phases of industrial development. Certainly the 'regime' and 'coalition' features of bureaucratic-authoritarianism have been experienced in other regions of the Third World. What may be distinctive about the Latin American case is the association with a particular policy, that of promoting advanced industrialisation. Further refinement of the concepts would make it possible to identify whether one type of policy is a necessary condition for a bureaucratic-authoritarian state, or whether certain kinds of regime and coalition are consistent with other policies for the distribution of resources within a society. As Collier notes for Latin America, interaction between regimes and policy changes seem to cut across the BA/non-BA distinction. The possible explanations of the rise of authoritarianism are many and varied. Not all confirm the 'deepening of industrialisation' hypothesis, or the preceding strength of the 'popular' sector.

If bureaucratic-authoritarianism turns out to be highly variable in the composition of its 'constellation', if the line between BA and populism appears blurred, if there is a wide range of explanations of BA, and if industrialised and non-industrialised countries can experience similar results from their relations with the international capitalist system, the concept's usefulness in the analysis of Third World states is reduced.

7. Conclusion

Interest in post-colonial state and society, including some states whose post-colonial histories are extensive, has concentrated on the need to explain the failure of democratic systems to survive. The progress towards liberal democracy predicted by modernisation theory has failed to occur in so many Third World societies, despite economic development, that an analysis of the problem was imperative. Theories of political stability will be examined in Chapter 13 in order to explore the correlates of democratic development in the Third World. Political functionalism seems not to offer the possibility of an explanation since its very definitions of political modernisation implied the inevitable emergence of liberal democracy and pluralism on the Anglo-American model. The alternative opportunity provided by class-based analysis of the post-colonial state offers a number of ways forward. What is most striking about all attempts to theorise about the post-colonial state or the modernising political system is the preponderance of bureaucracy in the explanations and models produced. Clearly this institution requires a degree of attention even beyond that necessary in the analysis of developed political systems. Bureaucracy in the Third World is accordingly the subject of a separate chapter (Chapter 9).

8

Political Parties and Pluralist Politics

1. Introduction

The purpose of this chapter is to consider the experience of Third World countries with political parties, the most important institutions of political mobilisation in the context of mass politics. Whatever the nature of a civilian regime – whether based on the principles and institutions of liberal parliamentary politics, monopolistic forms of political leadership, or on some interpretation of Marxism–Leninism – political parties reflect the fact that government is no longer the prerogative of a hereditary élite or alien oligarchy but rests to some degree on the support of the masses. Parties emerge whenever the notion of political power comes to include the idea that 'the mass public must participate or be controlled' (LaPalombara and Weiner, 1966, p. 3).

A party may mobilise and control support through ideological devices or even repression, but it has to be managed so that power can be captured and the legitimacy of constitutional office secured. The objectives of parties may be many and varied, seeking revolutionary change or maintaining the status quo, but they all require the mobilisation of mass support. Political parties are both a consequence of a process of political change and a cause of further change by increasing a society's capacity to cope with crises of integration, participation and distribution (LaPalombara and Weiner, 1966, pp. 41–2).

Defining a political party is difficult, especially in the Third World, because of the immense variety that is found (Apter, 1965, pp. 180–1). A satisfactory definition is that provided by Coleman and Rosberg (it was used in a recent study of a sample of Third World parties: see Randall, 1988):

associations formally organized with the explicit and declared purpose of acquiring and/or maintaining legal control, either singly or in coalition or electoral competition with other similar associations, over the personnel and the policy of the government of an actual or prospective sovereign state. (1964)

It is easier to classify what Third World parties do than provide a definition that will encompass all manifestations of them. Classification is also easier than explanation of change in party system and organisation, two issues to be explored later. The main classifications to be used by political science have been based on functions, ideology and organisation. Typologies have also been formed from a combination of these factors.

2. Functions

Political parties in developing countries have been found to perform the following functions (Coleman and Rosberg, 1964; LaPalombara and Weiner, 1966, pp. 400–33; Randall, 1988; Cammack *et al.*, 1993). First they can in some circumstances endow regimes with legitimacy by providing ideologies, leadership or opportunities for political participation, or a combination of all three. By providing a means of peaceful political succession within a competitive party system they legitimatise the authority of government based on mass participation and representation. In competitive situations parties permit a degree of rotation of power among the different élites which they sustain.

Secondly, they can act as a medium for political recruitment, perhaps simultaneously creating opportunities for upward social mobility. In developing countries political parties provide the most important civilian route into a political career. Parties accommodate demands for greater political participation and, in various ways including repression and patronage, help manage the conflict that such mass participation in politics inevitably produces.

Thirdly, parties provide opportunities for the formation of coalitions of powerful political interests to sustain a government. This is what the functionalists refer to as 'interest aggregation', a function of parties which is more important in competitive systems when electoral and legislative majorities have to be formed by the broadening of political support. Such coalition formation can assist in the process of political integration if parties are successful in drawing support from across regions to which people feel an attachment greater than that to the nation-state. In Nigeria such importance is attached to the potentially destructive force of regionally or ethnically-based political mobilisation that parties are required by law to draw their membership from across the country (Oyediran and Agbaje, 1991). This indicates that parties can, under some circumstances, impede political integration by aggregating primarily ethnic and regional interests.

Parties also act as the conduits of upward pressure from the rank and file membership, affiliated organisations representing special interests such as women, youth or trade unions, and, if they are forced to compete for office through the ballot box, the electorate. Some parties have represented traditional oligarchies, as in parts of West Africa, where traditionalists adapted the modern institution of the party to their own political ends. The Northern People's Congress in Nigeria, for example, represented the interests of the aristocratic lineages that provided social, political and religious leadership in the north of the country. In a constitutional arrangement that assigns one person one vote, even an aristocracy has to obtain mass support. It has the advantage of being able to trade on the traditional allegiances of naturally deferential societies within the wider context of more egalitarian principles. Other parties have been based on the demands of the professional classes such as teachers, lawyers and low-ranking officialdom. Ethnicity is often a parallel defining factor, limiting membership and cutting across occupational and economic interests.

Parties perform the function of political socialisation, affecting the attitudes of party members and the wider public on such matters as the management of the economy, national identification and the legitimacy of government.

Within certain ideological perspectives parties perform a different kind of mobilising role. They mobilise people into self-help projects at the local level in an attempt to supplement government interventions under conditions of extreme scarcity of resources. Such mobilisation is often associated with the socialisation function referred to above, as local party organs attempt to spread the party's doctrine among the masses.

In theory political parties should also be major influences on public policy as a result of devising programmes to attract a workable aggregation of interests or through the application of official ideology to current problems. However, there is a great deal of evidence that parties usually have a minimal impact on public policy in Third World countries, and even more rarely exercise any effective supervision of policy implementation (Randall, 1988, p. 185–6).

Finally, political parties have been seen as necessary for political stability. Huntington has produced the most explicit statement on this relationship. In his view, stability depends on a society being able to absorb the increasing level of political participation by the new social forces generated by modernisation. Parties offer the principal institutional means of organising that participation in constructive and legitimate ways, especially if the parties are created before the level of participation gets too high. A combination of high levels of participation and strong party organisation provides a defence against anomic politics and violence. The risk of military intervention, for example, increases if political parties are too weak. So 'the stability of a modernising political system depends on the strength of its political parties. A party, in turn, is strong to the extent that it has institutionalised mass support' (Huntington, 1968, p. 408).

3. Ideology

Inevitably, given their appeal to certain class interests, the ideological positions of Third World parties have often resembled those of their First and Second World counterparts. Western ideologies have been adapted to provide a common framework of values for very heterogeneous societies and to strengthen national integration. Both socialism and communism have been deployed in the Third World for such aims. But they have been adapted to the particular context in which they are to be a guide to action. Special versions have been developed, such as Tanzania's African socialism, which purports to draw on traditional communal values as well as European ideas about equality. Chinese Marxism–Leninism developed its own distinctive qualities.

Where capitalism has developed over a prolonged period, as in the relatively lengthy post-independence histories of Latin American countries, parties most clearly reflect class interests in their ideological stances. Conservative parties are supported in Argentina, Colombia and Equador by coalitions of landlords and the Catholic Church. Liberal parties are supported by coalitions of urban business interests. They compete for the support of workers and peasants with socialist and communist parties (where these are not proscribed). Most European ideologies have been represented in Latin American politics at one time or another.

In most parts of the Third World, however, ideological developments and the political organisations based on them have been distinctive in a number of important respects. First, the ideologies of Third World political parties have often been derived more from religion than from materialistic ideologies of the West which were expected to take a hold in many post-colonial societies. Examples are the Hindu communal parties in India, the Muslim party in Indonesia and the Islamic party in Libya. The development of Islamic political ideologies is increasingly significant in many regions of the Third World.

Secondly, some parties have developed to defend the way of life of different ethnic communities, for example Malays, Chinese and Indians in Malaysia. Ideologies reflect the culture of these distinctive communities rather than class interests. In India caste may provide the foundation for a political party, as in the case of the Dalits Party representing Untouchables. This party was successful in state elections in 1993, forming part of the coalition government in India's most populous state, Uttar Pradesh. The party aims to promote social justice for India's most oppressed and deprived people. Since 40 per cent of Indians belong to lower castes, this could be a very significant political development. Elsewhere, however, and especially in Africa, the tendency of political parties to reflect ethnicity and regional consciousness, rather than identities that cut across such cleavages and unite people on a national scale, has been seen as a cause of their weakness and the weakness of governments built on such party competition (Diamond, 1988, p. 19).

Thirdly, political parties in the Third World are frequently populist. This is a style of leadership rather than an ideology. It seeks to mobilise people regardless of class by denying the significance of class and of any class-based ideology. Populism tries to mobilise all interests under a single conception of the national interest. It rejects the idea that groups have irreconcilable interests. Political leaders such as Sekou Toure of Guinea have claimed that though their societies might be divided into occupational, age and other groups, all share a common interest represented by a particular party and its leadership. Society is presented as 'cellularized' into factions whose common interests outweigh their particular and possibly conflicting interests as illiterates or intellectuals, young or old, producers or consumers, men or women, peasants or urbanites, bureaucrats or clients.

Populism is thus a way of presenting a view of society that stresses homogeneity rather than diversity. In order to appeal to all interests in society, populist parties and leaders define special interests in ways that make them ultimately reconcilable. Issues associated with particular interests, or which are divisive, are, where possible, avoided. Leaders specifically aim to prevent the development of a consciousness of conflicting interests. The methods used include building support on the basis of rewards rather than ideological conviction, and expressing contradictory policy objectives incoherently. Populism is inevitably conservative, since it seeks to prevent alternative perspectives to the status quo developing.

Social diversity is not regarded as a barrier to the identification of a more important common interest. In some countries the structure of post-colonial society lent some support to this way of viewing the political world, particularly in those that did appear to be devoid of significant class distinctions simply because economic underdevelopment had prevented classes from emerging fully. Congress in India must rank as one of the most successful populist movements. It attracts support from very different sections of society whose interests might appear to be incompatible and it has proved able to manage an alliance between different kinds of class structure, those of the rural and urban areas, even when such stratification has been overlaid with linguistic, ethnic, communal and religious differences.

Ideology and organisation

Observations of the tendency in the early 1960s for single-party regimes to emerge in Africa led Coleman and Rosberg to produce a typology of parties based on a combination of ideological, participative and organisational variables. This enabled them to contrast a 'pragmatic pluralist' pattern with a 'revolutionary-centralising' pattern. Pragmatic pluralist parties were those that generally tolerated the persistence of traditional politics, only partially and intermittently tried to mobilise support, and assimilated group interests to a limited extent. Revolutionary-centralising parties in contrast espoused a modernising ideology, were highly committed to mass political participation, and developed monolithic and centralised organisations.

This classification was used to explain the level of success achieved by African countries in solving the problem of national integration, both in the sense of 'transcending the élite-mass gap' and in the sense of territorial integration. However, it proved difficult to develop a theory of successful political integration as distinct from identifying integration as a function that parties can perform, especially in the single-party system of government. Coleman and Rosberg are able to go little further than stating that 'In all but a few of Africa's new states the primary structure . . . for coping with the myriad parochial and ethnic pressures is the national political party, the single or dominant party currently governing the state' (Coleman and Rosberg, 1964, p. 691).

Regime and ideology

A similar combination of regime and ideology is employed by LaPalombara and Weiner in their classification of parties in developing countries. They distinguish first between competitive and non-competitive *systems* and then two dimensions along which parties differ within each system. Competitive systems are associated with large and/or ethnically fragmented countries such as India, Nigeria, Malaysia and Sri Lanka. One dimension of such a system ranges from 'hegemonic', where one party dominates for a long period, to 'turnover', where change in the party of government is frequent. The other dimension refers to parties themselves rather than regimes, and distinguishes between ideological and pragmatic parties. The hope is that this typology will have theoretical value in so far as 'the particular combination of hegemony or turnover, ideology or pragmatism that a party pattern manifests may tell us something about how the parties relate to social, economic and political development' (LaPalombara and Weiner, 1966, p. 37). The typology was also useful if one was interested in the ability of parties to manage conflict effectively:

> in competitive systems the ideological-hegemonic and the ideological-turnover systems are less able to cope (short of repressive measures) with conflicts than either pragmatic-turnover or pragmatic-hegemonic systems. (p. 418)

Another hypothesis offered is that any drive for hegemonic control is likely to be made by parties with a strong ideological position. -
Party control in a non-competitive system is by definition likely to be hegemonic rather than 'turnover'. Combinations of hegemonic party systems and the ideological variable produce three main types of single-party system. The one-party authoritarian system (such as Mali, Ghana and South Vietnam in the 1960s) treats opposition as a threat to revolutionary or nationalistic objectives. The one-party pluralist system is characterised by a pluralistic party organisation and a pragmatic ideology, as in Mexico's Institutional Revolutionary Party. The one-party totalitarian system has the state itself as an instrument of the party whose objective is social and economic transformation, as in China, Vietnam and North Korea.

4. Party systems

There have been two dominant preoccupations in the analysis of Third World parties. One concerns the development and survival of party systems and in particular the emergence of single-party systems. The other concerns the survival of parties as institutions.

Single-party systems

In some cases party systems in the Third World have resembled their Western counterparts, offering a degree of electoral choice, legitimate political opposition, and acountability to the interests ranged in support of them electorally. Others have resembled the democratic centralism of the former Soviet Union and Eastern bloc. But the Third World has produced important variants of its own, most notably the single-party system in the context of parliamentary government and capitalist economy, as in Kenya until 1991. In some countries multi-party politics has survived more or less intact since independence, as in India. Elsewhere it has appeared intermittently, as in Nigeria. Single-party regimes in the context of capitalism prove that this form of economy often requires the negation of liberal democracy rather than guaranteeing it.

With the emergence of independent states whose institutions were based on Western models of government, it was assumed that parties would become the main institutions for the political mobilisation of different sections of society, aggregating different interests into workable coalitions that could constitute majorities, sustain governments, and provide for the alternation of governments at regular intervals (Kilson, 1963). This alternation is often regarded as the crux of a modern democracy. Political development in both the pre-colonial and post-colonial eras had seen the emergence of parties based on the nationalist movements that fought for independence. The Indian Congress is a classic case of an organisation with a long pre-independence history. In some colonies more than one nationalist movement emerged to develop into parties, especially in Africa where nationalist movements often represented different tribal groupings, each with its own ideas about the ending of colonialism. This again lent support to the expectation that this was the origin of multi-party systems of government.

Multi-partyism is also usually seen as the natural alternative in states ruled by the military and preparing for a return to civilian rule. In Pakistan, for example, three National Assembly elections have been held since the restoration of democracy in 1988. In October 1993, 43 political parties contested the 217 states in the National Assembly, though the contest was really a two-party fight between the Pakistan People's Party and the Pakistan Muslim League. The narrowness of the PPP's victory required it to form a coalition with smaller parties in order to form a government.

The emergence of single-party systems of government was a distinct departure from the expectations of the constitution-builders on the eve of independence. Consequently, considerable effort has been made to uncover convincing explanations for what was often regarded as deviation from the normal developmental path (see, for example, Coleman and Rosberg, 1964, pp. 655–64; LaPalombara and Weiner, 1966, pp. 31–2).

One reason for the emergence of the single-party system that was propounded was the nature of nationalism and the overwhelming support received by a single organisation at the moment of independence. Kilson (1963, p. 266) refers to an 'aura of nationalist legitimacy' and the status that is achieved as a result of being seen as the victor over imperialism. Such an achievement was taken as evidence that the organisation could continue to reflect the common interests of all sections of society. Winning independence acquired a legitimacy that overshadowed all others, especially in electoral terms.

Such popular support then enabled the dominant party to make it unlawful for other parties to exist so that a single-party state is established *de jure* as well as *de facto*. Not all single-party regimes outlaw other parties, but when they do not it has been very common for them to put obstacles other than the law in the way of effectively organised opposition. Gaining control of the mass media has proved one of the most effective ways of making it difficult for opposition parties to function.

Another explanation of the single-party tendency refers to the autocratic form of government which it is said was the new state's inheritance both from colonialism and traditionalist government. Pluralism and multi-party democracy are not inherited from the past. Rather, autocracy is the dominant aspect of political history. Coleman and Rosberg (1964) argued that the situation that party leaders confronted at independence had been formed by the autocratic power of the departing colonialists, a culture supported by, in the case of African societies at least, elements that were predisposed towards more authoritarian forms of government. Multi-party democracy was too alien an importation for it to survive in the local political culture, traditions and history. Perceptions of tradition and what was appropriate for society combined with the colonial legacy such as a centralised administrative apparatus, paternalism, and electoral systems giving unfettered control to a party that has not necessarily gained a plurality of the votes. Where the legacy was different, a plurality of parties stood a better chance of survival (Randall, 1988).

The political culture of the new indigenous leadership was also élitist – government was believed to possess a monopoly of wisdom and legitimacy. Since there were few if any other social or political organisations that could compete with the concentration of professional knowledge that existed within government, it was difficult to dispute this claim. The leadership culture was also statist.

The state was regarded as the moderniser. In the context of a weak private sector, powerful bureaucracy and sometimes socialist ideology, the state was seen as the agent of development. The leadership was also nationalist, emphasising national unity as the paramount goal, condemning any subnational sentiment to tribe, religion, region or other centres of political attachment and loyalty as destructive of national integration.

All such elements fed what many have regarded as a natural predisposition towards more authoritarian forms of government. There were relatively few states in the position enjoyed by India at independence, with a long history of political organisation, mass mobilisation and representative government. Few had had such a preparation for independence (and even India did not settle to democratic politics until after the horrors of partition). Multi-party democracy was often perceived as a luxury that could not be afforded. The immense problems confronting the governments of new states meant that discontinuities in the pursuit of public goals was an indulgence. Developed democracies could afford to have changes of direction every four or five years, but poor and dependent countries could not.

Tied up in such an explanation of the single-party system there is obviously an element of self-justification. Sociological explanation should not incorporate the rationalising of political leaders seeking to hold on to public office unless such rationales were widely supported within society. The conclusion that scientific explanations are sometimes tainted by the self-justificatory rhetoric of national political leaders is lent some support by the obvious fact that political office is not readily relinquished, least of all in the Third World context. The rewards of political office in the context of underdevelopment are so great that there must always be a temptation to manipulate politics to exclude the organised opposition.

This goes further than mere corruption, serious though this problem is. The problem is rather that the state, being the main engine of economic development, is something that those who aspire to benefit socially and economically from such development have to control. An emerging bourgeoisie cannot look to other sources of capital. Production, trade and commerce all depend upon capital channelled through the state, which also controls licences, the law governing the labour force, and access to foreign exchange and import and export permits. The state is an organisation which has to be captured by any group that wishes to accumulate economic resources. Political power as well as political careers bring huge rewards that are not lightly conceded to opponents, whether that opposition is in terms of class, tribe, religion, ethnicity or race.

Fourthly, the classless nature of some Third World societies seems to negate the need for more than one party. In Tanzania, for example, the fact that society was composed of a number of more or less equally balanced ethnic groups without any major forms of social and economic stratification was said to remove the need for a multi-party system. Society was too homogeneous to need more than one party to represent interests effectively.

Fifthly, not all new states came into existence on the basis of a preparation for independence in a Western European constitutional mould. The preparation for independence in Algeria, Indo-China, Angola and Mozambique was rather different. Marxist-Leninist ideology has played its part. Such an ideology, perhaps having its origin in mobilisation for a war of liberation, identifies party with state and nation. Anything outside the party, and certainly anything that opposes it, is almost treasonable by definition. An organisation founded to wage war under such ideological motivation would have an automatic propensity to form the sole leadership in the context of post-war civilian politics.

There is also an explanation in terms of national integration. Political leaders in the new states undoubtedly encountered many separatist tendencies. There was a need to produce an organisation that could act as an agent of integration. This was a reaction to the potential for political instability arising from ethnic, religious and regional rivalries. Carter (1962) and Huntington (1968, ch. 7) both adopted this line of explanation. The need for political order made the single-party system attractive. So some Western political scientists discussed single-party systems approvingly as well as descriptively and analytically. Huntington noted the relative success of communist states in providing political order, seeing it as derived from the priority given to 'the conscious act of political organisation'. The number of political parties was more important for development than the strength and adaptability of the party system. A strong party could assimilate the social forces generated by modernisation that would otherwise threaten political stability. The number of parties was only important if political stability required more than one institutional channel. Multi-party systems were likely to perform this role weakly.

Huntington could find no stable multi-party system in any modernising country. Modernising states found one-party systems to be more stable than multi-party systems and less prone to military intervention, though 'real' competition between parties, according to Huntington, can contain divisive pressures. It all depends how parties institutionalise and regularise political conflict and competition. Single parties seemed better able to do this than parties in a multi-party system. This introduces the question of the 'decay' or survival of party *systems*, a topic returned to later.

Much of the debate about party systems has focused on whether developing countries can afford the luxury of democracy. Economic development is said to require planning and policy continuity. Political stability requires strong institutions to contain the divisive forces released by the modernisation process. However, research has failed to reveal evidence which consistently supports either the view that the absence of party competition is better for policy outcomes, such as economic development and social equality, or that democracy involving real political competition for votes leads to better economic growth and distribution of income (Sirowy and Inkeles, 1991).

Acceptance of single-party government was made easier by apparently democratic tendencies within some sole parties. It appeared as if some parties could sustain democratic decision-making within the party sufficient to compensate for the lack of choice between parties. Intra-party democracy could perhaps allow for just as much or just as little discussion of alternatives as inter-party democracy.

Tanzania has often been cited as a case in point. Its one legal political party, the Chama Cha Mapinduzi (CCM) is democratically organised, with the national conference electing delegates to the national executive council which in turn elects the central committee. For parliamentary elections the party selects two candidates for each constituency, sometimes from a large number of nominations – 85 in one constituency in 1990, for example. Seats are vigorously contested in a carefully regulated campaign. It is not uncommon for incumbents, including ministers, to be defeated.

Some political leaders in the Third World once claimed, not without some justification, that the policy choices offered by, say,

Democrats and Republicans in the USA were no greater than the choices being made within the mass organisations of sole parties and between the candidates which those parties sponsored in parliamentary elections. Different factions within a single party could also compete for political office. The idea of a formal opposition was also denounced as being alien to indigenous modes of decision-making (Emerson, 1963, pp. 640–2).

Consequently, following independence in many new states, the political leadership argued that traditional society had its own forms of democratic decision-making that could be adapted to contemporary conditions without needing more than one political party. Leaders such as Julius Nyerere of Tanzania and Leopold Senghor of Senegal claimed that traditional African decision-making was based on consensus, unity and egalitarianism, claims on which historical research has thrown some doubt (Hodder-Williams, 1984, p. 11; Riley, 1991, p. 3). Pre-colonial African village communities were said to have had 'a sense in which basic political democracy functioned. . . . The tribal elders might make the decisions, but they would be decisions that reflected the consensus' (Nursey-Bray, 1983, pp. 97–8). Such communities corresponded to Tonnies' *Gemeinschaft* rather than *Gesellschaft*. A more convincing explanation for the appeal to a pre-colonial golden age might be that it was necessary for political leaders to distance themselves from the institutions and values associated with the colonisers.

The development of an alternative form of democracy to that of Western liberalism appears more natural still when it is recognised that for much of the post-independence period Third World countries lacked the two vital conditions, one economic and one political, which preceded liberal revolutions in the seventeenth and eighteenth centuries in the West: the availability of capitalist enterprise, finance and skills; and a loyalty to the nation rather than an ethnic community. It was therefore to be expected that there would be 'a painful, long period of accumulation of capital and of productive skill. . . . A pre-political or pre-national people has to be brought to a political and national consciousness. This puts a premium on the mass movement with strong ideological leadership' (Macpherson, 1966, p. 27).

There have been some notable deviations from the tendency towards single-party systems. In 1983 Senegal, which soon after independence from France and under the charismatic leadership of

Leopold Senghor became a single-party state, decided to revert to a two-party system. More recently, international influences have encouraged such reversals. The exception is Zimbabwe, the only country whose political leadership has in recent years been attempting to justify a move away from a multi-party system, though a referendum on the subject has yet to be held.

The demise of party government

A more alarming tendency has been for parliamentary and party politics to collapse altogether under the impact of political crises. Party systems have often given way to military systems. Single and multi-party regimes seem to have fared equally badly in terms of the political stability which they were able to secure. It is difficult to find any pattern in the decay of party systems. Single-party systems sometimes survive, as in Kenya or Tanzania; sometimes they succumb to military *coups*, as in Ghana. Multi-party systems have sometimes survived, notably in India, but elsewhere they have not (for example in Pakistan after 1958 or Nigeria). Between 1960 and 1969 ten of the fifteen multi-party states in Africa had experienced military intervention. Of the twenty single-party states, eleven had *coups*.

It is not surprising that some commentators started to write off party systems generally as a total failure. This is reflected in the general down-playing of the political significance of Third World parties (see Randall, 1988, which is an attempt to restore a sense of their importance). Yet in some countries parties and party systems have survived for a very long time. The continuity of some Third World party systems is now greater than those of Eastern Europe. There is no shortage of examples of countries with long histories of party government. There are also examples of the military being instrumental in the reinstatement of parties, albeit to legitimise the military's role in politics.

Randall's book examines explanations for the survival of *systems*. Note that here we are entering the discussion of one aspect of political instability, namely the problem of sustaining democracy as represented among other things by a plurality of political parties. (This is a matter that will be returned to in Chapter 13). However, there is also the question of the survival of single-party systems (especially since in some cases the single-party system is more democratic than the most likely alternative, a military regime).

There are no obvious explanations for the survival of party politics. Economic growth, which might be expected to increase prosperity and therefore a sense of satisfaction with the regime, does not guarantee the survival of party systems, although the World Bank pointed out in 1989 that the African countries with the best economic records (Botswana and Mauritius) had parliamentary democracies. Support for this conclusion was seen to be provided by The Gambia, which has had multi-party democracy since independence in 1965 despite a GNP per head of only $US 240 and an average life expectancy of 43 years in 1989 (Riley, 1991, pp. 7 and 29) but which succumbed to the military in 1994.

Alternatively it might be hypothesised that social structure might offer an explanation, in that stratification based on class seems to provide a better basis for competitive politics than vertical cleavages based on race, language or religion. However, social factors such as class and related indicators of stratification such as urbanisation and literacy do not appear to be systematically related to patterns of party politics (Randall, 1988, p. 188).

It is more difficult to account for the stability of a party system than to explain variations between systems. Patterns of survival and stability are more difficult to discern than variations accounting for differences in party system. These include the legacy of colonialism, the time that parties have to take root and become established (India and Jamaica are examples of countries in which political parties have long histories), and whether independence was won by war or negotiation, the former method leading to the creation of the 'party-army' of national liberation, such as the FLN in Algeria which had great difficulty in transforming itself into a civilian political movement after the French withdrew. Not all nationalist movements have histories of guerrilla warfare, having been able to negotiate the end of colonialism rather than engage in armed struggle.

To these factors must be added foreign influences. Aid donors have added political pluralism, 'good governance', democracy and respect for human rights to their list of conditions attached to international development assistance. For example, in 1990 President Mitterrand of France warned African leaders at the sixteenth Franco–African Congress that 'France will link its contribution to efforts designed to lead to greater liberty and democracy'. In 1991 the British Minister for Overseas Development announced that British aid policy would require recipient governments to move towards pluralism, the rule of law, democracy and respect for human rights. Multilateral aid agencies such as the World Bank have added to the pressures demanding 'good government' in return for aid. Interpretations of 'good governance' as a condition for multilateral and bilateral assistance have been quite varied (Williams and Young, 1994, pp. 84–6).

Such pressure combined in the early 1990s with the influence of the momentous events in Eastern Europe and the Soviet Union on domestic political groups demanding political reforms and especially an end to the single-party regime. Competitive party politics have emerged in a number of countries as a consequence, most notably Nepal, Angola, Ghana, the Ivory Coast and Zambia. However, resistance to multi-partyism has been strong. The one-party state continues to be defended by reference to the threat of tribal factionalism (Zimbabwe), the need to concentrate on economic development (Tanzania), and the lack of readiness for democracy among the people (Kenya).

5. Institutional survival

There is now a growing interest in how parties as institutions survive rather than in why party systems decay, a question that is difficult to disentangle from the more general problem of political instability. The organisational characteristics of the parties themselves that sustain them has become a topic of scientific interest. This is a very difficult task because it is hard to know whether something that a party does to its internal organisation is crucial to its long-term existence.

Analysis of parties in French-speaking West Africa in the early 1960s led R. S. Morgenthau to distinguish between 'mass' and 'patron' parties (Morgenthau, 1964, pp. 336–41). This distinction, 'less neat in fact than in definition', indicated differences in organisational structure (particularly at the local level), size of membership (including its social composition), finances, functions, methods and patterns of authority. All such organisational factors reflected the way in which party leaders related to the rest of the population. Mass parties, such as the Democratic Parties of the Ivory Coast and Guinea or the Union Soudanaise, sought the adherence of all individuals, whereas patron parties such as Niger's Union Nigerienne 'usually terminated their structure simply with the adherence of influential notables or patrons' (p. 337). Patron parties were weakly organised and undisciplined, with little direct membership participation. Local patrons were relied upon to reach the local community. The individual was of interest to patron parties 'only in so far as he happened to be included in the franchise, provided candidates for election and the minimum machinery for bringing the voter to the polls'(p. 340). Mass parties in contrast had extensive organisations, performed the function of 'social integration' through their mass membership and were interested in all aspects of their members' lives, not just their voting choices.

Randall (1988) refers to the importance for organisational survival of making the party leadership representative of its former opponents as well as its own supporters. The United National Independence Party in Zambia has been quite successful in making the leadership representative of a wide range of social élites and interests. According to Huntington, parties become stronger the more they can institutionalise mass support, develop a complex organisation linked to socio-economic bodies such as trade unions, and recruit leaders that identify themselves with the party rather than using it as a means to office elsewhere, such as in the government bureaucracy (1968, pp. 408–12). Huntington is here referring to the loss to political parties when scarce talent is drawn off into other loyalties. He is not denying that parties should seek office for their leaders when they compete for positions in legislatures, executives and other parts of the state whose personnel are recruited by electoral competition.

Also important to the strength of party organisation is the distribution of patronage, and the allocation of state resources and positions within the military and bureaucracy, at the disposal of governments. The distribution of rewards to supporters and clients on a personalised basis can be crucial for the survival of a political party. Within parties different interests are often expressed through factionalism and patronage.

Factionalism refers to informal party organisation. It is an inevitable consequence of alliances and coalitions between leaders and followers that have no ideological foundation but which are designed to secure electoral support for particular groups of leaders. The relationship between the leader of a faction and his followers may be based on feudalistic tenure systems, such as when a landowner can guarantee electoral support from tenants because of their economic dependency, cultural loyalties and other traditional obligations. The factions within modern political parties can be built upon traditional allegiances. Alternatively the factional linkage may be tribal or linguistic. There are many different ways that the leaders of political parties can manage their electoral support. In India, party factions take on some of the characteristics of traditional family structures, castes and village organisations (Weiner, 1957, p. 238).

Factionalism within political parties is one manifestation of a more fundamental dimension of politics in the Third World (and elsewhere), namely clientelism. Patron–client relations reflect interdependencies between people with economic and political power and those who look to them for security and the performance of duties and who, in return, offer personal services, gifts, loyalty, deference and political support (Powell, 1970, pp. 412–13). Though expressing interdependency, clientelism is essentially an unequal form of political exchange. It is a relationship between the powerful and the weak. It represents a rational form of behaviour for people under conditions of inequality and when the state's rulers need the support of regional, ethnic and personal factions (Clapham, 1982). Eisenstadt and Roniger identify nine 'core analytical characteristics' of the social interactions and exchanges involved in patron–client relations:

- they are particularistic and diffuse;
- resources are exchanged, both economic and political (support, votes, protection, solidarity);
- resources are exchanged as a 'package', not separately;
- the relationship is strongly unconditional and long-term;
- there is a varying amount of solidarity in the relationship;
- it is based on informal and not necessarily legal understandings;
- patron–client relations are entered into voluntarily;
- the vertical nature of patron–client relations undermines horizontal solidarities, especially of clients; and
- the relationship is based on strong inequality and power difference. (Eisenstadt and Roniger, 1981, pp. 276–7)

Political and economic changes, particularly the development of the state and the spread of capitalism, have fundamentally altered the nature of patronage. Patron–client relations take the form of brokerage and mediation between clients in their dealings with government and the market (Powell, 1970; Lemarchand, 1981). They also become key components of the electoral process: political parties are compelled to recruit from among the local patrons and brokers in order to secure the political support of their clients.

The links between leaders and followers in party factions are therefore highly personalised. Special interests pursue their objectives through such links with the political authorities. People with power offer support and protection to those who accept and support their leadership. Identity with a leader will cut across conflicting interests, so that the leaders of factions have to mediate between the groups who support them. In India, for example, political parties and notably Congress have had to incorporate many different kinds of loyalty – those based on caste, landlord–tenant relations, language, tribe and religion.

Factionalism leads to a segmentary form of politics. The internal structures of factions are very much alike and political relations within them are always transactional, instrumental and dependent. Factionalism is stimulated by the rewards which are accessible to those in political office. Class interests and conflicts are overlaid by the common interest of patron and client. Factional conflict is about obtaining a broader basis of followers, but the outcome of conflict does not change the social structure.

If a leader fails to mediate successfully between different economic interests within his own faction, it may split into two. If the split runs the length of the party, factional conflict may lead to a new party being formed. The conflicts between factions are not ideological: they are conflicts over resources, over influence at key points in the decision-making structure of party and government, and over the ability to gain enough followers to win office so that patronage can be extended and the size and power of the faction can be increased. Success breeds success in a system of patronage. Leaders who win office can be expected to use their powers of patronage to enlarge their faction, drawing others into their sphere of influence. Leaders can then seek higher office, greater patronage and an enlarged following. Factional politics within parties and patron–client relationships produce a distinctive image for Third World parties.

Thirdly, decentralisation in the party organisation appears to be important. When the stable single-party states of the Third World such as Kenya, Tanzania and Cuba are compared, each with very different ideological foundations, it would appear that one of the reasons they have survived is because they have developed an elaborate internal apparatus to mobilise society, and penetrate it through a mass membership involved in a local as well as a national organisation. Then it becomes easier for the party to create a sense of national identity and a sense of legitimacy. It becomes a more successful instrument of political recruitment. Parties survive, it may be hypothesised, because they have firm grassroots. Single parties seem to have been better at political mobilisation in support of civilian institutions, at building a consensus, and at nation-building. Tanzania, for example, has been successful in this respect, though it may be said that it did not have too much of problem compared with many other African states, the population being predominantly Bantu, speaking a similar language and having similar customs. Single parties also seem to have been better at solving the problem of political succession – how one set of leaders is replaced by another when necessary. They have been able to resolve the leadership problem, a factor that has a lot to do with the political cultures of the societies concerned. It may also have something to do with the way in which governments based on those kinds of party distribute resources and plan economic development. In some of the African countries the single parties that squandered resources on uneconomic projects, or misappropriated resources by directing them into the hands of the political élite, fared less well than others.

It does seem that where parties, whether in single or multi-party regimes, have failed to create a machinery for transmitting interests, opinions and needs upwards to the policy-making élite, and have only created channels of communication and coercion downwards from the leadership to the masses, they have experienced difficulty surviving. Decentralisation of the party has significance beyond just organisational structure and embraces a whole approach to the management of society and economy as well as political education, indoctrination and control. Developing an ideology and communicating it is crucial to creating a sense of legitimacy.

Funding and institutional autonomy – that is, freeing the party from domination by the civil bureaucracy or military – are other important organisational features of Third World parties (Randall, 1988). (It has to be noted that India's Congress Party, with considerable bureaucratic infiltration, seems to be the exception to this.) Then there is support, both in terms of membership and votes, achieved by promoting an ideology, providing leadership and having a good record of performance while in office. Manipulating electoral rules, such as ballot-rigging, obstructing the registration of candidates, restricting political rallies and meetings, and intimidating opposition candidates and supporters, are also ways of securing 'support'. Such risky strategies may have to be followed up with repressive machinery if they are not to lead to civil disorder on a major scale. In Nigeria, for example, military intervention has usually been preceded by civil disorder arising directly from electoral irregularities and rigging of the population census on which constituencies are based.

6. Conclusion

The question of survival of party government and representative politics leads on to the question of political stability generally. Variations in party system may be relevant to the stability of the political system as a whole. Huntington, for example, predicted that in the long term, two-party and dominant-party systems were more likely than single or multi-party systems to produce political stability because they provide a form of party competition that is more effective in assimilating new groups into the political system. Single parties find it difficult to incorporate the new social and economic interests created by modernisation without coercion and therefore instability. In the multi-party system, the assimilation of new social forces into politics can only be done by increasing the number of parties: 'The two-party system . . . most effectively institutionalises and moderates the polarisation which gives rise to the development of party politics in the first place' (Huntington, 1968, p. 432).

The 'problem' of political instability is primarily seen in terms of the demise of parliamentary politics. The failure of a military regime is not seen as quite such a problem. Not surprisingly the attention that has been paid to political instability in the Third World has focused particularly on the supplantment, usually by the military, of a civilian form of government based on a system of parties. Military intervention and the general question of political stability are the subjects of later chapters.

9

Bureaucracy and Political Power

1. Introduction

Bureaucracies are important political organisations in all political systems. We no longer think of bureaucrats as merely the neutral implementers of the political decisions of others. In the Third World the bureaucracy has come to be regarded in some circumstances as *the* most important political institution. We have already touched upon ways in which the bureaucracy is so regarded. Theories of the post-colonial state have employed the concept of a bureaucratic oligarchy, clearly implying that government is in the hands of the paid officials of the state.

Some indication of the significance of bureaucracy in developing countries is gained from the scale of public employment, which accounts for over 50 per cent of non-agricultural jobs in Africa, 36 per cent in Asia and 27 per cent in Latin America. A sample survey of 28 developing countries revealed that an average of 27 per cent of salaried jobs in non-agricultural sectors were in government. In India the level was 54 per cent and in Tanzania 46 per cent. In the 1970s public service employment in some developing countries increased three to four times faster than in developed countries, and two to three times faster than the general population. African states in particular have seen uncontrolled expansion of the staff of government departments and public enterprises which, according to the World Bank, have often functioned as job-creation schemes for school-leavers, leading to chronic over-manning. For example, by 1986 the wages bill for Guinea's 75 000 civil servants accounted for 50 per cent of current expenditure. In the Central African Republic the figure was 63 per cent. Gambia's civil service doubled in size between 1974 and 1984 and Ghana's increased by 14 per cent each year between 1975 and 1982 – five times the growth of the labour market (World Bank, 1983, pp. 101–2; and 1989, pp. 55–7). Since independence in 1990 Namibia's civil service has expanded from 43 000 to 70 000.

Part of the explanation for the growth in the size of public bureaucracies lies in the demands that have been made on governments to stimulate development by providing a social and economic infrastructure and engaging directly in production. After independence, state bureaucracies were seen as promoters of social and economic change through planned development programmes (Jain, 1992, p. 15). Growth in the share of public services in GDP was faster in developing low-income and middle-income countries between 1960 and 1980 than in Western developed economies (see Table 9.1). In 1990 the proportion of GDP accounted for by government consumption in developing countries averaged 12 per cent.

Controlling the bureaucracy is one of the main challenges facing democratic political leaders. The pre-eminence of senior officials in Third World government presents reformist politicians with one of the greatest obstacles to change. Dependence on the bureaucracy is an inescapable feature of political life for incoming politicians, however sound their popular support and democratic credentials. When Begum Zia became Prime Minister of Bangladesh in 1991 she was unable to dispense with the services of the ten most senior officials – the so-called G-10 – despite their known collaboration

Table 9.1 *General government consumption^a as % of GDP*

	1970	1965	1991	1989
Sub-Saharan Africa	12	10	15	14
East Asia and Pacific	9	13	10	8
South Asia	10	8	12	12
Middle East and N. Africa	18	13	. .	14
Latin America and Caribbean	10	9	13	9
High-income economies	16	22	17	17

SOURCES: World Bank 1991 and 1993, Table 9.
NOTE: ^{a} Current expenditure on goods and services, and capital
   expenditure on material defence and security.

with the military dictator General Ershad. One became the PM's principal secretary.

Controlling bureaucrats at the other end of the hierarchy is equally daunting, especially when there are, as in India, 18.5 million of them. Making such huge bureaucracies accountable and honest seems an impossible task, as the victims of the Bophal disaster are only too aware. Ten years after an explosion at the Union Carbide plant released a lethal gas, killing 12 000 people and leaving half a million chronically ill, thousands of victims still await compensation from the $470 million paid by the company. Bribes are necessary to secure court hearings to rule on eligibility and at other stages of the claims process. Some have given up their quest for compensation because the process is too expensive. Civil servants living in a neighbourhood unaffected by the escape of gas have secured compensation to which they are ineligible. Corruption is rife throughout the whole relief operation. The bureaucracy has been so slow in awarding compensation payments that by 1994 only one-sixth of the interest earned by Union Carbide's out-of-court settlement has been used. At this rate it will take twenty years before all claims are settled. By then many of those eligible will have died. Other schemes promised by the Indian government, such as industrial retraining, have yet to be implemented (McGirk, 1994).

2.   Concepts of bureaucracy

One of the problems when studying bureaucracy is that the term carries different connotations for different people. These will appear as we examine the way in which political science has integrated the study of bureaucracy into the analysis of Third World politics. A number of different definitions have been attached to the term. This conceptual ambiguity can, however, be put to good use. If we remind ourselves what the different meanings of bureaucracy are, we can explore the full significance of bureaucracy as a political force in LDCs, a significance which extends well beyond the implementation of public policy.

'Bureaucracy' is sometimes used simply to refer to government administrative agencies staffed by public servants. It is synonymous with public administration, consisting of organisations set up as part of the modern state to carry out the policies of decision-makers. The state needs specialised institutions for implementing public policy and employs large numbers of people who make it their career to serve the state in a professional capacity. The bureaucracy thus refers to the public services and the organisations into which they are structured. It is a category of governmental personnel and offices that are filled in a particular way. It tells us no more about the way those organisations function or about the political power that the bureaucracy might exercise either over the formulation of public policies or their mode and even degree of implementation.

Another meaning of bureaucracy that may be identified, however, identifies a particular kind of organisational structure in which people are recruited into positions of authority in a special way. This is the classic Weberian concept of bureaucracy. Bureaucracy for Weber was the most advanced form of human organisation that society had devised and the most rational means for the performance of collective tasks, especially those requiring large-scale organisation. This clearly implies that organisations are not all bureaucratic. Some may be more bureaucratic than others. In so far as they are, they have clearly distinguishable features. They have clear lines of command from one level of a hierarchy to another. Recruitment to positions or offices within a bureaucracy will be on the basis of merit demonstrated by the acquisition of relevant qualifications or success in a competitive entry test. Officials are dependent on a salary. They do not own the means of administration. They cannot take personal possession of a share of any tax revenues that they might be empowered to collect. Officials are merely paid a salary in return for their services to the state.

This reinforces the demarcation of official jurisdictions. There is a clear division of labour within a bureaucratic organisation. It is divided into different offices to which attach certain clear-cut powers – regular, stable and precisely defined authority. This is sometimes represented graphically in an organigram or organisational chart set out as a pyramid of offices. The officials occupying such offices have clearly defined powers laid down in abstract rules. Their authority will be closely prescribed by those rules. They will be engaged in applying general rules to specific cases. This is a particular feature of government bureaucracies and especially those bureaucrats who encounter members of the public on a face-to-face level. They deal with the public as claimants or people who feel they are entitled to something that the state has to allocate, and that they fall within the category that the state has defined as being in need of, and entitled to, some benefit. The task of the bureaucrat is to make the allocation in a fair, impersonal and impartial way, treating like cases alike and having regard for nothing other than the factors that the regulations deem to be relevant. The bureaucrat is interested in nothing about a claimant other than what the regulations define as significant for arriving at a decision. If, for example, the official works for a small farmers development programme which defines entitlement in terms of size of land-holding, all the official needs to know is how much land the applicant occupies. All other aspects of the claimant's life – age, gender, race, tribe, caste, language, family size, place of origin – are irrelevant unless the law brings one or more of them into the calculation.

This brings us to another meaning of bureaucracy and one which most readily occurs to the ordinary person if they use the term. That is inaccessible administration, rigid decision-making bound up in 'red tape', and insensitivity to personal circumstances and needs as defined by the applicant rather than the bureaucracy. This is what Robert Merton referred to as the 'dysfunctional' or 'pathological' traits of bureaucracy. Rational organisation and procedures deteriorate into inefficiency. In particular, 'strict adherence to regulations' induces 'timidity, conservatism and technicism' as well as conflict with clients (Merton, 1952, p. 367). Bureaucracy becomes an end in itself and thus self-defeating. It becomes characterised by buck-passing, red tape, rigidity, inflexibility, excessive impersonality, oversecretiveness, unwillingness to delegate and reluctance to exercise discretion (Heady, 1959). Such bureaucrats are perceived as being unconcerned with personal problems, limiting their attention to narrowly defined circumstances that rules happen to define as significant. Bureaucrats are caught within a double-bind. If they do not administer the rules rigidly in order to avoid appearing to be inflexible and inhuman, they will be accused of abusing their power, exercising too much discretion and moving outside their circumscribed jurisdiction; if they apply the rules rigourously, they will be accused of being bureaupathological. The bureaucrat treads a difficult path between those two alternatives.

Finally, bureaucracy may be taken to mean a form of rule, a category of governmental system along with democracy or aristocracy. Bureau*cracy* means government by officials rather than government by the people, a single person or a hereditary class.

In many Third World societies that is precisely the kind of government that is in place, a kind of government that in many ways is very reminiscent of colonial government, which was also government by appointed officials, both military and civil. In such regimes, exemplified by today's military oligarchies and dictatorships, the bureaucracy is not merely a powerful political organisation exerting a lot of influence within the political process. The political process is coterminous with the bureaucracy, which may also be taking on some of the characteristics of a ruling class as well as a ruling stratum.

3. The political power of bureaucracy

So the first theoretical issue that may be identified concerns the political power of the bureaucracy and how this may be conceptualised. Ideological and methodological choices have been important here. Functionalists and Marxists have both had distinctive things to say about the bureaucracy in the Third World. What they chose to focus upon and the way they have interpreted the role of the bureaucracy has depended very much upon their wider views and theories of society and the state.

Knowledge

One source of political power is knowledge. In the Third World, bureaucracies are often said to monopolise the knowledge and expertise relevant to government. The concentration of technical, professional and administrative expertise within the bureaucracy is unrivalled. Even when there is strong parliamentary government and virile political parties and other centres of political power, and when the bureaucrats have a constitutional role which permits them merely to advise the political executive, they do so from positions of great influence. In many developing countries there are no political institutions which can compete with the bureaucracy in terms of a monopoly of technical and professional expertise. In addition, the majority of such professionals have for many years been employed in the public sector and public services. This again limits the availability of countervailing forces that can present political leaders with alternative plans, policy advice and techniques of implementation to those put up by government officials. Development planning has consequently tended to be highly centralised, technocratic and of the 'top down' variety, where the experts at the top make the decisions about what the masses need in terms of programmes of development, whether in health care, agriculture, education or other areas of planned development. This feature of bureaucracy reflects the concept of a specially recruited group appointed on the basis of merit to produce rational and efficient methods of working. A system of recruitment that admits only those that can demonstrate the required level of expertise and competence is bound to produce organisations which lay politicians find it difficult to dominate.

Dependency

Another source of power is dependency. Effective administration is a necessary if not sufficient condition for planned change in developing countries (Abernethy, 1971, p. 94). In so far as the state has been at the forefront of planning change in economy and society through programmes of investment, education, family planning, nutrition, sanitation and the like, it has been dependent for the success of those plans upon a powerful and effective administration. It is one thing for a government to pass a decree that, for example, unpaid labour is to be abolished. The subsequent land reform programme requires thousands of land-titles to be registered, compensations to be settled and paid, and disputes to be processed and adjudicated upon. Without officialdom, nothing is implemented. What the politicians might win through electoral support or force of arms has to be consolidated by administrative proceedings and by the multitude of development programmes formulated by governments in the Third World.

Status

A third source of bureaucratic power, recognised long ago by Weber, is the social esteem and status enjoyed by senior bureaucrats. This may originate from a number of different sources – the public's acknowledgement of the impartiality of the public service, or of its professional expertise; and the legacy of colonialism when, particularly in the rural areas, officials stood at the apex of the power structure and when the post-colonial officials inherited the posts, pay scales and perks of the colonial expatriates, so inheriting the same prestige and status in the community. When also there are few other opportunities for educated people to find employment, posts in the public service become the goal of the technocratic élite. For many years the private sector could not offer the opportunities which government service could and still does in many societies of the Third World. Even egalitarian ideology is no match for the bureaucrat's drive for prestige and status, as Meillasoux showed in the case of Mali:

> officially, all distinctions of castes or slavery were abolished and no mention could be made of inferior status in an official document. Marriage prohibitions between castes or classes were removed; monogamy was encouraged. Although these policies were actively supported by the minority of young literate people forming the rank and file of the US–RDA, majority popular prejudices were stronger and contributed to confine the bureaucracy to the traditional way of living. Attempts by party members (of high rank but low status) to marry outside their condition were definitely suppressed even by the most progressive leaders. Polygamy was widely practised among the top political personnel. Indeed, a tendency to imitate the traditional forms of power crept in among the leaders, both as a means to impress the masses and as an excuse to neglect democratic practices. Ties with prestigious ancestors were emphasized and invented. (1970, p. 107)

Employment in the national government also offers the tempting possibility of secondment to an international bureaucracy of a UN agency such as the FAO, UNDP or WHO, with the World Bank, the IMF or even a regional organisation such as the OAS or the ECLA. The universal values that are disseminated through such movements and contacts further enhance the élite status of bureaucrats in their own countries. This may lead to a bureaucracy which performs a kind of hegemonic role disseminating an ideology and a particular view of the state and its role in development. In the functionalist literature this has been especially identified as aimed at national integration through the enunciation of universalistic, Westernised and modern values. Bureaucrats were identified as pulling countries along the path to progress. They not only influence the policy choices of governments but also the way people outside government perceive the role of the state in development.

The weakness of other political institutions

A fourth factor was alluded to in the earlier discussion of the post-colonial state. This is the relative power of the bureaucracy as a political institution *vis-à-vis* others (Wallis, 1989, pp. 24–30). This perception is common to both Marxist and functionalist political science. The functionalist position was first put most persuasively by Riggs (1963). A very similar line of argument appears in Alavi's neo-Marxist analysis of Pakistan and Bangladesh (1972). Both schools of thought emphasise that one colonial legacy was the retarded development of political institutions that might have held the bureaucracy accountable. Colonialism developed bureaucracies at the expense of other institutions. It was more interested in the power of officials in relation to society than in the power of representative assemblies, political parties, pressure groups and other organisations representative of different sections of society and expected to evolve into institutions capable of controlling the bureaucratic apparatus of the state.

Colonialism left behind a well-organised bureaucracy which new governments had to staff with their own people, often in the context of a great shortage of qualified indigenous manpower. Crash programmes of training were launched to produce people capable of replacing the expatriates who were not invited to stay on and assist the newly independent governments to function. New states thus inherited bureaucracies that were prestigious, well-organised and with a strong sense of corporate identity, and other political institutions lacking the same power and legitimacy. As party organisations became stronger, this situation changed. As mass parties threw up leaders not dependent upon the bureaucracy but on mass support at elections, and the longer that parliamentary institutions had to establish themselves, the stronger techniques for controlling the bureaucracy grew. The more that groups outside the state, in business, agriculture, the labour movement, and the professions developed and produced their own organisations, the more the bureaucracy was further held accountable to other groups of policy-makers.

However, the political power of the bureaucracy is not necessarily matched by administrative competence. It frequently has to work with inadequate information, particularly statistical. The fact that it monopolises policy-relevant knowledge does not mean that it will have the quantity of skilled manpower for the tasks allotted to it. It may be reluctant for political reasons to complete projects started under the preceding political leadership (Milne, 1972). Riggs argued long ago that the greater the political power of the bureaucracy, the weaker the incentives for effective administration and the more ineffectual the bureaucracy. He also claimed that *efficiency* varied inversely with the weight of bureaucratic power, largely as a result of the imbalance between bureaucracies and other political institutions and the consequent preoccupation among bureaucrats with furthering their bureaucratic interests rather than serving political masters (Riggs, 1964).

Riggs also found historical and contemporary evidence to support the conclusion that bureaucratic power and expansion had adverse consequences for the development of political systems. The merit system, represented most strongly by bureaucratic recruitment methods, undermines one of the strongest supports of an emergent party system, namely the 'spoils' of office. Bureaucratic centralism and control of local governments weaken the educative effects of political participation. The bureaucratic mobilisation of interest groups weakens centres of autonomous political pressure. Parliamentary legislative institutions cannot thrive on a foundation of weak parties, pressure groups and popular participation. Bureaucracies rather than parliaments control revenue raising, expenditure and policy initiatives. Bureaucratic 'formalism', whereby laws are enacted but not implemented, further undermines representative institutions. The judicial system, lacking popular support, can be exploited by the bureaucracy to assist its abuse of power. Riggs concluded that 'too rapid expansion of the bureaucracy when the political system lags behind tends to inhibit the development of effective politics . . . separate political institutions have a better chance to grow if bureaucratic institutions are relatively weak' (1963, p. 126).

Heeger argues that the bureaucracy can positively discourage the development of institutions which can ensure accountability and function as alternative policy-making bodies. The development process of different political institutions such as bureaucracies and parties are not separate and unrelated. In effect the bureaucracy has been known to create political vacuums for it to fill itself. In post-independence Pakistan, for example:

> civil servants were allowed to dominate the national and provincial governments completely, a situation which considerably hampered efforts to build up the Pakistan Muslim League. . . . Active civil servants and civil servants-turned-politicians occupied the principal political offices at all levels of the Pakistani political system. These élites continually manipulated the party system through their control of government and fragmented the Muslim League beyond repair. . . . The expansion of the bureaucracy in Pakistan seems to have been less a flow into an institutional vacuum than a pre-emption of the offices through which political party institutions could be built. (Heeger, 1973, pp. 605–6)

The functionalists conceptualised this imbalance as 'multifunctionality', arguing that in transitional societies political structures have not become as specialised as they would ultimately when society had become fully modern (for a review see B. C. Smith, 1988, ch. 8). Riggs, for example, saw traditional societies as having a very limited differentiation of structures 'for the wide variety of functions that must be performed in any society. . . . A single set of officials or authorities, as in feudalism, may exercise undifferentiated military, political, administrative, religious and economic functions' (Riggs, 1963, p. 122). The functionalist idea of modernity was that institutions would become increasingly specialised in the functions that they performed. The bureaucracy would become fully specialised in rule application. In advanced societies as defined by the functionalists, power resides with the people and public servants are there to obey orders. Transitional society has political structures that have not become fully specialised, but are multifunctional. It becomes logically possible for bureaucratic structures to perform all the input and output functions of the political system. G. A. Almond, for example, believed the bureaucracy to be one of the most important sources of legislation in non-Western societies and therefore as much concerned with the function of rule-*making* as rule-*application* (Almond, 1960, p. 17). However, there was always difficulty in fitting the behaviour of Third World bureaucrats into the functionalist taxonomy (Smith, B. C., 1988, p. 120).

Marxist social theorists have adopted a different approach to bureaucratic overdevelopment which tries to explain the power of the bureaucracy in class terms; if not seeing the bureaucracy as a new class in its own right, then seeing its role in the state as being related to the class structure. Meillasoux, in his study of Mali, places the bureaucracy in a class context, though adopting at the same time a Weberian perspective in the way he analyses the instruments of power with which the bureaucracy was entrusted by the colonial regime, particularly its expertise. He notes the 'crisis of colonialism' which brought about independence before any viable political structures other than the bureaucracy had had a chance to develop. He also describes the post-independence bureaucracy as using its access to political power to acquire some of the characteristics of a social class. It controlled the infrastructure of the economy; it controlled the means of repression and used them to maintain its dominance, particularly in its conflict with weak indigenous social classes, notably the landed aristocracy and the petty-bourgeois class of traders; above all it created a nationalised sector of the economy which under the label of socialism enabled the economy to be brought under bureaucratic control.

The study of Pakistan and Bangladesh by Alavi reveals the power of a military-bureaucratic oligarchy in mediating the competing interests of the indigenous bourgeoisie. The bureaucracy's power in the state derives from the need for a state which can rise above class conflict in order to manage it and to protect the long-term interests of the established and emerging propertied classes. Alavi also refers to the overdevelopment of the bureaucracy relative to other political institutions. The alliance between the military and the civil bureaucracy at this stage of Pakistan's history was functional to the needs of a state requiring a degree of autonomy from class interests. The result of the 'superstructure' in a colony being overdeveloped in relation to the 'structure' of indigenous social classes is that the colonial state is 'equipped with a powerful bureaucratic-military oligarchy and mechanisms of government'. This is inherited by the post-colonial state. Once freed from direct metropolitan control, this oligarchy is able to extend its dominant power in society, assume a new economic role, proliferate bureaucratic controls and public agencies, manipulate the facade of parliamentary government, and eventually even seize power from the democratic regime, though 'it often prefers to rule through politicians so long as the latter do not impinge upon its own relative autonomy and power'.

Though Alavi insists that the bureaucratic-military oligarchy in Pakistan was in effective command of state power from the inception of the new state, and not only after the *coup d'état* of 1958, he was analysing a military regime for most of the period under consideration. Other writers, using Alavi's theory of relative autonomy in different contexts of class structure and regime type, particularly when the regime is orientated towards socialism, either found it inoperative or in need of modification. For example, when Colin Leys tried to apply Alavi's mode of analysis to Kenya he did not find it appropriate to refer to the state as 'overdeveloped'. He also reminds us that any bureaucracy in the sense of public administration is divided into different branches and strata. Civil servants do not always have identical interests to the managers of state-owned enterprises and the latter 'are especially exposed to the bourgeois values embodied in the technology, management practices, "efficiency" ideology, etc. of the firms they take over' (Leys, 1976, p. 44). The career bureaucrats also need to be distinguished from party officials inserted into the civil administration, particularly in terms of their respective class linkages.

Saul's analysis of East Africa (1974) suggested other important qualifications, because East African societies revealed a greater imbalance between the propertied classes than in South Asia. The weakness of indigenous classes meant that the 'oligarchy' was to a greater extent the instrument of the metropolitan bourgeoisie. Furthermore, the state was so central to the development of economy and society that the personnel of the state enjoyed considerable autonomy from class control. The bureaucracy's privileged access to the economic surplus arising from the role of the state in production gave it an interest comparable to that of a class, especially when control over property combined with political power. Similarly the Tanzanian critic Shivji interpreted the weak social classes of Tanzania as having allowed a 'ruling clique' to become a 'bureaucratic bourgeoisie' consisting of ministers, senior civil servants, high military and police officers and high-level party bureaucrats. This 'bureaucratic bourgeoisie' developed from being essentially politico-administrative with a regulative role in the economy to being, after the Arusha Declaration, the 'dominant actors in the economy': 'political power and control over property now came to rest in the same class' (Shivji, 1976, p. 85).

Obviously interpretations of the political power of the bureaucracy depend upon the ideological position of the regime under analysis and the consequent structure of the economy and property relations, whether predominantly capitalist or socialist. The extent of public ownership is a major influence on the social and political development of the bureaucracy as a political force (see below, pp. 235–6).

Other authorities have qualified the post-colonial model by seeing it as a passing phase and one that in some Third World societies has been left behind – notably in India, where the colonial administration was overdeveloped and had enormous prestige supported by a complex ideology of racial superiority, paternalism, and tolerance of indigenous institutions deemed to be compatible with metropolitan interests. But after independence a fairly well-established Indian middle class increasingly articulated its interests through the formal institutions of political democracy. Arguing from the basis of a case-study of the Kosi Development Region of North-East Bihar, Wood shows that administrative behaviour in post-colonial India had become increasingly bureaucratic and instrumental 'as a response to the emergence of legislatures, political parties, and new forms of class differentiation which together have functioned to undermine the autonomy of the state administrative apparatus' (Wood, G. D., 1977, p. 307). In particular, a class of capitalist farmers had emerged as dominant in the formation of agrarian policies. The establishment of democratic institutions meant a loss of authority, power and status for the bureaucracy. To protect itself from class interests seeking to oppose reforms by undermining administrative authority, the bureaucracy retreated into ideologies of professionalism, instrumentalism and neutrality. It was obstructed in this partly by the power of those who dominated the agrarian political structure and partly by the bureaucracy's own class and caste interests. Indeed, bureaucrats attempted to compensate for their loss of status as administrators by asserting their status as members of prestigious castes. Class interests were pursued through property investments, corruption, patronage, nepotism and discrete partisan affiliations.

Continuity

A final source of administrative power is bureaucratic stability or the continuity of the bureaucratic élite compared with other political élites. Governments come and go, *coups* bring about changes of regime, but the bureaucracy remains. Other élites come to be dependent on it: 'it seldom occurs to the men leading a *coup* to throw the administrators out' (Abernethy, 1971, p. 95). In the case of Pakistan, it seems that the bureaucracy has been in control from the very inception of 'military' rule (Alavi, 1990, pp. 48–9). Under conditions of political instability the continuity of the bureaucracy enhances its power. It is impossible to dispense with it as an institution and often extremely difficult to replace its personnel with those who have the ideological commitment needed by the leaders of a new government or regime, especially if administrative expertise is monopolised by the old guard.

4. The class position of the bureaucracy

Political power has been discussed in terms of the resources and assets at the disposal of bureaucrats. There has also been the claim that the bureaucracy is more than just an institution with power, but is developing socially in a particular way – as a new kind of class, and a ruling class at that. This has long been a controversy among historians of bureaucratic development, especially in the Soviet Union and East European states (for a survey see Smith, B. C., 1988, pp. 107–18). There are a number of reasons why this conclusion has been reached for some Third World states.

The main reason is that some developing countries have had what has been called a bureaucratic mode of production. The bureaucracy controls and manages the means of production through the state. It provides the necessary organisation. It proliferates opportunities for bureaucratic careers by the creation of public bodies needing public managers – marketing boards, development corporations and other parastatal organisations and their subsidiaries (Hirschmann, 1981). It articulates an ideology of state ownership and planning. It organises the means of its own reproduction by passing on to the offspring of bureaucrats disproportionately advantageous opportunities to obtain the qualifications needed for entry into bureaucratic occupations and therefore the new class.

In Tanzania, for example, African Socialism is a special ideology that justifies public ownership and bureaucratic management and direction of, at the very least, the commanding heights of the economy. If the state controls most of the economic surplus created rather than leaving it to be privately appropriated, and where surplus extraction is through institutions that are part of the state apparatus, the bureaucracy is said to be acting in relation to the means of production in a way analogous to a property-*owning* ruling class. In Tanzania this argument has been taken to the extent of saying that it is the bureaucracy that not only manages on behalf of the public the means of production through state-owned enterprises, but also controls the different prices of the factors of production to ensure that direct producers generate a surplus which the bureaucracy then accumulates and deploys. Removing the rights of workers to strike, initiating government controls of the trade unions, imposing statutory wage ceilings, engaging in manpower planning, taking control of agricultural marketing, and controlling the prices paid to agricultural producers, are all part of the bureaucracy's control over the means of production and the surplus created (Shivji, 1976).

The expertise which the bureaucracy has can be seen as another factor of production, in addition to land, labour and capital. The bureaucracy supplies the organisations necessary and the managerial, scientific and technical knowledge required. It takes over that legacy of colonialism in which the bureaucracy dominated embryonic indigenous classes. The bureaucracy monopolises organisation and all its attributes necessary for the management of the economy. It articulates an ideology in support of this. Any mode of production requires a set of ideas to justify control of the surplus by the ruling element in society. In Tanzania the ideology has been African Socialism (Stein, 1985), but different brands of socialism have been articulated by leaders in other parts of the Third World: Mali's version of socialism has similarly acted as a justification for state-directed development.

There are, then, bureaucratic features which have been taken to be signs of the emergence of a new kind of ruling class. The fact that ownership resides with society and not the bureaucracy is taken to be a legalistic fiction. Control is what matters, as indeed has been said about capitalism – that the managers not the owners of corporate assets are the power-holders. In addition there is the ability to restrict access to the bureaucratic stratum from outside by increasingly supplying new recruits from bureaucratic families. This is assisted by the accumulation of personal wealth made possible by a career in the bureaucracy. Hirschmann describes how the salaries enjoyed by the upper ranks in many African states, their easy access to credit, and their control over permits, licences and tenders have enabled them to acquire urban and rural real estate and business ventures (Hirschmann, 1981).

This line of argument has been deployed in relation to developing societies that have adopted some form of socialism, and especially Tanzania, which has been more exposed to this type of analysis than any other comparable country. Tanzania has bred a particular kind of political analyst in its universities and development institutes who have taken a radical and critical look at the Tanzanian experience and found indications of the creation of a new kind of ruling class that monopolises the means of repression and exploits the producers at the point of production. Rights are thus acquired over the economic surplus which is then allocated bureaucratically.

The greater the degree of public ownership the stronger the new class will appear to be. But even in societies such as the NICs of South East Asia and Latin America, the state and the bureaucracy has been highly interventionist. Even when the ideology has been predominantly capitalist and free-market, the state has intervened to support private capital. Such different combinations of administrative roles and social formations remind us once again, as Leys did using African experience, that the class interests of the state bureaucracy will not necessarily be an indication of the class character of the state. For Leys the dominant class in African society in the 1970s was the *foreign* bourgeoisie. Any class interests which the personnel of the state might have will only be reflected in state policy in a secondary way (Leys, 1976). Senior members of the bureaucracy might be able to embourgeoise themselves through the opportunities to acquire property made available by their official positions, siphoning off 'a large part of the economic surplus that is generated in society to accumulate wealth for themselves' (Alavi, 1990, p. 23) and even enjoy substantial social mobility for themselves and their families as a result, but this alone does not amount to evidence of the emergence of a new class structure.

5. Bureaucracy, rationality and access

If we reconsider the different meanings attached to bureaucracy, and in particular bureaucracy as a certain kind of rationality, we find that in the context of the bureaucratic allocation of scarce resources rationality takes on a special political significance. High levels of need, particularly among the poorer sections of society but also among other sections, such as private capital, mean that the bureaucracy has to allocate scarce resources according to its own politically determined categories of need. The market is not left to make such allocations, it is done through official action.

The needs of poor people are not being met by the market because they do not have the resources to create an effective demand. If the lower strata of society are deemed to be in need – of an income, work, land, health care, agricultural inputs, food, education and so on – it is because they are unable to acquire through the market what is required to maintain life at a certain officially designated standard. If the policy-makers define need in terms of income, for example, steps may be taken to create jobs such as a public works programme into which will be recruited labour from a target group whose need has been officially identified and which the public intervention has been set up to meet. Or the need may be identified as land so that people can support themselves. The policy might then be a land-reform programme which allocates land to the landless or to increase the size of uneconomic holdings by means of official rules determining eligibility. The need might be for shelter which cannot be demanded in the private housing sector. Similarly the private market for education may be beyond the reach of certain categories of people who are politically defined as 'needing' educational provision. Health care is in a similar category. The ways in which development planners identify the needs of different people are extremely numerous. Particular categories of agricultural or industrial producers might be identified as having a need for inputs which should increase levels of productivity. A potentially productive group may be unable to obtain credit in the financial markets because of the lack of secure collateral or ability to repay at the market rate of interest, so the state provides loans at a subsidised rate. The need for increased productivity may be seen in terms of physical inputs such as fertiliser, seeds or equipment, which again will be allocated by the state.

A wide range of state interventions aimed at particular groups of beneficiaries is virtually synonymous with development planning in many parts of the Third World. Those state interventions should be managed bureaucratically by officials acting according to the Weberian model of public service. Rules and regulations will be applied to specific cases. Entitlements to public benefits are created for specified groups. According to bureaucratic theory the intended beneficiaries will be able to identify themselves as such, will be informed of their newly defined rights under a governmental programme and will be able to comprehend the way bureaucratic organisations arrive at final decisions in individual cases. Officials correspondingly behave according to norms which structure the decision-making process, seeking relevant information to test whether specified conditions have been met. The conditions may be numerous and complex. Nevertheless a claim can still be systematically examined to see whether a claimant falls into the category of eligibility or not (Smith, B. C., 1986).

For many people, there is no problem in understanding the way public organisations plan such expenditure and interventions, and the way they make decisions about its allocation. There may be political interference with the process of administrative allocation, leading to deviation from the bureaucratic norm. Allocations may then not be made impartially and according to the rules. It is a highly politicised process, but for the more Westernised and educated sections of society the processes of decision-making are comprehensible. However, for other sections of society in poor, agricultural economies that are in the process of change, bureaucratic methods of decision-making are difficult to adjust to.

In a peasant community such bureaucratisation may appear very alien. This is not because people lack intelligence, are irrational or are too backward. It is because bureaucratic rationality does not coincide with peasant rationality. The behaviour of the bureaucrat, who can only deal with information that is relevant to the case that falls within his jurisdiction, may appear very strange in the context of rural society in many parts of the world. To dismiss information about a person's current situation as irrelevant is difficult for a person to accept when they are part of a community in which aspects of different lives interact. People do not see themselves as standing in a single-stranded relationship with others, but in multi-stranded relationships (Wood, G. D., 1977). A money-lender rather than an agriculture extension officer may be approached for credit, but the relationship with the money-lender will be very different from that with a government official. The multi-stranded relationships of peasant communities combine debt, kinship, tenancy, employment, reciprocity, political factionalism, and patronage. A bureaucrat treating like cases alike and concerning himself exclusively with officially selected aspects of an individual's circumstances is using a peculiarly Westernised form of rationality that rich and educated farmers in the community may be able to appreciate and co-operate with. But poor, illiterate, uneducated and *dependent* members of the community, at whom the programmes of public expenditure may have been specifically and deliberately targeted, may find the process difficult to adapt to. A bureaucrat cannot be approached in a multi-stranded way. Other aspects of an individual's economic and family circumstances which are currently all-pervading will be defined as irrelevant to the bureaucrat. Needs will have been defined in terms of officially selected attributes of a person's existence. The claimant, on the other hand, will not want to present a case. He will want to present a story about the integrated parts of his whole existence.

Bureaucrats perhaps should not be surprised to discover that their programmes do not have the impact which the policy-makers hoped for. Resources provided by officialdom are often used to satisfy what the beneficiaries regard as more pressing needs (Wood, G. D., 1977). Nor should they be surprised that the intended beneficiaries do not come forward and claim their rights. Entering a government programme may be risky if it involves disengaging from the traditional obligations of the community. If the bureaucratic allocation fails to work as intended and if one has removed oneself from the local community and no longer seeks the protection, assistance and reciprocity of local relationships, the consequences could be disastrous. A position of dependency and even exploitation may be preferred to the position of recipient of a state programme.

Pressures on the bureaucrat, on the other hand, may mean that the resources to be allocated are not received by the target group but instead find their way to other destinations. They may be allocated to those who can produce the results which can be translated into the levels of administrative performance that the officials need to demonstrate to their superiors. Bureaucrats need to be able to demonstrate success. To achieve this they swing their attention towards the groups that they think will be able to use the resources as intended. These are likely to be farmers who have experience of modern agricultural techniques and the commercial foundation needed for the resources to be used as they were intended. Bureaucrats will have a certain amount of discretion and will use it as far as possible to satisfy the needs of political and administrative superiors. Different classes, particularly in the rural areas of poor societies, vary in their ability to secure resources from the development programmes that are administered bureaucratically in their localities.

In addition to bias in agricultural development *policies* towards the needs and capacities of capitalist farmers, and the bias in *implementation* arising from the power of wealthy farmers to use the law courts, the police, the local bureaucracy and patronage to block land reforms and manipulate other public programmes, there is a third dimension of bias arising from the appropriateness of administrative *procedures*. The bureaucratic rationality on which such administration is based is not that of the poor peasant, whose rationality is

'derived from their poverty which is at variance with the model of them held by bureaucratic administration. . . . In this situation there is a discontinuity of values between official and client. The former is seeking the security of compartmentalized bureaucratic behaviour and the latter the familiar safety of low status in a known system. (Wood, G. D., 1984, p. 352)

Since it is the capitalistic, rationally economic, literate and market orientated *farmer* who corresponds to the model of behaviour on which bureaucratically administered programmes are predicated, such programmes will inevitably favour him rather than the survival-orientated, indebted, dependent, marginal and vulnerable poor peasant.

There is, then, a problem of 'access' about which social scientists have had some important things to say in recent years (Schaffer, 1973; Schaffer and Lamb, 1974; Schaffer and Huang Wen-hsien, 1975; Lamb and Schaffer, 1981. For a survey see Smith, B. C., 1988, ch. 11). It is a problem experienced by some social classes more than others. As such it affects the allocation of resources in society away from the egalitarian objectives of much development planning. In so far as bureaucracy again determines its own consequences, it provides yet another reason for placing it at the centre of our analysis of Third World politics.

6. Conclusion

In this chapter definitions of bureaucracy have been used to structure an examination of its political role in Third World states. The definition of bureaucracy as a form of government stands in stark contrast to the definition in terms of a neutral administrative instrument. The former rests on a perception of bureaucracy as being able to exercise power in its own right, either relative to other political institutions of parliamentary democracy or party government, or as a consequence of having usurped them in alliance with the military, or as having emerged as a new kind of politically *and* economically dominant class. The definition of bureaucracy as rational administration opposes the pejorative definition in terms of procedural rigidity. Both have great political significance in that they reflect a style of public administration that has serious implications for the distribution of resources and ultimately power between social classes, especially in poor, mainly agrarian societies.

10
Military Intervention in Politics

1. Introduction

Direct military intervention in the politics of Third World countries has been a depressingly regular occurrence since the high-water mark of post-war independence. Between 1960 and 1980 three-quarters of Latin American states experienced *coups*, as did half of the Third World Asian states and over half of the African states (Clapham, 1985, p. 137; see also Woddis, 1977, pp. 7–10). The 1980s saw the trend continue strongly. Not a year passed without there being a *coup* or an attempted *coup* in some part of the Third World. Since 1948 there has been at least one *coup* attempt per developing country every five years (World Bank, 1991, p. 128). So far in the 1990s there have been *coups* or attempted *coups* in Chad (1990), Togo (1991), Peru, Sierra Leone and Haiti (1992), Guatemala and Nigeria (1993) and Gambia (1994).

Thirty years ago expectations were very different (Wells, 1974; Charlton, 1981). Military intervention in politics, including the *coup d'état*, was nothing new in historical terms, but that it should became such a remarkably common occurrence in Third World states surprised and dismayed many national politicians and outside observers, including Western social scientists who had shared the view that the military was unlikely to be a threat to civilian regimes. In the late 1950s and early 1960 many social scientists were fairly confident that though the military might be a problem in Latin America, conditions were so different in other regions of the world, including Africa, that it was unlikely to be so there. It was widely believed that there was little chance in the newly-independent states of the world that the military would play other than a constitutional role in politics. The organisation of the military and the circumstances in those countries were not such that it need be feared that the military would perform any other role than that of professional servants of the state. Yet no sooner had the complacency been expressed than events were to prove such optimistic predictions false. In one African state another civilian government succumbed to the military, and in other parts of the Third World military support became a necessary condition of regime survival even if the military did not take over complete and direct power.

The question soon arose in social science circles as to why the military became the political force that it did in so many newly-independent Asian and African countries and remained a dominant force in Latin America, despite its longer experience of independence and economic development. In particular, attention focused on the *coup d'état* and how, often with apparent ease (First, 1972, pp. 4–6), the military is able to supplant civilian regimes. This is the problem with which this chapter is concerned. It does not deal with what kind of government the military is capable of providing a Third World country with once it has taken control by force (an important theoretical framework for the analysis of this question is to be found in Clapham and Philip, 1985).

No single explanation has achieved total acceptance, as might be expected with such a complex phenomenon occurring in such widely differing societies (Dowse, 1969, p. 217). Many of the explanations produced of military intervention have dwelt more on why the preceding civilian regimes were so fragile and unstable, almost taking it for granted that if a civilian regime collapses in less developed societies the military will inevitably be the successor. In the context of underdevelopment this is not an altogether unwarranted assumption. In some circumstances of political instability the military 'represent the only effectively organised element capable of competing for political power and formulating public policy' (Pye, 1966, p. 283). A more recent example of this assumption is O'Kane (1981). Other explanations, however, have looked at the problem in terms of the political advantages which the military enjoy under such conditions.

2. Forms of intervention

The main focus of academic interest has been supplantment – the act of taking political control by force and replacing civilian institutions with military leadership forming a self-appointed junta with absolute power unconstrained by any civilian political institutions. Government is then by decree. Constitutional niceties such as parliamentary procedures, popular consent, or political representation are ignored, because elected assemblies are dissolved immediately upon taking power, elections are suspended, and political parties are abolished. Some constitutional principles might be observed if it is judged necessary to obtain a modicum of legitimacy, such as leaving the judiciary intact, with the power to declare on the legality of some administrative decisions. But supplantment may be defined as the substitution of a civilian regime by a military one by means of armed coercion.

The political influence of the military

This is by no means the only role which the military can perform. It is an important organised interest or pressure group in all states. It is one of the best endowed organisations in terms of access to the state apparatus. The military leadership is always incorporated into the machinery of government through various consultative and executive arrangements such as defence councils, advisory committees, and the close working relationships between top political, bureaucratic and military personnel. In no system of government should the political importance of the military be underestimated. It is an organisation capable of very effective political pressure on behalf of the interests and values that it represents. One of the key questions about the military in politics is how far it has values that extend beyond decisions about how best to defend a country and wage war, to those which express not only a corporate interest in good pay, good conditions, and the highest level of weapons technology but also a sense of how society should be organised. In Indonesia, for example, the military sees itself as having a political as well as a military role, one that requires it to protect the unity and integrity of the nation against regionalism and sectarianism. Such values can be a critical factor in the decision and ability to intervene more overtly in politics than merely as adviser to governments on defence policy.

Furthermore, in its normal constitutional role the military is very difficult to subject to democratic control and accountability because it is so easy for it to surround itself with secrecy and so avoid parliamentary scrutiny. This secrecy commonly extends far beyond what it is necessary to keep from potential or actual foreign aggressors, to include detailed financing of expensive projects for which the taxpayer has to pay.

The power behind the throne

Another form of intervention is when the military displaces one civilian regime and replaces it with another. A refusal to act as the instrument of the government against its opponents is one way in which the military can bring about a change of government (Woddis, 1977, p. 23). In any revolution control of the army is a vital factor. This was clearly the case in the Iranian revolution and could be so in Algeria if the Islamic revolt gathers momentum. Already there are signs that the lower ranks of the army are reluctant to fire on demonstrators. Whether a new regime has control of the army and can use military power against remnants of the *ancien regime* is a critical factor determining the outcome of a period of revolutionary upheaval. Changes of government resulting from the military switching its allegiance from one group of political leaders to another can also occur and have frequently done so in recent Latin American history. The military is often the power behind the throne. Clear examples of this are also found in Southeast Asia, where in both Indonesia and Thailand the military has long been the final arbiter in political conflict. The Suharto regime in Indonesia has been backed by the military for over twenty-five years. In Thailand, changes of government are usually brought about by the military replacing one civilian prime minister with another, as in 1991.

When military regimes hand back power to civilian politicians, it is often to people of their own choosing in a constitution of their own design. In Chile, for example, the Pinochet regime created a constitution in which the military has veto powers. The civilian government has to be extremely careful in what it does. It operates within a set of rules that allows the military to justify any future intervention which it deems desirable. The courts have been 'packed' with supporters of the Pinochet regime, so that the decisions of the civilian government are adjudicated upon by people favourably disposed towards the policies of the junta. Civilian politics in developing countries is often a veneer behind which lies military power that is ready to take full control.

3. Explaining military intervention

Much of the research that has been done on the military in Third World politics has been from a macro and quantitative standpoint. Here the literature is based on statistical analysis of a large number of countries which are ranked by variables that measure levels of instability or military intervention. These are then correlated with socio-economic factors that seem likely to have explanatory value. A good example of the genre is Wells' study of 31 countries in Sub-Saharan Africa in 1970. Wells related, through multivariate analysis, social and economic variables to military *coups* in order to explain why some African countries had experienced them and others had not. Population size and growth rate, urbanisation, literacy, mass-media availability, GNP per capita, economic growth rate and measures of 'centrality' (the geographical concentration of political and economic life) were taken as relevant indicators of social and economic conditions that might be thought a priori to be related to the likelihood of military intervention. Indicators of the size of the military and police force, and of defence expenditure, were used to establish the significance of organisational characteristics in military intervention. The level of loans from the USA was taken as indicative of external influence on vulnerability to the *coup d'état*. The results were disappointingly inconclusive. Even combining all the independent variables only explained 56 per cent of the variation in *coup* activity. The final explanatory model produced owed more to case studies than statistical analysis (Wells, 1974).

Problems of quantitative analysis

This is fairly typical of the problems that are encountered when making quantitative statistical analyses to explain and predict military *coups* (Dowse, 1969, pp. 217–22; Jackman, 1986; Johnson *et al.*, 1986; O'Kane, 1986). First there is the question of which states should be included in the analysis. Were colonies 'states'? Should they have been included in the populations at risk from military intervention as they have been in some analyses? Statistical explanations require the rule of *ceteris paribus* to be satisfied, so the cases compared have to have things other than military intervention equal. With nation states 'other things' are hardly ever 'equal'. Grouping together 'Black African states', for example, could be said to produce heterogeneity rather than homogeneity. Aggregating a meaningfully comparable collection of countries produces problems, the solutions to which do not repay the effort put into finding them.

The second source of doubt about such analysis is how far the specific measurable variables chosen represent dependent and independent factors such as social mobilisation, characteristics of the military itself, degrees of political development, international economic dependence and so on. For example, how well do 'voter turnout' or 'degree of multi-partyism' represent 'political development' as an independent variable? How satisfactory is the total of US loans and credit in a single year as an indicator of the external influences that might encourage a military take-over? The weak conceptual foundation of much multivariate analysis can result in unjustifiable conclusions being drawn from the statistical results.

Thirdly, measures used as dependent and independent variables should cover the same time periods, otherwise temporal variation introduces problems of 'simultaneity bias'. How, for example, can it reasonably be claimed that 'party fractionalisation' in 1975 caused *coups* starting fifteen years earlier, especially when the military commonly banish political parties and therefore determine themselves the level of pluralism (or 'fractionalisation') in the political system?

Fourthly, there are tautological pitfalls that await the quantitative analyst, when some part of what is to be explained is contained within the definition of the *explicandum* (the explanatory or independent variable). An example is when 'increased military expenditure' is used as an independent variable but has resulted from military domination of the state, the dependent variable that is to be explained by expenditure on the military. The same problem is found in the attempt discussed later to explain military *coups* by reference to the level of the political culture in a society, when political culture is defined by reference to a lack of consensus, evidence for which is found in the failure of the civilian system to withstand military supplantment.

The use of doubtful indicators of the variables under consideration and the unwillingness of researchers to replicate each others' methods in different regions undoubtedly accounts, along with the problems of correlational analysis already mentioned, for the widespread dissatisfaction with this mode of analysis. However, it would be wrong to be too dismissive, either on the grounds that there are no identifiable patterns of military intervention – that it is totally random – or that statistical comparisons and correlations force the use of indicators of political, social and economic development that are of doubtful validity. Quantitative analysis generate interesting hypotheses. The fact that so far they have produced nothing more conclusive and leave us still needing a convincing theory – and are probably incapable of meeting these needs – possibly explains some of the frustration and irritation which they engender.

4. A typology of *coups*

However, such analysis may be able to generate some hypotheses which can be useful in guiding the investigation of specific cases. The factors which have been causally associated with the *coup d'état* will be taken in turn in order to clarify the hypotheses which have been formulated and which may prove fruitful in the analysis of specific cases in the future. These factors may be grouped into social, economic, political, organisational and international categories. But first it is useful to classify the major types of military *coup*. Huntington (1962 and 1968) provides the following typology.

- the governmental or **guardian coup** – for example, Nigeria in 1966, 1979, 1983 and 1993 after the military annulled the elections, placed a civilian in the presidency and then took back full control after a general strike and High Court ruling that the government of the military's puppet was illegal. The military's role is one of guardianship in the sense that the new regime leaves the prevailing economic system intact, brings about little fundamental change in government policy, and bases its right to rule on the claim that its task is to provide a period of stability before handing power back to civilians. The leadership of the government is changed, but not the social or political structure. Perlmutter sees this type of *coup* as the result of an 'arbitrator army' which accepts the existing social order, creates no independent political organisation, and expresses an intention to return to barracks once the civilian disputes are settled or an alternative and acceptable regime is established (Perlmutter, 1971, pp. 315–18).

- the **veto coup** – for example, Chile in 1973 and Haiti in 1991 when the army ousted President Aristide, Haiti's first democratically elected President who, because of his liberationist theology and reformist programme was idolised by the poor and hated by the rich and their military allies. Here 'veto' refers to the military supplanting a civilian government that is committed to radical social and economic reform that will be to the cost of the wealthier classes in society.

- a sub-set of the 'veto' *coup* is the **anticipatory veto**, when the military intervene to pre-empt power passing to a revolutionary or radical government as distinct from the overthrow of an existing progressive and reformist government. Ajub Khan's *coup* in Pakistan in 1958 may be seen as one to pre-empt the electoral success of a left-wing party (Woddis, 1977, pp. 66–8). Similarly in Algeria in 1991, when the Islamic Salvation Front, with a programme of social change, won twice as many votes as its nearest rival in the first of two ballots and the military cancelled the second round, appointed a 'High State Council', and embarked on repression of the fundamentalist movement. Burma in 1990 is another example.

- the **reforming coup,** when the military seeks to change the social order and place state and society on a new ideological foundation. Perlmutter distinguishes three sub-types within what he calls the ruler-type praetorian army which rejects the existing order, challenges its legitimacy and creates its own political organisation to legitimise and maximise military control over the state: (i) the anti-traditionalist, radical reformer (for example, Argentina, 1945–55); (ii) the anti-traditionalist, anti-radical reformer (for example, Nasser's Egypt); and (iii) the anti-traditional, republican reformer (for example, Turkey under Ataturk).

5. Social explanations

Social mobility

Social explanations of military intervention have focused mainly on the destabilising effects of social mobility. As societies become more open and fluid, people can use the opportunities provided by new economic activities and institutions to change their status in society. Wealth, education and skills confer status on groups that in traditional society had lacked such opportunities. Social mobilisation is followed by political mobilisation as the new socio-economic interests brought into existence as a result of modernisation, particularly in the economy, seek effective means of expression within the political system. Such political mobilisation will be encouraged by the democratic milieu and participative ethos of post-colonial society.

Some analysts of military intervention have argued that the social mobility following the spread of industrialisation and its associated developments in education, urbanisation, mass communications and the commercialisation of all walks of economic life, including agrarian society, increases the rate of political participation and mobilisation and places intolerable burdens of conflict management on civilian regimes. The division of society into more complex groups and structures has to be politically articulated through unions, voluntary associations, political parties, professional bodies, trade associations, industrial bodies, and chambers of commerce. These are rarely sufficiently developed for the task. Political resources become spread over a larger number of actors than in traditional societies where a privileged minority has command of political decision-making. In modern society power becomes more dispersed, at least in principle if not in practice. Expectations of a more equal dispersal of power are aroused. This is reflected in the right to vote and to share in the selection of political leaders. Such participation needs institutions through which it can operate in a structured and ordered way. Procedures and organisations have to be created through which political demands can be expressed effectively and decisions can be made which will be regarded as legitimate and binding. Processes of government represent the latter kind of organisation. Parties and pressure groups represent the former, required for people to protect and promote their interests effectively.

The propensity for military intervention will be reduced, the more such institutionalisation occurs (Huntington, 1968; Perlmutter, 1971). The higher the levels of social mobilisation, the higher the levels of political participation. If this is accompanied by the development of organisations through which political participation can be channelled, the population will develop a commitment to their civilian institutions and regime (see Chapter 13). They will see them as effective means of obtaining access to power and the resources that follow from it. The military will not find themselves in an environment conducive to their intervention, over and above that of a technical and professional élite in whose hands a major function of the state rests, that of national defence.

There is a related technological argument. Social mobility results from changes in the level of economic development. This not only increases the wealth and political significance of a wide range of groups with an interest in preserving civilian forms of government. It also increases the technological complexity of government and puts it beyond the grasp of the military.

A problem with such theories is that they are of too high a level of generality because they try to provide a framework that can encompass all instances of military intervention (Dowse, 1969). As soon as one tries to apply them to specific countries, all sorts of exceptions and variations begin to appear (see, for example, Philip, 1984). However, the hypothesis that rapid social change will lead to political violence and military intervention has received some support from comparative studies (Jackman, 1976; Johnson *et al.*, 1984).

The military and the middle class

Social explanations of military intervention have sometimes had a class dimension. Social mobilisation leads to the development of a middle class. The more developed the indigenous middle class, the stronger the political foundation of civilian democracy. The middle class is seen by modernisation theorists as a stabilising force which in the early stages of development is 'small, weak, ineffective, divided and therefore politically impotent'. The economic and political interests of a fragmented middle class diverge, thereby encouraging 'praetorianism' or a potential for the military to dominate the political system (Perlmutter, 1971, p. 309).

Perlmutter explained the lack of alternatives to the military when social cohesion breaks down by reference to divisions within all sectors of society, including the middle class. In an underdeveloped society 'its various sectors tend to be further fragmented and incapable of mounting unified action even for the narrower benefit of a particular sector'. Praetorianism occurs when the middle class is too weak to defend democratic civilian institutions. But it can equally happen when it is large, growing and more cohesive, as in Latin America where 'military intervention assures the middle class of power if and when they fail to come to power by electoral means' (p. 309). This is consistent with Huntington's view that in societies that are too underdeveloped to have produced a middle class the military will be a radical force (trying to abolish feudalism), but that when a middle class has developed, the military will side with it as a conservative force (Huntington, 1968, p. 221; Jackman, 1976, p. 1080). Unfortunately, attempts to prove this quantitatively have failed, throwing serious doubt on the proposition that the effects of military government change systematically as countries become wealthier.

It might be assumed that a new middle class will have a vested interest in civilian government which represents their interests rather than those of the classes of the pre-industrial era. Putnam tested this hypothesis with data from Latin America. An index of social mobilisation was used to reveal a negative relationship with military intervention. An economic development index was made up of scores from indicators such as GNP per capita, annual rates of growth, and the proportion of the population in industrial employment. Economic development was found to be correlated with social mobility. Controlling for this effect, Putnam found that economic development was moderately positively correlated with intervention. A middle-class index, based on the percentage of the population classified as in the middle or upper social strata, was correlated with military intervention and confirmed the obstacle which such social development produces to military intervention. A country equal to another in terms of its level of economic development will be less prone to military intervention if it is more socially mobilised. If two countries are equal in their levels of social mobility and one has had more economic development, it will be more likely to experience a *coup* (Putnam, 1967).

The findings for political development were more surprising. If constitutional restrictions on the military can be taken as reflecting public commitment to civilian rule, they nevertheless were unrelated to military intervention. Putnam acknowledged that this might be because constitutions and popular aspirations are unrelated. Military intervention was related statistically to political participation and the strength of parties and pressure groups, but the correlations were negligible, leading Putnam to conclude that Huntington was mistaken in thinking that stable civilian rule depends on strong political institutions (p. 107).

Jackman carried out a similar type of analysis, using African data from 1960 to 1975, but came to rather different conclusions: notably that social mobilisation has a destabilising effect and that political participation, when measure by electoral turnout, decreases the probability of *coups*, suggesting the conclusion that '*political* mobilisation in the form of higher levels of mass electoral participation may reflect a higher degree of acceptance of conventional non-violent processes of élite succession' (Jackson, 1978, p. 1274). Johnson *et al.* also found party competition, especially between mass parties with nationwide rather than ethnic or regional support, to be strong protection against military intervention (1984, p. 634).

An alternative interpretation of the significance of class development is to see it as a source of fragility in civilian institutions. The key development is not that there is a new middle class, but that there can be conflict between factions within the middle class particularly under conditions of dependency and underdevelopment. Such conflict has often preceded the *coups* that have been staged in the Third World. The very category of a 'guardian' *coup* reflects awareness of this possibility. This may be accounted for by the centrality of political power to the needs and interests of the middle class in less developed societies, when capital comes largely from state sources. If sections of the middle class feel disadvantaged by the operation of the political system, they may support its overthrow by a military that is allied to their interests.

If the political consensus and ideological foundation of the system are weak, as was often the case in the immediate post-independence period, when the remnants of pre-capitalist social relations such as forms of feudalism remained in rural areas, support for modern, democratic, civilian institutions can be fragile. The rules of politics are not firmly established in such a context. If one middle-class faction attempts to secure a permanent monopoly of power and therefore of the limited resources available for the generation of wealth, there is a strong temptation for other factions to resort to extra-constitutional means to gain power. This is the classic Bonapartist scenario where the pure form of bourgeois rule through liberal democratic institutions is impossible to sustain during crisis, and where other classes become increasingly difficult to manage and incorporate into the social order, again because of a weak ideological base.

The 'crisis of hegemony' in post-colonial societies to which a form of Bonapartism responds includes conflicts between tribes and regions as well as interests founded on pre-capitalist, capitalist and *comprador* class structures. Military intervention often represents a way of managing such conflict rather than a way of profoundly changing the power structure of society. In many instances *coups* just 'speed the circulation of élites and the realignment of factions of the ruling classes more often than they bring about fundamental change in the organisation of state power and its allocation between (rather than within) social classes' (Luckham, 1991, p. 368).

However, Latin American experience suggests the following reasons why the middle class might not feel that its interests are best served by military dictatorship:

- it is fragmented and the military may deny political power to newly emerging factions of the bourgeoisie;
- repression of the workers may reduce the profits derived from mass consumption;
- the state may encroach upon the private sector;
- the intellectual element of the bourgeoisie may have a different ideological position from that of the dictatorship;
- the economic performance of the military regime may be disappointing;
- state oppression of the working class may be costly in its disruption of production;
- bourgeois politicians resent being ousted from power;
- foreign aid and investment may be dependent on showing a democratic face to the world. (Therborn, 1979, pp. 106–9)

Military embourgeoisement

Another plausible class explanation of intervention is that it provides opportunities for social mobility on the part of the armed forces themselves. Take, for example, the 1971 *coup* in Uganda. One interpretation was that the *coup* reflected the interests of the army as a marginalised group subordinate to a post-independence élite based on Westernised educational attainment and the use of English as a *lingua franca*. This excluded the armed forces from élite status because army personnel operated in the vernacular Swahili. The *coup* therefore provided an opportunity for social mobility for an uneducated *lumpen militariat*. Thus without altering the class basis of political power, the *coup* produced a realignment of ruling groups and an opportunity for upward mobility for sections of the political élite not prominent under the previous civilian regime because they were drawn from underprivileged sections of society or regions of the country that had not been a major source of political recruitment for leadership positions. Other examples from Africa would include the 'middle belt' tribes of Nigeria, and the northerners of Togo. Political power for a minority group, especially one with an ethnic identity, has often 'flowed from the barrel of a gun' (First, 1972, p. 435; Lloyd, 1973, pp. 167–8).

Embourgeoisement may take an even more literal form when the senior ranks of the military use their political power after a successful *coup* to enrich themselves with wealth and property. Members of the armed forces can rise from petty-bourgeois status, with social origins among rich peasants, technocrats, intellectuals, state bureaucracy, industrial management and small-scale private capitalists, into the new bourgeoisie through the accumulation of wealth from commissions, corruption, land acquisition and speculation, trade and rents (Woddis, 1977, p. 87).

6. Economic interpretations

Economic development

An alternative explanation, which emphasises the importance of economic factors, sees economic development as securing the stability of civilian regimes. It is a lack of economic development that encourages military intervention. When civilian governments are perceived as having failed to modernise the economy via industrialisation, they run the risk of being ousted by frustrated sections of the modernising élite that are out of office. Evidence to support this is offered by McGowan and Johnson, who examined military intervention in Sub-Saharan Africa between 1956 and 1984, and found that the lower the economic growth and level of industrial employment, the higher the incidence of military intervention in politics. However, as the authors recognise, causation is unlikely to run in one direction: the political instability caused by *coups* hinders economic development. 'We are left with the image of a vicious circle in which economic stagnation and decline lead to military interventions, which themselves in turn usually produce more economic uncertainty and stagnation' (1984, p. 659; see also Johnson *et al.*, 1984, p. 635).

Another theory stresses the significance of economic factors relating to underdevelopment. O'Kane argues that the most important responsibility of a Third World government is for the economy. Certain economic conditions give rise to economic instability. Dependence on primary export products whose world prices can fluctuate wildly produces damaging effects. A lack of a diversified economy means there are no alternative goods and services to offset those fluctuations. Instability arising from such economic specialisation and its trading consequences is conducive to *coups*, because it produces problems which can be blamed on governments. When a very high proportion of tax revenues comes from the export of a single commodity, the terms of trade have an immediate impact on the ability of a government to develop the economy and provide for the welfare of society. Government inevitably is the focus of attention when the value of the country's commodities falls in world markets. So in a country which has a high level of specialisation because of the nature of its exports and a high level of dependence of its economy on those export revenues, the probability of a successful *coup* is increased.

There will always, however, be factors which will reduce the likelihood of a *coup*. First there is the proximity of independence. *Coups* are more likely the longer a country is independent, giving governments time to demonstrate an inability to cope. Secondly, there is the experience of military intervention – what might be called internal contagion. Once a *coup* has occurred, there is likely to be another. A country with no experience of the *coup d'état* is less likely to have one than a country where one has already taken place. The military gain skills in domestic coercion, popular support for government is discouraged by experience under the military, and subsequent periods of civilian rule become increasing difficult to sustain. Thirdly, the presence of foreign troops is an obstacle. They would not be present with the approval of the domestic government in the first place if there was any chance of them being sympathetic to military take-over. Even though there is evidence of foreign powers encouraging rather than hindering *coups*, the presence of foreign troops invited in by the civilian government will deter interventions by the local military. The absence of these three conditions removes the obstacles to military supplantment and increases the probability of a *coup*.

These hypotheses were tested statistically, and not refuted by the data used, leading to the conclusion that 'the *coup d'état* is the drastic response to an unstable and sometimes hopeless economic situation' (O'Kane, 1981). Economic underdevelopment thus leads to conditions conducive to military *coups*. This conclusion lends some support to the explanation that associates the survival of civilian regimes with economic development and the social mobility that accompanies it.

A methodological problem here is to know how recent is 'recent'. Nigeria had five years of civilian government before it succumbed to its first military *coup*. It did not appear to need a long time for government to reveal its inability to cope with the tensions and conflicts of an underdeveloped economy and an ethnically divided society.

7. The political culture

The most influential political explanation of military intervention relates it to the level of the political culture. Finer (1962) classified political cultures as mature, developed, low and minimal in a descending scale of modernity. Each level is related to the propensity of the military to intervene, and to different kinds of military intervention. A mature political culture is one in which the military are an important force in defence policy-making, but have no wider role ascribed to them by social values, attitudes and expectations. A sense of legitimacy supporting the regime is widespread. At the other end of the scale are found countries with 'minimal' political cultures, where the legitimacy of civilian government is almost totally lacking. Such countries are likely to experience the most extreme form of military intervention, the *coup d'état*.

Low levels of political culture and a weak sense of political obligation are found predominantly in the Third World. Here there is a lack of confidence that political demands will be heard, and a lack of trust in other groups which might gain power. Because political values and beliefs do not coincide with the presuppositions upon which the regime is built, there may well be widespread popular support for direct military intervention. The destruction of democracy and the rise of authoritarianism may be tolerable in societies that do not feel that the form of civilian government which they have is the best that could have been devised:

> Where public attachment to civilian institutions is strong, military intervention in politics will be weak. It will take the form, if it occurs at all, of working upon or from behind these institutions – be they throne or parliament – according to the political formula current. By the same token, where public attachment to civilian institutions is weak or non-existent, military intervention in politics will find wide scope – both in manner and substance. (Finer, 1962, p. 21)

Critics of Finer have pointed out that this sounds tautological. A low level of political culture is defined as a lack of consensus. It is defined by reference to what it is supposed to explain. Rather than offering an explanation of a lack of political consensus, the concept of political culture offers a statement that is true by definition. There is further circularity in the argument, in that military intervention is taken to be evidence of a low political culture because it is evidence of the breakdown of consensus. So military intervention is being explained by reference to conditions which are represented by that intervention itself. In so far as there is explanatory value in the theory of political culture, it is more about how civilian governments fail than why the military should be the inevitable successor. Furthermore, the theory does not explain why *coups* occur in some states with minimal political cultures but not others (First, 1972,

p. 14). The only solution to this problem is to make intervention itself an indicator of the level of political culture, but this makes the explanation even more tautologous.

8.   Organisational factors

Knowledge of why the military have usurped power in so many states may depend more on observations of the military itself than the socio-economic context in which Third World governments find themselves. There has been a long-standing debate between the supporters of an 'environmental' approach to military intervention, emphasising the influence of social and economic factors on the propensity for intervention, and the 'organisationalists' (Charlton, 1981, pp. 51–6). The organisational characteristics of the military may be crucial to understanding military intervention, especially when the socio-economic conditions of different countries, such as India and Pakistan, look similar, yet their experience of military intervention has been so markedly different.

Organisational strengths

The military appears to have many political advantages over other organisations involved in politics. 'Even the most poorly organised or maintained of such armies is far more highly and tightly structured than any civilian group' (Finer, 1962, p. 6). It has a clear chain of command, with a well-understood and rigorously observed set of superior–subordinate relationships. Decisions are obeyed, not debated until some consensus is reached. The military is well-organised for striking at civilian institutions. However, when the military intervenes, the leadership of the *coup* is often drawn not from the top-ranking officers but from the middle echelons of younger officers, perhaps because their senior officers are too closely associated with the civilian regime; or because that particular stratum of the officer corps is drawn from an ethnic group that is concerned about the way political power is being used. Even if the decision to stage a *coup* is not taken by the most senior ranking officers, those who do lead the overthrow have at their disposal an organisation that is likely to respond to their commands.

The organisational unity of the military in the Third World should not be exaggerated. They are riven with factions based on age, education, rank and tribe, reflecting divisions within the wider political community (Charlton, 1981, pp. 58–60). The military needs to be viewed as thoroughly integrated into society in this respect and not as a self-contained entity. It is also worth noting that when Putnam tried to test the importance of variations in organisational characteristics to the propensity for intervention, using Latin American data – a difficult feat given the availability of 'only a few gross characteristics of the armed forces' – he found a negative correlation between the size of the military establishment and the extent of military intervention. Of course, as with all such quantitative analysis, it is easy to reject the indicator used on the grounds that it is an unreliable proxy for the variable under investigation (Putnam, 1967, pp. 110–11; Wells, 1974). However, Johnson *et al.* found from their study of politics in thirty-five Black African states between 1960 and 1982 that military 'cohesion' (a large and ethnically homogeneous armed forces) and political 'centrality' (its role in repression against the government's opponents and its share of public expenditure) to be positively related to military intervention, leading them to recommend strongly 'that variables specific to African military establishments must be considered in any search for the structural determinants of military intervention in African politics' (1984, p. 634).

Symbolic status

The military also have a symbolic status which may endow them with legitimacy should they intervene in the world of civilian politics. Without articulating this as part of a corporate philosophy or belief system, the military may symbolise something valuable to the rest of society. They may represent modernity because of their technological expertise, structures of authority, and training. Symbolic status may derive from successful performance. Shortly before the first military *coup* in Nigeria in 1966 the army had been involved in a UN peacekeeping force in the Congo in which it acquitted itself well, gained an international reputation for being well-disciplined and effective, and so brought credit to the country internationally.

Modernity

The apparent modernity of the military, according to some developmentalists such as Pye, is a major reason why the military is an obvious alternative to a democratic government that has failed to function effectively: 'the armies created by colonial administration and by the newly emergent countries have been consistently among the most modernised institutions in their society'. Their rational structures, capable of relating means to ends and associated with rapid technological development and specialist skills, enable them to be viewed as 'possible saviours' where there is 'a sense of failure in the country' (Pye, 1971, pp. 278–83). However, as Mazrui has argued, though the military may be a modern organisation in structural terms, in Africa, where soldiers are frequently recruited from the rural and less Westernised areas,

> the attitudes of the soldiers to the wider society is probably more deeply conditioned by traditionalist sympathies than by the modern characteristics of a particular profession . . . the military as an organisation might in part be a carrier of scientificity, while the soldiers remain carriers of more primordial habits. (Mazrui, 1976, pp. 251–2)

Consequently the military, in Africa at least, may play a traditionalising role.

The monopoly of modern weapons is clearly an organisational asset to the military, providing it with a near-monopoly of physical force. If the civilian regime lacks military support, but the idea of a military government lacks legitimacy, then the deciding factor will be the deployment of coercion. Communications too are vital in this kind of political intervention, particularly in a large country with many administrative centres. The military's communications system enables them to strike at different centres of government simultaneously and to co-ordinate their activities in the immediate disorderly aftermath of the *coup*. Such organisational advantages offset the political weaknesses of the military such as its lack of legitimacy and administrative expertise.

Professionalism

Finally, there is the question of professionalism. This may mean that the professional ethic and code of conduct within the military, into which recruits are trained and socialised, support the supremacy of the civilian government. The professional soldier's duty is to obey the directives of the properly constituted civil authorities (Rapaport, 1962, p. 75). Professionalism is made up from expertise, social responsibility and corporate loyalty. According to Huntington, the more professional in this sense the military is, the more 'politically sterile and neutral' it will be (Huntington, 1957, p. 84).

However, military professionalism in some cultures can mean something quite different: that the army sees itself as having a duty to defend the state against forces that would undermine its integrity, even though such forces might be the civilian politicians. The military is guardian of the nation's integrity (Finer, 1962, p. 25). Finer therefore questions Huntington's association of professionalism with the principle of the supremacy of the civil power. If the politicians appear to be weakening the nation and making it vulnerable to external forces, economic as well as military, the army might give priority to the defence of society's basic values. The military is then not a neutral instrument of the government of the day, but rather an instrument of the nation, whose interest is capable of interpretation by the military itself. If the military contains within its corporate culture such a set of attitudes, it might provide sufficient justification for direct intervention in politics, especially since there will almost certainly be sections within civil society that will approve of the military taking such responsibility. Military involvement in politics may have a powerful ideological foundation such as nationalism, *dirigism*, a moral code and 'a deep distrust of organised civilian politics' (Janowitz, 1970, p. 145).

9.   Foreign influence

External involvement by foreign powers has often been thought to be crucial in the decision of the military to stage a *coup d'état*. Chile is an example of US support for the overthrow of the Allende regime. Continuity of links with developed countries through military aid, training and equipment have also strengthened national armies in the Third World relative to the civilian authorities. The influence of foreign support, through clandestine military, security and intelligence agencies such as the US CIA, has been critical in a number of Third World *coups*. Through 'covert operations' involving political advice, subsidies to political organisations and individuals, propaganda, training, economic interventions, paramilitary support to domestic groups, and infiltration and co-option of local agents and allies in trade unions, corporations, political parties, the media and the military itself, foreign influence has penetrated deeply into Third World societies (Woddis, 1977, pp. 56–60).

Foreign influence has sometimes been defined in terms of 'contagion' (First, 1972, pp. 20–2). There have been times when it appeared as if the reason why some states experienced *coups* was because neighbouring states had shown how easily it could be done, and the advantages that accrued to the armed forces as a result. There is some evidence from West Africa that military commanders did 'learn' from the experience of their counterparts in other countries as to how to take power, and about the financial attractions of it, lessons which entered into their calculations about whether and when to intervene. However, this argument cannot be taken too far in general explanatory terms, since the logic of it would be that there would be no end to military intervention as it spread like wildfire from one state to another. Neither Putnam for Latin America nor Wells for Africa found empirical evidence to confirm the contagion hypothesis (Putnam, 1967, p. 102; Wells, 1974). There are clearly effective barriers to contagion.

External influences also include the international context in which domestic conflict and insecurity occur. When Third World countries were at the periphery of the Cold War or at the centre of regional conflicts, the strength and significance of the armed forces, concerned with both national security and national pride, were enhanced and their motivation to intervene strengthened (Luckham, 1991, p. 376).

10. Conclusion

Many of the factors associated with military intervention, particularly social and economic variables, have also figured in attempts to understand the context of political instability within which military *coups* may occur. Military intervention is by no means the only form of political instability. Communal violence, separatist movements and ethnic conflicts can escalate into civil war and create prolonged instability. This more general and widespread picture of instability is the subject of a later chapter. The present chapter has identified the circumstances surrounding military interventions in Third World politics in order to explore how successful explanations of the phenomenon have been. An understanding of military intervention is particularly important when it undermines democracy either by the *coup d'état* or by refusing to reinstate democratic politics in response to widespread popular demand. There are implications for public policies and governmental strategies if it can be shown that the propensity for military intervention is related to the level of political institutionalisation, economic development, political participation, economic specialisation, the development of mass political parties, the centrality of the state in the process of capital accumulation and the development of a middle class, or the professional culture of the military itself.

Part IV
Challenging the Status Quo

11
Nationalism and Secession

1. Introduction

Throughout the Third World there are political movements campaigning, in many cases through armed struggle, for political self-determination on behalf of minority groups. In the Western Sahara, Polisario fights for liberation from Morocco. In Western Somalia the Liberation Front aims to restore the Ethiopian Ogaden to Somalia. The Kurds of Turkey, Iran, Iraq and Syria seek an independent and united Kurdistan. The National Resistance Council in Iran aims to establish an autonomous Baluchistan. In India there are movements for autonomy among the Sikhs, Nagas, Mizos and Tripuras as well as in Kashmir. The Shanti Bahini of Bangladesh seek autonomy for the Chittagong tribes. In Burma the programme of the Federal National Democratic Front includes a federal union based on self-determination for the Shan, Karen, Mon, Arakan, and Kachin peoples. The Tamil minority in Sri Lanka have been waging civil war with the objective of forming a separate state in the north of the island. Indonesia has three movements struggling for independence – in West Papua, East Timor and Acheh. In the Philippines the Moro National Liberation Front seeks independence of the Muslim Moros in the south. There has been a strong ethnic revival since 1960 and a corresponding growth of interest among social scientists (Brown, 1989, p. 1).

Such organisations are to be distinguished from revolutionary movements seeking to overthrow the incumbent regime. Secessionist movements do not want to overthrow national governments: they want to withdraw from their jurisdiction. This, from the perspective of the centre, may appear very revolutionary; and the movement itself may have a revolutionary agenda in addition to independence, though this is not inevitable. Only in Latin America are revolutionary movements almost exclusively concerned with a different kind of independence – that of a whole country from repression by an authoritarian regime. Separatism in Latin America is largely an aspect of nineteenth-century history (Anderson *et al.*, 1974, ch. 3).

Few secessionist movements are likely to be successful in achieving full independence for the people they represent, but it is unlikely that they will give up the struggle and disband. They may, however, be crushed by the superior military might of the national government – as in Nigeria, Zaire, the Sudan and, it would seem, East Timor. Occasionally, however, a separatist movement succeeds, as in the case of the violent separation of East Pakistan to form the state of Bangladesh, the secession of Somaliland from Somalia in 1991 (yet to receive international recognition), and the secession of Eritrea from Ethiopia in 1993. Military conflict often marks the passage from integration to autonomy, as with the birth of Bangladesh.

The political movements fighting for separation often do so in the name of nationalism. Their aim is secession, though other organisations and factions may be prepared to negotiate for less than full separation. Before examining the causes of ethnic separatism, the main aim of this chapter, it is necessary to clarify some of the terms that are central to the analysis.

2. Secession

'Secession' may be defined as the formal separation of a region from a nation state of which it formerly constituted an integral part. The region may have experienced considerable decentralisation of power. The Eastern Region of Nigeria, for example, which attempted to break away in 1967 to form the independent state of Biafra, had been part of a federation in which extensive powers were allocated to the regional level of government. Secession, however, is not further decentralisation but complete separation so that the breakaway region becomes a state in its own right, with its own constitution and recognised as such in international law. Normally secessionist movements aim at autonomy rather than integration with a neighbouring country. Such autonomy, which may win international recognition and give the new state rights in international law, does not necessarily mean that all political and economic links with the 'parent' state will be severed. Economic relationships are particularly likely to persist, especially in the form of trade.

The central authorities of the parent state may attempt to contain secessionist tendencies by offering various concessions, such as constitutional autonomy which stops well short of separation (Brass, 1991, pp. 21 and 50–5). Alternatively the state may resist separatism with repression. Responses to nationalism and separatism have included genocide, expulsion, assimilation, language policies, quotas in political and bureaucratic élites, revenue allocation formulae, positive discrimination, cultural autonomy and political decentralisation. In South Asia, at least eight different types of governmental response to secessionist movements can be identified: military action, police restrictions, constitutional obstacles, electoral manipulation, economic subsidies, policy concessions (such as job quotas, the co-option of separatist leaders, and language rights), constitutional accommodation and, in principle only, the granting of autonomy (Wright, 1976, pp. 12–13; Brass, 1991, pp. 154–6). Brass has placed state management of ethnic conflict at the centre of attempts to understand nationalist political mobilisation, arguing that central élites (which in Third World countries usually means bureaucrats, whether civil or military, partisan or professional) form alliances with local ethnic organisations, either to oppose or support local élites. For Brass

It is a principal task of research on ethnic groups and the state to determine how privileges are distributed among different ethnic categories, with which élites within an ethnic group state leaders tend to collaborate, and what the consequences are both for ethnic group identity formation and political mobilization. (Brass, 1991, p. 256)

It is unusual for national governments to approve the breaking away from the nation-state of a distinctive region, especially if part of that region's distinctiveness is its endowment with valuable natural or other economic resources. Demands for independence are revolutionary from the perspective of the centre (Connor, 1973; Clay, 1989, pp. 230–1) and history teaches us that 'attempts at secession are generally seen by governmental leaders as a threat to the authority of their regime which is so intolerable that it is worth spilling blood to prevent it' (Birch, 1978, p. 340). In South-east Asia, for instance, responses to separatism prove conclusively that 'the nation-state clings above all to territory' (McVey, 1984, p. 13). In 1994 Morocco's King Hassan threatened a return to war if the people of the Western Sahara voted for independence in any referendum which the UN might organise. As Chaliand pointed out:

> the fact is that during the last three decades it has been far easier for a country to achieve formal independence from ex-colonial power than for a minority to obtain a measure of (effective) autonomy within a Third World state. The reaction of demands of every kind has been almost universally negative. (Chaliand, 1980, p. 9)

National governments may be assisted in their negotiation of a compromise by nationalist factions which are prepared to accept less than complete political independence. Surveys of political attitudes mainly, it has to be admitted, in developed countries, have revealed that significant numbers and often majorities within the ethnic groups concerned are prepared to accept constitutional autonomy rather than separation for their country – a finding that almost certainly applies to developing countries. However, surveys also show that even among those who do not favour separation and who reject violence as a means to that end, there are many who sympathise with those engaged in violent resistance – explaining 'how guerrilla struggles have been maintained for years in the face of overwhelming odds' (Connor, 1988, p. 216).

The demands of political movements may be significantly modified over a period of time, so that national independence is displaced by lesser objectives, such as the creation of a new territorial unit within a federation, official recognition of a language, and symbolic distinctions. Equally, modest demands can escalate under pressure of events, such as East Pakistan's progression from linguistic equality to autonomy in a loose federation and from there to secession (Wright, 1976, p. 9). The ultimate goal of secessionists is the creation of a new nation-state. Decentralisation is unlikely to provide a lasting solution if there is widespread support within the affected region for the secessionist cause, and there is likely to be widespread support if the secessionist movement is founded on a sense of nationalism within the aspirant state.

3. Nationalism

Such nationalism, which may extract concessions in the form of political decentralisation of various kinds, including federalism, has become increasingly widespread in recent decades. It has been argued that it, rather than ideology built on class, is 'the dominant political passion' of the second half of the twentieth century (Payne, 1975, p. 249), though it may now have given way to religion.

Nationalism presupposes some cultural distinctiveness on the part of the inhabitants of a particular region. Nationalism in the context of colonialism is a relatively straightforward concept, but nationalism among minorities indicates cultural identity and uniqueness, often strengthened by linguistic distinctiveness, that unites a particular population and which may inspire a nationalist movement. But what constitutes a 'nation', which may seek the status of a nation-state, is a question that has occupied the minds of political theorists for many decades.

A sense of nationhood will be based on some combination of religion, language, customs, institutions, mythology, folklore, culture, history and race, though it should not be assumed that each type of identity will have the same effect on political behaviour (Connor, 1978, p. 396 and 1988, pp. 201–2; Clay, 1989, pp. 224–6; Kellas, 1991, pp. 2–3). None, however, is sufficient in itself to define a nation, not even language (Smith, A. D., 1971, pp. 181–6). Economic and political features may be considered necessary conditions of nationhood, in addition to cultural factors and group sentiment. Smith lists the following seven features of a nation, and distinguishes 'tribes' and ethnic groups as having some but not all of these:

- cultural differentiae;
- territorial contiguity with internal mobility;
- a relatively large population;
- external political relations;
- considerable group sentiment and loyalty;
- direct membership with equal citizenship rights;
- vertical economic integration around a common system of labour.

According to Smith, tribes have only the first and second characteristics. 'Ethnie' have the first five. Nations have all seven.

Some post-colonial societies are collections of tribes and/or ethnie and therefore lack at least two of the seven features – cultural differentiae and group sentiment – because of the arbitrary nature of colonial boundaries (pp. 186–90).

Groups supporting secessionist movements, though usually having a sense of cultural identity, are not universally distinct ethnically. Secessionist groups may be ethnically heterogeneous. Nationhood may be claimed, but whether this is justified raises many problems of subjective and objective definition (Symmons-Symonolewicz, 1965; Rustow, 1967; Snyder, 1976; Wood, J.R., 1981). The subjectivity is captured in the definition of 'nation' employed by Rejai and Enloe:

> a relatively large group of people who feel that they belong together by virtue of sharing one or many such traits as common language, religion or race, common history or tradition, common set of customs, and common destiny. As a matter of empirical observation, none of these traits may actually exist: the important point is that people believe they do. (Rejai and Enloe, 1969, p. 143; see also Paribatra and Samudavanija, 1984; Connor, 1988)

A subjective belief that people constitute a nation that deserves political recognition is more important than the objective definitions of historians and social scientists. Emerson's judgement about anti-colonial nationalism may well apply to ethno-nationalism: 'The simplest statement that can be made about a nation is that it is a body who feel that they are a nation; it may be that when all the fine-spun analysis is concluded this will be the ultimate statement as well' (Emerson, 1960, p. 102; Erikson, 199, pp. 11–12).

Secessionist alienation arises from a perception of special bonds between people which distinguish them from other communities within the nation-state (Enloe, 1973, p. 15). Referring to secessionist movements in South Asia, Wright claims that 'the sociological characteristics of the various provincial populations are at the heart of their demands for autonomy or secession. All of the movements have asserted the primacy of particular criteria of identification which render the populations minorities in the country as a whole even if majorities locally' (Wirght, 1976, p. 8). In Kashmir and Nagaland the principal factor is religion, in Tamil Nadu, East Bengal and Baluchistan, it is language.

The ethnic foundation for nationalism is important not only because it provides a criterion for defining a nation, but also because it is central to the debate about what causes nationalism and separatism, and whether ethnicity is a sufficient or necessary condition for the existence of demands for political autonomy.

Any attempt to find a simple causal explanation of nationalism and separatism is probably doomed to failure by the sheer diversity of the phenomenon. The history of nationalism reveals wide differences in the size, cohesiveness and mobilisation of ethnic communities, in the goals of nationalist movements, in the threats that they pose to existing states, in the economic contexts in which ethno-nationalism is found, and in the political methods chosen by nationalist movements (Zubaida, 1978; Kellas, 1991, pp. 132–4). An exhaustive review of the literature on nationalism in the Third World is beyond the scope of this chapter. All that can be attempted is a critical look at the theoretical perspectives which seem to be of greatest heuristic value for future research.

4. Political integration

The theory which attaches the greatest weight to ethnicity in explaining separatism is that of 'political integration'. In the Third World context this emphasises the fact that new states were frequently the arbitrary creations of colonialism. They consist of a multiplicity of ethnic groups bound together under colonial domination and a common administrative and economic system after the European powers had divided their tropical dependencies among themselves with scant regard to existing social and political boundaries. Differences of caste, region and ethnicity were further exacerbated by the representation of these incorporated societies in racial and tribal categories, and by the unequal impact of colonial educational, economic and political experiments (Nafziger and Richter, 1976). The nationalism which subsequently drew such communities together was based solely on opposition to subjugation by an alien power. They were united (and often far from completely) only in their desire to throw off colonial domination. The state created by the achievement of independence is said to 'precede' nationalism, in that there is no other common identity than anti-colonialism. The nation-state is not built on a basis of common religious, cultural, linguistic or racial factors as it is when nationalism precedes the state (Kohn, 1945; Coleman, 1954, p. 419).

The crisis of integration

For Anderson, von der Mehden and Young, for example, it is 'uncontroversial' that:

> Afro–Asia, in particular, is dominated by new states that face agonizing problems in winning the full commitment of their citizenry which is taken for granted in most Western societies. In equipping the state with a mystique of nationhood, the new leaders face intense competition from diverse forms of subnational loyalties, which we have referred to as cultural pluralism. These loyalties may be based on race, ethnic identity, language, caste, religion, or region; they have in common the capability of evoking sentiments in men very similar to those described as nationalism. What seems to us crucial to know is the direction of change. Are subnational loyalties giving way to the imperative of nationalism, as many seem to assume? Our evidence suggests to us that this is not the case in Africa and Asia. Both national identification and subnational loyalties are growing stronger as modern communications and education penetrate and the self-enclosed, small-scale rural subsistence communities are progressively eliminated. (1974, p. 9)

Eventually parochial loyalties should be eroded by a diffusion of cultural values during the process of modernisation. The diffusionist school of modernisation theory argues that when countries modernise, cultures become diffused and sub-cultures lose their significance. Ethnic loyalties become superseded by loyalties to the wider state. There are four factors involved in this process: bureaucratic penetration, social mobilisation, industrialisation and mass communication. In conjunction these developments produce cultural diffusion that may even extend beyond the boundaries of the nation-state.

A 'crisis of integration' is therefore likely to occur after independence unless a sense of territorial nationality can be created by unifying the independent social, cultural and political entities. National integration is at risk not only when a minority is threatened by a single numerically and politically dominant group (as in Sri Lanka); self-determination may also be demanded where there is a more 'balanced' pluralism of ethnic groups (as in India and Nigeria) (Weiner, 1965).

Demands for self-determination by ethnic groups are viewed from this perspective as deviations from the path to modernity. The 'problem' for the post-colonial state is one of 'nation-building' – creating loyalties and attachments to the new nation-state which supersede the parochial loyalties evoked by traditional values. Secession may then reflect a failure to integrate at all (for example, during colonialism) or a process of disintegration after a relatively stable period of unity (Wood, J. R., 1981, p. 111).

Evaluation of integration theory

In common with the theories of modernisation and development from which this concept of integration springs, it mystifies rather than illuminates the sources of political conflict which may lead to attempts at secession. Integration theory presents the 'crisis' of integration as a deviation from the functional process of political change. Political 'disintegration', of which secession is one form, is portrayed as the consequence of an incompatibility between traditional and modern values, rules and modes of behaviour. Failure to incorporate regions successfully into the state system is regarded as evidence of persistent parochial loyalties, often founded on tribal communality, which elevate the legitimacy of traditional community above that of the modern form of political association – the nation-state. The 'primordial' attachment to tradition is thus seen as an obstacle to development.

The 'integration' approach to the phenomenon of secession suffers from all the teleological and ethnocentric defects of development theory generally. Although it is true that political hostility to the inequalities of contemporary states may be reflected in an appeal to a sense of common identity and historical continuity, such 'parochialism' is itself the consequence of other factors rather than the prime mobiliser of political action. These other factors have to be understood. It is inadequate to dismiss them as failures on the part of disaffected sections of society to understand how to articulate political demands through an essentially imaginary egalitarian and pluralistic political system. To talk about national integration as if it is simply a question of minorities becoming aware that new nation-states are the modern forms through which politics must be carried on, is to present an explanation of political crisis in terms that are not very meaningful. It is necessary to analyse what lies behind ethnic unrest. Ethnicity cannot be regarded as a primordial 'given'. It is subject to a range of economic and political forces such as economic competition between regions, the manipulation of ethnic identity by ruling élites to divert attention from other forms of socio-economic conflict, and the attraction of communalism in the absence of other effective forms of political participation (Nafziger and Richter, 1976, p. 92). One reason for turning to ethnically-defined activism is despair at ever protecting one's interests through other forms of political association.

Furthermore, there is also evidence to support an interpretation of post-colonial history which sees ethnicity supporting national integration. Wallerstein has argued that in West Africa ethnicity assists national integration in at least four ways. First, it provides the social support needed during periods of social upheaval that cannot be provided by either the state or the extended family. Secondly, ethnic groups aid the process of resocialisation during periods of rapid social change by providing opportunities for a range of social and political contacts to be made. Thirdly, by offering opportunities for social mobility, ethnic groups help to prevent the formation of castes and so assist in the maintenance of a fluid stratification system. Finally, they are an important 'outlet for political tensions'. Such potentialities have to be recognised and set against the inevitably particularistic and separatist potential of ethnic sentiment (Wallerstein, 1960).

5.   Internal colonialism

As an explanation of why a minority group should feel compelled to seek greater autonomy and even separation, the theory of internal colonialism offers some interesting hypotheses. The concepts of uneven development and internal colonialism were developed by Hechter with reference to the UK, where it was used to explain Celtic nationalism. But it is a theory that owes its origins to interpretations of Third World colonialism and dependency. It would seem to have considerable resonance as an approach to territorial economic and political differentiation in the post-colonial states of the Third World and the consequent demands for autonomy on the part of the groups experiencing discrimination and exploitation.

Core and periphery

This thesis argues that contemporary societies will be divided into a 'core' community and one or more peripheral communities, exploited by the core from a position of primarily economic advantage. The economy of the periphery is usually highly specialised and thus more vulnerable to fluctuations in world markets than the economy of the core community. This core–periphery distinction is a function of capitalism which entails territorial as well as class inequalities and conflicts through a process of uneven development. (For a survey, see Orridge, 1981, pp. 6–7.) A cultural division of labour is created in the course of such development: 'a system of stratification where objective cultural distinctions are superimposed upon class lines' (Hechter, 1975, p. 30). The survival of nationalism depends on this cultural division of labour, a stratification system which links a person's life chances to cultural distinctions, thereby giving culture a political salience. People see a shared material interest in cultural terms. This is a necessary but not sufficient condition of group solidarity and collective action. Other conditions are necessary to encourage solidarity with a nationalist organisation, namely a high level of dependence on a nationalist movement as a source of benefits, and the monitoring of members' 'compliance with the movement's goals and procedures' (Hechter, 1985).

The politics of the peripheral regions are controlled by the core. Influential positions in the state are disproportionately occupied by people from the core community. This applies to the central state apparatus as well as to its local arms in the minority areas. Political organisations seeking to represent the interests of minority cultures may be restricted or banned. The repressive instruments of the state may be used selectively to counter expressions of dissent by a nationalist group. Repression has often been justified by means of a racist ideology.

In addition to such economic discrimination, the marginalisation and exclusion of an ethnic or regional minority may take the form of cultural discrimination, by stereotyping the cultural group as backward, uncivilised, unreliable, inferior or dangerous. It may even involve attempts by the core group to deny any ethnic distinctiveness, as in the case of Turkish efforts to prove the Turkishness of the Kurds, or the Iranian government's claim that the Kurds are 'pure Iranians' (Bullock and Morris, 1993, p. 51). Such claims can easily become self-fulfilling prophecies when, because of economic deprivation, a disproportionately large number of people from the minority group are found to be suffering from unemployment, low incomes, poor health, bad housing, illiteracy, low life-expectancy, high crime rates, high rates of suicide and other indicators of social disadvantage. Discrimination may be more overt, as when minorities are denied the use of their own language in education, the media and local administration. Indirect measures include requiring that education, information and social advancement generally are only available to those using the official language (Kendal, 1980). Discrimination may well escalate as regimes retaliate against the agitation of nationalist groups, involving forced migration and even attempted genocide.

The case of Bangladesh

The internal colonialism thesis would seem to fit some parts of the Third World, such as Bangladesh. West Pakistan began with an initial economic advantage in receiving most of the entrepreneurs who migrated at independence and who were central to the West's industrial development. Then the new nation's capital was established in the West, further encouraging industrial and infrastructural development. Development funds, foreign aid, economic and fiscal policies, foreign exchange controls and licensing powers were used disproportionately to the benefit of West Pakistan. The positive discrimination that would have been necessary for the East to catch up was not forthcoming, further encouraging the flow of resources to the more developed region.

But the main factor that led to a feeling of exploitation and discrimination among the Bengalis of East Pakistan was the diversion of the East's foreign exchange earnings to the West. The differential between the two 'wings' of the country in terms of per capita income, the relative contribution of agriculture and industry to regional incomes, school and university enrolments, and the infrastructure generally and transportation in particular, increased throughout Pakistan's post-independence history (Jahan, 1973, pp. 30–2).

Political developments during this period confirm the broad outline of the 'internal colonialism' model. In the years immediately following independence Bengali representation in the national power élite was limited. Because over half the population of Pakistan lived in the East, the Bengalis had nearly 50 per cent representation in the political institutions which were based on democratic recruitment. But only 5 per cent of the military élite, 30 per cent of the senior bureaucracy and 10 per cent of the entrepreneurial class were Bengali. This became particularly significant with the abolition of representative government after the military *coup* in 1958, and the consequent dominance of the bureaucratic-military oligarchy. Bengali representation in the political élite declined and their sense of alienation increased. Following the government's refusal to accept the results of the 1965 and 1971 elections, the Bengali élite concentrated its efforts on radical autonomist demands (Rahman, 1976). Provincial autonomy was reduced in a way which was more to the disadvantage of the East than the West. Administrative and political centralisation gave rise to demands for Bengali autonomy which were fuelled by the central government's economic policies (Jahan, 1973, pp. 23–30).

The case of Bangladesh, though unique, suggests some conclusions regarding nationalism and secession that may have wider applicability in the Third World. Though Bengalis had long been conscious of their cultural distinctiveness, and had found it necessary to assert this from time to time in the face of assimilationist policies (notably the one-language issue of 1950–2), it was not until their gains through the democratic process had been vetoed by the central authorities that they were driven towards secession. Until then their programme had been for reforms within the state of Pakistan (such as the Six Point Programme which called for a confederal constitution, fiscal devolution, and separate trading and commercial relations with foreign countries). Nationalism and secessionist demands were precipitated more by the intransigence of the central authorities than by spontaneous articulation.

The liberation movement was strengthened by the existence of a political movement, the Awami League, which gained support as its dominance in national politics was resisted by Western Pakistani political factions. The national cause, on the other hand, was weakened by the costly logistical problems of controlling an area separated by a thousand miles of Indian territory, and by eventual Indian military support to the Bengalis.

Internal colonialism: an assessment

Despite the evident relevance of the internal colonialism thesis to some Third World situations, there are serious problems with it as a theory of nationalism and secession. The main difficulty, as has frequently been pointed out with reference to developed countries, is that there have been prosperous regions that have demanded political autonomy from the state, and many poor ones that have not (Orridge, 1981, pp. 181–2; Wood, J. R., 1981). It is arguable that Katanga (now Shaba) in the Congo, Bougainville in Papua New Guinea, and Biafra in Nigeria attempted to secede because of their relative wealth, based on their natural mineral resources, rather than their backwardness. The internal colonialism thesis is further weakened by the phenomenon of ethnic nationalism and separatism in regions yet to be extensively penetrated by capitalist development – the Kurds, Naga and Eritrea, for example (Smith, A. D., 1979).

'Uneven development', producing overdeveloped peripheral regions within poor countries, is awkward to fit into the internal colonialism model. A 'power disparity' can develop, when an economically better off region with *de facto* power demands *de jure* equality within the state. For example, although the Kurdish areas of Turkey and Iran are among the least developed regions of those countries, Kurdistan in Iraq has been favoured by natural conditions and resources, notably oil. However, being rich in natural resources does not guard against exploitation. The Kurdish parts of Iraq have consistently received disproportionately small quantities of development expenditure, industrial projects and infrastructure, despite the fact that they contribute some 80 per cent of Iraqi oil production and over 53 per cent of state revenue (Vanley, 1980).

Thus it may be theorised that if a region combines 'ethnic potential' with an improved economic position (or a faltering core economy) it may become politically assertive (Gourevitch, 1979; Wood, J. R., 1981). Part of the 'faltering core' may be a failure to develop effective political bargaining, notably through national political parties. The development of powerful regional parties in Nigeria and Pakistan is felt to have increased secessionist instability by focussing political conflict on regional rivalries (Wood, J. R., 1981). Competition for economic and political power in Pakistan and Nigeria after independence became increasingly regional in character. The regional orientation of political élites intensified regional identities, conflict and the subordination of national class differences to tribalism.

This still leaves a need for an explanation of nationalism in the context of 'even' development, such as the nationalism in East Africa, French Saharan Africa and the West Indies which prevented workable federal amalgamations between more or less evenly developed territories. There is also the problem of why uneven development can exist without nationalist and secessionist movements, though this may be a puzzle more for the developed than the developing regions of the world.

A possible answer to the question of why inter-ethnic inequality is not sufficient to produce nationalism, and why dominant groups sometimes become nationalistic, is relative deprivation, in the sense of aspirations to standards of living which have yet to be reached but to which the 'deprived' group feels it has a right (Hah and Martin, 1975). Brass is critical of this theory because it is not possible to specify and measure the level of relative deprivation needed to turn an ethnic group towards nationalism. The theory accepts as evidence of relative deprivation the claims made by the nationalists themselves. And 'deprivation theory cannot explain the nationalism of privileged groups, such as that of Afrikaners in South Africa' (Brass, 1991, p. 42). However, it is not clear why objective measures of relative deprivation should not be constructed to compare two ethnic groups in conflict about political autonomy; nor why the theory cannot be applied to the examples of relative privilege for which it was designed. So the theory of relative deprivation would appear to retain some heuristic value.

A further problem with the theory of internal colonialism is that it does not explain why *nationalism* should be the response to uneven development and internal, colonial-style exploitation rather than, say, a return to pre-modern politics or revolutionary class consciousness. Why should a deprived community aspire to become a nation-state? (Orridge, 1981, pp. 183–4).

Then, as Orridge convincingly argued, the theory of uneven development requires a clearer definition of what constitutes unevenness than has so far been provided: 'we need to be given some clearer idea of how much unevenness is necessary for the maintenance or growth of a sense of separate ethnic or national feeling' (Orridge, 1981, p. 187). Unless it is known how to identify the significant spatial variations between regions, it is impossible to test whether or not the theory applies to a particular country. Application of the Hechter model to other countries is also made difficult by the fact that the inequalities between parts of the UK identified for analysis are not derived from the general statements about internal colonialism and so consequently do not explain relationships that may need to be explored in other countries (Page, 1978, pp. 302–3).

The case of Nigeria

Some of the problems with the internal colonialism thesis are illustrated by the failure of the Biafran secession attempt. Although there certainly were (and are) profound cultural differences between the major ethnic groups of Nigeria, and considerable competition and hostility between them, conflict was more the consequence of competition for power, patronage and wealth than the exploitation of the Ibos or the region in which they were politically dominant. Indeed, much of the hostility to the Ibos among other ethnic groups stemmed from fear of the opportunities which education had given them to become dominant in many walks of life. Most significantly in the history of the secession attempt, the first military *coup* of 1966 was widely regarded among other ethnic groups as an 'Ibo *coup*' because most of the young army officers were Ibo (Lloyd, 1970). In many respects the Ibos had become the most 'national' of Nigeria's ethnic groups, taking their economic opportunities wherever they happened to be located (Clendenen, 1972). Plans for secession did not begin to emerge until the communal violence of 1966 began to look like a genocide attempt. Even then, the political unit referred to as 'Biafra' consisted of the whole of the Eastern Region of the federation, including minorities of 5 million non-Ibos in a population of 12 million.

Until the discovery of oil in the East made secession look like an economically viable option, Ibo reaction to problems in the region, such as land shortages, had been to look for opportunities in other regions of Nigeria. Secession began to look attractive to Ibo members of the bureaucratic and commercial classes working in other parts of the country only when they sensed that discrimination in employment opportunities would await them even if they survived the pogrom which began in 1966 in retaliation for what other ethnic groups, particularly in the North, perceived as an Ibo *coup*. Hitherto the Eastern Region had not suffered discrimination in either revenue allocation or economic investment. The Western Region had experienced a severe drop in revenues from export duties as a result of the slump in cocoa prices between 1960 and 1965 and lost its oil to the newly-created Mid-West Region, but the East derived a rapidly growing yield from mining rents and royalties. In terms of total revenues the East did better than both the West and the North between 1958 and 1965. There was concern that in the post-independence period economic development was being concentrated in the North, but this was as much at the expense of the Yorubas in the West as the Ibos in the East. Until 1964 the East had received the largest *increase* in industrial investment.

Politically the Ibos played a major role in national as well as regional politics from the earliest years of the independence movement. The first major political party to operate nationally, the National Convention of Nigeria and the Cameroons (NCNC), was led by an Ibo, Nmandi Azikiwe, who became the first President of Nigeria. The NCNC originally attracted support from all parts of Nigeria, but was eventually accused by some Yoruba leaders of Ibo chauvinism. As politics at regional level became more important, the NCNC became the dominant political party in the East, but continued to have a considerable following in the non-Yoruba areas of the West and minority areas of the North. At independence it became a coalition partner in the federal government. With the demise of electoral politics in 1966, Ibos were dominant at the national level through the military regime. Thus it was not by secession that the Ibos sought the advancement that would have been theirs in a country without regional obstacles to recruitment and promotion. The concept of an independent Biafra did not emerge among Ibo leaders until after the army rank and file had mutinied and assassinated hundreds of Ibo officers and men and after pogroms in Northern cities raised the spectre of genocide.

In 1966 the East was by no means the only region proposing a loose confederation for the future of Nigeria. All parts of the country were ambivalent about the desirability of Nigerian unity. The West had used the threat of secession from the federation more than any other region since preparations for independence from Britain began, and secession had also been considered prior to independence by the leaders of the Muslim majority in the North (Panter-Brick, 1976, pp. 31–3). It was largely the fears of the minorities in all regions, including the East, for their futures under a fragmented Nigeria that united the rest of the country against Biafra.

Arguing that 'the probability of secession of a regional unit from a nation-state is dependent upon the expected costs and benefits to the region from the maintenance of the national unit and those of secession from it', Nafziger (1972, p. 185) points out that 'the benefits of regional autonomy for the East increased relative to the benefits of continued membership of the federation as a result of the discovery and commercial exploitation of crude oil centred in the region in the late 1950s'. However, oil did not prompt secession. It simply made it a viable strategy in the eyes of the Biafran leadership against the national level of government. The share of revenue from oil accruing to the East became a major source of political friction – specially after 1959, when a new revenue allocation system left the East with a fraction of its earlier oil revenues. Another major factor was the decision in 1967 to increase the number of states in the federation from 4 to 12. Dividing the Eastern Region into three states meant that the Ibos would be in a majority in only one and would be reduced to one-sixth of the region's oil output. The Ibo heartland would be severed from the oil resources and landlocked.

The Biafra case also suggests that levels of economic integration may be an important factor in the build-up of ethnic consciousness and demands for self-determination. In Nigeria at the time of the Biafran secession the value of inter-regional trade was low. Indigenous firms tended to sell to local markets. Virtually no capital moved between regions. Ethnic conflict between 1965 and 1967 further discouraged economic integration. The cost of secession was therefore perceived to be less than the benefits of integration, especially when opportunities for economic advancement through migration, from which the Ibos had formerly benefited, were discouraged, first by policies of regionalisation in employment and then by pogroms (Nafziger, 1972).

Ethnic identity

The lack of correlation between peripheral economic status and nationalistic mobilisation draws us back to the significance of ethnic identity, which some would argue is the main cause of nationalism. All national movements have some unifying feature such as language, culture or race. Cultural differences are perceived by the groups they define, while spatial economic differences may or may not be. Ethnicity would seem to be a necessary condition for separatism: 'uneven development theorists assume the existence of a large number of pre-existing ethnic identities and see uneven development as working upon them and transforming them into modern ethnic or national identities' (Orridge, 1981, p. 188). But economic exploitation by the core community does not seem to be a necessary, let alone a sufficient, condition of nationalism. The roots of separatism must be sought in other than economic factors. People must see themselves as a distinct nation before they will contemplate independence (Polese, 1985, p. 112). Yet ethnicity seems not to rank as a sufficient condition. The history of nationalism clearly shows that

> the objective existence or subjective perception of inequality is indispensible to justify nationalism, but it is not in itself an explanation for it. The only certainty is that every nationalist movement has always justified itself in terms of existing oppression or anticipated oppression by a rival group. (Brass, 1991, p. 43)

Not all 'objective' cultural groups are nationalistic. Group identity becomes important under external threat, especially from the state (through assimilationist policies, discrimination, environmental damage, and the expropriation of natural resources, for example – Brown, 1989, pp. 5–10; Clay, 1989, pp. 228–30). The claims of both Eritrea and Somaliland to self-determination were based on a 'consciousness of oppression' (Adam, 1994, p. 35). Hence the appeal of political integration theory, which concentrates on interpretations of ethnicity and the conflicting cultural values, particularly those relating to politics, of different ethnic groups.

6.   The balance of advantage

The idea that communities weigh up the costs and benefits of integration and separation was introduced in one interpretation of the Biafra case. Birch has developed a cost-benefit perspective on nationalism into a general explanation of the phenomenon. He sees ethnicity as an independent variable, producing identities and loyalties which persist over long periods, largely regardless of other factors. 'In comparison with the rapid changes in economic development and political organisation of the past hundred years, ethnic and cultural loyalties are durable and relatively permanent' (Birch, 1978, p. 333). Therefore ethnicity should be treated as given and not explained in terms of political discrimination, economic exploitation or relative deprivation. Birch is arguing largely on the basis of evidence from developed countries, but his contribution to the debate about nationalism is too important for it not to be considered in the present context.

Political integration involves costs and benefits to peripheral communities. There will be a changing balance of advantage from time to time in being incorporated into a wider community, and the incorporation is unlikely to be total, contrary to the basic premise of the diffusionist school that ethnic loyalties will be superseded by loyalties to the wider political unit because of bureaucratic penetration, social mobilisation, industrialisation and mass communication. Ethnic groups resist the erosion of their cultural identity, even gaining 'psychic income' from pride and satisfaction with the assertion of an identity which compensates for a sense of inferiority and deprivation engendered by a dominant culture.

Since the Second World War the balance of advantage between the small community and the large state has swung in favour of the former, first because 'changes in the international order have removed one of the main benefits to be derived from membership of a sizeable state' (p. 335), namely diplomatic and military security. Secondly, the development of international organisations such as the EC, OECD and the IMF give small states access to markets, loans, employment and investment that make their small economies more viable than they would otherwise be. Thirdly, the impact of the mass media on minority cultures and languages has heightened consciousness of, and hostility to, cultural imperialism and homogenisation. Finally, political agitation for minorities is less costly than in the past. Rights are more readily demanded and conceded. Agitation and terrorism are easier and get instant and extensive publicity. National energy supplies are more vulnerable to sabotage. Hence a decline in the acceptability to minorities of piecemeal reforms and in the value attached to the benefits of integration in the wider nation-state.

This explanation sounds highly plausible in the context of both developed and developing regions of the world. There are problems associated with it, however. First, it concentrates more on the relative ease with which the break can be made, rather than on the factors that prompt disillusionment among some ethnic minorities and not others with the existing territorial jurisdiction of the state. It implies that the demand for separation is constant, only awaiting an easing of the circumstances under which a new, small state can be born and survive. Yet the demand is clearly not constant, so the factors precipitating nationalist mobilisation have to be identified.

Secondly, it pays insufficient attention to the organisational requirements of a successful bid for independence and the variable political context in which it is made. Brass has identified the following organisational factors affecting a nationalist movement's chances of political success: command of community resources; identification with the community represented; an ability to shape the identity of the group to be led; continuity in leadership; and exclusive or dominant representation of ethnic demands. The intensity and form of nationalist politics is also affected by contextual factors, especially the realignment of political and social forces (as when an organisation based on class proves more attractive to members of an ethnic group than a nationalist body), the willingness of élites from dominant ethnic groups to share political power, and the availability of alternative political arenas, such as federalism (Brass, 1991, pp. 49–62).

Thirdly, it is important not to underestimate the ideological, governmental and repressive apparatus which the state can bring to bear on separatist movements. Enloe provides a revealing catalogue of the impressive powers available to central governments in dealing with separatist regions, in addition to the more obvious and risky strategies of military coercion and the withholding of public funds:

- the ability to conduct a census which defines social categories for the purpose of internal comparisons;
- the authority to define the issues and conflicts that are to be politically managed;
- an internationally recognised right to negotiate with the separatists;
- control over taxation (and therefore redistribution), the definition of economic strata, the collection of information and the investment of capital;
- an ability to recruit skilled and professional personnel;
- the right to control internal migration which can 'alter drastically the ethnic composition of certain regions, usually diluting the indigenous populations and thus undermining possibly separatist tendencies. (Enloe, 1976, p. 82)

Central governments can call on diplomatic, administrative and political resources, blocking external sponsorship of separatist dissidents and exploiting divisions within regional communities. Sometimes they can add foreign interference to the list of reasons for not conceding independence, as in the case of India's handling of the Kashmir crisis.

Finally, it should not be assumed that the international context is wholly supportive of aspirant nation-states, though the conditions identified by Birch are undoubtedly significant and should inform further investigations. The attitudes of world powers and neighbouring states to Bangladesh and Biafra were important factors in the contrasting outcomes of these two instances of secession (Wood, J. R., 1981, pp. 130–1). External influences are usually critical to the outcome of independence struggles (Wright, 1976, pp. 8–9; Tinker, 1981, p. 115). They were conclusive in the history of the short-lived Kurdish Republic of 1946 (Ghassenbie, 1980; Roosevelt, 1980). But support from outside is a difficult commodity to acquire, even when ethnic groups straddle national frontiers. In South-east Asia, for instance, there has been surprisingly little support for ethnic separatism from neighbouring states when ethnic minorities are located in frontier regions: 'Boundaries left by the receding colonial tide have usually been viewed as sacrosanct, no matter how little relevance they have had to geographic, economic and ethnic realities' (McVey, 1984, p. 18).

Eritrea's secession depended much more on the internal political situation, and the fact that its liberation movement had assisted the coalition which eventually ousted the Mengistu regime, than on external support. However, its long-term viability is probably dependent on the international co-operation identified by Birch as easing the path to independence – something like a Horn of Africa Common Market, the nucleus of which already exists in the Intergovernmental Authority on Drought and Development (Adam, 1994, pp. 37–8).

7. Élites and class

It is a mistake to expect all sections of an ethnic minority to arrive at the same conclusion after calculating the costs and benefits of integration. Cultural minorities are not homogeneous societies, they are socially stratified. Different classes in a peripheral community will experience different costs and benefits from incorporation into a wider economy, society and polity. A major influence on the degree of mobilisation of ethnic groups for nationalistic ends is the relationship between élites and classes in the core and peripheral communities.

Élite integration

An economically dominant class within the minority community may be well-integrated into the wider state and economy. Brass found that 'locally powerful economic, religious and political élites find it to their advantage to co-operate with external authorities and adopt the language and culture of the dominant ethnic group in order to maintain or enhance their own power' (1991, p. 26). In the Kurdish region of Turkey, for example, the Kurdish landed class and wealthy merchants have been integrated into the Turkish economy through trade and investment in urban property and small-scale industry in the major urban centres. Since the 1950s the Turkish authorities have needed less repression against the Kurds because the corruption and self-interest of the Kurdish ruling class achieve the government's aims for it (Kendal, 1980). The newly-emerging Kurdish bourgeoisie also co-exists with the Turkish economic and political élite, serving as a regional section of the Turkish commercial network and enjoying representation within the national political parties.

Nationalism is often a weapon which regional élites use in their competition for national political power. Appeals to ethnic loyalties to build and sustain political support may be a consequence of a struggle for power between ethnic élites, rather than a cause of mobilisation on the part of minority groups. McVey demonstrates this from Indonesian experience of separatist regionalism in the 1950s. This was not an assertion of primordial loyalties, but an attempt to consolidate political support. Eventually the regionalist movements came to nothing because their ethnic base was insufficiently meaningful:

> Both Sumatra and Sulawesi were patchworks of culturally, linguistically and religiously diverse peoples, and the unification of either into a nation-state would have replicated Indonesia's problems in achieving consensus among the claimants for power, with much less basis for credibility. (McVey, 1984, p. 11)

In Nigeria, on the other hand, the reinforcement of political mobilisation on the basis of ethnicity by politicians exploiting growing inter-ethnic competition was a major factor in the descent into civil war (Melsom and Wolpe, 1970).

Élite competition

Brass also sees ethnic conflict as reflecting competition between élites for 'political power, economic benefits and social status'. In modernising societies the development of ethnic consciousness is heavily dependent upon industrialisation, the spread of literacy, urbanisation and the growth of government employment opportunities, and the new social classes which such developments produce. This is the way in which conflict between élites precipitates nationalism – by challenging the distribution of resources and political power between ethnic groups. According to Brass the potential for nationalism is not realised 'until some members from one ethnic group attempt to move into the economic niches occupied by the rival ethnic group' (Brass, 1991, p. 47). Secession is a strategy likely only to be adopted when minority élites have no chance of acquiring economic and political power within the existing state and when there is a good chance of foreign support.

The bureaucratisation of society is linked to separatism by Smith, who argues that trained and educated people from minority groups ('ambitious and qualified professionals') find themselves excluded from bureaucratic occupations for which they are qualified as the supply of such professionals outstrips the capacity of bureaucracies to absorb them. The state bureaucracy is particularly discriminatory when the state itself is dominated by a core community. Separatism provides 'a new set of avenues to power and privilege for members of strata hitherto excluded from a share in both', especially when the state in developing countries has boundaries that are recent and artificial, few constitutional outlets for 'minority grievances', a lack of resources for helping poor regions, and a form of government that is prone to discrimination rather than conciliation (Smith, A. P., 1979, pp. 21–35).

Class interests

Responses to nationalist demands for self-determination will depend upon the class interests in the rest of the country. In Pakistan, for example, the landowning class in the West felt threatened by the Eastern leadership's proposal to tax hitherto exempt agricultural incomes in order to provide development capital. The Western bourgeoisie had an interest in retaining the East as a market for their manufactured goods and as a source of foreign exchange earnings. At the same time, however, Western agriculture was becoming an increasingly profitable source of investment to them, and they were concerned about revolutionary stirrings in the East. It was mainly the bureaucratic-military oligarchy that opposed secession and used armed force in the attempt to prevent it. Punjabi bureaucrats resented the promotion of Bengalis as a response to pressure from a political movement seeking to redress the regional imbalance within senior ranks. Regional autonomy also threatened their control over resources. The army was even more directly threatened by regional autonomy, which would have deprived the centre, responsible for defence, of funds. The Awami League was committed to a substantial reduction in expenditure on the military. The army's hostility was further strengthened by its belief that Bengali nationalism had been engineered by India to destabilise Pakistan.

The case of East Pakistan and Bengali nationalism is particularly illuminating to the question of how different classes respond to regional disparities. In the 1960s the central government under President Ayub Khan decided to create an East Pakistani bourgeoisie to provide the President with a political base in the province and restrict the spread of socialist ideas. Educated Bengalis with useful contacts in the bureaucracy and political élite were given permits, licences, construction contracts, loans, official support and equity. However, this new Bengali bourgeoisie also benefited from the pressures created by Bengali nationalism, and so was inclined to be favourably disposed towards it. Greater economic autonomy for the East increased nationalism's appeal among Bengali industrialists and businessmen when they found themselves unable to compete with the stronger West Pakistan businesses. At the same time they were uncertain as to whether an independent East Bengal could continue to provide the support and protection that the government of Pakistan could offer (Jahan, 1973, pp. 185–98).

One conclusion was that 'the movement for independence in East Bengal cannot, therefore be explained by reference to the aspirations of the Bengali bourgeoisie' (Alavi, 1971, p. 63). It existed before the Bengali bourgeoisie was created. The class basis of the movement was mainly petty-bourgeois. The urban salaried classes believed economic independence would reduce prices by removing the power of West Pakistan cartels. Bengali bureaucrats looked forward to freedom from the central government's fiscal policies. The radical intelligentsia supported autonomy because they believed it would provide greater opportunity for economic reform in a region with few indigenous capitalists. Alavi concluded that Bengali secession

> emphasises the political role in post-colonial societies of the educàted middle class, whose aspirations are directed primarily towards positions in the bureaucratic-military oligarchy which dominates such societies. The ideology of 'national' solidarity is put forward . . . On the other hand, under-privileged groups put forward their demands in the idiom of regional culture or linguistic or ethnic identity. These demands are reinforced by the phenomenon of economic disparities which are a necessary concomitant of the unevenness of capitalist development. (Alavi, 1971, p. 65)

8. Conclusion

Even if investigations are restricted to the Third World, the phenomenon with which this chapter has been concerned is far too complex and diverse for simple generalisations of a causal nature to be arrived at. Each situation is unique in what prompts nationalism, how central governments respond to nationalist demands, and what further political forces are mobilised as a reaction to such responses. There are important aspects of the subject that have hardly been touched upon in this brief excursion, especially the internal dynamics of separatist movements and the different organisations that make them up.

Apart from the hypotheses generated by the theories reviewed above, the following matters should form part of any research into ethnonationalism:

- the kind of political agenda which a nationalist movement has, whether there is more than one, and what those agenda prescribe for the future governance of the territory should independence be achieved;
- why nationalist movements persist despite the odds against success, and what resources sustain them;
- the socio-economic make-up of the factions within ethnic communities and nationalist movements that are prepared to negotiate for less than complete separation and how these negotiations with the state authorities are conducted;
- what diplomatic and economic relationships develop with the former 'parent' state after independence has been achieved and how far they constitute a continuation of earlier links and interdependencies between regions;
- how states attempt to manage ethnic separatism, the basis on which minority élites are selected for collaboration and accommodation, and the influence of such co-option on the movements involved in the struggle for independence;
- whether the dominant cultural feature identifying a self-perceived national group affects the structure of the nationalist movement and its choice of strategy (how cultural identity affects political behaviour);

- the variability of nationalist movements in terms of organisation, objectives and strategy (including the extent to which they are prepared to resort to violence); and
- how variations in the size, cohesiveness and mobilisation of ethnic communities can be specified and measured for comparative purposes.

12
Peasants, Workers and Revolution

1. Introduction

A paradox in Third World politics that needs to be addressed is that if the production of wealth and the numbers of people involved were indicators of power, the peasantries and proletariats would be powerful groups in all developing countries. As Shanin points out for the peasantry, being food producers, being dispersed and being numerically preponderant should make them a powerful political force. With some exceptions, however, it is their political weakness that stands out (Shanin, 1971, p. 256). Peasants and workers account for large proportions of the populations and produce the goods that earn the foreign exchange, yet experience levels of deprivation that are extreme by any standards. The gap between them and the richer middle classes is widening. Their conditions might be expected to lead them to be highly mobilised in politics, demanding reform and change.

Yet the basic political rights of the poor are notoriously difficult to protect in post-colonial societies. The power of the ballot box is easily emasculated by electoral frauds of one kind or another. In poor societies votes can easily be bought: shoes, mattresses, sacks of beans and T-shirts will suffice in some poor rural communities in Latin America.

Rural people experience various kinds of oppression, not least that of nature, as we see from those parts of the Third World that suffer from drought and famine, poor land, deteriorating soils and climatic failure (Johnson and Bernstein, 1982). In addition to the oppression of nature, the rural poor live in a precarious position as regards life and work. Their land-rights are generally weak, and they live under the threat of dispossession, landlessness and therefore destitution. There are always powerful landowners and their allies willing to obstruct even what governments might initiate in the way of land reform. It is always difficult for the rural and urban poor to assert their rights. Successful appeals to the judiciary are rarely made, even if they can be attempted, because of the costs involved.

As producers on the land the existence of the rural poor is insecure. They operate with crude tools, they are dependent on human or at best animal energy, they are often unable to afford better equipment, seeds, fertiliser, pesticides or irrigation; there are no savings or reserves to fall back on; a crop failure or illness to a member of the family, a fall in the price of produce, or an increase in the price of some input can lead to crisis, indebtedness, and further exploitation. The government may step in to provide inputs at subsidised prices to increase productivity and security, and land reform programmes may be initiated, sometimes with considerable success. However, these often benefit a small number of rich farmers and further impoverish the rural poor.

Rights to land for peasant cultivators or share-croppers are threatened by the commercialisation of agriculture and capital-intensive methods of cultivation, creating not only landless but jobless people. Such people become marginalised into the informal sectors of the urban areas trying to survive by small-scale trade and petty crime – marginalised in all respects: on the fringe of the law, on the edge of subsistence, and with only marginal access to health care, shelter and education or anything else that makes for a decent standard of living. The new urban proletariat being created under pressures of land-shortages, commercial agriculture, population pressures, and the attractions of the cities (mainly in the form of job opportunities created by industrialisation) experience overcrowding in slums and shanty-towns, poverty, inequality, and long-term unemployment. In the formal sector, industrial employment is precarious, often dependent on corrupt employers and officials.

There are therefore large numbers of people who would appear to have everything to gain from political struggle. Yet there are many obstacles standing in the way of their political participation. The social science literature has tended to focus on two themes: the problems experienced by industrial and agricultural workers in effectively articulating their political demands; and the revolution-ary potential of the peasantry. The first aspect provides insights into the social realities of life for the majority of people, even in contemporary democracies, where there are in principle equal political rights and the institutions of representative government.

2. Concepts

The conceptual apparatus required distinguishes between participation, revolt and revolution. 'Participation' refers to normal involvement in constitutional politics through membership of pressure groups and political parties and through voting. The poor in post-colonial societies face special obstacles to such involvement in the politics of their community or their nation.

'Rebellion' refers to extra-constitutional action, perhaps involving violence, when the rural or urban poor take direct action against the governmental authorities or local power-holders in an attempt to resist the intensification of exploitation through higher workloads, declining real wages, victimisation of trade unionists, police harassment, loss of land, or the raising of rents and taxes. Here the political activism is short term. The objective is to redress a wrong. There is no long-term programme or ideology for fundamental change in social and economic relations.

'Revolution' involves the replacement of a whole social order, and not just a political regime, by another. Ideologies and new forms of organisation are required. Solidarity is mobilised, mainly along class lines, but religion may be significant in raising class consciousness, as in the case of Islamic fundamentalism in Iran and Algeria. Existing social and political structures, particularly property relations, are defined as exploitative and oppressive and are challenged as such. The objective is an alternative form of society (Shanin, 1982, p. 313; see also Migdal, 1974, p. 226).

Peasantries

Various definitions of 'peasantry' have been produced. The most frequently cited are those of social anthropologists and particularly Robert Redfield, Lloyd Fallers and Eric Wolfe. Redfield (1956) defined peasants as being involved in economic exchanges and markets (rather than producing for subsistence), political and administrative hierarchies (rather than self-contained primitive communities), a country-wide network of social relations (for example, castes), and two cultural traditions – the 'great' culture of the educated élite and the 'little' culture of the unlettered masses. Fallers (1961) also defines peasants as producing for the market as well as for family subsistence, and belonging to political hierarchies as well as communal structures. Wolfe (1966) focuses specifically on the process of extraction which characterises the relationship between the peasantry and the ruling class. He defines peasants as 'rural cultivators whose surpluses are transferred to a dominant group of rulers' to be used to support the rulers and other social groups who do not farm but who provide goods and services (pp. 3–4). What distinguishes the peasant from the communal cultivator is the production of rent and his integration into a social and political system wider than that of his immediate community: 'it is only when a cultivator is integrated into a new society with a state – that is, when the cultivator becomes subject to the demands and sanctions of power-holders outside his social stratum – that we can appropriately speak of peasantry' (pp. 10–11; see also Geertz, 1962; Shanin, 1971, p. 240; Saul and Woods, 1971, pp. 104–5; and Migdal, 1974, pp. 24–5).

Thus investigation of the politics of the peasantry is complicated in so far as rural societies are not all organised in ways which produce 'peasantries' in the sense of a group that owes a proportion of the product of its labour to a land-owning aristocracy in return for the right to occupy and cultivate the land. In tribal societies in Africa, for example, land was traditionally deemed to be held in common. Landlord–tenant relationships were absent. In tribal societies the individual held land from a corporate descent group of which he was a member. Only the descent group was able to sell land. Individual cultivators might find it difficult to raise credit, because of the restrictions on land alienation, but this reduced dependence on moneylenders. Land shortages did not deprive people of rights assigned by membership of a descent group and did not produce a landless labour force. Problems of land shortage during colonialism were met by migration to sources of employment in industry or plantations. There was no land-owning aristocracy dominant economically and politically.

When the cultivation of cash crops produced a stratum of wealthy cultivators, any further accumulation was dependent upon other economic activities such as trade and transportation. In centralised kingdoms dues might be paid to administrative overlords (village and district heads in the Emirates of Northern Nigeria, for example), but the exactions were slight compared to those of Indian or Latin American landlords (Lloyd, 1973, p. 99; see also Post, 1972). In tribal societies the state, rather than the landlord, has become the agent of exploitation through direct and indirect taxation. The production of cash crops, where this existed, required no alteration in the traditional rules of land tenure.

Colonialism had an immediate impact on such socio-economic systems and may be said to have instituted a process of 'peasantisation' as defined above. It ended 'primitive agriculture' over most of Africa, bringing cultivators into a wider economic and political system and so creating African peasantries and, eventually in some regions, a class of capitalist farmers and a landless rural labour force. Such participation in a wider economic system varied according to whether there were sectors of the economy needing wage labour (mines, plantations, and manufacturing industry), whether there existed an environment and infrastructure conducive to the production of cash crops, whether there was European settlement, and the rate at which an indigenous bourgeoisie developed (Saul and Wood, 1971, p. 108).

To the extent that rural communities are not peasant-based, theories of political behaviour derived from the analysis of peasant societies will be of limited applicability. The question of why peasant-based revolutions have occurred in some underdeveloped societies and not others may thus in part be explained by the form of social organisation which distinguishes one agrarian society from another. The case of Africa is informative here, and will be considered later when attempts to apply the conclusions of comparative historical analysis to Africa are reviewed.

A further complication with the term 'peasantry' needs to be noted in this context. It may imply greater homogeneity in the countryside than actually exists among rich and poor cultivators, sharecroppers, landless labourers, small farmers and even slave labour (revealed in some Brazilian plantations, ranches and sugar cane distilleries in 1992 by the Catholic Church). It has sometimes been useful to distinguish between poor, 'middle' and rich peasants in attempts to locate any revolutionary potential (see below). The difference between a peasant and a farmer is also important, the latter owning land and controlling the disposal of the produce, the former renting land and owing other obligations to landowners. Farmers hire labour, peasants rely on their own or that of members of their family. Different categories of rural people and even the rural poor will experience the problems of political participation and mobilisation with different degrees of intensity.

3. Political Participation

Isolation

A factor that has been widely noted as significant for the political mobilisation of poor people, is their isolation as economic actors (Wolfe, 1968). Peasants work their own land with their own labour in scattered fields. Work is in isolation rather than in co-operation with others. The peasant family is 'atomised' (Migdal, 1974, pp. 42–4). There is little experience of collective exploitation of the kind that landless labourers know, especially if working on a plantation. So the isolation will vary depending upon the social relations of production. Class, or even group, consciousness is difficult to create as a basis for political organisation.

Similar experiences may be felt in some industrial situations, such as mining, where workers are isolated in industrial villages and provided with their needs at the point of employment. They may become unionised, and that may constitute an important basis for political agitation. But union activity may be restricted to concerns in the workplace rather than political issues that affect people in their other roles. The political strength of numerically weak industrial workers in the Third World is further limited by the fragmented structure of small firms which creates 'obstacles to a strong collective organisation of the working class'. Awareness of growing inequalities may breed a degree of radicalism, but this is easily contained by state repression and by clientelist and populist modes of political incorporation 'which facilitate state control and regimentation' (Mouzelis, 1989, pp. 20–6).

In urban areas problems of political organisation similar to those in rural areas are found. In the informal sector of the urban economy households and units of production can be as isolated as they are in peasant society. Separate producers act in isolation to acquire minimal levels of capital, confronting antagonistic social classes in isolation – landlords, merchants, money-lenders, bureau-crats, and wholesalers who can exploit and further weaken them because of these personalised relationships. Hence the efforts being made in developing countries to establish non-governmental organisations to try to strengthen through co-operation people who would otherwise be isolated in their dealings with better organised and more powerful sections of society.

Competition

A related factor is that the rural and urban poor are in competition with each other, rather than sharing a common experience that can form a basis for a common sense of identity and exploitation (Wolfe, 1968; Harris, 1970, p. 20). Unemployment is a major source of competition among urban and rural workers. It is no coincidence that in Namibia some of Africa's most repressive employment practices exist alongside an employment crisis in which each year 16 000 people enter a labour market offering 4000 jobs in the formal sector. The experience of poverty, far from acting to unify people, intensifies the competition for scarce resources – rights to land occupancy, land purchase or rent, employment, loans, particularly during lean times, and access to grazing, water and implements. The members of the informal sector are in competition for cheap items with which to trade. Such experiences do not lead to solidarity among such people. Harris cites the case of radical attempts in India to create alliances representing the lowest castes, and the huge difficulties encountered: 'The natural identification of village Untouchables is, sadly, with the dominant peasant castes of the village (even when they murder some of them) rather than with the millions of Untouchables in other districts' (Harris, 1970, p. 21). Solidarity is further undermined for those who have exchanged rural for urban poverty by the precariousness of their existence in shanty-towns and the constant threat of eviction.

There is no single role uniting the peasantry into a homogeneous group. An individual may be part subsistence farmer, part agricultural labourer, part urban labourer, part sharecropper, part cash crop farmer. Each occupation links the peasant to a different socio-economic interest, again undermining solidarity. For the purposes of politics the poor are caught up in vertical alliances or factions. Patron-client relations spill over from the economy into political organisation. Allegiance to a patron may mean participation in political conflicts that are in pursuit of the patron's interests rather than the client's.

Tribal attachments, encouraged by the competitiveness of urban life and employment, have been a major source of conflict among the rural and urban poor in Africa. Competition for jobs has been an especially potent force in exacerbating ethnic rivalries, and ethnic associations have been one way of providing mutual support and protection for immigrants into the urban areas. In such a context, tribalism may be seen as a form of false consciousness, especially when it is manipulated by political leaders for their own purposes (Post, 1972, p. 248).

The tyranny of work

Then there is what Wolfe refers to as the 'tyranny of work', the daily grind of hard manual labour with little opportunity to take part in political activity when the burden of toil is rarely lifted. It is not easy to escape the harsh regime of subsistence living, whether in the agricultural sector or on the fringes of the urban economy. The intensity of this problem again varies between different categories of people, especially in this case between men and women. Poor women in Third World societies have heavy domestic chores in addition to cultivating, marketing, and engaging in wage labour. This may include carrying large quantities of water long distances to service the home. With energy consumed at such a rate and inadequately replenished by a poor diet, it is not easy to persuade people to spend what little free time they have travelling by foot to and from political meetings. The physical effort and malnourishment experienced by the poor cannot sustain political activism.

The risks of participation

There are also great risks in getting involved in politics and neglecting the few assets that are owned (Worsley, 1984, pp. 119–22). Such neglect could mean disaster for lives at near subsistence level. Migdal concluded from his comparisons of Third World peasant societies that:

Innovations were looked upon sceptically, for the peasant was aware that so-called advances could leave him worse off than before, and this could be an intolerable risk to those already hovering near the brink of survival. (1974, p. 53)

There are other risks. There is the risk of alienating the people upon whom one is dependent – landlord, employer, money-lender, and people of higher status (Migdal, 1974, p. 233). These are all participants in the local political process whose interests may be threatened by successful political agitation by the poor. Relations of dependency support the poor through systems of reciprocal obligations within the traditional framework of the local community. Kinsmen will help in times of need and adversity. Kinship networks consist of rich and poor, making it difficult for poor people to engage in political activism which appears threatening to their own kin. Similarly political action may be seen as putting other members of the kinship group at risk, even though the objective is the improvement of conditions for people of that class. Kinship ties may strengthen the obligations of the poor peasant to the rich. Such ties cut across class lines, further reducing political consciousness (Wolfe, 1968). Finally, political action often risks severe repression by an authoritarian state.

Reciprocity

There are many dimensions of village reciprocity. In peasant communities with feudalistic landowners, 'lords' can prevent peasants from becoming outward-looking because of the resources and services which people of wealth, power and status control, especially land, capital and knowledge. Migdal hypothesizes that the more such resources are controlled by the peasants' overlords, the more those services are important to the peasant and his family, and the greater the monopoly the lord has over their supply, then the firmer the control that the lord can exercise. Historically the Latin American *hacienda* or *latifundia* present the most extreme cases of restrictions on peasant participation in life outside his immediate community (Migdal, 1974, pp. 34–42).

The whole social and political organisation of the peasant village was initially geared to the community's survival through reciprocal relations in which all were required to participate. Consequently mechanisms were put in place to block the formation of alliances extending beyond the village and releasing people from dependence on it, thus undermining its self-sufficiency. Success in enforcing such self-sufficiency might vary, depending, for example, on the strength of community organisation. 'Yet the striking characteristic of the historical village is the degree to which inward-oriented forces generally dominated' (Migdal, 1974, p. 84). The major pressures eroding this self-sufficiency and inward-orientated behaviour were increased taxation, the decline in handicraft production brought about by industrialisation, growing urban demand for food, imperialism and population growth.

Organisational factors

The potential for political organisation and communication on the part of the poor is further reduced by low levels of literacy and education, extreme parochialism, respect for traditional authority, religion and custom. Access to the mass media is limited. It is also difficult to organise and unionise when there are substantial reserve armies of labour available to much better organised employers. Women may feel reluctant to join male-dominated organisations such as trade unions. Another factor inhibiting organisation, whether of workers or peasants, is that leadership needs to be drawn from people with education and experience outside the countryside and from the intelligentsia (Migdal, 1974, pp. 223 and 232; Shanin, 1982, p. 311). The Chinese revolution had the support of the peasantry, but was led by a party whose leadership was drawn mainly from the urban intelligentsia. It was not even an agent of the Chinese peasantry but drew support more widely from Chinese rural society. The bulk of the party's rank and file was made up of people from peasant origins, but they were soldiers or party officials rather than cultivators (Harris, 1970, pp. 22–3; Post, 1972; p. 245). In parts of Latin America today the Roman Catholic clergy have provided badly-needed leadership, organisation and consciousness-raising.

But peasants are often suspicious of knowledge that appears to be part of the social system in which they are oppressed. Towns are seen as places where the wealthy, powerful and educated are concentrated. Peasants cannot identify easily with people whose work is so different from their own. Their experiences of outsiders is often a negative one (Migdal, 1974, pp. 210–11). Government officials, in particular, are prone to collaborate with the wealthy and powerful members of local society to deny the poor their rights (Allen and Williams, 1982, pp. 84–6).

Cultural subordination

Finally the peasantry and unskilled workers experience cultural subordination. This can be traced back at least as far as colonial racialism and forms the bedrock of contemporary racialism in South Africa. Domination is exercised through ideological devices which confer subordinate status on exploited groups such as Latin American indians, untouchables and tribals in India, and women in many countries. An important task of such ideology is to instil the belief that subordination is natural and irreversible. Research in rural Tanzania revealed that officials 'believe the poorer peasants to be lazy, ignorant and prone to practice witchcraft. . . . Such opinions are sometimes sincerely held, and sometimes no more than rationalizations of their own interest in aligning with the richer peasants' (Allen and Williams, 1982, p. 87).

Developing peasant participation

There have, despite these impediments to successful political mobilisation, been some important developments that have extended peasant politics beyond parochial and primordial associations and relationships. Migdal points to the decline in the political significance of the village, especially as a centre for the settlement of disputes, as the critical factor leading to a changed political orientation on the part of the peasantry, drawing them into formal organisations representing their interests, such as unions, political parties and other types of political association, albeit initiated by non-peasants, such as union leaders, party officials and even government administrators. This decline was caused by the growing importance of interactions with institutions beyond the village, especially the state which, in varying degrees, incorporated village institutions into its administrative hierarchy (Migdal, 1974, pp. 200–1).

Then there is universal suffrage, which forces élites to seek the support of peasants and workers, even if through vertical factions and patron–client relations. As peasant communities have become increasingly integrated into wider social and economic networks under the influence of commercialism, so patron–client relations have become part of hierarchies extending from the village to the city. At all levels patrons provide protection and favours, while clients provide political support. For example, in India

> Leadership in the village council was usually exercised by the economically more powerful of the dominant caste members, since they had the resources to perform the favours required in order to establish a political network of supporters. (Rosen, 1975, p. 171)

Patron–client relations eventually governed relations between office-holders and voters, the structure of political parties, and the conduct of political life at State level. Hierarchical relationships between families expressed through patron–client relationships permeated all the countries studied by Rosen – the Philippines, Indonesia, Thailand and India. Variations depended upon the strength of the family as an institution, population pressures on land, food production, land ownership, and the structure of political and religious authority. As was noted in Chapter 8, the essence of the relationship is reciprocity:

> Patron–client relationships serve to protect individual families against minor disasters through a redistributive ethic that ensures a subsistence flow of goods from patron to client . . . in exchange the client provides labour and (perhaps more important) a variety of social, political and religious services to the patron. (Rosen, 1975, p. 206)

The vote is a political resource which others need. The leverage which this gives should not be underestimated. In 1969 impoverished villagers in Brazil's north-east, where 80 per cent of the population was illiterate or semi-literate, 70 per cent earned £40 or less a month, and employment conditions verged on slavery in some areas, voted successfully for the Workers Party candidate in the first round of presidential elections rather than, as in the past, for the candidates of those on whom they depended for survival, the large landowners. Peasants give their support to political organisations claiming to represent their interests in exchange for concrete benefits. They exchange their votes and other forms of political participation for goods and services: credit, public investments, tax relief, water and electricity supplies, agricultural extension services, or marketing facilities.

There has also been a gradual spread of education leading to an enhanced awareness of social causality and to stronger class consciousness. A sense of common identity among industrial workers in particular develops an awareness and resentment of widening gaps between their living standards and those of the political and business classes increase. This awareness can become more important than ethnic or religious divisions (Allen and Williams, 1982, p. 149). A significant growth in the number of non-governmental organisations, many of which combine collective action for production with political agitation and pressure, is another important development.

Migdal identified different levels of peasant political action beyond passive accommodation of the demands imposed by the political system: active pursuit of individual material or social gains; action to secure gains for an identifiable group; and action to secure gains for their entire class. It was then hypothesized that peasants do not move to the second and third levels of action until they have had successful experience of the previous one (1974, pp. 218–21). A similar classification of patterns of peasant political action is drawn up by Shanin, who distinguishes independent class action from guided political action by the peasantry, when external organisers come from millenial movements, secret societies or a people's army. Shanin's conclusion that under some circumstances the peasantry is an object of leadership or manipulation, 'used' by an external leadership for aims that may not be in the peasants' interest, is one that, as we shall see, has been rejected by other scholars. But his category of 'fully spontaneous, amorphous political action' taking the form either of local riots or 'peasant passivity' which causes government decrees to be negated by 'spontaneous, stubborn and silent non-fulfilment' is one worth testing in contemporary contexts.

4. Peasant rebellions

Occasionally groups of peasants will rise up against their oppressors in order to extract concessions from the governmental authorities or local landowners and merchants. Peasant political consciousness tends to be localised. It is also likely to be directed towards adjustments to the existing economic and political regime rather than towards restructuring and transformation.

> Peasant movements strike at local targets, and as such do not attempt to reach out and attack their enemies at source. A violent attempt to adjust local relationships would thus be a rebellion, rather than a revolutionary attempt to destroy classes completely. Peasant revolutions, as opposed to rebellions, are thus unusual and infrequent phenomena, and depend on the movement's ability to extend beyond the rural areas. (Post, 1972, p. 241)

A notable recent example is the 1994 uprising in the southern Mexican state of Chiapas by the Zapatista National Liberation Army (ZNLA). The grievances expressed by the ZNLA concerned homes, work, land, education and electoral fraud. This is but one of many indigenous peasant groups campaigning for land, democracy and equal rights which is unlikely to benefit from Mexico's participation in the North American Free Trade Agreement. The uprising has forced the government to listen to the grievances of the peasantry in a country where, according to World Bank estimates, 32 million of the population of 85 million live in poverty and 95 per cent of the country's wealth is in the hands of a few hundred thousand people. The public sympathy that it has elicited may even undermine the dominance of the Institutional Revolutionary Party which has ruled Mexico since 1929. The success of the ZNLA has encouraged other indian groups to seek the support of left-wing workers, students and intellectuals. In the state of Chiapas 140 peasant groups declared their intention to establish a state-wide autonomous organisation. The consequences of this rebellion may be far-reaching, but it does not amount to a revolutionary movement and it is unlikely that the plight of the rural poor and indian peasants in Mexico will be much affected in the long run. A comparable instance from Africa is the peasant uprising which took place in the Western State of Nigeria in 1969 (Anediran, 1974).

What is true for peasants is also true for industrial workers. According to Shanin, it can equally be said of them that they are 'preoccupied with local day-to-day concerns rather than with general long-term aims and complex ideologies'; for workers, wages, pensions and holidays take the place of land, rents and taxes which form the limited horizons of the peasantry (Shanin, 1982, p. 310).

Political opposition has in some instances taken the form of 'social banditry' when small, armed groups prey on the rich and powerful, offering their protection to poor villagers in return for refuge. 'Banditry is the most primitive form of taking sanctions against the system, where self-interested criminality is scarcely distinguishable from socially conscious rebellion, and where the sanction is no more than a marginal irritant to the system' (Harris, 1970, p. 20; see also Hobsbawm, 1959). A recent example is Phoolan Devi, the 'Bandit Queen' of Uttar Pradesh, released from prison in 1994 after awaiting trial for eleven years. This is how she was described by Michael Fathers of the *Independent* on 20 February 1994:

> scourge of high caste Hindus and darling of the country's rural downtrodden. . . Like Robin Hood she was loved by the poor and feared by the rich. She roamed the countryside, usually on horseback, exacting retribution and revenge from wealthy landowners whom she believed tormented and exploited their tenants.

5. Revolution in the Third World

It is appropriate to set a discussion of revolution in a context that is largely concerned with agrarian politics because, as Shanin reminds us, 'every successful self-generated revolution for over a century has taken place in a "developing society"', peasant revolt being central to all of them (Shanin, 1982, pp. 319 and 321; see also Dunn, 1972, p. 234). The analysis of such events has been largely dominated by a search for the conditions necessary for a peasant-based revolution. Historians and social scientists have asked why these should occur in some societies and not others which seem to be comparable in respect of the social and economic factors which a priori might be thought likely to lead to revolution (Dunn, 1972, p. 226; Goodwin and Skocpol, 1989). The search has thus been for the necessary conditions associated with revolution in predominantly agrarian societies.

This is an extremely difficult project. As Dunn points out, because there have been relatively few revolutions, they are difficult to study sociologically. They are not sufficiently homogeneous in terms of their causes to provide categories large enough for the formulation of explanatory hypotheses that are other than historical (Dunn, 1972, p. 241). Nevertheless the importance of revolutionary events in the history of the world is so great that social scientists have felt obliged to identify uniformities and causal explanations: and historical explanations, as distinct from predictions, are not to be dismissed as unimportant in the quest for knowledge.

Capitalism and crisis

Shanin identifies four major characteristics of the processes preceding the revolutions of the twentieth century:

(1) A major crisis causing severe dislocation of society and its day-to-day functioning; (2) a major crisis of the governing élite, affecting its ability to govern; (3) a crystallization of classes and subclasses expressed in a sharp increase in self-identification, organization, and militancy along class lines; and (4) an effective revolutionary organization providing leadership in the political struggle. (1982, p. 313)

This categorisation of the immediate preconditions leaves still to be explained the reasons why the crises should occur and why classes should become more militant.

Shanin is here influenced by Wolfe's comparative study of the major social and political upheavals of the twentieth century fought with peasant support: the Mexican revolution of 1910, the Russian revolutions of 1905 and 1917, the Vietnamese revolution, the Algerian liberation struggles of the 1950s, and the Cuban revolution of 1958. Though Wolfe studied revolutions his analysis distinguishes between the causes of peasant rebellions and uprisings, and the conditions which are needed to turn such events into factors contributing to revolution. He is concerned with the transition 'from a movement aimed at the redress of wrongs, to the attempted overthrow of society itself' (Wolfe, 1968, p. 294). Though peasants initially rebel to redress wrongs 'the iniquities against which they rebel are but, in turn, parochial manifestations of great social dislocations. Thus rebellion issues easily into revolution, massive movements to transform the social structure as a whole' (p. 302).

The dislocations of which peasant rebellions are local manifestations are both economic and political. Economically revolutions in which the peasantry has participated have been associated with the development of capitalism and the commercialisation of agriculture (see also Shanin, 1971, pp. 249–51; Rosen, 1975, p. 15). As labour, land and wealth are turned into commodities the peasant's fragile equilibrium is threatened:

> in Russia land reform and commercialization together threatened the peasant's continued access to pasture, forest and plowland. In Mexico, Algeria and Vietnam commercialization menaced peasant access to communal land; in Mexico and Cuba it barred the peasant from claiming unclaimed public land. In Algeria and China, it liquidated the institution of public granaries. In Algeria, it ruptured the balance between pastoral and settled populations. In Mexico, Vietnam, Algeria and Cuba, finally, outright seizures of land by foreign colonists and enterprises drove the peasants back upon a land area no longer sufficient for their needs. (Wolfe, 1968, p. 280)

Pressures on land were increased by population growth which worsened the imbalance between population and resources.

Politically the advent of capitalism precipitated another crisis – in the exercise of power. Traditional power-holders were undermined by groups associated with commodity production and the sale of labour (Wolfe, 1968, p. 282; see also Zagoria, 1974). A political vacuum is created when those with economic power have yet to obtain political legitimacy and those with traditional legitimacy are losing it rapidly. Migdal's research confirms this, but shows that those who traditionally held power were often the beneficiaries of the market forces that eventually destroyed traditional forms of authority in the peasant village (Migdal, 1974, p. 135).

All of the cases studied by Wolfe showed that the political vacuum is filled by a central executive power which attempts to rise above the contending groups by playing them off against each other. A further political crisis occurs for the peasantry when the market forces at work in the economy make the reciprocal supports between peasants and landlords redundant. New economic groups may be responsive to market forces, but they are unresponsive to the disrupted population because they are ignorant of or indifferent to its plight.

Forms of leadership

These factors make the peasantry rebellious. What turns the peasantry into a revolutionary force? First, the situation through-out society is likely to be in a state of crisis under the impact of capitalism and industrialisation. The social, economic and political orders will all be in decay. Wolfe's case material also confirms that peasants need outside leadership to make a revolution. The importance of a coalition between peasants, intellectuals, students, professionals, clerics and industrial workers, whose class distinctions may be very fluid, in providing a forward-looking revolutionary consciousness in place of the peasant's inclination to seek inspiration from a lost 'golden age', is confirmed by White (1974) in the case of Vietnam, and Goodwin and Skocpol ((1989) for Iran, Cuba and Nicaragua. Revolutionary leadership generally takes the form of an 'intelligentsia-in-arms', either as a military organisation or a paramilitary political party. In Mexico and Algeria it fell to the army to stabilise the new regime. In Russia, China and Vietnam it was the party which reorganised the state and the social order. Wolfe is able to identify the *consequences* of the task of social reconstruction falling to these two different organisations, but admits that it is difficult to say why 'in some cases it is the army that generates the new political controls, while in other situations this task falls to the party' (1968, p. 301).

The history of Africa since 1960 may offer a clue to this conundrum. Here revolutionary action has either come from the military, as in Ethiopia in 1974, or from a guerrilla war of liberation against colonialism (as in Angola and Mozambique). The peasantry has been involved in liberation movements, but more because of the appeal of nationalism than because of economic dislocation. Chaliand, concerned mainly but not exclusively with the experience of guerrilla wars of national liberation against colonialism, especially in Africa between 1960 and 1975, focuses on the driving force behind the political movements involved, and identifies a single common denominator – nationalism. Revolutionary forces stand for 'authentic national values', whether the opposition is a regime, a coloniser or an external aggressor (Chaliand, 1977, pp. 178–84).

Land reform has not generally been a rallying point for political action on the part of the peasantry in Africa. After independence power passed into the hands of the new commercial and bureaucratic bourgeoisie which incorporated support from the rural masses into the political parties which emerged from the nationalist movements. Even in those rare cases when peasant rebellions had posed a serious challenge to the colonialists, as in the Mau Mau emergency of 1952–56 in Kenya, middle-class politicians rather than peasant leaders emerged to negotiate independence. Peasant political identity was secondary to ethnic identity as politicians exploited tribalism in their competition for power, and secured the support of the peasantry in return for a share in the spoils of office. Political instability caused by economic crises has been followed by military intervention, and very few military *coups* have been motivated by revolutionary objectives (First, 1972, pp. 457–65).

Social exchange

The relationship between the leaders of revolutionary organisations and the peasantry is central to Migdal's explanation of why peasants should be induced to participate in revolutionary struggles. Migdal rejects explanations based on 'frustration with deprivation', ideological altruism, or a view of the peasantry as an inert mass which bends to 'the cajoling or coercion of outsiders' (see also Dunn, 1972, p. 238). He stresses the interdependence between the peasantry and revolutionary organisations. A revolutionary peasantry results from a process of social exchange. The peasantry seek to solve local problems with the benefits offered as incentives to participate in revolutionary action. The problems and crises which confront the peasantry and make them susceptible to revolutionary leadership are caused by increased participation in economic markets, a participation which is fraught with dangers associated with corruption, monopolistic merchants and economic insecurity – an economic network that is 'full of shortcomings and injustices'. The faster the disruption to the normal social organisation of the peasantry (speeded up, perhaps, by a succession of crop failures), the more responsive will the peasantry be to outside revolutionary organisers.

Revolutionary organisations, for their part, need to expand their power through recruitment among the peasantry. They need to be able to demonstrate that they can deliver what peasants need. This must be more than other political organisations because of the risks involved, not least that of severe retaliation by the state. Delivering what peasants need includes substitutes for the socio-economic arrangements that are to be replaced by the revolution. Migdal's studies showed revolutionary organisations to have offered marketing arrangements; land reform; co-operatives; harvest labour; public utilities such as roads, communications and irrigation ditches; social services such as health care and education; and, most importantly, destruction of the power of corrupt officials, monopolistic merchants and landlords. Revolutionary organisations, such as parties and armies, also offer opportunities for social mobility. Revolutionary participation by the peasantry involves

> various segments of the peasantry seeking to solve certain very specific problems that arise as villages move from an inward- to an outward-orientation. These problems stem from the conditions of monopoly, corruption and structural incompleteness peasants face in their expanded outside involvement. (p. 238)

Race (1974) relates the social exchange between revolutionary organisations and their potential recruits to the governmental crisis that is so often associated with Third World revolutions. Revolutionary organisations, such as those in southern Vietnam and northern Thailand, may be able to step in when the government forfeits its opportunity to develop influence among disaffected rural communities (see also Goodwin and Skocpol, 1989).

Class structure

Alavi compared the Russian and Chinese revolutions and peasant movements in India in order to enquire under what circumstances the peasantry become revolutionary. Recognising that the peasantry is not an undifferentiated mass, Alavi also asked 'what roles different sections of the peasantry play in revolutionary situations' (Alavi, 1973, p. 292). He was particularly concerned with the respective roles of 'middle' and poor peasant, and the conditions likely to lead to the revolutionary mobilisation of the latter. Poor peasants are landless sharecroppers working land owned but not cultivated by landowners. Included here are farm labourers employed by rich peasants. Middle peasants are independent smallholders who own their land and produce enough with their own labour to be self-sufficient. Rich peasants own substantial amounts of land, requiring the exploitation of wage labour. These three classes of peasant are thus distinguished in terms of modes of production rather than merely wealth or poverty. Though there is overlapping between these categories, the distinction between the economic independence of the middle peasants and the subordiantion and dependence of poor peasants is crucial for Alavi's analysis.

Comparison of Russia, China and India shows the poor peasants to be the least revolutionary in the initial stages of class conflict. This is largely because of extreme economic dependency and a servile mentality. However the morale and militancy of the poor peasant can be mobilised when anti-landlord or anti-rich peasant action is taken by the middle peasantry. Poor peasants need to be shown that the power of landlords can be resisted, before they will become revolutionary. The middle peasants are initially the most militant, but may become fearful for their interests as a revolution gathers momentum.

Wolfe's conclusions differed from Alavi's findings in two important respects. First, poor peasants and landless labourers were found to need some external power to challenge the power of landlords and employers. In Mexico it was the Constitutionalist army in Yucatan, in Russia the return of peasant soldiers from the army to their villages, in China the Red Army. 'Where such external power is present, the poor peasant and landless labourer have latitude of movement; where it is absent, they are under near-complete constraint' (1968, p. 289). Wolfe agrees with Alavi that the middle peasants have the autonomy to challenge the power of their overlords (see also Yoo, 1974), but includes in this category peasants located in peripheral areas, whether they be poor or 'middle'. In such areas the poor can supplement their resources from casual labour, smuggling and livestock-raising which, not being under external control, give the peasantry some 'latitude of movement'.

We have marked the existence of such a tactically mobile peasantry in the villages of Morelos, in the communes of the Central Agricultural Region of Russia; in the northern bastion established by the Chinese Communists after the Long March; as a basis for rebellion in Vietnam; among the fellahin of Algeria; and among the squatters of Oriente in Cuba' (Wolfe, 1968, p. 290).

The revolutionary potential of poor peasants is further increased when they are located in regions that the state finds it difficult to control, such as frontier areas. The 'tactical mobility' of the peasantry in such areas as Morelos in Mexico, Kabylia in Algeria and Oriente Province in Cuba was further enhanced by ethnic or linguistic identity: 'Ethnic distinctions enhance the solidarity of the rebels; possession of a special linguistic code provides for an autonomous system of communication' (Wolfe, 1968, p. 292).

The destruction of the peasantry

Wolfe identifies the middle peasants as those who conform to the model later provided by Barrington Moore of revolutionary potential under the impact of commercial agriculture. The middle peasants in the countries studied by Wolfe were most vulnerable to the changes brought about by commercialisation – population growth, competition from other landlords, the loss of rights to grazing land and water, falling prices, interest payments and foreclosures – while remaining locked into traditional social structures of mutual aid between kin and neighbours.

Barrington Moore's comparative study of India, China, Japan, England and Russia at different moments in their histories ranks as one of the most authoritative pieces of historical scholarship comparing peasant societies in which revolution occurred with those where it did not though it might have been expected to. Moore tested a number of hypotheses offering explanations of why the peasantry had been 'decisive in China and Russia, quite important in France, very minor in Japan, insignificant in India to date, trivial in Germany and England after initial explosions had been defeated'. His aim was to 'relate these facts to each other systematically in the hope of discovering what kinds of social structures and historical situations produce peasant revolutions and which ones inhibit or prevent them' (Moore, B., 1973, p. 453).

Moore is able to discard a number of plausible explanations. First, the theory that revolution among the peasantry occurs when the situation of the peasantry deteriorates markedly under the impact of commerce and industry is dismissed because of the case of India, where the deterioration in the economic position of the peasantry during the nineteenth and twentieth centuries has been as great as in China but where the political behaviour of the Indian peasantry has been very different.

Secondly, there is the hypothesis that a massive threat to the whole way of life of a peasantry – property, family and religion – will stimulate revolution. But for this to be true, the English peasantry, destroyed by the enclosure movement in the seventeenth century, should have risen in massive revolt and the French and Russian peasantries, whose societies remained largely intact, should not have.

A third thesis is that absentee landlordism encourages peasant revolution – contrast the behaviour of the French and English aristocracies of the eighteenth century, for example. However, Russian landlords in the nineteenth century lived on their estates, 'a fact that did not deter peasants from burning manors and finally driving the *dvorianstvo* from the historical stage' (pp. 454–5). Moore also questions the belief that the French aristocracy spent more time at court than on their estates.

The next hypothesis to be discarded by Moore is that 'a large rural proletariat of landless labour is a potential source of insurrection and revolution'. This falls foul of the historical evidence from Russia, where 'no rural proletariat of this type was important in the Russian Revolutions of 1905 and 1917', and China, where the 'revolutionary upsurges of 1927 and 1949 were certainly not those of a rural proletariat working huge landed estates' (p. 455).

Religion might be thought to be the crucial variable, with Hinduism accounting for the passivity of the Indian peasantry. However, Moore argues that religions teaching resignation, acceptance, fatalism and the legitimacy of the social and political order are the product of urban and priestly classes and by no means necessarily part of peasant beliefs. Even though heretical movements in Europe and Asia have broken out from time to time, they have not universally accompanied the important peasant upheavals. For example, there is little evidence of religious motivation in the peasant disturbances preceding the French or Russian revolutions.

Moore's conclusion is that these explanations have concentrated too much on the actions of the peasantry and not enough on the actions of the upper classes in revolutionary situations. When the analysis was broadened, Moore found that what determined whether the peasantry will be revolutionary was the response of the upper class to the challenge of commercial agriculture. Revolution is most likely when the aristocracy damages the interests of the peasantry as a class by exacting a larger surplus from it, but leaves it intact by failing to develop a sufficiently powerful commercial impulse in the countryside. This factor links the revolutions in eighteenth-century France, nineteenth-century Russia and twentieth-century China. When the commercial interest in rural life is sufficiently strong to destroy the peasantry as a class, peasant-based revolution is less likely. Moore concludes:

> the success or failure of the upper class in taking up commercial agriculture has a tremendous influence on the political outcome. Where the landed upper class has turned to production for the market in a way that enables commercial influences to permeate rural life, peasant revolutions have been weak affairs . . . a revolutionary movement is much more likely to develop and become a serious threat where the landed aristocracy fails to develop a really powerful commercial impulse within its own ranks. Then it may leave beneath it a peasant society damaged but intact. . . The main areas where peasant revolutions have in modern times had the greatest importance, China and Russia, were alike in the fact that the landed classes by and large did not make a successful transition to the world of commerce and industry and did not destroy the prevailing social organization among the peasants. (pp. 459–67)

Moore's historical researches found two other factors to be related to a society's vulnerability to peasant revolution. One was the existence of a centralised agrarian state bureaucracy used to extract an economic surplus from the peasantry. The other was the social organisation of peasant societies. Three features of this organisation appeared to be particularly significant. First was the link between the peasant community and its overlord: 'where the links arising out of this relationship between overlord and peasant community are strong, the tendency towards peasant rebellion (and later revolution) is feeble' (p. 469). Strong links supporting social stability depend upon there being enough land for both peasants and overlord, and upon the existence of fair extractions in return for the lord's protection and justice: 'the contribution of those who fight, rule and pray must be obvious to the peasant, and the peasants' return payments must not be grossly out of proportion to the services received' (p. 471). The other two features of peasant social organisation significant for the political behaviour of the peasantry were the existence of class divisions within the peasantry and the level of solidarity and cohesiveness within peasant communities.

6. Conclusion

Revolution is a manifestation of the political instability of the previous regime. Rebellions also indicate that constitutional procedures for resolving conflict have been rejected by disaffected minorities that have no confidence in the justice or effectiveness of the alternative methods open to them for the redress of their grievances or the protection of their interests. Much of what has been explored in this chapter thus relates to the widespread instability of regimes in the Third World. It leads to a consideration of the broader phenomenon and its conceptualisation in political science.

The focus in this chapter has been on the poor, the obstacles to their effective political participation and the crises which precipitate extreme reactions against those who dominate them economically and politically. It might be expected that as societies develop economically and become richer, poverty will be reduced and the appeals of radical and violent political change will be greatly weakened for a growing number of people. Political stability should follow and be reinforced by political change designed to facilitate political participation and engender consensus about the prevailing social, economic and political order. Such possibilities and the hypotheses that have been prompted by the study of economic growth, social mobility, national integration, institutional development and political cultures are the subject of the next chapter.

13
Stability, Democracy and Development

1. Introduction

The number of military *coups*, civil wars, communal conflicts and other manifestations of political instability in the Third World has been too great not to attract a great deal of attention in the social sciences. But at first glance the failure of parliamentary politics seems not to fall into any particular pattern. Assuming for the moment military intervention to be an indicator of instability, rich and poor countries alike have succumbed. Senegal is relatively rich in African terms and has not experienced severe instability. Nigeria, also rich by African standards, has not been able to maintain democratic politics since independence for more than five years at a time. Ideology equally does not seem to provide a clue. Both capitalist and socialist developing countries have experienced instability. Capitalist countries such as Kenya, India and South Korea have survived (though not without considerable politically-inspired violence). Capitalist Zaire and Nigeria have succumbed over and over again to military intervention. Socialist regimes such as Tanzania and North Korea have been stable whereas the Central African Republic has fallen to the military. Federal and unitary constitutions alike have experienced such manifestations of instability.

2. Conceptual difficulties

It is not surprising then that considerable effort has been expended on explaining political instability in the Third World. But the concept of 'stability' is fraught with difficulties which need to be recognised before a proper evaluation can be made of why regimes survive.

A normative concept

The first thing to be recognised is that 'stability' is a highly normative concept. What is instability for one person might well constitute the welcome overthrow of a detestable regime for another. (Many in the West welcomed instability in communist Eastern Europe and the Soviet Union.) The US has produced many of the political scientists interested in political instability, while at the same time being actively engaged in destabilising regimes that it does not like. One person's stability is another person's repression. It is not easy to exclude values from the analysis of political stability. Outside the Marxist tradition, instability is seen as deviancy, a slip on the path to progress. It is an aberration that has to be explained. In the Marxist tradition, instability is accepted as inevitable in the progression of history. Class conflict is an unavoidable stage in the movement of society towards its end-state. Crisis is the inevitable consequence of the contradictions of economic development.

Consequently some would argue that it is not possible to handle the concept in a scientific way at all. An analytical obsession with instability simply indicates a preference for the regime that is under threat. Understanding a particular type of political change, especially one that often entails violence, loss of life and severe economic dislocation, has to be based on an objective analysis of the conditions leading to such change. This is not easy when there are so many values at stake when instability is experienced.

Democratic stability

Secondly there is the question of whether the analysis is concerned with stable government or stable *democratic* government. The answer might seem obvious, in that few would presumably want to concern themselves with stable totalitarianism. But whether the alternative to democracy is totalitarianism depends on one's definition of democracy. The analysis of stability is complicated when democracy has been superceded, not necessarily with great political instability, by a single-party regime which the analysts concerned do not regard as democratic.

Identifying the necessary conditions for the survival of democratic regimes has long been a preoccupation of political science, and is particularly relevant today when so many attempts are being made to establish or restore Western liberal democracy in so many parts of the world (Pinkney, 1993, ch. 2). But interest has not concentrated exclusively on the travails of democracy. Whereas the attention of political science focused on the preconditions of stable democracy in the 1950s and early 1960s, interest shifted in the 1960s and 1970s to a concern with political order, whether in democracies or other types of regime. In the 1970s US political science in particular concentrated more on the prerequisites of order and control, rather than pluralism and democracy, revealing a strong ideological impulse (Leys, 1982).

Concern for the maintenance of regimes and élites, political order and stability in policy-making arose from changing political realities in the Third World, the pessimism which developed during the first Development Decade, and perceptions of continuing external influence over supposedly independent nation-states and sovereign governments. Attention concentrated on the policy-making capabilities of national élites, their ability to bargain with foreign interests, and the need for centralised government. Successful governmental interventions were seen to be obstructed by competition between national and local élites and passive traditionalism. High rates of growth were seen as requiring authoritarianism, democracies apparently having relatively poor economic records both in terms of growth and distribution (Higgott, 1983, pp. 19–39; Huntington, 1987).

Stability is still sometimes seen as an end in itself, if not regardless of the regime involved, then at least with grudging respect for what can be achieved with less than full democracy. Consider, for example, the reference by Diamond to political restructuring in Malaysia, which has limited political competition and restricted freedom of expression: 'While this restructuring has levelled parliamentary democracy down to semi-democratic status, it has also brought considerable ethnic peace, political stability and socio-economic prosperity' (1989, p. 2).

Nevertheless, recent reforms in the direction of pluralist democracy and away from military rule and other forms of authoritarianism have revived interest in how to identify the prerequisites of stable democracy (an excellent example being Diamond *et al.*, 1990). Though the enquiry has not always been couched in terms of the conditions required for political stability, the current concern is with the maintenance of stable democracy. However, it has to be recognised that stable democracy might be replaced by stable authoritarianism or even a stable regime which may not conform to some definitions of democracy, particularly those entailing multi-partyism, but which would be regarded by few as authoritarian. The failure of democracy should not be equated with the breakdown of stable government. It may simply be that a particular definition of democracy determines the scale of the failure, as in Diamond's analysis of the 'failure' of democracy in Sub-Saharan Africa where, by the early 1970s, multi-party democracy had disappeared in all but Botswana, Gambia and Mauritius (Diamond, 1988, p. 5).

Handling the concept of stability is also made difficult by the fact that it is often used in a way which fails to distinguish between countries that have experienced the overthrow of a democratic regime and its replacement with a stable but authoritarian one, and countries where there is constant civil disorder and change of regime. Much of the concern for the health of democracy over the past thirty years has been prompted by tendencies to 'drift away' from democratic standards (Emerson, 1963, p. 637) rather than a drift into instability, though the two trends are usually closely related. Huntington falls into this trap when he cites 'going communist' as evidence that Cuba and the Indian State of Kerala are unstable (Huntington, 1965, p. 406).

Currently 'democracy' is defined in Western liberal terms (Pinkney, 1993, ch. 1). For example, Diamond *el al.* require a system of government to provide meaningful and extensive competition between individuals and groups, highly inclusive levels of political participation in the selection of leaders and policies, and civil and political liberties sufficient to ensure such competition and participation, before it is classified as democratic, though they acknowledge that countries satisfy such criteria to differing degrees, and that rules and principles may be contaminated by practice (1990, pp. 6–8). Rueschmeyer *et al.* look for realistic possibilities rather than philosophical ideals: 'modest' popular participation in government though representative parliaments, the responsibility of government to parliament, regular free and fair elections, freedom of expression and association, and an extensive suffrage (1992, pp. 10 and 41–4).

Defining stability

Thirdly, there is the problem of finding a satisfactory operational definition of 'stability'. Various indicators have been employed, such as the turnover rate for chief executives, deaths from internal group violence per million population, and the total number of violent incidents (Russett, 1964). Attempts have been made to measure the aggression of groups within the political system, the longevity of governments, the freedom of elections, and the constitutionality of governmental acts (for reviews see Hurwitz, 1973 and Ake, 1974). None of these completely captures a sense of what is involved in political instability. Even when political structures change, it may not necessarily be destabilising. Ake's formulation of instability in terms of members of society deviating from 'the behaviour patterns that fall within the limits imposed by political role expectations' has the advantage of extending the types of events that are to be considered beyond the élite interactions which are conventionally regarded as indicators of political instability – *coups*, electoral violence, political assassinations and so on – as well as acknowledging that what is destabilising to one political structure may not be to another. For example, a refusal of leaders to seek an electoral mandate may be destabilising to a constitutional democracy, but not to a hereditary monarchy (Ake, 1974 and 1975; a similar approach to instability is found in Castles, 1974).

Timing stability

Fourthly, there is the time factor. In addition to knowing what it is a country must remain free from, it is necessary to specify some time period during which it must remain free from destabilising factors for it to be labelled stable.

Despite such difficulties, a great deal of effort has been put in to analysing the failure of systems of government to persist over a prolonged period. These need to be categorised.

3. Economic explanations

One set of factors that has been associated with political stability relates to various aspects of economic development.

Economic growth

First, increasing affluence is said to improve the chance of stability, especially in countries with democratic regimes. Lipset (1959; 1960) was the initiator of this diagnosis. He set out a proof that the stability of democratic government is positively correlated with measures of affluence and economic modernisation. Indicators of wealth such as per capita income, the percentage of the population owning motor cars, and the number of doctors, radios and telephones per thousand population, were combined with measures of industrialisation such as the proportion of the population still engaged in agriculture, and measures of social development such as literacy rates, educational enrolments and levels of urbanisation. Correlations were found with democratic stability in Latin America, Europe and the English-speaking countries.

Lipset's interpretation of the correlations was in terms of affluence reducing lower-class discontent. He argued that his data confirmed the age-old view (traceable back to Aristotle) that

> only in a wealthy society in which relatively few citizens lived in real poverty could a situation exist in which the mass of the population could intelligently participate in politics and could develop the self-restraint necessary to avoid succumbing to the appeals of irresponsible demagogues. (Lipset, 1959, p. 71)

Other observers have similarly identified poverty as a major cause of political instability. For example, writing about Asia, Brecher states that 'people who live at the margin of subsistence are either indifferent or hostile to government . . . it remains true for most of the new Asian states that all-pervasive poverty undermines government of any kind' (1963, p. 623).

Not only the average wealth, but also the levels of industrialisation, urbanisation and education were found to be higher for the more democratic countries investigated. Lipset argued that economic development led to greater economic security and better education, both of which allow 'longer time perspectives and more complex and gradualist views of politics'. Increased wealth and education also contribute to pluralism 'by increasing the extent to which the lower strata are exposed to cross pressures which will reduce the intensity of their commitment to given ideologies and make them less receptive to supporting extremist ones'.

Economic development also enlarges the middle class, whose interest is in moderating conflict – which it is able to do by rewarding moderate political parties and penalising extremist ones. The greater the wealth of the lower class, the less opportunity there is for the upper class to deny them their political rights. The wealthier a country, the less important it becomes if some redistribution takes place; losing political office becomes less significant and, therefore, non-democratic means of holding on to power become redundant, as does nepotism: 'The wealth level will also affect the extent to which given countries can develop "universalistic" norms among its civil servants and politicians'. Lipset also argued that wealth proliferates countervailing sources of power and opportunities for political participation, communication and recruitment, all of which are supportive of democracy.

Critics of Lipset have pointed out that when more regions of the world were examined, poor and underdeveloped *stable* societies were found. What they seemed to have in common was that they were authoritarian rather than democratic regimes. In fact it seemed that the poorer the dictatorship the more stable it was likely to be. Stability seemed to be possible without either wealth or democracy. Europe's unstable democracies and authoritarian regimes were also shown to have had higher levels of development than Lipset's group of Latin American democracies. The problem with Lipset's analysis was that it revealed correlation without accurately indicating the direction of causality. It did not use multivariate analysis which allowed the causal weight of variables to be estimated by controlling for other causal factors. All that Lipset's data showed was a causal tendency (Diamond, 1992, pp. 94–5).

It also seems feasible that political stability might cause affluence and economic growth rather than be the consequence of it. Some politically stable nations achieved stability before they achieved their affluence. Similarly, totalitarian regimes were also able to produce stability before producing economic change. So Lipset's explanation, despite the superficial attractiveness of the idea that as a society gets richer there will be fewer discontented people and greater consensus in favour of a democratic status quo, has problems associated with it.

Nevertheless, almost all of the large number of quantitative studies using multivariate analysis as well as cross-tabulations published since Lipset's original paper find a positive relationship between democracy and various indicators of socio-economic development. The finding of greatest significance for an understanding of political stability is that 'high levels of socio-economic development are associated with not only the presence but the stability of democracy' (Diamond, 1992, p. 108). There are, inevitably, some exceptions to the rule but, after an extensive review of the literature and a new cross-tabulation of per capita GNP with type of regime, Diamond felt it safe to theorise that 'the more well-to-do the people of a country, on average, the more likely they will favour, achieve and maintain a democratic system'. Considering the different quantitative methods, time-spans and indicators used 'this must rank as one of the most powerful and robust relationships in the study of comparative national development' (Diamond, 1992, pp. 109–10; see also Rueschmeyer, 1991 and Rueschmeyer *et al.*, 1992, pp. 13–20).

There is still a fundamental problem with this type of analysis, however. It actually tells little about the reasons why democracy breaks down, other than that there is likely to have been a drop in the level of some statistically significant socio-economic indicators. Such a mode of analysis cannot explain why a fall in, say, per capita income is likely to reduce the chances of democratic survival. For this a more qualitative and historical approach to individual countries needs to be taken (Potter, 1992).

Case studies, most notably by theorists of Latin American dependency, have often challenged the relationships which quantitative analysis purports to establish. Latin America shows no simple correlation between socio-economic development and democracy, with some relatively rich countries losing democracy (Argentina in 1930) and some relatively poor countries developing democratic institutions (for example, Chile in the first half of the nineteenth century). Economic performance (that is, broadly distributed growth) has been more important for democracy than high levels of socio-economic development (per capita income or structure of production). The process of socio-economic development in Latin

America may be supportive of democracy, depending on how élites respond to the new political demands generated by increased urbanisation, industrialisation, education and communications. Whether new groups are included in the political process through institutional developments, especially political parties, and given access to economic opportunities and rewards (such as land, jobs, health care and consumer goods) is also relevant. So democracy has fared better in countries such as Venezuela and Costa Rica, where the new social forces unleashed by development are accommodated within the political system, than in Brazil and Peru where too often they have been excluded: 'the contribution of socio-economic development to democracy illustrates again the powerful and indeed inescapable mediating role of political leadership, choice and institutionalization' (Diamond and Linz, 1989, p. 44).

Asia also reveals that the relationship between development and democracy is by no means simple. The case of India shows that democracy is not necessarily incompatible with a low level of development. A high level of development can increase the demands and supports for democracy through increases in income, education, participation, the political consciousness of the middle class, pluralism or foreign contacts; or be destabilising by loosening traditional forms of authority, generating political demands from newly created political interests, and deepening ideological cleavages. Such developments can push authoritarian regimes in the direction of democracy, or present democracies with unmanageable problems. The consequences of development for democracy are very ambivalent (Diamond, 1989, pp. 33–4).

Nevertheless, case studies have confirmed many of the hypotheses generated by quantitative analysis: that education strengthens commitment to democracy; that political violence is greatest in poor countries; that the growth of a middle class is conducive to democracy; that the centrality of politics to economic opportunity is a fundamental cause of democratic breakdown; and that the development of a plurality of interest associations supports stable democracy (Diamond, 1992, pp. 117–25).

The rate of growth

An alternative hypothesis is that the *rate* of economic development is crucial to political stability. The more rapid the rate of development, the more difficult it is to maintain stability (Huntington, 1968). Rapid economic growth produces social groups that find themselves left behind in the progress being made. Their skills, occupations and economic activities become less important than they were. When a society is modernising and transforming its economy from subsistence or small-scale production via industrialisation or the commercialisation of agriculture, and introducing new technology, formerly important groups find themselves excluded from the new economic opportunities. For example, peasant proprietors would be turned into a rural proletariat. Discontent would arise from a loss of status and autonomy.

Mass movements seeking revolutionary change will be made up from people whose bonds to the established order are changing. Rapid economic growth increases the number of such *déclassés*: by changing the methods of production and the distribution of income, and by weakening the bonds of family, class, caste, tribe and guild. The *nouveaux riches* use their economic power to challenge the social and political order. The *nouveaux pauvres* resent their poverty, a particularly significant fact given that economic growth can significantly increase the number of losers. Rapid growth concentrates material gains in relatively few hands as prices increase faster than wages and technological change replaces people with machines. At such times, and especially in the early stages of industrialisation, there are unlikely to be welfare arrangements to compensate for economic hardship. There will also be those who, though making some absolute gains from economic growth, find that their relative position has deteriorated, a further source of dissatisfaction and of contradiction between the structure of economic and political power. Furthermore, levels of consumption can decline with rapid economic growth. Standards of living may have to be reduced to produce the required rate of savings. Consequently 'it is economic stability – the absence of rapid economic growth or rapid economic decline – that should be regarded as conducive to social and political tranquillity' (Olson, 1963, p. 550).

This convincing a priori reasoning needs to be queried in view of the growth rates in many Western countries since 1945 which have been higher than at any previous period in their histories without causing political instability (Castles, 1974). The fact that there are examples of countries which have experienced high rates of economic growth and political stability, in Europe and Scandinavia, suggests that there is another problem of causality here.

In developing countries, however, there may be circumstances which, when combined with rapid growth, produce political instability. It may also be that political stability makes it possible for a country to enjoy a high rate of economic growth. If political stability and high rates of growth go hand in hand in advanced industrialised countries, it does not necessarily follow that this would be the case in poor agrarian societies. Booth's research on Central America found that rapid growth in agriculture together with industrialisation reduced the relative and absolute living standards of the working class, who then revolted against their governments. Only when, as in Costa Rica and Honduras, governments responded with policies to reduce inequalities and increase the real value of wages, did popular protest subside. Where the state responded with repression (Nicaragua, El Salvador and Guatemala) 'opposition mobilisation and unity increased and led to a broad, rebellious challenge to regime sovereignty' (Booth, 1991).

In Third World countries, political factors are again an intervening variable, particularly the speed at which democracy has been introduced. Thus in Latin America the abrupt and violent seizure of independence followed by civil and foreign wars produced political turmoil in the nineteenth century that made progress towards any kind of stable government very difficult to achieve. With the exception of Venezuela, the countries in Latin America that have been most successful in developing democracy have had long histories of élite competition, supporting Dahl's (1971) thesis that democracy is most likely to be successful when political competition becomes institutionalised before the expansion of the suffrage and other forms of political participation. Latin American history supports the hypothesis that democracy is likely to be more stable if based on a historical sequence that establishes national identity first, followed by the creation of legitimate state structures, followed by the extension of rights to political participation to all members of society (Diamond and Linz, 1989, pp. 5–9). Inadequate preparation for constitutional democracy by colonial powers has been seen as another factor contributing to the difficulties in coping with change experienced by many newly-independent regimes (Brecher, 1963, p. 624; Diamond, 1988, pp. 6–9 and 1989, p. 13; Pinkney, 1993, ch. 3), though it has to be recognised that a common colonial legacy can be followed by very different experiences of political stability, as the cases of India and Pakistan confirm.

The revolution of rising expectations

A period of rapid economic growth can be followed by an economic down-turn. Then there may be a 'revolution of rising expectations' meaning that if there is a set-back in prosperity after a period of rapidly rising economic growth, frustration would be experienced by people whose expectations are rising faster than the economy. This frustration among people who are denied the increase in the standard of living which they had anticipated can be politically destabilising, because of the ways in which their frustration is likely to be expressed. Building upon Marx's observation that we measure our desires and pleasures by social comparison and not by the objects that provide the satisfaction, and de Tocqueville's conclusion that 'Evils which are patiently endured when they seem inevitable become intolerable when once the idea of escape from them is suggested', Davies offers a largely psychological explanation of revolution which postulates that: 'Revolutions are most likely to occur when a prolonged period of objective economic and social development is followed by a short period of sharp reversal' (Davies, 1972, pp. 136–7).

The reversal in economic circumstances produces anxiety and frustration as an intolerable gap opens up between what people expect and what they actually get. 'Political stability and instability are ultimately dependent on a state of mind, a mood, in a society . . . it is the dissatisfied state of mind rather than the tangible provision of "adequate" supplies of food, equality, or liberty which produces the revolution' (Ibid., p. 137). Deprivation, it is argued, does not lead to revolution, but rather a sudden decline in the opportunities to continue improving one's condition in line with expectations. A 'revolutionary state of mind' requires an expectation of improvements in the satisfaction of needs (for physical, social and political benefits) to be under 'a persistent, unrelenting threat'. The 'crucial factor' is the fear that 'ground gained over a long period of time will be quickly lost'. The relationship between *expectations* of needs satisfaction and their actual satisfaction can be demonstrated by a J curve:

Figure 13.1   *Needs satisfaction and revolution*

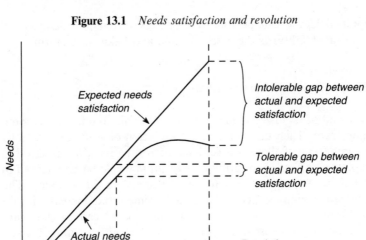

Source: Davies, 1972, p. 137.

Davies claims that this theory fits not only the American, French and Russian revolutions, but also the Egyptian revolution of 1952 after a series of strikes, peasant uprisings and urban riots was rounded off by a *coup d'état* by army officers. He points out that expectations of improvements began in 1922 with a grant of limited independence by the British, and continued with industrialisation and an increase in exports following the Second World War. Expectations of continued progress were dashed between 1945 and 1951 by a collapse in the world demand for cotton, unemployment among a third of the work force, high inflation, humiliating defeat by the new state of Israel, government corruption and shortages of wheat and oil. The promises made by nationalist groups contribute to such problems when the anticipated benefits of independence failed to materialise.

Foreign influences

Some economistic explanations of instability emphasise the importance of foreign factors. In Latin America debt and dependency have destabilising implications as they affect the legitimacy of democracy by adversely affecting the economic performance of government.

However, more overtly political factors act independently of such economic influences or mediate their impact. International demonstration and diffusion may be important, as in the case of the Cuban revolution within Latin America, military *coups* in neighbouring countries, or the attitude of the USA towards dictators and democracies. Aid has been used as a weapon against undemocratic practices. Threats, real or perceived, to a country's security have fostered authoritarianism, militarisation and curbs on civil liberties in Asia, encouraging two interesting hypotheses:

> international effects on democracy (positive and negative) tend to be greater the smaller and more vulnerable the country

and

> international influence . . . is more pro-democratic when the regional or global trend is towards democracy, and when the powerful external actors make the promotion of democracy a more explicit foreign policy goal. (Diamond, 1989, p. 42. See also Diamond, 1988; Diamond and Linz, 1989, pp. 50–1; Diamond *et al.*, 1990, p. 33).

4. Sociological explanations

The distinction between developed and developing countries when considering the impact on politics of the rate of economic growth is important for other reasons than those already noted. In moving from an economy based on agriculture to an economy based on manufacturing there is a serious shift of population from rural to urban areas. In industrialising countries with high rates of economic growth, with industrial capital derived from surpluses generated one way or another from the commercialisation of agriculture, one is likely to find rapid urbanisation. What is happening in the countryside will dislocate life there, removing livelihoods from people and displacing rural populations that have to seek work in urban centres. Towns are attractive for other reasons than economic opportunity.

Hence some explanations of political instability have stressed social rather than economic factors, or at least that the two cannot be disentangled, so that though in industrialised countries a high rate of economic growth will not be destabilising, in an industrialising country it will be, because of social factors and in particular the process of urbanisation.

Urbanisation

Third World urban areas are said to harbour extremism and activism. High levels of unemployment are most severe within such areas. Urban people are attracted to volatile forms of political expression. Urban political organisations provide opportunities for power, status and social mobility to otherwise underprivileged groups, so political activism becomes even more attractive. When cities are full of 'marginalised' people, the opportunity costs of political activism may be very low. With poverty, unemployment, inequalities of income, insecurity, bad working conditions and poor health, accompanied by a lack of governmental provision for the poor and by disparities in political power that exacerbate disparities in wealth, it is not surprising that the process of urbanisation is thought to be a major cause of political instability in the Third World.

Social mobility

Another sociological explanation of instability emphasises social mobility. Mobility is made possible by the economic changes associated with development. When new economic activities are introduced into the economy with new technology and methods of financing, new roles and occupations come into existence in both the urban and rural areas. Workshops, factories, warehouses and public utilities need managers, technicians, mechanics, wage labourers and professionals. Such new economic roles create new opportunities for economic independence for individuals who in a traditional society would not expect to enjoy such opportunities. The unity and bonds of family, kin group and village community will be undermined by these new roles and values.

When those new roles recognised in the modern economic context fail to receive recognition in the traditional context, they come into conflict with those who are being displaced from their positions of status and power by the new sets of values – village elders, tribal chiefs, traditional healers, magicians, craftsmen, priests (Pirages, 1976, ch. 3). Such groups are displaced by people whose ties with their extended families, castes, classes and kinship groups are being loosened by the processes of industrialisation and commercialism. Economic development produces opportunities for social mobility by releasing the bonds that fitted people into a social order. Subsistence agriculture and cottage industries become less significant in the wider economy, and the significance of the village as a community is weakened. Communities that consist of atomised individuals are brought into existence. The conflicts that are generated by such developments may be reduced by continuing bonds of ethnicity such as were referred to earlier. But these themselves may then become competitors for the rewards available under the new economic arrangements and a new focal point for political conflict which the system may not be able to contain (Pye, 1966; Eisenstadt, 1964; Apter 1965; Huntington, 1968).

We must be wary of the somewhat crude models of 'traditional' and 'modern' contained in this line of analysis. Ake points out that role confusion and disorientation can stimulate group identity and associational sentiments; industrialisation can be integrative, creating new foundations for social linkages, such as classes; structural differentiation can eliminate some sources of conflict and reduce tension; new forms of political participation can be supportive rather than destabilising. Consequently the fact that modernisation can generate political instability does not mean that it necessarily will (Ake, 1974, pp. 576–84).

Ethnicity

The destabilising effect of modernisation is related to another factor that has received extensive attention. This is ethnicity and the problems that many societies have had when loyalty to an ethnic group transcends loyalty to a new state. As we saw in Chapter 11, that problem is sometimes referred to as the crisis of integration or nation-building. Nation-building is sometimes seen as an ethical and psychological activity designed to reorientate people's loyalties towards a new political entity. But primordial attachments based on tribe, language, religion or race have been and still are enormously powerful in most regions of the Third World. They have been extremely divisive (Ake, 1967).

The problem of national integration was that when new states came into existence primary loyalties were focused on groups other than the national community. So public authorities had difficulty in sustaining a sense of legitimacy because the nation, its political institutions and its methods of government did not enjoy the same level of legitimacy as more primary points of attachment and loyalty (Saravanamuttu, 1989, p. 2).

Whether ethnic diversity threatens political stability depends very much on how it is structured and managed. Recent research on Asian and African countries shows that ethnicity is reduced in significance when there are cross-cutting identities rather than a correspondence between ethnic, religious, regional and linguistic cleavages. Instability is also more likely where there are a few large ethnic groups whose conflicts dominate politics, and less likely when there is a multiplicity of small ethnic groups – compare Nigeria and Tanzania in this regard. The cultural pluralism which has been cited as almost a hallmark of political underdevelopment has often meant a lack of consensus about political values. There is then what is often regarded as a crisis of political culture.

5. Political explanations

The political culture

This leads to a consideration of a group of influences on stability that are explicitly political. One explanation of instability has been in terms of the political cultures found in Third World societies. A landmark in this line of analysis was an attitude survey carried out in the early 1960s by Almond and Verba, the results of which were published as *The Civic Culture* in 1963. Samples of people from different societies held to be at different stages of political development were interviewed to test how strong their commitment to their political system was. It was posited that there is a pattern of political attitudes that supports democracy – a 'civic' or balanced culture 'in which political activity, involvement and rationality exist but are balanced by passivity, traditionality, and commitment to parochial values' (Almond and Verba, 1963, p. 30).

The political culture is usually defined as the way people evaluate and judge political acts and institutions (Pye and Verba, 1965; Kavanagh, 1972; Rosenbaum, 1975). It is a system of beliefs, values and ideals about the way a system of government should function. Subject to some variations, 'political culture' refers to standards of evaluation about the rules of the political game. Some political scientists have limited the concept to values concerning the procedures of politics, and how political leaders should be selected, how they ought to behave, and how authoritative decisions ought to be made. Others, such as Almond, add to this the scope of government action and the legitimacy of government intervention in certain areas of social and economic activity.

Cultural values will include the means for transferring power and the legitimate boundaries of the state. Nationalism and secession are the consequence of values about territorial boundaries and where they ought to be drawn. Ideas about personal political involvement, about who is entitled to participate and about whether political action is likely to be effective within a given political system also form part of the political culture. Included too are attitudes towards other participants and their roles as political actors. A political culture may not endorse the involvement and participation of all sections of society. For example, women may be excluded.

A great deal of attention has been paid to the way political cultures are transferred from generation to generation. The influences of early stages of life, the family, the school, churches, youth movements, political parties and the interpretation of one's political history are all said to be formative influences on the young, which enable political cultures to be transmitted through processes of socialisation.

The idea of shared values in the context of cultural heterogeneity as being a major problem for Third World states is closely related to the importance attached to the political culture as a source of either consensus or conflict. Stability is seen as a consequence of a widely accepted set of values and orientations towards the political system (Diamond, 1993a, pp. 427–8). There is much convincing evidence that a 'low' level of political culture can undermine democracy. A lack of commitment to democratic principles, procedures and beliefs on the part of African political élites, for example, has made it difficult to sustain democracy – even though some traditional values support consensus, moderation, consultation, the rule of law and controlled political authority (Diamond, 1988, pp. 14–15). Similarly in Latin America democratic cultures have helped to maintain democracy and make it more difficult to consolidate and perpetuate authoritarian government, as in Uruguay in 1980 and Chile in 1988 where 'both the fact of the plebiscites and the ultimate popular rejections of the military at the polls reflected the continuing vitality of democratic culture' (Diamond and Linz, 1989, p. 13).

However, there is no simple, deterministic link between political culture and democratic stability because experience of democracy is itself a powerful socialising influence. In Latin America democratic political cultures have been strengthened by the successful performance of democratic government in accommodating new interests, expanding the economy, developing education and securing the welfare of the lower classes. The legitimacy created by governmental success helps explain the strong correlation between the economic performance of democratic regimes in Latin America and their stability (Diamond and Linz, 1989, pp. 11 and 44). Furthermore, studies of Asian society show that political cultures are often mixed, with countries having 'some significant values and orientations that press in a democratic direction and others that press in an authoritarian one' (Diamond, 1989, p. 17).

The secret is knowing what creates the critical level of consensus. Following de Tocqueville, Lipset argued that democratic values are more likely to be preserved at a time of great social change (such as when democracy is first introduced) if all major social groups are given some access to the political system early on, and the status of major pre-democratic institutions (for example, monarchy) is not threatened during the transition period. Legitimacy is also preserved by governmental effectiveness: efficient political and administrative decision-making which enable governments to meet the needs of the population. In many African states the squandering of resources by mismanagement, corruption, waste and greed has alienated support for democratically constituted regimes. It is no coincidence that Botswana is the most stable African democracy and has moved from being one of the poorest African countries to one of the richest in a decade and a half (Diamond, 1988, p. 16). A problem for many Third World countries is that they are locked into a vicious circle of low legitimacy and ineffective performance (Diamond *et al.*, 1990, p. 10).

The values and orientations found to be associated with the stability of democracy are moderation, cooperation, bargaining and accommodation. 'Moderation' and 'accommodation' imply tolera-tion, pragmatism, willingness to compromise, and civility in political discourse (Diamond *et al.*, 1990, pp. 16–17; Diamond, 1993b, pp. 10–11). Time is often seen as a critical variable here, producing (for example) a contrast between the time available to India to acquire democratic values and have them disseminated from élites to the masses, and the limited opportunity to develop democratic values in Africa before independence (Diamond, 1993b, pp. 16–27).

Research has revealed strong statistical relationships between per capita GNP and personal beliefs and values supportive of democracy, suggesting that the political culture may be an important intervening variable in the relationship between develop-ment and democracy (Diamond, 1993b, pp. 1–2). As countries become richer and improvements in education and communications are felt, people have been observed to become politically more aware, effective, and defensive of their political and civil liberties. Evidence from Taiwan, Thailand, Turkey and Brazil has been adduced to support this hypothesis (Diamond, 1993a, pp. 419–20). The causal relationships, however, are not simple and in a single direction. The political culture influences behaviour and the operation of institutions, but is itself influenced by the development of new social forces, modes of socialisation, leadership and international influences. Hence the political culture can sustain democracy despite relatively low levels of economic development. For example, both India and Costa Rica show 'surprising democratic persistence despite low or moderate economic develop-ment' because 'political culture at both the élite and mass levels clearly plays a strong supporting role' (Diamond, 1993a, p. 425).

Problems with the concept of political culture

Reservations have been expressed about the concept of political culture and explanations of change in terms of it. First there is a problem of causality in assuming that certain types of political culture are conducive to the maintenance of certain sorts of political system, and that if there is no congruence between culture and system the system will change as a result of being undermined by a lack of consensus and legitimacy. Political culture must not be viewed too deterministically (Diamond, 1993b, pp. 9–10). There is a presupposition in much of the literature that the line of causality runs in this direction. For example, the work by Almond and Verba on the 'civic' culture and democracy implies that a set of values about the rightness of certain political structures, a high level of political competence on the part of individuals, and a sense of trust in other individuals and groups, are not only the mark of a modern society but also lead to stable democracy. It could equally be argued that all such values could be a consequence of the experience of democratic government. When attitude surveys are carried out to determine what the predominant political culture is, all that may be revealed are the expectations that people have as the result of their experience of a political system. If there is the possibility that the political culture is not cause but consequence, it ceases to have theoretical significance for understanding change and the loss of critical levels of support.

There is a further problem with the argument that instability stems from the plurality of political cultures found in many Third World societies and the transformation of a set of relatively discrete communities, with their own sets of values about how government should be conducted and, in particular, the legitimacy and trustworthiness of other actors in the system, into a nation. This is that a good deal of the political instability which Third World countries have experienced would seem to be associated with widely shared values. The idea that the only way to protect one's own interests is to acquire and hold on to a monopoly of power to the complete exclusion where possible of other groups, has characterised the behaviour of many political movements in the post-independence era, as it did the behaviour of some of the fragmented nationalist movements fighting for independence. Because of the significance of the state in social and economic terms it has been the object of attention of political groups seeking to monopolise power, rather than share it in a spirit of trust with other groups. Such widely disseminated attitudes towards power have been very destabilising.

So if some shared values are conducive to stability and others are not, the use of the concept of culture implying shared values as an explanation of stability no longer works. At the very least it becomes a circular argument: stability occurs if members of society share values conducive to stability. It depends what those shared values are. It is not enough to say that a society will be stable when a sufficiently large number of people share common values about how to conduct political affairs.

This is quite apart from the problem of how many is enough. Writers on political culture acknowledge that in any particular society one is likely to find more than one set of beliefs about the role of government in society, the way it should be conducted, and the proper political roles of different sections of the community. The question of what proportion of society there must be supporting one view of how government should be conducted before there can be said to be sufficient consensus to sustain a political system that corresponds to those shared values, is left unanswered. How homogeneous does the culture have to be, and how widely shared?

Another difficulty arises if we assume that there is a crisis of legitimacy when some proportion of society feels that the rules of government lack moral authority and so dispute them, not seeing it as immoral to manipulate the constitution for its own ends. It is not easy to predict, simply by knowing that they believe some or all of those rules to lack moral worth, how far people will deviate from the established norms. People might believe that the rules do not deserve their moral approval without being prepared to break them. This is a universal dilemma in politics. A system can lose moral authority if it is proved easy to abuse. But acting contrary to some rules because others are being bent and broken may be more damaging than going along with the outcomes of the rules as they are presently being played.

This creates another problem for the idea of the political culture as a determinant of stability. If it is not possible to know how far people will deviate simply because they lack moral respect for government, it is equally impossible to know whether when they deviate it is because of that lack. In the Third World there is frequent flouting of the rules, with electoral malpractices very widespread. Does this signify a crisis of legitimacy? It does not always lead to instability, unless instability is defined as breaking the rules. So it again does not seem to be a very useful theoretical explanation to say that if consensus is lacking, there will be political instability.

Finally the concept of political culture implies that attitudes and feelings about politics reflect rational choices and high levels of awareness about what a political system means as far as individual interests are concerned. There is no place for the idea of false consciousness or hegemony. Yet what people believe to be in their interest in terms of structures of government may be ideas and cultures that are promulgated by socio-economic groups intent on maintaining their own domination. Alternative sets of values would undermine that dominance. The political culture literature to some extent takes that notion on board with the idea of socialisation and the way sets of political values are passed from one generation to another. But socialisation is described as a generational process rather than as a class problem, whereby one generation passes on to another values that are contrary to their class interests. The idea of political power being in part expressed through false consciousness and an ability to gain acceptance of ways of organising society has very wide implications throughout the study of politics. The political consciousness of specific groups in Third World societies is an important issue if we are to understand why so much deprivation, injustice and inequality is accepted in societies where such features are most severe. The political culture idea does not really tackle what must be regarded as an important dimension of political power.

Inequality

A proposition concerning political instability which can be traced back to Aristotle is that equality in society will secure peace and stability (Pinkney, 1993, pp. 86–90). This is relevant to the Third World where generally there is great inequality and where 'deep, cumulative social inequalities represent a poor foundation for democracy' (Diamond *et al.*, 1990, p. 19). A common-sense view suggests that if there are profound inequalities there will be resentment and discontent with a system of decision-making that is unable to redress the imbalance or is controlled by those intent on preserving the status quo.

The idea of hegemony might lead to an obvious qualification of such a simplistic assumption. Socialisation may effectively lead people to accept their station in life. However, there is some evidence supporting a relationship between political instability in poor countries and material inequality, such as in land-holdings (Rueschmeyer *et al.*, 1992). The poorest countries with unequal land distribution are more unstable than countries that have inequalities in land but also have alternative sources of wealth and reasonable levels of income (Russett, 1964; Huntington, 1968). This relates to the economic backwardness argument that poor countries cannot produce enough wealth to satisfy all needs, whereas richer countries satisfy basic needs and make the standard of living of the poorest reasonable and not too insecure.

The converse argument is that stable countries have relatively egalitarian distributions of income. Lipset presented evidence to support this. But it has to be recognised that the hypothesis would seem to be falsified by inegalitarian societies that have nevertheless experienced considerable stability. India would be a case in point, frequently cited as a stable democracy, at least in Third World terms (Castles, 1974). It obviously depends on how stability is measured. Evidence from Latin America suggests that the relationship between inequality and stable democracy is more complex than a simple correlation. Although not incompatible with the development of democracy, inequalities in land distribution and wealth are less conducive to democracy than a more egalitarian social structure, suggesting 'a tension between extreme inequality and (or) class polarisation on the one hand, and stable democracy on the other' (Diamond and Linz, 1989, p. 39).

The poor are not necessarily a source of resistance and revolt, possibly because they do not perceive there to be any alternative to their condition. There is also the fact that violent changes in politics have often been instigated and supported by those who have benefited most from the distribution of ownership and rewards in the economy and the allocation of status in society. Inequalities in society do not necessarily mean that it will be those at the lower end of the socio-economic spectrum who will resort to violent resistance to the laws and institutions of the political system. The inequality argument leaves us needing some other explanation of the poor's acquiescence and the wealthy's subversion.

Class conflict

From a Marxist perspective a theoretical explanation of instability would be in terms of class conflict. As classes develop within capitalist economy and society, their interests become increasingly irreconcilable. The impoverishment of the labouring class is accompanied by the growth in its size until eventually revolution becomes inevitable. But at least one of the problems with this line of thought in the Third World context is that if class consciousness is developing, it is in a unique way. It is less in terms of the ownership of the means of production and more in terms of political power. Those who control and manage the means of production, such as bureaucrats earning salaries, often confront a peasant society that has yet to develop class consciousness derived from its material position in society.

Then there is the problem alluded to earlier, that it is often the privileged members of society who indulge in destabilisation. In LDCs it has been noted how far conflict and crisis within the newly emerging middle class have been a source of political instability. Factionalism, perhaps along ethnic lines, among the propertied classes and classes in charge of the state apparatus has often led to military *coups* or the illegal manipulation of political processes. Rather than peasantries rising up against their oppressors, or workers revolting against their exploiters, sections of the middle class compete for control of the state, using methods that fall outside the law and the constitution.

A crisis of authority

Another answer to the problem of instability stresses the crisis of authority. Third World states lack the power to make their presence felt throughout society. They lack a legal and administrative capacity to rule. Bureaucracies might be overdeveloped in terms of political power but they are not necessarily effective in terms of administration. The state cannot deliver the services which taxpayers believe they are paying for; it cannot extract the resources from society that it needs to finance its activities; it cannot maintain law and order; it cannot police its territory effectively. The case of Uganda in the 1980s seems to support this kind of explanation. Too many areas were under the control of criminals, bandits and other groups which had no legitimate authority. There are other societies in which this is a problem. The Thai government does not control its northernmost provinces – they are under the control of drugs barons. In Colombia there has been virtual civil war between the state and organisations that want to remain outside the scope of the state's authority and the enforcement of its laws.

The reservation that must be expressed about this explanation of instability is that regimes are more often overthrown by those who control the coercive apparatus of the state than by those who control extra-legal means of coercion, whether as criminal organisations or opposition groups. The military is the most obvious case in point. The crisis of authority comes because the coercive apparatus of the state turns against its civil masters, not because that apparatus is so weak that it cannot resist an external challenge to the state's authority. In the Philippines in the mid-1980s there appears to have been an effective expression of 'people power' and the overthrow by the masses of a weak and corrupt regime, but even here the army was crucial. The strength of the state apparatus, or the military part of it, has been and still is crucial to the survival of regimes. Some regimes are far more dependent on coercion than others. Democracy in South Africa was eventually achieved by popular pressure supported by international opinion against a formerly highly effective coercive state. So the crisis of authority explanation has its shortcomings, because we do not know how much coercion is needed to maintain order, or how effective the state has to be in enforcing compliance with its laws before it can be deemed stable.

The balance of power

A recent attempt to theorise about the conditions necessary for the survival of democracy employs the methodology of comparative history applied to Southern and Central America to develop a 'balance of power' approach (Rueschmeyer *et al.*, 1992). A balance of power between classes (and coalitions of classes), between the state and civil society, and between international and national pressures is seen as the crucial determinant of whether democracies survive even under adverse conditions. The stability of democracy was found to vary according to different historical contexts, depending on the overall balance of power.

The relative power of social classes was found to be dependent upon the reaction of the new middle class, emerging with the development of capitalist economies, to the rising power of the working class. The working class had supported democracy and the landed upper class had consistently opposed it, especially when controlling a large supply of cheap labour and forming a significant part of the economic élite, as was the case in South and Central America throughout the first half of the twentieth century. The relative weakness of the working class in Latin America has always been a contributory factor in the instability of democracy in the region (Rueschmeyer *et al.*, 1992, p. 282).

The middle class supported representative government, but opposed the inclusion of the working class. Middle-class support for democracy was apt to disappear when its interests were threatened by lower-class pressures, the middle class often supporting military intervention which curtailed civil rights and parliamentary government even though it found its own access to the state restricted. Political parties were found to be crucial in consolidating a balance of power between classes – in mobilising the working class and in protecting the interests of economically dominant classes so that they had no need to resort to authoritarianism (Rueschmeyer *et al.*, 1992, p. 9).

A balance between state power and civil society was found to be necessary for the stability of democracy and the avoidance of authoritarianism. In developing countries the state's autonomy at the time of the emergence of mass pressure for democratisation was greater than in the history of European democracy, a factor of significance to the balance of power and therefore the stability of democracy. Autonomous social organisations, supported by religion, could act as a counterbalance to the state, but their class content is important for democratic outcomes, as they have sometimes served as the repositories of authoritarian ideologies.

Other research has supported this aspect of the balance of power argument. Case studies on Latin American countries have revealed the importance to democracy of a state capable of maintaining order and territorial integrity through the rule of law, but balanced by 'a pluralistic, autonomously organised civil society to check the power of the state and give expression to popular interests . . . there is a strong correlation between the strength and autonomy of associational life and the presence and vitality of democracy'. Democracy was more viable when state interventions were accountable and controlled rather than authoritarian and corporatist. Decentralisation also secured legitimacy and effectiveness, both crucial to stability (Diamond and Linz, 1989, pp. 27–35).

The importance of a countervailing power to that of the state is confirmed by post-colonial African history. Here the state has been 'the primary arena of class formation' and the 'primary means for the accumulation of personal wealth', leading to corruption, the concentration of power, the emergence of a parasitic bureaucratic bourgeoisie, and the absence of a middle class to demand 'the expansion of democratic rights and limitation of state power'. With a few exceptions, the state has not been balanced by a plurality of autonomous associations – intellectuals, traditional leaders, professionals, trade unions, business associations, religious groups, students, journalists and so on – that are necessary for stable, responsive and accountable government: 'unless the people are incorporated in the development process, their alienation from the state will intensify and the possibility of any kind of stable authority will diminish' (Diamond, 1988, pp. 21–7). In Asia, similarly, wherever bureaucratic and military dominance has restricted the autonomy of interest groups, voluntary bodies and political parties, a foundation of democracy has been removed with authoritarian consequences (Huntington, 1984; Diamond, 1989, p. 22; Diamond *et al.*, 1990, pp. 22–4).

The concept of a balance between international and national forces refers to the varying impact which foreign influences can have on the internal balance of power. Economic dependence of agrarian exports strengthens the power of large landholders. Capital-intensive industrialisation using imported technology blocks the development of a working class. Foreign-owned mineral extraction for export, and import-substituting industrialisation, weakens landowners, and strengthens urban classes, both the working class and the domestic bourgeoisie. When the repressive apparatus of the state is reinforced by foreign powers concerned about their strategic and economic interests, the balance between state and civil society is altered (Rueschmeyer *et al.*, 1992, pp. 69–75).

Political institutionalisation

Finally, political institutions have long been recognised as important for stability in developing countries. The significance of institutional development was first recognised by Huntington, who believed that the most important political consequence of modernisation in a pre-industrial society is a rapid increase in political mobilisation and participation (Huntington and Dominguez, 1975, pp. 33–47). If political instability is to be avoided, such participation needs to be matched by a corresponding level of institutional development. By and large this had not happened in developing countries. On the contrary, 'institutional decay has become a common phenomenon of the modernising countries' (Huntington, 1965, p. 407). Violence and instability have been the consequence of political institutions developing more slowly than the rate at which new socio-economic groups were being politically mobilised (Huntington, 1968, p. 5).

In the absence of alternative opportunities for social mobility, such as economic participation, political participation is resorted to. But the lack of effective political institutions makes it impossible for demands to be channelled through effective and legitimate procedures. Huntington saw the relationship between political participation and instability as follows:

(1) $\dfrac{\text{Social mobilisation}}{\text{Economic development}} = \text{Social frustration}$

(2) $\dfrac{\text{Social frustration}}{\text{Mobility opportunities}} = \text{Political participation}$

(3) $\dfrac{\text{Political participation}}{\text{Political institutionalisation}} = \text{Political instability}$

The problem with this explanation is that it contains a tautological element (Leys, 1982). 'Institutionalisation' refers to a process through which conflict can be managed in a peaceful and structured way. It does not just mean the creation of organisations. This seems tantamount to saying that if individuals and groups are prepared to participate in politics by playing according to the rules and abiding by the outcomes of so doing, there will be stability. In other words, there will be stability when there is no instability. We are left needing an explanation of why people should behave in ways that are not constitutionally sanctioned.

However, recent research has confirmed that political institutions and leadership have implications for democratic stability. Democracy in Asia has been threatened by the willingness of rulers to abuse their constitutional powers to strengthen their position. Military intervention in the region has often been preceded by the severe erosion of democratic constitutionalism by civil politicians seeking to perpetuate their power. A willingness to accept the consequences of democratic practices has been exceptional among Asian political leaders (Diamond, 1989, pp. 6–11). In Latin America democratic instability has followed 'shifts in political leadership strategies and styles from consensus .to confrontation, from accommodation to polarization' (Diamond and Linz, 1989, p. 15). In Africa the values and skills of political leaders have been crucial in undermining or sustaining democracy. Democracy in all regions of the Third World requires commitment to democratic values and an accommodating, compromising and consensual style on the part of political leaders (Diamond *et al.*, 1990, pp. 14–15).

Other institutional weaknesses have been reflected in political parties that are internally divided, unable to articulate interests clearly and unable to mobilise a significant mass base. In Latin America stable democracy has been associated with parties that satisfy Huntington's (1968) criteria of coherence (in policy), complexity (of organisation), autonomy (from the state) and adaptability (to social change). There is evidence that a party system with only a small number of parties is most conducive to democratic stability. Conversely in Thailand the military and bureaucracy have dominated politics because:

> with 143 parties crossing the Thai political stage between 1946 and 1981, political élites have been unable to build strong bases of popular support, to articulate, aggregate and mobilise political interests, to incorporate emerging interests into the political process, and to cooperate with one another in achieving policy innovations. (Diamond *et al.*, 1990, p. 27)

In Africa weak 'input' institutions, and especially political parties, have excluded the mass of the population from constitutional politics, encouraging élitism and clientelism, and forcing people into 'non-formal' modes of participation (Diamond, 1988, pp. 19–20).

Vigorous legislative and judicial institutions capable of controlling an excessively zealous executive have also been important: 'in Asia, as elsewhere in the world, the strength and autonomy of the judiciary is roughly proportional to the condition of democracy' (Diamond, 1988, p. 31). A comparison of Latin American, Asian and African cases suggested that a parliamentary system of government is preferable to a presidential one because of its greater flexibility and avoidance of concentrated executive power and a 'winner takes all' approach. A parliamentary system might have helped Brazil and Peru in the late 1980s 'where presidents whose programmes had failed catastrophically and whose political support had evaporated were forced to limp through their remaining terms with virtually no capacity to respond effectively to the deepening economic and political crises' (Diamond *et al.*, 1990, p. 28).

6.   Conclusion

The contemporary interest in the prospects for democracy in the Third World and in the lessons that can be learned from the experiences of democracy in different countries has extended the field of inquiry well beyond the prerequisites of stable government. Recent investigations have included the historical conditions necessary for the original establishment of democratic government; the standard of economic performance achieved by democracies at different stages in their development; and the factors affecting the ability of democracies to match political practice with legal and constitutional procedures and safeguards. Political instability is just one possible outcome among many for a Third World democracy, unless 'stability' is defined in such a way as to make any deviation from a model of democracy a sign of instability.

At the same time the focus has narrowed. Few people are now interested in the conditions necessary for the stability of any other form of government than a democratic one. This is because the dominant ideology prescribes a free-market economy, and it is assumed that for this to operate successfully it must be accompanied by liberal democratic values and institutions. There are very powerful pressures being applied to Third World countries to liberalise their economies and transform their polities in the direction of pluralism. Hence the current interest in what is needed to restore democracy as well as how to make it function effectively so that its legitimacy becomes firmly established.

Many different factors have been related to political instability, though the direction of causality has not always been clear. None is sufficient in itself to explain the complexity of political instability. The significance of each factor will vary according to the circumstances of region, history, level of economic development and place within the international system. It thus becomes important to know, as Ake implied in his formulation, under what circumstances is a factor such as economic inequality, rapid economic growth, or social differentiation likely to lead to political instability. One answer is when the expectations of political participants of appropriate social, economic and political action are not met by changes in social organisation:

> if changes in the nature of social organisation are in accord with the dominant image of society, they will be conducive to the promotion and maintenance of political stability, if they are not, they will lead to instability. (Castles, 1974, p. 294)

So if, for example, extreme inequalities in pre-industrial societies are found to be associated with political stability, contrary to the expectations of analysts, this can be explained by reference to the absence of egalitarianism from the dominant image of society. When that image is changed as a result of mass mobilisation, inequality becomes less acceptable and political instability can result. Similarly,

> one can explain the fact that rapid economic growth in contemporary Western societies is not destabilising as a consequence of the fact that such changes have become institutionalised expectations of the dominant ideology. (Castles, 1974, p. 297)

The advantage of such a paradigm is that it provides a framework for understanding why supposedly causal factors operate under some circumstances but not others. In stressing the importance of the response to changes in society and economy by the dominant protagonists of current images it also helps to explain why a group or class that might be expected a priori to be violently dissatisfied with their lot expresses no political dissent likely to undermine political stability. It is furthermore a paradigm that can be applied to all societies and political systems, regardless of whether they satisfy some stipulative definition of democracy.

Part V
Conclusion

14

Conclusion

The main challenge facing Third World societies today is the creation of a political system with legitimacy in the eyes of the majority. Without legitimacy in government there can be no stability, and without stability, no social and economic progress. Legitimacy is increasingly seen to reside with democratic forms of government as pro-democracy movements gather momentum in most regions of the Third World. Yet the most pronounced feature of democratic regimes is their fragility. The establishment of peaceful, democratic politics is obstructed by civil war in Afghanistan, Burundi and Sudan, political assassination in Mexico, ethnic conflict and separatism in Rwanda, Somalia, Sri Lanka and Liberia, religious fundamentalism in Egypt and Algeria, bankrupt absolutism in Zaire and El Salvador, and the West's willingness to sell arms to any regime, no matter how repressive. The threat of economic crisis hangs over the fledgling democracies of Brazil, Malawi, Nepal, Uganda, Angola and Mozambique. Communal violence persistently mars India's democratic record. Many Third World countries are faced with accumulations of such factors, and some combine them with severe ecological problems.

Although there have been impressive transitions away from military dictatorship in many parts of the Third World in the last decade, the military as a political force is present everywhere, growing stronger, and should never be underestimated politically. It remains dominant in parts of Asia, the Middle East and Africa. The armed forces pose an overt threat to democracy in the Philippines, Haiti, Guatemala, Thailand, Uruguay, Chad, Venezuela and Cambodia, and block its reinstatement in Nigeria, Burma, Algeria, Mali, Peru, Sierra Leone and Gambia. Foreign intervention has often been a Third World democracy's only protection against the militarisation of politics.

Much of the hope for stability in the new pluralist political systems rests on the organisational strength of political parties whose ideologies support the democratic process. How long some of the diverse coalitions for the restoration of democracy can survive the enormous expectations of them is a subject of much speculation. Elections in Mozambique, Kenya and Nepal have introduced competitive party politics into inhospitable social and economic environments. The African National Congress in South Africa encompasses a broad spectrum of regional, racial, cultural, class and ideological positions. Democratic stability in the country will be very dependent on how far such divisions, especially ethnic, can be held together after Nelson Mandela ceases to be leader. Elsewhere parties themselves constitute the greatest threat to democracy, either because of their refusal to accept majority decisions (such as Renamo in Mozambique, Unita in Angola or the South African Conservative Party), or because of their inherent authoritarianism, contempt for human rights or religious intolerance.

The apparent globalisation of political values and institutions represented by the dissolution of the communist regimes in the Second World and their replacement by systems of government broadly subscribing to liberal democratic beliefs and practices, has lent credence to the view that there is an inevitable trend towards a universal form of government on which all societies will eventually converge. Such interpretations of recent world history gain encouragement from the extent to which pluralist democracy has replaced military regimes or single-party states in Latin America and Africa.

There would seem to be echoes of modernisation theory in such predictions and interpretations (Leftwich, 1993, p. 605). Assumptions about the importance of the development of civil society as a counterbalance to the power of the state are reminiscent of the importance attached by modernisation theory to the 'organic solidarities' which are a function of the increased complexity and specialisation of modernising social structures. Similarly ideas about 'good governance' which are likely increasingly to inform Western aid policy and which prescribe the separation of powers, the accountability and efficiency of public bureaucracy, and the rule of law as indispensable components of a democratic polity and free society, find their counterpart in the concept of structural differentiation that is central to political functionalism. The development of differentiated and specialised political structures serves to strengthen the extractive, regulative, distributive, symbolic and responsive capabilities of governments, as well as preserving the independence of different parts of the machinery of government, thus inhibiting the concentration of power in a small and personalised executive élite which is so often the hallmark of Third World politics.

However, as Leftwich reminds us, modernisation theory, unlike much contemporary Western political rhetoric, did not assume that democracy could take root regardless of economic and social conditions. Rather it sees economic development as preceding the modernisation of politics – which is precisely what has happened in the newly industrialising states of the Third World, where democracy has until very recently been conspicuously absent in some of the fasting growing capitalist economies, notably Brazil, Singapore, South Korea, Taiwan, Thailand and Indonesia (Leftwich, 1993, pp. 612–13). The Asian Tigers are sometimes offered as evidence that authoritarianism is better than democracy for rapid economic development, though it should be recognised that the conditions which were crucial to economic success – including a high rate of domestic savings and a large number of small and medium-sized enterprise – do not appear to be dependent on an authoritarian political regime (Sandschneider, 1991).

The resurgence of religious fundamentalism in parts of the Third World appears to undermine much of modernisation theory's conclusions about secularisation as a feature of modern society and polity. However, the modernisation theorists did not simply equate secularisation with the separation of theology and politics. Secularisation also meant a particular kind of rationalisation seen as characteristic of efficient economic and political organisation. In this respect modernisation theory is relevant to the analysis of the performance of theocratic regimes, and of which category of autocratic regime they join – that with dismal records of social and economic development or that with records of economic growth and relatively high per capita incomes. The concepts of 'community' and 'association' will be central to such analysis. Although the diversity of political developments in the Third World, and the absence of a clear direction of political change even in individual countries, obviate any theory of progress towards a single goal, the sociological concepts of modernisation theory (though not the psychological) are indispensable for distinguishing between the different values that underpin social relationships and conflicts, especially those based on ethnicity.

As we saw in Chapter 13, democratic stability is unlikely to be achieved unless there is economic growth. However, this needs to be used to support social progress. Much will depend on whether opportunities for social betterment are provided for formerly excluded groups. Rapid economic growth may increase inequalities and lead to powerful expressions of political discontent, with destabilising consequences. The economic and social conditions of the urban and rural poor are likely to decline, at least in the short term. Under the neo-liberal economic policies required by structural adjustment programmes, the correlates of political resistance remain of great significance to the analysis of politics among the Third World's poor. There are few countries where the poor are experiencing much progress. The drift from countryside to towns is unlikely to improve their position, either economically or politically, and therefore provides fertile ground in which to test theories of political action and inaction among marginalised people. The constraints on effective political mobilisation among such groups remain strong, as does the inter-dependency between them and leaders from more prosperous and organised sections of society, such as the Church in parts of Africa and Latin America, which mediate between them and the public authorities.

New democracies are also threatened by the possibility of a 'revolution' of rising expectations, as in Nepal where price increases have led to riots, and South Africa, where the ANC government will have to struggle to meet the expectations of a politically conscious and mobilised black population for jobs, land, housing, safe water, health care and education.

Institutional developments, and particularly the emergence of political parties strong enough to defend class interests in competitive politics, are crucial for democratic stability, and for the development of civil society as a counter-balance to the power of the state. Of particular significance here is the tendency for Third World parties to secure their support through patronage, clientelism and traditional affiliations, rather than by mobilising people with a common socio-economic status. This makes it difficult to organise political action along class lines, and enables ruling élites to maintain their position even when faced with the need to secure mass support.

The reactions of dominant socio-economic groups to demands for greater social equality and political participation will also be crucial to the future of fragile democracies. As we saw in Chapter 10 the social dislocation and extended political mobilisation occasioned by economic change and growth has often been associated with military intervention on behalf of sectional interests threatened by democratic politics. Political institutionalisation has been found to provide some protection against a reactionary military–middle class alliance, which again points to the importance of mass political parties attracting support from across all regions and ethnic divisions. Military intervention has often responded to intra-class conflict by managing the state on behalf of fundamental social structures and economic philosophy that seemed threatened by the democratic process, or by siding with one middle-class faction (perhaps associated with a particular ethnic group) and dismantling the political institutions through which other factions articulated their interests.

The political culture may include anti-democratic values which endorse such authoritarian modes of government, especially among classes which believe their privileges to be threatened by a wider distribution of political power. There are still plenty of examples to remind us that in the rural areas of the Third World landlords are in a position to employ armed force and a corrupt judicial system to ward off land reform.

The extent to which political autonomy is limited by external control of parts of a country's economy, and the internal power structure affected by dependency, were the subjects of Chapters 5 and 6. The ability of a country to secure substantial aid in return for buying arms from the aid donor, as evidenced by Malaysia's Pergau hydro-electric project, is indicative of the changing relationship between metropolitan centres and the wealthier of their former colonies. When aid is used to finance uneconomic projects as a 'sweetener' to secure arms deals in countries where the need for development assistance is much less than in many others, an ideal testing ground is provided for some of the contesting hypotheses in the neo-colonialism debate, especially those pertaining to the autonomy of governments to negotiate with richer countries and the beneficiaries of the outcomes of those negotiations within the Third World country concerned.

A key question for the future is how far Third World countries can diversify their economies and so reduce their reliance on the fluctuating values of a few vulnerable commodities. Indonesia, for example, reduced its export dependence on oil and gas from 80 per cent in 1981 to 35 per cent in 1989 by diversification into other minerals and timber. Malaysia has reduced its dependence on rubber and tin by manufacturing steel and motor cars and becoming the world's largest producer of electronic equipment. Such development requires substantial foreign investment of a kind which will always render a Third World economy vulnerable to the extraction of valuable surplus, growing disparities of income between the new industrial and business classes and the rural poor, and increasing international debt (Indonesia's foreign debt of over £50 billions is Asia's largest).

The effect on the domestic social structure of penetration by the global market of rapidly-growing economies in the Third World continues to present a challenge to political analysts. The exploitation of labour for low wages in unsafe working conditions is on the increase. Associations to represent the rights of workers are often banned, but as inequalities increase it is difficult to see how governments can continue to suppress legitimate demands. While it may be good for such abstractions as growth rates and levels of production that investment by developed countries in developing economies, mainly Asian and Latin American, increased from $13 billions in 1990 to $61 billions in 1993, it is questionable how good it is for the people in the low-pay occupations that make these regions attractive to foreign investment. Economic liberalisation may be accompanied by very limited political liberalisation. The latter is of much less concern than the former to private foreign investors. The concepts related to the theories of dependency and neo-colonialism provide a framework for analysing the behaviour of foreign interests within the developing and industrialising society, their relations with indigenous interests, especially the local business class and political élite, and the consequences of these relationships for the urban and rural proletariats.

Bibliography

Abernethy, D. B. (1971) 'Bureaucracy and economic development in Africa', *The African Review*, vol. 1, no. 1.

Abrahamson, M. (1978) *Functionalism*. Englewood Cliffs: Prentice-Hall.

Adam, H. M. (1994) 'Formation and recognition of new states: Somaliland in contrast to Eritrea', *Review of African Political Economy*, no. 59.

Ake, C. (1967) 'Political integration and political stability', *World Politics*, vol. 19, no. 3.

Ake, C. (1974) 'Modernisation and political instability: a theoretical explanation', *World Politics*, vol. 26, no. 4.

Ake, C. (1975) 'A definition of political stability', *Comparative Politics*, vol. 7, no. 2.

Alavi, H. (1971) 'The crisis of nationalities and the state in Pakistan', *Journal of Contemporary Asia*, vol. 1, no. 3.

Alavi, H. (1972) 'The state in post-colonial societies: Pakistan and Bangladesh', *New Left Review*, no. 74.

Alavi, H. (1973) 'Peasants and revolution' in K. Gough and H. P. Sharma (eds) *Imperialism and Revolution in South Asia*. London: Monthly Review Press.

Alavi, H. (1990) 'Authoritarianism and legitimation of state power in Pakistan', in S. K. Mitra (ed.) *The Post-Colonial State in Asia. Dialectics of Politics and Culture*. London: Harvester Wheatsheaf.

Allen, C. and G. Williams (eds) (1982) *Sociology of 'Developing Societies': Sub-Saharan Africa*. London: Macmillan.

Almond, G. A. (1960) 'Introduction', in G. A. Almond and J. Coleman (eds) *The Politics of the Developing Areas*. Princeton: Princeton University Press.

Almond, G. A. (1963) 'Political systems and political change', *American Behavioral Scientist*, vol. 6, no. 10.

Almond, G. A. (1965) 'A developmental approach to political systems', *World Politics*, vol. 17, no. 1.

Almond, G. A. (1987) 'The development of political development', in M. Weiner and S. P. Huntington (eds) *Understanding Political Development*. Boston: Little, Brown.

Almond, G. A. and J. Coleman (eds) (1960) *The Politics of the Developing Areas*. Princeton: Princeton University Press.

Almond, G. A. and G. B. Powell (1966) *Comparative Politics: A Developmental Approach*. Boston: Little, Brown.

Almond, G. A. and S. Verba (1963) *The Civic Culture. Political Attitudes and Decomocracy in Five Nations*. Princeton: Princeton University Press.

Amin, S. (1976) *Unequal Development: An Essay on the Social Formation of Peripheral Capitalism.* Brighton: Harvester Press.

Amin, S. (1982) 'The disarticulation of economy within "developing societies"', in H. Alavi and T. Shanin (eds) *Introduction to the Sociology of 'Developing Societies'.* London: Macmillan.

Anderson, C. W., F. R.von der Mehden and C. Young (1974) *Issues of Political Development.* Englewood Cliffs: Prentice-Hall, 2nd edn.

Anediran, T. (1974) 'The dynamics of peasant revolt: a conceptual analysis of the Agbekoya Parapo uprising in the Western State of Nigeria', *Journal of Black Studies,* vol. 4, no. 4.

Apter, D. E. (1965) *The Politics of Modernisation.* Chicago: University of Chicago Press.

Apter, D. (1980) 'The passing of development studies – over the shoulder with a backward glance', *Government and Opposition,* vol. 15, no. 3/4.

Aron, R. (1968) *Peace and War. A Theory of International Relations.* New York: Praeger.

Banuazizi, A. (1987) 'Socio-psychological approach to political development', in M. Weiner and S. Huntington (eds) *Understanding Political Development.* Boston: Little, Brown.

Baran, P. A. (1957) *The Political Economy of Growth.* New York: Monthly Review Press.

Barratt Brown, M. (1963) *After Imperialism.* London: Heinemann.

Barratt Brown, M. (1972) 'A critique of marxist theories of imperialism', in R. Owen and B. Sutcliffe (eds) *Studies in the Theory of Imperialism.* London: Longman.

Barratt Brown, M. (1974) *The Economics of Imperialism.* Harmondsworth: Penguin.

Bauer, P. (1971) *Dissent on Development.* London: Weidenfeld & Nicolson,

Bauer, P. (1981) *Equality, the Third World and Economic Delusion.* London: Weidenfeld & Nicolson.

Bendix, R. (1967) 'Tradition and modernity reconsidered', *Comparative Studies in Society and History,* vol. 9, no. 3.

Berger, M. T. (1994) 'The end of the "Third World"?', *Third World Quarterly,* vol. 15, no. 2.

Berman, B. (1974) 'Clientelism and neocolonialism: centre-periphery relations and political development in African states', *Studies in Comparative International Development,* vol. 9, no. 1.

Berman, B. (1984) 'Structure and process in the bureaucratic states of colonial Africa', *Development and Change,* vol. 15, no. 2.

Bernstein, H. (1971) 'Modernisation theory and the sociological study of development', *Journal of Development Studies,* vol. 7, no. 3.

Bernstein, H. (1979) 'Sociology of underdevelopment vs. sociology of development', in D. Lehmann (ed.) *Development Theory. Four Critical Studies.* London: Frank Cass.

Bernstein, H. (1982) 'Industrialisation, development and dependence', in H. Alavi and T. Shanin, *Introduction to the Sociology of 'Developing Societies'.* London: Macmillan.

Bienefeld, H. (1980) 'Dependency in the Eighties', *IDS Bulletin*, vol. 12, no. 1.

Birch, A. H. (1978) 'Minority nationalist movements and theories of political integration', *World Politics*, vol. 30, no. 2.

Black, C. E. (1966) *The Dynamics of Modernisation. A Study in Comparative History*. New York: Harper & Row.

Blomstrom, M. and B. Hettne (1984) *Development Theory in Transition*. London: Zed Books.

Bock, K. (1978) 'Theories of progress, development, evolution', in T. Bottomore and R. Nisbet (eds) *A History of Sociological Analysis*. London: Heinemann.

Bodenheimer, S. (1971) 'Dependency and imperialism: the roots of Latin American underdevelopment', in K. Fann and D. Hodges (eds) *Readings in United States Imperialism*. Boston: Porter Sargent.

Booth, J. A. (1991) 'Inequality and rebellion in Central America', *Latin American Research Review*, vol. 26, no. 1.

Brass, P. R. (1991) *Ethnicity and Nationalism. Theory and Comparison*. London: Sage Publications.

Brecher, M. (1963) 'Political instability in the new states of Asia', in H. Eckstein and D. E. Apter (eds) *Comparative Politics. A Reader*. New York: Free Press.

Bretton, H. L. (1973) *Power and Politics in Africa*. London: Longman.

Brewer, A. (1980) *Marxist Theories of Imperialism. A Critical Survey*. London: Routledge & Kegan Paul.

Brown, D. (1989) 'Ethnic revival: perspectives on state and society', *Third World Quarterly*, vol. 11, no. 4.

Bulloch, J. and H. Morris (1993) *No Friends but the Mountains. The Tragic History of the Kurds*. Harmondsworth: Penguin.

Cammack, P., D. Pool and W. Tordoff (1993) *Third World Politics. A Comparative Introduction*, 2nd edn. London: Macmillan.

Cardoso, F. H. (1972) 'Dependency and development in Latin America', *New Left Review*, no. 74.

Cardoso, F. H. (1973) 'Associated-dependent development: theoretical and practical implications', in A. Stepan (ed.) *Authoritarian Brazil. Origins, Policies and Future*, New Haven: Yale University Press.

Carnoy, M. (1984) *The State and Political Theory*. Princeton: Princeton University Press.

Carter, G. (1962) *African One-Party States*. Ithaca: Cornell University Press.

Castles, F. G. (1974) 'Political stability and the dominant image of society', *Political Studies*, vol. 22, no. 3.

Chaliand, G. (1977) *Revolution in the Third World. Myths and Prospects*. Brighton: Harvester Press.

Chaliand, G. (1980) 'Introduction', in G. Chaliand (ed.) *People Without a Country. The Kurds and Kurdistan*. London: Zed Press.

Charlton, R. (1981) 'Plus ça change. . . A Review of two decades of theoretical analysis of African *Coups d'état*', *Culture et Developpement*, vol. 13, no. 2.

Chiriyankandath, J. (1994) 'The politics of religious identity: a comparison of Hindu nationalism and Sudanese Islamism', *Journal of Commonwealth and Comparative Politics*, vol. 32, no. 1.

Clapham, C. (1982) 'Clientelism and the state', in C. Clapham (ed.) *Private Patronage and Public Power. Political Clientelism in the Modern State.* London: Frances Pinter.

Clapham, C. (1985) *Third World Politics. An Introduction.* London: Croom Helm.

Clapham, C. and G. Philip (eds) (1985) *The Political Dilemmas of Military Regimes.* London: Croom Helm.

Clay, J.W. (1989) 'Epilogue: the ethnic future of nations', *Third World Quarterly*, vol. 11, no. 4.

Clendenen, C.C. (1972) 'Tribalism and humanitarianism. The Nigerian-Biafran civil war', in R. Higham (ed.) *Civil Wars in the Twentieth Century.* Lexington: University Press of Kentucky.

Cohen, B.J. (1973) *The Question of Imperialism. The Political Economy of Dominance and Dependence.* New York: Basic Books.

Cohen, R. and J. Middleton (eds) (1967) *Comparative Political Systems. Studies in the Politics of Pre-Industrial Societies.* New York: Natural History Press.

Coleman, J.S. (1954) 'Nationalism in Tropical Africa', *American Political Science Review*, vol. 48, no. 2.

Coleman, J.S. (1960a) 'Conclusion: the political systems of the developing areas', in G.A. Almond and J. Coleman (eds) *The Politics of the Developing Areas.* Princeton: Princeton University Press.

Coleman, J.S. (1960b) 'The politics of Sub-Saharan Africa', in G.A. Almond and J. Coleman (eds) *The Politics of the Developing Areas.* Princeton: Princeton University Press.

Coleman, J.S. and C.G. Rosberg (eds) (1964) *Political Parties and National Integration in Tropical Africa.* Los Angeles: University of California Press.

Collier, D. (1979) 'The BA model: synthesis and priorities for future research', in D. Collier (ed.) *The New Authoritarianism in Latin America.* Princeton: Princeton University Press.

Connor, W. (1973) 'The politics of ethnonationalism', *Journal of International Affairs*, vol. 27, no. 1.

Connor, W. (1978) 'A nation is a nation, is a state, is an ethnic group, is a . . . .', *Ethnic and Racial Studies*, no. 4, Oct.

Connor, W. (1988) 'Ethnonationalism', in M. Weiner and S.P. Huntington (eds) *Understanding Political Development.* Boston: Little, Brown.

Crow, B. (1990) 'The state in Bangladesh: the extension of a weak state', in S.K. Mitra (ed.) *The Post-Colonial State in Asia. Dialectics of Politics and Culture.* London: Harvester Wheatsheaf.

Dahl, R. (1971) *Polyarchy: Participation and Opposition.* New Haven: Yale University Press.

Davies, J.C. (1972) 'Toward a theory of revolution', in D.H. Wrong and H.L. Gracey (eds) *Readings in Introductory Sociology*, 2nd edn. London: Collier-Macmillan.

Debray, R. (1967) 'Problems of revolutionary strategy in Latin America', *New Left Review*, no. 45.

de Selincourt, K. (1993) 'Future shock', *New Statesman and Society*, 3 Dec.

Diamond, L. (1988) 'Introduction: roots of failure, seeds of hope', in L. Diamond, J.J. Linz and S.M. Lipset (eds) *Democracy in Developing Countries*, vol. 2, Africa. Boulder: Lynne Rienner Publishers.

Diamond, L. (1989) 'Introduction: persistence, erosion, breakdown and renewal', in L. Diamond, J.J. Linz and S.M. Lipset (eds) *Democracy in Developing Countries*, vol. 3, Asia. Boulder: Lynne Rienner Publishers.

Diamond, L. (1992) 'Economic development and democracy reconsidered', in G. Marks and L. Diamond (eds) *Re-examining Democracy. Essays in Honor of Seymour Martin Lipset*. London: Sage Publications.

Diamond, L. (1993a) 'Causes and effects', in L. Diamond (ed.) *Political Culture and Democracy in Developing Countries*. Boulder: Lynne Rienner Publishers.

Diamond, L. (1993b) 'Introduction: political culture and democracy', in L. Diamond (ed.) *Political Culture and Democracy in Developing Countries*. Boulder: Lynne Rienner Publishers.

Diamond, L. and J.J. Linz (1989) 'Introduction: politics, society and democracy in Latin America', in L. Diamond, J.J. Linz and S.M. Lipset (eds) *Democracy in Developing Countries*, vol. 4, Latin America. Boulder: Lynne Rienner Publishers.

Diamond, L., J.J. Linz and S.M. Lipset (eds) (1990) 'Introduction: comparing experiences with democracy', in Diamond, Linz and Lipset (eds) *Politics in Developing Countries. Comparing Experiences with Democracy*. London: Lynne Rienner Publishers.

Dos Santos, T. (1970) 'The structure of dependence', *American Economic Review*, vol. 60, no. 2.

Dos Santos, T. (1973) 'The crisis of development theory and the problem of dependence in Latin America', in H. Bernstein (ed.) *Underdevelopment and Development*. Harmondsworth: Penguin.

Dougherty, J. and R. Pfaltzgraff (1981) *Contending Theories of International Relations*. New York: Harper & Row.

Dowse, R.E. (1966) 'A functionalist's logic', *World Politics*, vol. 18, no. 4.

Dowse, R.E. (1969) 'The military and political development', in C. Leys (ed.) *Politics and Change in Developing Countries*. Cambridge: Cambridge University Press.

Dunn, J. (1972) *Modern Revolutions. An Introduction to the analysis of a Political Phenomenon*. Cambridge: Cambridge University Press.

Durkheim, E. (1965) 'On mechanical and organic solidarity' (from *The Division of Labour in Society*, 1893) in T. Parsons, E. Shils, K.D. Naegle and J.R. Pitts (eds) *Theories of Society. Foundations of Modern Sociological Theory*. New York: Free Press.

Durkheim, E. (1985) *Rules of Sociological Method*. 1962 edn. Glencoe, Ill.: Free Press.

Eckstein, H. (1982) 'The idea of political development: from dignity to efficiency', *World Politics*, vol. 34, no. 4.

Eisenstadt, S. N. (1964) 'Institutionalisation and change, *American Socio-logical Review*, vol. 29, no. 2.

Eisenstadt, S. N. (1966) *Modernisation: Protest and Change*. Englewood Cliffs: Prentice-Hall.

Eisenstadt, S. N. and L. Roniger (1981) 'The study of patron- client relations and recent developments in sociological theory', in S. N. Eisenstadt and R. Lemarchand (eds) *Political Clientelism, Patronage and Development*. London: Sage Publications.

Emerson, R. (1960) *From Empire to Nation: The Rise to Self-Assertion of Asian and African Peoples*. Cambridge, Mass.: Harvard University Press.

Emerson, R. (1963) 'The erosion of democracy in the new states', in H. Eckstein and D. E. Apter (eds) *Comparative Politics. A Reader*. New York: Free Press.

Emmanuel, A. (1972a) *Unequal Exchange: A Study of the Imperialism of Trade*. London: New Left Books.

Emmanuel, A. (1972b) 'White-settler colonialism and the myth of investment capitalism', *New Left Review*, no. 73.

Emmanuel, A. (1974) 'Myths of development versus myths of under-development', *New Left Review*, no. 85.

Emmanuel, A. (1976) 'The multinational corporations and the inequality of development', *International Social Science Journal*, vol. 28, no. 4.

Enloe, C. H. (1973) *Ethnic Conflict and Political Development*. Boston: Little, Brown.

Enloe, C. H. (1976) 'Central governments' strategies for coping with separatist movements', in W. H. Morris-Jones (ed.) *The Politics of Separatism*, Collected Seminar Papers no. 19. London: University of London Institute of Commonwealth Studies.

Eriksen, T. H. (1993) *Ethnicity and Nationalism. Anthropological Perspectives*. London: Pluto Press.

Eulau, H. (1963) *The Behavioral Persuasion in Politics*. New York: Random House.

Fallers, L. (1961) 'Are African cultivators to be called "peasants"?', *Current Anthropology*, vol. 12, no. 1.

Finer, S. E. (1962) *The Man on Horseback. The Role of the Military in Politics*. London: Pall Mall Press.

Finer, S. E. (1970) 'Almond's concept of "the political system": a textual critique', *Government and Opposition*, vol. 5, no. 1.

Finer, S. E. (1974) *Comparative Government*. Harmondsworth: Penguin.

First, R. (1972) *The Barrel of a Gun. Political Power in Africa and the Coup d'État*. Harmondsworth: Penguin.

Foster-Carter, A. (1976) 'From Rostow to Gunder Frank: conflicting paradigms in the analysis of underdevelopment', *World Development*, vol. 4, no. 3.

Frank, A. G. (1966) 'The development of underdevelopment', *Monthly Review*, vol. 18, no. 4.

Frank, A. G. (1969a) *Capitalism and Underdevelopment in Latin America. Historical Studies of Chile and Brazil*. London: Monthly Review Press.

Frank, A. G. (1969b) *Latin America: Underdevelopment or Revolution*. New York: Monthly Review Press.

Frank, A. G. (1972a) 'Economic dependence, class structure and under-development policy', in J. D. Cockcroft, A. G.Frank and D. L. Johnson (eds) *Dependence and Underdevelopment: Latin America's Political Economy*. New York: Doubleday.

Frank, A. G. (1972b) *Lumpenbourgeoisie: Lumpenproletariat*. London: Monthly Review Press.

Frank, A. G. (1972c) 'Sociology of development and the underdevelopment of sociology', in J. D. Cockcroft, A. G.Frank and D. L. Johnson (eds) *Dependence and Underdevelopment: Latin America's Political Economy*. New York: Doubleday.

Freedom House Survey Team (1992) *Freedom in the World. Political Rights and Civil Liberties 1991–92*. New York: Freedom House.

Galtung, J. (1971) 'A structural theory of inperialism', *Journal of Peace Research*, vol. 2, no. 1.

Geertz, C. (1962) 'Studies in peasant life: community and society', in B. J. Siegel (ed.) *Biennial Review of Anthropology, 1961*. Stanford: Stanford University Press.

Ghassemlou, A. R. (1980) 'Kurdistan in Iran', in G. Challiand (ed.) *People Without a Country*. London: Zed Press.

Godfrey, M. (1980) 'Editorial: is dependency dead?', *IDS Bulletin*, vol. 12, no. 1.

Goodwin, J. and Skocpol, T. (1989) 'Explaining revolutions in the contemporary Third World', *Politics and Society*, vol. 17, no. 4.

Goulbourne, H. (1979) 'Some problems of analysis of the political in backward capitalist social formations', in H. Goulbourne (ed.) *Politics and State in the Third World*. London: Macmillan.

Gourevitch, P. A. (1979) 'The re-emergence of "peripheral nationalisms": some comparative speculations on the spatial distribution of political leadership and economic growth', *Comparative Studies in Society and History*, vol. 21, no. 2.

Griffin, K. and J. Gurley (1985) 'Radical analyses of imperialism, the Third World, and the transition to socialism: a survey article', *Journal of Economic Literature*, vol. 23, no. 3.

Gusfield, J. R. (1967) 'Tradition as modernity: misplaced polarities in the study of social change', *American Journal of Sociology*, vol. 72, no. 2.

Hagen, E. (1962) *On the Theory of Social Change*. Homewood, Ill.: Dorsey Press.

Hagen, E. (1963) 'How economic growth begins: a theory of social change', *Journal of Social Issues*, vol. 19, no. 1.

Hah, C. and J. Martin (1975) 'Towards a synthesis of conflict and integration theories of nationalism', *World Politics*, vol. 27, no. 3, Apr.

Harris, N. (1970) 'The revolutionary role of the peasants', *International Socialism*, no. 41, Dec.–Jan.

Harrison, P. (1979) *Inside the Third World*. Harmondsworth: Penguin.

Hawthorne, G. (1992) 'Sub-Saharan Africa', in D. Held (ed.) *Prospects for Democracy. North, South, East, West*. Cambridge: Polity Press.

Heady, F. (1959) 'Bureaucratic theory and comparative administration', *Administrative Science Quarterly*, vol. 3, no. 4.

Hechter, M. (1975) *Internal Colonialism. The Celtic Fringe in British National Development, 1536–1966*. London: Routledge & Kegan Paul.

Hechter, M. (1985) 'Internal colonialism revisited', in E. A. Tiryakian and R. Rogowski (eds) *New Nationalisms of the Developed West*. London: Allen & Unwin.

Heeger, G. A. (1973) 'Bureaucracy, political parties and political development', *World Politics*, vol. 25, no. 4.

Hein, W. and K. Stenzel (1979) 'The capitalist state and underdevelopment in Latin America: the case of Venezuela', in H.Goulbourne (ed.) *Politics and State in the Third World*. London: Macmillan.

Herbst, J. (1990) 'The structural adjustment of politics in Africa', *World Development*, vol. 18, no. 7.

Higgott, R. A. (1978) 'Competing theoretical perspectives on development and underdevelopment', *Politics*, vol. 13, no. 1.

Higgott, R. A. (1983) *Political Development Theory. The Contemporary Debate*. London: Croom Helm.

Hilferding, R. (1910) *Finanz kapital (Finance Capital)*. (Vienna: Verwörks, 1923).

Hirschman, A. O. (1961) 'Ideologies of economic development in Latin America', in A. O. Hirschman (ed.) *Latin American Issues. Essays and Comments*. New York: Twentieth Century Fund.

Hirschmann, D. (1981) 'Development or underdevelopment administration? A further "deadlock"', *Development and Change*, vol. 12, no. 4.

Hobsbawm, E. J. (1959) *Primitive Rebels. Studies in Archaic Forms of Social Movement in the Nineteenth and Twentieth Centuries*. Manchester: Manchester University Press.

Hobson, J. A. (1902) *Imperialism. A Study*. London: George Allen & Unwin.

Hodder-Williams, R. (1984) *An Introduction to the Politics of Tropical Africa*. London: Allen & Unwin.

Holt, R. T. and J. E. Turner (1966) *The Political Basis of Economic Development*. Princeton: D. Van Nostrand Co.

Holt, R. T. and J. E. Turner (1972) 'The methodology of comparative research', in R. T. Holt and J. E. Turner (eds) *The Methodology of Comparative Research*. New York: Free Press.

Holt, R. T. and J. E. Turner (1975) 'Crises and sequences in collective theory development', *American Political Science Review*, vol. 69, no. 3.

Hoogvelt, A. M. M. (1978) *The Sociology of Developing Societies*, 2nd edn. London: Macmillan.

Hoogvelt, A. M. M. (1982) *The Third World in Global Development*. London: Macmillan.

Hopkins, A. G. (1975) 'On importing Andre Gunder Frank into Africa', *African Economic History Review*, vol. 2, no. 1.

Hoselitz, B. F. (1964) 'Social stratification and economic development', *International Social Science Journal*, vol. 16, no. 2.

Hume, D. and M. Turner (1990) *Sociology and Development. Theories, Policies and Practices.* London: Harvester Wheatsheaf.

Huntington, S. P. (1957) *The Soldier and the state: The Theory and Practice of Civil–Military Relations.* Cambridge, Mass.: Harvard University Press.

Huntington, S. P. (1962) 'Patterns of violence in world politics', in S. P. Huntington (ed.) *Changing Patterns of Military Politics,* International Yearbook of Political Behaviour Research, vol. 3. Glencoe: Free Press.

Huntington, S. P. (1965) 'Political development and political decay', *World Politics,* vol. 17, no. 2.

Huntington, S. P. (1968) *Political Order in Changing Societies.* New Haven: Yale University Press.

Huntington, S. P. (1971) 'The change to change', *Comparative Politics,* vol. 3, no. 2.

Huntington, S. P. (1984) 'Will more countries become democratic?', *Political Science Quarterly,* vol. 99, no. 2.

Huntington, S. P. (1987) 'The goals of development', in M.Weiner and S. P. Huntington (eds) *Understanding Political Development.* Boston: Little, Brown.

Huntington, S. P. and J. I. Dominguez (1975) 'Political development', in F. I. Greenstein and N. W. Polsby (eds) *Micropolitical Theory,* Handbook of Political Science vol. 3. Reading, Mass.: Addison-Wesley Publishing Co.

Hurwitz, L. (1973) 'Contemporary approaches to political stability', *Comparative Politics,* vol. 3, no. 3.

Hymer, S. (1982) 'The multinational corporation and the law of uneven development', in H. Alavi and T. Shanin (eds) *Introduction to the Sociology of 'Developing Societies'.* London: Macmillan.

Inkeles, A. and D. H. Smith (1974) *Becoming Modern: Individual Change in six Developing Countries.* Cambridge, Mass.: Harvard University Press.

Jackman, R. W. (1978) 'The predictability of *coups d'état*: a model with African data', *American Political Science Review,* vol. 72, no. 4.

Jackman, R. W. (1986) 'Explaining African *coups d'état*', *American Political Science Review,* vol. 80, no. 1.

Jahan, R. (1973) *Pakistan: Failure in National Integration.* New York: Columbia University Press.

Jain, R. B. (1992) 'Bureaucracy, public policy and socio-economic development', in H. K. Asmerom, R. Hope and R. B. Jain (eds) *Bureaucracy and Development Policies in the Third World.* Amsterdam: VU University Press.

Janowitz, M. (1970) *Political Conflict. Essays in Political Sociology.* Chicago: Quadrangle Books.

Jessop, R. (1977) 'Recent theories of the capitalist state', *Cambridge Journal of Economics,* vol. 1, no. 4.

Johnson, D. L. (1972) 'Dependence and the international system', in J. D. Cockcroft, A. G. Frank and D. L. Johnson (eds) *Dependence and Underdevelopment: Latin America's Political Economy.* New York: Doubleday.

Johnson, H. and H. Bernstein (eds) (1982) *Third World Lives of Struggle*. London: Heinemann.

Johnson, T. H., R. O. Slater and P. McGowan (1984) 'Explaining African military *coups d'état, 1960–1982*', *American Political Science Review*, vol. 78, no. 3.

Johnson, T. H., R. O. Slater and P. McGowan (1986) 'Explaining African coups d'etat', *American Political Science Review*, vol. 80, no. 1

Kamrava, M. (1993) *Politics and Society in the Third World*. London: Routledge.

Kasfir, N. (1983) 'Relating class to state in Africa', *Journal of Commonwealth and Comparative Politics*, vol. 21, no. 3.

Kaufman, R. R., H. I. Chernotsky and D. S. Geller (1974) 'A preliminary test of the theory of dependency', *Comparative Politics*, vol. 7, no. 3.

Kavanagh, D. (1972) *Political Culture*. London: Macmillan.

Kay, G. (1975) *Development and Underdevelopment: A Marxist Analysis*. London: Macmillan.

Kedourie, E. (1992) *Politics in the Middle East*. Oxford: Oxford University Press.

Kellas, J. G. (1991) *The Politics of Nationalism and Ethnicity*. London: Macmillan.

Kemp, T. (1972) 'The Marxist theory of imperialism', in R. Owen and B. Sutcliffe (eds) *Studies in the Theory of Imperialism*. London: Longman.

'Kendal' (1980) 'Kurdistan in Turkey', in G. Challiand (ed.) *People Without a Country*. London: Zed Press.

Kiernan, V. G. (1974) *Marxism and Imperialism*. London: Edward Arnold.

Kilson, M. L. (1963) 'Authoritarian and single-party tendencies in African politics', *World Politics*, vol. 15, no. 1.

Kohn, H. (1945) *The Idea of Nationalism: A study of its Origins and Background*. London: Macmillan.

Kothari, R. (1968) 'Tradition and modernity revisited', *Government and Opposition*, vol. 3, no. 2.

Kuznets, S. (1973) 'Notes on the take-off', in P. A. Samuelson (ed.) *Readings in Economics*, 7th edn. New York: McGraw-Hill.

Laclau, E. (1971) 'Feudalism and capitalism in Latin America', *New Left Review*, no. 67, May–Jun.

Lall, S. (1975) 'Is "dependence" a useful concept in analysing under-development?', *World Development*, vol. 3, no. 4.

Lamb, G. B. and Schaffer, B. B. (1981) *Can Equity be Organised?* Farnborough: Gower Press.

Lane, R. (1994) 'Structural-functionalism reconsidered. A proposed research model', *Comparative Politics*, vol. 26, no. 4.

LaPalombara, J. (1963) 'Bureaucracy and political development: notes, queries and dilemmas', in J. LaPalombara (ed.) *Bureaucracy and Political Development*. Princeton: Princeton University Press.

LaPalombara, J. and M. Weiner (eds) (1966) *Political Parties and Political Development*. Princeton: Princeton University Press.

Larrain, J. (1989) *Theories of Development. Capitalism, Colonialism and Dependency*. Cambridge: Polity Press.

Leftwich, A. (1983) *Redefining Politics*. London: Methuen.

Leftwich, A. (1993) 'Governance, democracy and development in the Third World', *Third World Quarterly*, vol. 14, no. 3.

Lemarchand, R. (1981) 'Comparative political clientelism: structure, process and optic', in S. N. Eisenstadt and R. Lemarchand (eds) *Political Clientelism, Patronage and Development*. London: Sage.

Lenin, V. I. (1917) *Imperialism. The Highest Stage of Capitalism. A Popular Outline*, 1939 edn. New York: International Publishers.

Lerner, D. (1958) *The Passing of Traditional Society. Modernizing the Middle East*. New York: Free Press.

Levine, D. (1986) 'Religion and politics in contemporary historical perspective', *Comparative Politics*, vol. 19, no. 1.

Levine, D. (1988) 'Assessing the impacts of liberation theology in Latin America', *The Review of Politics*, vol. 50, no. 2.

Levy, M. J. (1952) *The Structure of Society*. Princeton: Princeton University Press.

Levy, M. J. (1966) *Modernisation and the Structure of Society*. Princeton: Princeton University Press.

Leys, C. (1975) *Underdevelopment in Kenya. The Political Economy of Neo-Colonialism*. London: Heinemann.

Leys, C. (1976) 'The "overdeveloped" post-colonial state: a re-evaluation', *Review of African Political Economy*, vol. 5, no. 1.

Leys, C. (1977) 'Underdevelopment and dependency: critical notes', *Journal of Contemporary Asia*, vol. 7, no. 1.

Leys, C. (1978) 'Capital accumulation, class formation and dependency – the significance of the Kenyan case', in R. Miliband and J. Saville (eds) *The Socialist Register, 1978*. London: Merlin Press.

Leys, C. (1982) 'Samuel Huntington and the end of classical modernisation theory', in H. Alavi and T. Shanin (eds) *Introduction to the Sociology of 'Developing Societies'*. London: Macmillan.

Lipset, S. M. (1959) 'Some social requisites of democracy. Economic development and political legitimacy', *American Political Science Review*, vol. 53, no. 1.

Lipset, S. M. (1960) *Political Man*. New York: Doubleday.

Lipton, M. (1977) *Why People Stay Poor. Urban Bias in World Development*. London: Temple Smith.

Lloyd, P. C. (1970) 'The ethnic background to the Nigerian crisis', in S. K. Panter-Brick (ed.) *Nigerian Politics and Military Rule. Prelude to the Civil War*. London: Athlone Press.

Lloyd, P. C. (1973) *Classes, Crises and Coups. Themes in the Sociology of Developing Countries*. London: Paladin.

Long, N. (1977) *An Introduction to the Sociology of Rural Development*. London: Tavistock.

Lonsdale, J. (1981) 'States and social process in Africa: a historiographical survey', *African Studies Review*, vol. 24, nos. 2–3.

Love, J. L. (1980) 'The "Third World". A Response to Professor Worsley', *Third World Quarterly*, vol. 2, no. 2.

Luckham, R. (1991) 'Militarism: force, class and international conflict', in R. Little and M. Smith (eds) *Perspectives on World Politics*, (2nd edn). London: Routledge.

Luton, H. (1976) 'The satellite metropolis model: a critique', *Theory and Society*, vol. 3, no. 4.

Luxemburg, R. (1913) *The Accumulation of Capital*, 1951 edn. London: Routledge & Kegan Paul.

Mack, A. and R. Leaver (1979) 'Radical theories of underdevelopment: an assessment', in A. Mack, D. Plant and V. Doyle (eds) *Imperialism, Intervention and Development*. London: Croom Helm.

Mackintosh, J. P. (1966) *Nigerian Government and Politics*. London: George Allen & Unwin.

Macpherson, C. B. (1966) *The Real World of Democracy*. Oxford: Clarendon Press.

Magdoff, H. (1972) 'Imperialism without colonies', in R. Owen and B. Sutcliffe (eds) *Studies in the Theory of Imperialism*, London: Longman.

Magdoff, H. (1982) 'Imperialism: an historical survey', in H.Alavi and T.Shanin (eds) *Introduction to the Sociology of 'Developing Societies'*. London: Macmillan.

Mair, L. (1962) *Primitive Government*. Harmondsworth: Penguin.

Marx, K. (1969) *On Colonialism and Modernisation*, a collection of published and unpublished extracts edited by S. Avinieri. New York: Anchor Books.

Mazrui, A. A. (1976) 'Soldiers as traditionalisers: military rule and the re-Africanisation of Africa', *World Politics*, vol. 28, no. 2.

McCall, G. (1980) 'Four worlds of experience and action', *Third World Quarterly*, vol. 2 no. 3.

McClelland, D. C. (1961) *The Achieving Society*. Princeton: Princeton University Press.

McClelland, D. C. (1963) 'The achievement motive in economic growth', in B. F. Hoselitz and W. E. Moore (eds) *Industrialisation and Society*. The Hague: Mouton.

McClelland, D. C. (1966) 'The impulse to modernisation', in M. Weiner (ed.) *Modernisation. The Dynamics of Growth*. New York: Basic Books.

McGirk, T. (1994) 'Poisonous legacy', *The Independent Magazine*, 12 Nov.

McGowan, P. J. (1976) 'Economic dependence and economic performance in Black Africa', *Journal of Modern African Studies*, vol. 14, no. 1.

McGowan, P. J. and T. H. Johnson (1984) 'African military *coups d'état* and underdevelopment: a quantitative historical analysis', *Journal of Modern African Studies*, vol. 22, no. 4.

McGowan, P. J. and D. L. Smith (1978) 'Economic dependency in black Africa: an analysis of competing theories', *International Organisation*, vol. 32, no. 1.

McMichael, P., J. Petras and R. Rhodes (1974) 'Imperialism and the contradictions of development', *New Left Review*, no. 85.

McNall Burns, E. (1963) *Ideas in Conflict. The Political Theories of the Contemporary World*. London: Methuen.

McVey, R. (1984) 'Separatism and the paradoxes of the nation-state in perspective', in L. Joo-Jock and S. Vani (eds) *Armed Separatism in Southeast Asia*. Singapore: Institute of Southeast Asian Studies.

Meillasoux, C. (1970) 'A class analysis of the bureaucratic process in Malawi', *Journal of Development Studies*, vol. 6, no. 2.

Meier, G. (1976) *Leading Issues in Economic Development*, third edition. New York: Oxford University Press.

Melsom, R. and H. Wolpe (1970) 'Modernisation and the politics of communalism', *American Political Science Review*, vol. 64, no. 4.

Merton, R. (1952) 'Bureaucratic structure and personality', in R. Merton *et al.* (eds) *Reader in Bureaucracy*, Glencoe, Ill.: Free Press.

Migdal, J. S. (1974) *Peasants, Politics and Revolution. Pressures toward Political and Social Change in the Third World*. Princeton: Princeton University Press.

Milne, R. S. (1972) 'Decision-making in developing countries', *Journal of Comparative Administration*, vol. 3, no. 4.

Moore, B. (1973) *Social Origins of Dictatorship and Democracy. Lord and Peasant in the Making of the Modern World*. Harmondsworth: Penguin.

Moore, M. (1980) 'Public bureaucracy in the post-colonial state: some questions about "autonomy" and "dominance" in South Asia', *Development and Change*, vol. 11, no. 1.

Moore, W. E. (1964) 'Motivational aspects of development', in A. and E. Etzioni (eds) *Social Change. Sources, Patterns and Consequences*. New York: Basic Books.

Moore, W. E. (1977) 'Modernisation and rationalisation: processes and restraints', *Economic Development and Cultural Change*, vol. 25, supplement.

Moore, W. E. (1979) 'Functionalism', in T. Bottomore and R. Nisbet (eds) *A History of Sociological Analysis*. London: Heinemann.

Morgenthau, H. J. (1948) *Politics among Nations: the Struggle for Power and Peace*. New York: Knopf.

Morgenthau, R. S. (1964) *Political Parties in French-Speaking West Africa*. Oxford: Clarendon Press.

Mouzelis, N. (1989) 'State and politics in the parliamentary semi-periphery', in C. Thomas and P. Saravanamuttu (eds) *The State and Instability in the South*. London: Macmillan.

Muni, S. D. (1979) 'The Third World: concept and controversy', *Third World Quarterly*, vol. 1, no. 3.

Nafziger, E. W. (1972) 'Economic aspects of the Nigerian civil war', in R. Higham (ed.) *Civil Wars in the Twentieth Century*. Lexington: University of Kentucky Press.

Nafziger, E. W. and W. L. Richter (1976) 'Biafra and Bangladesh: the political economy of secessionist conflict', *Journal of Peace Reseach*, vol. 13, no. 2.

Naipal, S. (1985) 'The myth of the Third World: a thousand million invisible men', *The Spectator*, 18 May.

Nash, M. (1963) 'Approaches to the study of economic growth', *Journal of Social Issues*, vol. 29, no. 1.

Nisbet, R. (1969) *Social Change and History: Aspects of the Western Theory of Development*. Oxford: Oxford University Press.

Nkrumah, K. (1965) *Neo-Colonialism. The Last Stage of Imperialism*. London: Nelson.

Nove, A. (1974) 'On reading Andre Gunder Frank', *Journal of Development Studies*, vol. 10, nos. 3–4.

Nursey-Bray, P. (1983) 'Consensus and community: the theory of African one-party democracy', in G. Duncan (ed.) *Democratic Theory and Practice*. Cambridge: Cambridge University Press.

Nyerera, J. K. (1973) *Freedom and Development*. London: Oxford University Press.

O'Brien, D. C. (1972) 'Modernisation, order and the erosion of a democratic ideal: American political science 1960–70', *Journal of Development Studies*, vol. 8, no. 4.

O'Brien, P. J. (1975) 'A critique of Latin American theories of dependency', in I. Oxaal, T. Barnett and D. Booth (eds) *Beyond the Sociology of Development. Economy and Society in Latin America and Africa*. London: Routledge & Kegan Paul.

O'Connor, J. (1970) 'The meaning of economic imperialism', in R. I. Rhodes (ed.) *Imperialism and Underdevelopment*. New York: Monthly Review Press.

O'Donnell, G. (1979) 'Tensions in the bureaucratic authoritarian state and the question of democracy', in D. Collier (ed.) *The New Authoritarianism in Latin America*. Princeton: Princeton University Press.

O'Kane, R. H. T. (1981) 'A probabalistic approach to the causes of *coups d'état*', *British Journal of Political Science*, vol. 11, no. 3.

O'Kane, R. H. T. (1986) 'Explaining African *coups d'état*', *American Political Science Review*, vol. 80, no. 1.

Olson, M. (1963) 'Rapid growth as a destabilising force', *Journal of Economic History*, vol. 23, no. 4.

Omid, H. (1992) 'Theocracy or democracy? The critics of "westoxification" and the politics of fundamentalism in Iran', *Third World Quarterly*, vol. 13, no. 4.

Oyediran, O. and A. Agbaje (1991) 'Two-partyism and democratic transition in Nigeria', *Journal of Modern African Studies*, vol. 29, no. 2.

Orridge, A. W. (1981) 'Uneven development and nationalism', *Political Studies*, vol. 29, nos. 1 and 2, Mar. and Jun.

Packenham, R. A. (1973) *Liberal America and the Third World. Political Development Ideas in Foreign Aid and Social Science*. Princeton: Princeton University Press.

Page, E. (1978) 'Michael Hechter's internal colonialism thesis: some theoretical and methodological problems', *European Journal of Political Research*, vol. 6, no. 3.

Panter-Brick, S. K. (1976) 'Biafra', in W. H. Morris-Jones (ed.) *The Politics of Separatism*, Collected Seminar Papers no. 19. London: Institute of Commonwealth Studies.

Parfitt, T. W. and S. P. Riley (1989) *The African Debt Crisis*. London: Routledge.

Paribatra, M. R. S. and C.-A. Samudavanija, 'Factors behind armed separatism: a framework for analysis', in L. Joo-Jock and S. Vani (eds) *Armed Separatism in Southeast Asia*. Singapore: Institute of Southeast Asian Studies.

Parsons, T. (1951) *The Social System*, Glencoe, Ill., Free Press.

Parsons, T. (1960) *Structure and Process in Modern Societies*. Chicago: Free Press.

Parsons, T. (1966) *Societies: Evolutionary and Comparative Perspectives*. Englewood Cliffs: Prentice-Hall.

Payne, S. (1975) *Basque Nationalism*. Reno: University of Nevada Press.

Perlmutter, A. (1971) 'The praetorian state and the preatorian army: toward a taxonomy of civil-military relations in developing polities', in J. L. Finkle and R. W. Gable (eds) *Political Development and Social Change*, 2nd edn. London: John Wiley.

Petras, J. F. (1975) 'New perspectives on imperialism and social classes in the periphery', *Journal of Contemporary Asia*, vol. 5, no. 3.

Petras, J. F. (1981) *Class, State and Power in the Third World*. London: Zed Press.

Philip, G. (1984) 'Military-authoritarianism in South America: Brazil, Chile, Uruguay and Argentina', *Political Studies*, vol. 32, no. 1.

Philip, G. (1990) 'The political economy of development', *Political Studies*, vol. 338, no. 3.

Phillips, A. (1977) 'The concept of "development"', *Review of African Political Economy*, vol. 8, Jan.–Apr.

Pinkney, R. (1993) *Democracy in the Third World*. Buckingham: Open University Press.

Pirages, D. (1976) *Managing Political Conflict*. London: Nelson.

Polese, M. (1985) 'Economic integration, national policies and the rationality of regional separatism', in E. A. Tiryakian and R. Rogowski (eds) *New Regionalisms of the Developed West*. London: Allen & Unwin.

Portes, A. (1976) 'On the sociology of national development: theories and issues', *American Journal of Sociology*, vol. 82, no. 1.

Post, K. (1972) '"Peasantisation" and rural political movements in western Africa', *European Journal of Sociology*, vol. 13, no. 2.

Potter, D. (1992) 'Democratization in Asia', in D. Held (ed.) *Prospects for Democracy. North, South, East, West*. Cambridge: Polity Press.

Powell, J. D. (1970) 'Peasant society and clientelist politics', *American Political Science Review*, vol. 64, no. 2.

Pratt, R. P. (1973) 'The underdeveloped political science of development', *Studies in Comparative International Development*, vol. 8, no. 1.

Preston, P. W. (1982) *Theories of Development*. London: Routledge & Kegan Paul.

Putnam, R. D. (1967) 'Toward explaining military intervention in Latin American politics', *World Politics*, vol. 20, no. 1.

Pye, L. W. (1960) 'The politics of South East Asia', in G. A. Almond and J. Coleman (eds) *The Politics of the Developing Areas*. Princeton: Princeton University Press.

Pye, L. W. (1965) 'The concept of political development', *The Annals of the American Academy of Political and Social Science*, vol. 358, Mar.

Pye, L. W. (1966) *Aspects of Political Development*. Boston: Little, Brown.

Pye, L. W. (1971) 'Armies in the process of political modernisation', in J. L. Finkle and R. W. Gable (eds) *Political Development and Social Change*, 2nd edn. London: John Wiley.

Pye, L. W. and S. Verba (eds) (1965) *Political Culture and Political Development*. Princeton: Princeton University Press.

Race, J. (1974) 'Toward an exchange theory of revolution', in J. W. Lewis (ed.) *Peasant Rebellion and Communist Revolution in Asia*. Stanford: Stanford University Press.

Rahman, M. (1976) 'Bangladesh', in W. H. Morris-Jones (ed.) *The Politics of Separatism*, Collected Seminar Papers no. 19. London: Institute of Commonwealth Studies.

Randall, V. (1988) *Political Parties in the Third World*. London: Sage Publications.

Randall, V. and R. Theobald (1985) *Political Change and Underdevelopment. A Critical Introduction to Third World Politics*. London: Macmillan.

Rapaport, D. C. (1962) 'A comparative theory of military and political types', in S.P.Huntington (ed.) *Changing Patterns of Military Politics*, International Yearbook of Political Behaviour Research vol. 3, Glencoe, Ill.: Free Press.

Ray, D. (1973) 'The dependency model of Latin American underdevelopment: three basic fallacies', *Journal of Interamerican Studies and World Affairs*, vol. 15, no. 1.

Redfield, R. (1956) *Peasant Society and Culture*. Chicago: Chicago University Press.

Rejai, M. and C. H. Enloe (1969) 'Nation-state and state-nations', *International Studies Quarterly*, vol. 13, no. 2.

Rhodes, R. I. (1968) 'The disguised conservatism in evolutionary development theory', *Science and Society*, vol. 32, no. 3.

Ricci, D. (1977) 'Reading Thomas Khun in the post-behavioural era', *Western Political Quarterly*, vol. 30, no. 1.

Riggs, F. W. (1957) 'Agraria and Industria', in W. J. Siffin (ed.) *Toward the Comparative Study of Public Administration*. Bloomington: Indiana University Press.

Riggs, F. W. (1963) 'Bureaucrats and political development', in J. LaPalombara (ed.) *Bureaucracy and Political Development*. Princeton: Princeton University Press

Riggs, F. W. (1964) *Administration in Developing Countries. The Theory of Prismatic Society*. Boston: Houghton Mifflin.

Riggs, F. W. (1981) 'The rise and fall of "political development"', in S. C. Long (ed.) *The Handbook of Political Behaviour* vol. 4. New York: Plenum Press.

Riley, S. P. (1991) *The Democratic Transition in Africa. An End to the One-Party State?*, Conflict Studies 245. London: Research Institute for the Study of Conflict and Terrorism.

Riley, S. P. (1992) 'Political adjustment or domestic pressure: democratic politics and political choice in Africa', *Third World Quarterly*, vol. 13, no. 3.

Robinson, R. and J. Gallagher (1961) *Africa and the Victorians. The Official Mind of Imperialism*. London: Macmillan.

Rodinson, M. (1977) *Islam and Capitalism*. Harmondsworth: Penguin.

Roosevelt, A. (1980) 'The Kurdish Republic of Mahabad', in G. Challiand (ed.) *People Without a Country*. London: Zed Press.

Rosen G. (1975) *Peasant Society in a Changing Economy. Comparative Development in Southeast Asia and India*. Urbana: University of Illinois Press.

Rosen, G. and W. Jones (1979) 'The radical theory of development', in A. Mack, D. Plant and U. Doyle (eds) *Imperialism, Intervention and Development*. London: Croom Helm.

Rosenbaum, W. A. (1975) *Political Culture*. London: Nelson.

Rostow, W. W. (1952) *The Process of Economic Growth*. New York: Norton.

Rostow, W. W. (1960) *The Stages of Economic Growth. A Non-Communist Manifesto*. Cambridge: Cambridge University Press.

Rothstein R. L. (1977) *The Weak in the World of the Strong. The Developing Countries in the International System*. New York: Columbia University Press.

Roxborough, I. (1976) 'Dependency theory in the sociology of development: some theoretical problems', *West African Journal of Sociology and Political Science*, vol. 1, no. 2.

Roxborough, I. (1979) *Theories of Underdevelopment*. London: Macmillan.

Rueschmeyer, D. (1991) 'Different methods – contradictory results? Research on development and democracy', in C. C. Ragin (ed.) *Issues and Alternatives in Comparative Social Research*. Leiden: Brill.

Rueschmeyer, D. E. H. Stephens and J. D. Stephens (1992) *Capitalist Development and Democracy*. London: Polity Press.

Russett, B. M. (1964) 'Inequality and instability: the relation of land tenure to politics', *World Politics*, vol. 16, no. 3.

Rustow, D. A. (1960) 'The politics of the Near East: southwest Asia and northern Africa', in G. A. Almond and J. Coleman (eds) *The Politics of the Developing Areas*. Princeton: Princeton University Press.

Rustow, D. A. (1967) *A World of Nations. Problems of Political Modernisation*. Washington: The Brookings Institution.

Rustow, D. A. and R. E. Ward (1964) 'Introduction', in R. E. Ward and D. A. Rustow (eds) *Political Modernisation in Japan and Turkey*. Princeton: Princeton University Press.

Sandbrook, R. (1976) 'The crisis in political development theory', *Journal of Development Studies*, vol. 12, no. 2.

Sandschneider, E. (1991) 'Successful economic development and political change in Taiwan and South Korea', in J. Manor (ed.) *Rethinking Third World Politics*. London: Longman.

Saravanamuttu, P. (1989) 'Introduction to the problem of the state and instability in the South', in C. Thomas and P. Saravanamuttu (eds) *The State and Instability in the South*. London: Macmillan.

Sartori, G. (1970) 'Concept misinformation in comparative politics', *American Political Science Review*, vol. 64, no. 4.

Saul, J. (1974) 'The state in post-colonial societies: Tanzania', in R. Miliband and J. Saville (eds) *The Socialist Register, 1974*. London: Merlin Press.

Saul, J. S. and R. Woods (1971) 'African peasantries', in T. Shanin (ed.) *Peasants and Peasant Societies*. Harmondsworth: Penguin.

Schaffer, B. B. (1973) *Improving Access to Public Services*, IDS Discussion Paper no. 25, Institute of Development Studies, University of Sussex.

Schaffer, B. B. and Huang Wen-hsien (1975) 'Distribution and the theory of access', *Development and Change*, vol. 6, no. 2.

Schaffer, B. B. and Lamb, G. B. (1974) 'Exit, voice and access', *Social Science Information*, vol. 13, no. 6.

Schumpeter, J. A. (1951) *Imperialism and Social Classes*. Oxford: Blackwell.

Seers, D. (1981) 'Development options: the strengths and weaknesses of dependency theories in explaining a government's room to manoeuvre', in D. Seers (ed.) *Dependency Theory: A Critical Reassessment*. London: Francis Pinter.

Shanin, T. (1971) 'Peasantry as a political factor', in T. Shanin (ed.) *Peasants and Peasant Societies*. Harmondsworth: Penguin.

Shanin, T. (1982) 'Class, state and revolution: substitutes and realities', in H. Alavi and T. Shanin (eds) *Introduction to the Sociology of Developing Societies*. London: Macmillan.

Shivji, I. G. (1973) 'Tanzania: the silent class struggle, in L. Cliffe and J. S. Saul (eds) *Socialism in Tanzania*. Nairobi: East African Publshing House.

Shivji, I. G. (1976) *Class Struggles in Tanzania*. London: Heinemann.

Sirowy, L. and A. Inkeles (1991) 'The effect of democracy on economic growth and inequality', in A. Inkeles (ed.) *On Measuring Democracy. Its Consequences and Concomitants*. New Brunswick: Transaction Books.

Smelser, N. (1963) Mechanisms of change and adjustment to change', in B. F. Hoselitz (ed.) *Industrialization and Society*. The Hague: Mouton.

Smith, A. D. (1971) *Theories of Nationalism*. London: Duckworth.

Smith, A. D. (1979) 'Towards a theory of ethnic separatism', *Ethnic and Racial Studies*, vol. 2, no. 1.

Smith, B. C. (1986) 'Access to administrative agencies: a problem of administrative law or social structure?', *International Review of Administrative Sciences*, vol. 52, no. 1.

Smith, B. C. (1988) *Bureaucracy and Political Power*. Brighton: Wheatsheaf.

Smith, T. (1979) 'The underdevelopment of development literature: the case of dependency theory', *World Politics*, vol. 31, no. 2.

Smith, T. (1985) 'Requiem or new agenda for Third World studies', *World Politics*, vol. 37, no. 4.

Snyder, L. L. (1976) *Varieties of Nationalism: A Comparative Study*. Hinsdale: Dryden Press.

So, A. Y. (1990) *Social Change and Development. Modernization, Dependency and World System Theories*. London: Sage.

Stein, H. (1985) 'Theories of the state in Tanzania: a critical assessment', *Journal of Modern African Studies*, vol. 23, no. 1.

Sutcliffe, B. (1972) 'Imperialism and industrialisation in the Third World', in R. Owen and B. Sutcliffe (eds) *Studies in the Theory of Imperialism*. London: Longman.

Sweezy, P. (1942) *The Theory of Capitalist Development. Principles of Marxian Political Economy*. New York: Oxford University Press.

Symmons-Symonolewicz, K. (1965) 'Nationalist movements: an attempt at a comparative typology', *Comparative Studies in Society and History*, vol. 7, no. 2.

Taylor, J. G. (1979) *From Modernisation to Modes of Production. A Critique of the Sociologies of Development and Underdevelopment*. London: Macmillan.

Theodorson, G. A. (1953) 'Acceptance of industrialization and its attendant consequences for the social patterns of non-western societies', *American Sociological Review*, vol. 18, no. 3.

Therborn, G. (1979) 'The travail of Latin American democracy', *New Left Review*, nos. 113–14, Jan.–Apr.

Thomas, A. (1994) *Third World Atlas*, 2nd edn. Buckingham: Open University Press.

Thornton, A. P. (1959) *The Imperial Idea and Its Enemies. A Study in British Power*. London: Macmillan.

Tinker, H. (1981) "The nation-state in Asia', in L. Tivey (ed.) *The Nation-State. The Formation of Modern Politics*. Oxford: Martin Robertson.

Tipps, D. (1973) 'Modernization theory and the comparative study of societies: a critical perspective', *Comparative Studies in Society and History*, vol. 15, no. 2.

Tonnies, F. (1965) *Gemeinschaft and Gesellschaft*, 1887, extracts in T. Parsons, E. Shils, K. D. Naegele and J. R. Pitts (eds) *Theories of Society. Foundations of Modern Sociological Theory*. New York: Free Press.

Toye, J. (1987) *Dilemmas of Development. Reflections on the Counter-Revolution in Development Theory and Policy*. Oxford: Blackwell

Twitchett, K. J. (1965) 'Colonialism: an attempt at understanding imperial, colonial and neo-colonial relationships', *Political Studies*, vol. 13, no. 3.

United Nations Development Programme (1992) *Human Development Report 1992*. New York: United Nations.

United Nations Development Programme (1993) *Human Development Report 1993*. Oxford: Oxford University Press.

Valenzuela, J. S. and A. Valenzuela (1978) 'Modernization and dependency: alternative perspectives in the study of Latin American underdevelopment', *Comparative Politics*, vol. 10, no. 4.

Vanley, I. S. (1980) 'Kurdistan in Iraq', in G.Challiand (ed.) *People Without a Country*. London: Zed Press.

Varma, B. N. (1980) *The Sociology and Politics of Development: A Theoretical Study*. London: Routledge & Kegan Paul.

Vengroff, R. (1977) 'Dependency and underdevelopment in Black Africa: an empirical test', *Journal of Modern African Studies*, vol. 15, no. 4.

von Freyhold, M. (1976) 'The post-colonial state and its Tanzanian version', *Review of African Political Economy*, vol. 5, no. 1.

Wallerstein, I. (1960) 'Ethnicity and national integration in West Africa', *Cahiers d'Etudes Africaines*, no. 3, Oct.

Wallerstein, I. (1980) *The Capitalist World Economy*. Cambridge: Cambridge University Press.

Wallis, M. (1989) *Bureaucracy. Its Role in Third World Development*. London: Macmillan.

Warren, B. (1973) 'Imperialism and capitalist industrialization', *New Left Review*, no. 81.

Warren, B. (1980) *Imperialism: Pioneer of Capitalism*. London: New Left Books.

Webber, M. (1993) 'The Third World and the dissolution of the USSR', *Third World Quarterly*, vol. 13, no. 4.

Weber, M. (1965) 'On Protestantism and capitalism' (from *The Protestant Ethic and the Spirit of Capitalism*) in T. Parsons, E. Shils, K. D. Naegele and J. R. Pitts (eds) *Theories of Society. Foundations of Modern Sociological Theory*. New York: Free Press.

Weiner, M. (1957) *Party Politics in India. The Development of a Multi-Party System*. Princeton: Princeton University Press.

Weiner, M. (1960) 'The politics of South Africa', in G. A. Almond and J. S. Coleman (eds) *The Politics and Developing Area*. Princeton, NJ.: Princeton University Press.

Weiner, M. (1965) 'Political integration and political development', *The Annals of the American Academy of Political and Social Science*, no. 358, Mar.

Weiner, M. (1966) 'Political participation and political development', in M. Weiner (ed.) *Modernization*. New York: Basic Books.

Wells, A. (1974) 'The *coup d'état* in theory and practice: independent Black Africa in the 1960s', *American Journal of Sociology*, vol. 79, no. 4.

Westlake, M. (1991) 'The Third World (1950–1990) RIP', *Marxism Today*, Aug.

White, C. P. (1974) 'The Vietnamese revolutionary alliance: intellectuals, workers and peasants', in J. W. Lewis (ed.) *Recent Rebellion and Communist Revolution in Asia*. Stanford: Stanford University Press.

Whitaker, C. S. (1967) 'A dysrhythmic process of political change', *World Politics*, vol. 19, no. 2

Williams, D and T. Young (1994) 'Governance, the World Bank and liberal theory', *Political Studies*, vol. 42, no. 1.

Woddis, J. (1977) *Armies and Politics*. London: Lawrence & Wishart.

Wolfe, E. R. (1966) *Peasants*. Englewood Cliffs: Prentice-Hall.

Wolfe, E. R. (1968) *Peasant Wars of the Twentieth Century*. New York: Harper & Row.

Wolf-Phillips, L. (1979) 'Why Third World?', *Third World Quarterly*, vol. 1, no. 1.

Wolf-Phillips, L. (1987) 'Why "Third World"? Origin, definition and usage', *Third World Quarterly*, vol. 9, no. 4.

Wood, G. D. (1977) 'Rural development and the post-colonial state: administration and the peasantry in the Kosi region of North-East Bihar, India', *Development and Change*, vol. 8, no. 3.

Wood, G. D. (1980) 'Bureaucracy and the post-colonial state in South Asia: a reply', *Development and Change*, vol. 11, no. 1.

Wood, G. D. (1984a) 'State intervention and agrarian class formation: dimensions of the access problem in the Kosi Development Region of North East Bihar, India', *Public Administration and Development*, vol. 4, no. 4.

Wood, G. D. (1984b) 'State intervention and bureaucratic reproduction: comparative thoughts', *Development and Change*, vol. 15, no. 1.

Wood, J. R. (1981) 'Secession: a comparative analytical framework', *Canadian Journal of Political Science*, vol. 14, no. 1, Mar.

World Bank (1989) *Sub-Saharan Africa: From Crisis to Sustainable Growth*. Washington: World Bank.

World Bank (1990) *World Development Report 1990. Poverty*. Oxford: Oxford University Press.

World Bank (1991) *World Development Report 1991. The Challenge of Development*. Oxford: Oxford University Press.

World Bank (1993) *World Development Report 1993. Investing in Health*. Oxford: Oxford University Press.

Worsley, P. (1980) 'One world or three? A critique of the world-system theory of Immanuel Wallerstein', in R. Miliband and J. Saville (eds) *The Socialist Register, 1980*. London: Merlin Press.

Worsley, P. (1984) *The Three Worlds. Culture and World Development*. London: Weidenfeld and Nicolson.

Wriggins, H. (1966) 'National integration', in M. Weiner (ed.) *Modernization*. New York: Basic Books.

Wright, T. P. (1976) 'South Asian Separatist Movements', in W. H. Morris-Jones (ed.) *The Politics of Separatism*, Collected Seminar Papers no. 19. London: University of London Institute of Commonwealth Studies.

Yoo, S. H. (1974) 'The communist movement and the peasantry: the case of Korea', in J. W. Lewis (ed.) *Peasant Rebellion and Communist Revolution in Asia*, Stanford, Stanford University Press.

Zagoria, D. S. (1974) 'Asian tenancy systems and communist mobilization of the peasantry', in J. W. Lewis (ed.) *Peasant Rebellion and Communist Revolution in Asia*. Stanford: Stanford University Press.

Ziemann, W. and M. Lanzendorfer (1977) 'The state in peripheral societies', in R. Miliband and J. Saville (eds) *The Socialist Register 1977*. London: Merlin Press.

Zubaida, S. (1978) 'Theories of nationalism', in G. Littlejohn (ed.) *Power and the State*. London: Croom Helm.

Index